Selected Essays by

FRANK H. KNIGHT

Selected Essays by

FRANK H. KNIGHT

Volume Two
LAISSEZ-FAIRE: PRO AND CON

Edited by ROSS B. EMMETT

THE UNIVERSITY OF CHICAGO PRESS • CHICAGO AND LONDON

FRANK H. KNIGHT was the dominant influence in the economics department at the University of Chicago during the 1930s and 1940s. *Risk, Uncertainty, and Profit,* his best-known book, remains current today. He also made lasting contributions to economic theory and methodology, and wrote extensively about economics and social philosophy.

Ross B. EMMETT is the John P. Tandberg Associate Professor of Economics at Augustana University College.

The University of Chicago Press, Chicago 60637
The University of Chicago Press, Ltd., London
© 1999 by The University of Chicago
All rights reserved. Published 1999
08 07 06 05 04 03 02 01 00 99   1 2 3 4 5
ISBN: 0-226-44697-2 (cloth)

Library of Congress Cataloging-in-Publication Data

Knight, Frank Hyneman, 1885–
    Selected essays by Frank H. Knight / edited by Ross B. Emmett.
        p.   cm.
    Includes bibliographical references and indexes.
    Contents: v. 1. "What is truth" in economics? — v. 2. Laissez -faire : pro and con.
    ISBN 0-226-44695-6 (v. 1 : alk. paper). — ISBN 0-226-44696-4 (v. 1 : pbk. : alk. paper). — ISBN 0-226-44697-2 (v. 2 : alk. paper). — ISBN 0-226-44698-0 (v. 1 : pbk. : alk. paper)
    1. Economics.   I. Emmett, Ross B.   II. Title.
HB71.K55   1999
330—DC21   98-53133
                                                                                 CIP

∞ The paper used in this publication meets the minimum requirements of the American National Standard for Information Sciences—Permanence of Paper for Printed Library Materials, ANSI Z39.48–1992.

Contents

1

Ethics and Economic Reform

I. The Ethics of Liberalism

The problem of ethics is the most baffling subdivision of the social problem as a whole. For on the one hand, it seems clearly impossible to "talk sense" at all, in the way either of criticism of the existing state of affairs or of any proposal for change (which two things are properly inseparable, for to call a situation hopeless is for practical purposes the same thing as calling it ideal) unless we have a defensible, and hence reasonably clear and stateable ideal to indicate at least a direction of change if not an ultimate goal. Society depends upon—we may almost say that it *is*—moral like-mindedness. But on the other hand, an essential feature of the present social problem itself is the fact that our ethical common sense, the ethical common sense of modern Western civilization—now commonly referred to as "capitalistic"—seems to be little more than a tissue of vague generality and contradiction. It seems hardly possible to find ethical premises which can be used as a basis for reasoning and which are not matched by other premises equally valid or plausible in the abstract, and as generally accepted, often by the same people, yet which are opposite in sense and lead to different and conflicting conclusions.

Perhaps the basic contradiction, from the standpoint of such a discussion as this, is that which subsists between the absolutist, negativistic, personal idealism taught by Christianity, the religion generally professed in some form in Western civilization, on one hand, and on the

Reprinted with permission from *Economica* 6 (February, August, and November 1939): pp. 1–29, 296–321, and 398–422.

other the positive, activistic, relativistic, and practical norms of utilitarian mutualism and sportsmanship which actually prevail in workaday life, in so far as this rests on ethical ideals at all. According to the
first view, all that is good is the good will; according to the second, "good
intentions" are contemptible: it is "results" which count. The situation
is well pictured in a sports writer's newspaper headline: "The meek may
inherit the earth, but hits win ball games"; and some blasphemous wag
has also observed that faith will remove mountains, but engineers rec-
ommend dynamite, in spite of the expense.

Corresponding to this confusion is that which obtains in the attitude
towards power. The Christian ethic repudiates power as a virtue or a
value, viewing it rather as an evil temptation; but the ordinary behavior
of Christian-European man suggests as the reason for such professions
a sense of shame because he "really" admires or desires little else. Another inconsistency which is almost as fundamental as that just mentioned is the opposition between personal loyalty or fidelity and loyalty
to abstract principle, especially to truth. In the attitude towards truth is
centered, in fact, much of the paradox of modern ethical convictions.
On one hand, truth as integrity is the most essential value, the cornerstone of our ethical thought and our social life; and it is especially sacred
in science, where men typically pose as despising all sanctities and values. And yet the least effort to formulate the conditions under which it
is really good or proper, or conducive to the general peace and well-
being, to speak the truth, rather than some variety and some degree of
untruth, will surely bewilder anyone who undertakes the task. Plays
have, of course, been written on this theme, but writers find difficulty
in dramatizing it effectively without seeming to belabor the commonplace, a commonplace which is unpleasant without rising to the level of
the tragic.

What may conceivably be done, or reasonably attempted, in the
scope of an article on the ethical phase of the social problem is limited
at best. This paper will attempt only to give an intelligible statement of
the main ethical assumptions involved in free enterprise as a social-
economic form, i.e., the ethical axioms which are assumed and must be
assumed to be valid in accepting or defending the system—assuming
always that it can be and is made to work in accord with its theoretical
or mechanical ideal. We must always keep in mind the relations between ethical and mechanical aspects of the critical discussion of the
economic system. In so far as undesirable results are due to obstructions
or interference of a frictional character in the workings of the organi-

zation machinery, the correct social policy will be to remove these or to supplement the natural tendencies of the system itself. In so far as these natural tendencies are wrong, the effort must be to find and substitute some entirely different machinery for performing the right function in the right way. There is much confusion in the popular mind on this point: critics of enterprise economy who do not have a fair understanding of how the machinery works cannot tell whether to criticize it because it doesn't work according to the theory or because it does. And the same dilemma arises if the critic does not know what are his ethical ideals.

It may be well to say frankly in advance that the net constructive achievement of two articles will not be very large. We shall not get much beyond an elaboration of the negative theme already announced, that ethical reflection in modern civilization has hardly come to grips at all with the fundamental ethical problem of social organization. This is true whether we look at the ethical common sense of the man in the street, or at the assumptions taken for granted in our non-scientific literature, essays, and *belles lettres*, or at the ethical teachings of our religion, or, finally, at the ethical writings of philosophical specialists and the teaching in our universities. We shall be concerned here with that preliminary clearing and survey of the ground which study has seemed to show is necessary before construction on sound lines can begin.

For lack of a better term, we shall refer to the general type of social order accepted as a working ideal in European civilization in the later nineteenth century, and which until recently was supposed to be in process of realization, as "liberalism." It is the "ethics of liberalism" that this article will attempt to examine. The main content of the liberal ideal was economic and ethical individualism. The tenet which received most emphasis in political and social discussion was economic *laissez-faire,* or political negativism, with specific reference to economic relations. Stated positively, the essential principle of *laissez-faire* liberalism is that each "individual" (really meaning each family—see below) shall be free to use his own resources in his own way to satisfy his own wants. The primary ethical claim on behalf of free enterprise as a mechanism of economic organization is that it leads to this result, i.e., that under this system the "individual" gets the consequences of his own activities, takes out of the social enterprise what he puts into it. In so far as this is true, it is of course in a quantitative sense; the individual or family cannot get what it "produces" in the direct sense in which this is true of a primitive, self-sufficient household. The assumption is that in the ideal working of such an economic system each contributor takes from the joint product the "equivalent" of his contribution in productive service. The measure of equivalence is exchange value or money price, and the question of its validity involves a correct interpretation of the valuation process of the economic system as a whole, considered both in mechanical and in ethical terms.

At first sight, it seems arguable that in such a system there is little or no place for ethics, that it is non-ethical if not unethical; for it makes little reference to moral obligation, especially in a positive sense. But this view can be shown to be an error. Every social order, in fact all organized action, all social life, and all human life, is necessarily ethical, in so far as its character is a matter of deliberation and conscious acceptance on the part of its participants. Our main task in this article is to show that the social system of liberalism embodies a genuine ethical ideal and to make clear what the ideal is.

It is a political commonplace that in no society do its members obey the laws from sheer self-interest or purely because of "sanctions." They must be believed to be "right," in principle, and in the main. And personal rulers are followed or officials obeyed because their positions are accepted as, first, legal, and second, in accord with a law which itself is fundamentally "right." Social institutions must be in harmony with what those who live under them think to be moral—whatever theory one may hold as to the causal relation in history between institutions and moral ideas. Our point here is merely that the basis of social order is opinions on matters of right which are viewed as objective, i.e., as knowledge and not merely or mainly as individual and subjective interests, desires, wishes, or even opinions. As will appear throughout, the relation between interests and opinions is one of the crucial aspects of the social problem. One of the vices of Western thought in the social sciences and of certain of the most popular schools of philosophy is that of "reducing" value judgments to statements of preference, asserting that "this is better" or "ought to be done" "really" means merely, "I like it." Popular and practical thinking, on the other hand, characteristically shows the opposite tendency to erect every personal wish or comparison into a cosmic value.[1]

The essential social-ethical principle of liberalism or liberal individualism may now be stated, for the purpose of examination. It is that *all relations between men ought ideally to rest on mutual free consent, and not on coercion, either on the part of other individuals or on the part of "society" as politically organized in the state.* The function, and the only ideally right function, of the state, according to this ethic, is to use coercion negatively, to prevent the use of coercion by individuals or groups against other individuals or groups. Some of the main aspects and implications of this ideal principle may now be considered point by point.

1. In explaining what is involved in this notion and—of at least equal importance—what is not involved in it, we must in the first place maintain a clear distinction between the political and the personal aspects of ethical doctrine. The principle as stated is a theory of the right sphere of political coercion, not of what is right and wrong in individual conduct, or in social conduct, outside the single matter of the individual's role in determining the answer to this one question, in his own political group (or conceivably in other groups).[2] What the leading proponents of liberalism have thought about other ethical problems, such as the nature of the good life, the meaning and content of moral obligation, etc., is a separate question. As we shall see, it has a much less direct and vital bearing on the meaning of liberalism, and calls for notice chiefly for the purpose of illuminating the really central, positive issue, the sphere of politico-legal coercion.

2. Our second point is that this principle itself was never advocated in any strict or absolute interpretation. The *laissez-faire* economists of the straightest sect made exceptions of a sort which opened the way to much wider departures from the principle when and as changed conditions might seem to demand. This applies particularly to the great apostle of the movement, Adam Smith. All liberal individualists have recognized the necessity for restriction on individual freedom, and also for action by the state for purposes of defense [*sic!*] and police, and for carrying out various public functions, including "certain public works" of obvious public utility but which it would not be profitable for any individual or private group to construct and maintain. The state was to be supported, of course, by taxation, and the liberal notions of tax policy always inclined rather to equalizing the burden than to imposts in accord with benefit received. Moreover, liberalism has always accepted without question the doctrine that every member of society has a right to live at some minimum standard, at the expense of society as a whole—i.e., out of taxation levied as indicated above—if unable to provide such subsistence through his own efforts, the proceeds of sale of services, or through help from his family or voluntary private charity. Finally, Adam Smith and other liberals recognized as a legitimate function and task of the state provision for the education of the youth, and, in varying

degrees, for activities designed to promote the diffusion of knowledge and the advancement of science, art, and general culture.

3. Thirdly, the liberal ideal of mutual free consent applies in all relations of life and not merely in those called economic. The predominant emphasis on economic liberty in the nineteenth-century literature no doubt reflected some bias and some misunderstanding on the part of the liberal leaders; but this is explicable in terms of the particular problems which were important at the time and the historical background out of which liberalism took its rise. In its historical setting it was primarily a movement for the removal of restrictions on economic freedom which had prevailed in Europe in the preceding epoch—that of mercantilism or nationalism. This epoch had also greatly stressed the economic side of life, but had leaned in the opposite direction, namely, political control or direct political action. We must remember, too, that as a matter of historical fact, the struggle for freedom in its earliest phases related directly to religious freedom even more than to economic, and the mutual-consent principle was always meant to apply equally to all fields of human relations. But this tended to be taken for granted, because the situation did not seem to call for important changes in this respect in fields other than the economic, after the subsidence of the wars over religion. No doubt also, liberals were inclined for historical and other reasons to assume, rightly or wrongly, that it is primarily in the sphere of economic life that opportunity arises for the coercion of individuals by individuals, and that in consequence preventive coercion by the state is called for; and they were perhaps even more disposed to assume that the "temptation" of the state itself to exercise positive coercion is a danger chiefly in the economic sphere.

It should be emphasized that, apart from the historical circumstances under which the liberal political faith arose—as a reaction against measures of economic control which had become anachronistic—these assumptions have no high degree of validity. The truth is rather that the economic sphere of action is inseparable practically, and even theoretically, from other spheres, and the contrary position, in the form of the "economic interpretation," is one of the worst fallacies, or vices, of current thinking. But for various reasons, it was the "mode" in the nineteenth century to think of social problems of conflict and struggle between men (or "private" groups), and between the "individual" and the state, and between states primarily in economic terms. In general, this view cannot be maintained. Every form of human association necessarily gives rise to power relations and to conflicts of interests within the group and between groups, and to rivalry and struggle in both these areas. And these will ultimately lead to violent conflict, "human nature being what it is," in the absence of some regulatory restraint, i.e., of "law" and enforcement, in some form. In any fair appraisal, the casualty list of cultural rivalry and of purely personal clash is far longer than the list for conflicts of economic interest in any proper definition. And there is no reason to believe that if all properly economic problems were solved once for all through a fairy gift to every individual of the power to work physical miracles, the social struggle and strife would either be reduced in amount or intensity, or essentially changed in form, to say nothing of improvement—in the absence of some moral revolution which could by no means be assumed to follow in consequence of this change itself.

The idea that the social problem is essentially or primarily economic, in the sense that social action may be concentrated in the economic aspect and other aspects left to take care of themselves, is a fallacy, and to outgrow this fallacy is one of the conditions of progress towards a real solution of the social problem as a whole, including the economic aspect itself. Examination will show that while many conflicts which seem to have a non-economic character are "really" economic, it is just as true that what is called "economic" conflict is "really" rooted in other interests and other forms of rivalry, and that these would remain unabated after any conceivable change in the sphere of economics alone.

Especial emphasis on economic freedom might, however, be justified within very wide limits by the fact that it is basic to other forms of freedom, as historical fact and general considerations join in proving. But it is not clear, to the present writer at least, how far the leading nineteenth-century proponents of liberalism actually saw this relationship and took this ground.

4. It cannot be denied that liberal leaders propounded views on the nature of the good in individual life, and these were often vulnerable to criticism. The liberals inclined to hedonism, the doctrine that the good means pleasure. Indeed, they were much addicted to the absurdity of combining or confusing ethical and psychological hedonism,[3] holding that pleasure is at once what men do universally and necessarily pursue in conduct, and at the same time what they "ought" to pursue, the content of "duty." But whatever any individual, however great or important, may have thought, liberalism is not logically committed to any particular conception of the nature or content of the good, individual or

social. The importance of this fact can hardly be too much stressed. As an economic movement, the primary immediate objective of liberalism was freedom for the individual in relationships of exchange, of goods and services, i.e., relations of *quid pro quo*. Beyond freedom of transactions was the more remote objective of increasing "efficiency." This is a synonym for economy, which is not an end, but an auxiliary or instrumental conception relative to any end whatever, in so far as its achievement is a manner of degree, and the degree of achievement depends upon the mode of employing means. The relationship between economy or efficiency and various types of real end or value cannot be discussed here, though we may refer again to the "straddle" in our customary valuation axioms referred to at the outset that nothing is good but the good will, and that nothing is good but results; obviously the notion of efficiency fits the second axiom and not the first, and it is also irrelevant to such ideals as obedience and ascetic self-discipline. But the ideal of freedom is relevant to these also.

Regarding the end of action, it is of the essence of liberalism properly conceived to have no concrete position. The end of action is whatever the individual wants and strives to do, or to get, or to be, as the case may be—as far as the main issue, namely freedom from coercion, by others or by the state, is concerned, and as long as he does not infringe on the like freedom of other individuals to pursue their own ends in their own way. The theory is that the individual is, in general (but not without exceptions—cf. use of narcotics, etc.), the "best" judge of his own ends and of the procedure to be used in promoting them. The doctrine never meant that the individual is a perfect judge, but only that he is a better judge, and especially a more impartial judge, than "the government" or any other person likely to claim the right to judge for him. Consequently, according to the liberal view, a greater total achievement of ends actually desired and pursued, and in that sense a greater realization of "good," will result from a general application of the principle of freedom, with the limitation of mutual consent, than from the application of any other general rule.

5. The principles of liberalism involve no pressure on anyone to practice efficiency in any sense, or to pursue ends in connection with which it has meaning, rather than other ends. He is free to pursue such ideals as "poverty, chastity, and obedience" (assuming that he can find someone willing to be obeyed), or universal "love," or any form of ascetic practice, as long as he does not attempt to coerce others or infringe upon their similar freedom. He is also free to join with others in form-

ing groups voluntarily devoted to the practice of any ideal of life which is not so offensive to the tastes of the larger community as to create danger of violence.

6. In particular, liberalism allows any collection of individuals to organize economic life in any way they may choose. They do not have to establish markets or make exchanges under any form, to say nothing of conducting "enterprises" for profit. They may practice any type of cooperation, and adopt any mode of apportioning burdens and benefits upon which the members themselves can agree. And under the liberal regime groups have tried widely various schemes. But on seeing that cooperative, or planned, or controlled economic organization does not work out as it figures out (to some figurers), instead of learning their lesson, opponents of liberalism typically pour contempt and scorn upon such experiments as "Utopian" and demand political authority over whole nations or the whole earth. The reasons for this attitude are not so very far to seek in the nature of human nature, but they cannot be explored in detail here. The fact that such propaganda wins adherents among the educated as well as the masses, and threatens to subvert liberalism itself and replace it with a most extreme dogmatic and violent illiberalism, is of course a matter for the profoundest concern. But to return to our theme (and to repeat), liberalism means only that individuals and groups shall not coerce others, and not merely in economic relations, but in any department of life, though freedom for the conduct of enterprise economy was the main immediate objective of liberalism as a general political movement.

It should be pointed out, however, that liberal doctrine involved a tendency to oversimplification of values and motives, for which the hedonistic bias was no doubt partly to blame, or of which this bias was a consequence, as the case may be. The main argument for *laissez-faire* was instrumental, in the general meaning of the term; it was intended to increase efficiency. On one hand, this obviously involved taking the individual's actual endowment with means as a datum (either as "right" or as unalterable) along with his tastes and other characteristics. This is the main weakness of the system, from an economic standpoint, as will be emphasized presently. Freedom is freedom to use power, of which the individual may possess much or little or none at all, and be equally free.

Apart from this shortcoming, the liberal position itself can be maintained on quite different grounds, some at least as cogent as the tendency of freedom to increase efficiency, and different lines of argument are more or less confused in the literature. (In general, the writings of the utilitarians were not characterized by any great subtlety or analytic profundity.) The context, if not the explicit wording, frequently suggests more penetrating views. Freedom may be, and often was, considered an end or value in itself, and not merely as instrumental to efficiency in realizing other values. And going still farther, the writers would occasionally recognize that freedom is a "good," not merely in the sense that men actually want it, but in the deeper and more truly ethical sense that men "ought" to be free, more or less independently of whether they wish to be or not. This latter view, that it pertains to the dignity of human life to live responsibly, to make one's own decisions and take the consequences, is in keeping with the religious ethic of Puritanism, which certainly played an important role in the historical culture movement of which liberalism was a phase. Moreover, still another (a fourth) more "practical" line of argument for economic *laissez-faire* is important, and is occasionally met with. This is that the capacity of the state is limited, and that loading it with tasks which it cannot perform will cripple its effectiveness for functions which are possible for it as well as vital for the social life.

7. As already noted, the "end" of the enterprise economy is, in liberal theory, productive efficiency, which means the transformation of the ultimate productive capacity possessed by each individual into the maximum "income," consisting of "goods and services" reduced to a common denominator in terms of each individual's preferences. The notion of the economic individual will have to be further discussed presently. We now observe that the concept of income contains a twofold ambiguity which has been the source of much difficulty and confusion in technical economics itself. On the one hand, it includes "means of satisfaction," specifically the services of persons, logically including one's own services, and also services of "things," whether "owned" by oneself or by someone else. On the other hand, it also includes any accretion during the time interval for which it is measured in the total productive capacity belonging to the individual affected. The relation between income in the form of satisfaction-yielding services and income in the form of growth in productive capacity is further complicated by the relation first noted between services rendered to oneself—by one's own person or by things which one owns—and services rendered by other persons and instruments owned by them. And even more serious complications arise from the relation between accretions to productive capacity incorporated in the individual's own person (labor, power, skill,

knowledge) and that which is incorporated in external things which he owns (capital goods). All that it is in point to say on this problem here is that the use of resources actually owned at any moment in any form is subject to the control of the individual, who, in so far as he behaves in accord with the principle of economic rationality, apportions all his available productive capacity, without regard to its form, among all the alternatives of use open to him, in such a way as to "maximize" the total "return" in all forms, reduced to common units in terms of his own value-scale. (In economic jargon, his value-scale is represented by a "utility function," or satisfaction function, or system of indifference curves, including investment as well as consumption.) Opportunities for exchange with other persons (which must in some degree increase the total income of both) count to any one person as alternative modes of use to be considered in apportioning whatever resources he "owns." The result of intelligent apportionment, according to economic theory, is the maximum provision, to each individual, under the given conditions (especially the similar maximum for all others), of "means of life," realized either in the form of momentary satisfaction or in further addition to productive capacity; allocation between these two fields and among all the subdivisions of both should accord with the economic principle of a maximum, i.e., equalization at the margin. Beyond this maximum provision of *means,* the ideal of freedom as qualified by mutual consent obviously had nothing to say.

8. An outstanding ethical consequence of the theory of productive organization through freeing the urge to self-advancement is a new and sharp division in the field of conduct, a new ethical dualism (there are many such dualisms) or at least a bifurcation of the ethical problem. The situation is suggested by the vernacular expression, "Business is business," meaning that business is one thing, and "charity" another. There is a strong feeling that it is "right" to "play the business according to the rules," to make exchanges at the ratios objectively set or made possible by the market. That is, it is assumed to be ethically legitimate and even positively virtuous, to *desire* to maximize one's "income," as defined above, and to act in such a way as to do so, subject always to the sweeping reservation of mutual free consent in all relations with others. (Some problems in the nature of this freedom of consent, especially as regards "persuasion" and effects on persons not parties to a transaction will come up presently.)

The question of what is to be done with income when obtained, or the reasons on account of which it is desired, not only receive no answer or illumination from the social-ethical principle so far discussed; there is even a certain tendency to deny their reality as ethical problems through emphasizing the right of every individual to do as he will with his own and his duty to live of his own and to make it fruitful. In any event, liberalism was emphatic that exchange dealings involve no obligation beyond honesty and non-predation—both primarily negative, but their meaning will call for further consideration later. In the political connection the payment of taxes and assumption of a fair share of the "proper" obligations of society was added. But at that point it would seem that the ethical theory of liberalism as a distinctive principle stops. Certainly the use of income, or specifically the matter of obligation in its use, belongs to a completely separate ethical problem-field, and constitutes a different branch of ethical science or inquiry. This branch of ethics tended to be a stepchild.[4] We must keep in mind that in the ideal market economy of theory the individual has economic power only in the form of income and also that his income represents his own productive contribution to the aggregate social output.

However, the public mind or conscience of the civilization which in general accepted the liberal principle has never been clear or at ease on this question of obligation outside of and beyond the business code. Worse still, liberal thought has been much confused about the relations involved, and has never been happy even about the separation, the business-*versus*-charity dualism which we may call the second axiom or principle of liberalism (the mutual-consent principle being its first axiom). The issue raised is one of the most important factors in the current situation of unrest and crisis. A little headway may be made in the illumination of the problem by considering it briefly in the light of history.

What we call primitive society, as known, and back of which knowledge cannot penetrate, presents as one of its most fundamental phenomena the notion of *equity* as a normative ideal and pattern of individual relationships. The most pungent example of "primitive" equity is the *lex talionis,* "an eye for an eye," etc., which of course represents an almost inconceivably long development of legality and civilization beyond the really primitive anger reaction. The bulk of primitive law is, moreover, law of tort rather than criminal law; it prescribes "damages" to injured parties, rather than punishment for wrongdoers. In our own society the notion of equity is still largely that of the preliterate tribal stage; we try to get away from it to what we consider higher ethical norms, but make slow progress. "Reciprocity" in all our emotional and social life, the return of cordiality for cordiality, snub for snub, if not blow for blow, affection for affection, and the "repayment" of gifts, visits, and entertainments in kind, seems as inevitable as a precise calculation and explicit negotiation of terms (or compounding in money) is repugnant, so that one wonders about the realism of any ethical teachings which pretend to get very far away from this level, especially through discussion. But of course there are exceptions, a sort of fringe around the blanket of *quid pro quo* which moral progress may gradually extend from generation to generation.

Primitive equity also includes what we vaguely think of as economic reciprocity, the "exchange" of goods and services, but under very different conditions and forms from those of modern commerce. For the most part, trade is foreign trade, and in general is highly ritualized; and the ratios of exchange, the prices, are very rigorously fixed by traditional standards. Much intertribal exchange is a pure ritual, without economic significance, though involving a substantial "cost." When conditions change and the amounts of any ware or token which will be supplied and demanded at the traditional prices become too unequal, other forms of interchange, especially gifts, largely take the place of exchange before prices yield. We find the same phenomena in "backward" areas today.[5] One of the great historical-anthropological problems is that of the development of markets in the modern sense, with flexible prices responding freely and accurately (more or less!) to changes in supply and demand conditions. It can be said with confidence that this happened first in the field of foreign trade, trade between groups, and was introduced into intra-tribal relations much later.[6] Exchange of services is a late development, and it is an important fact that labor is a commodity which—apart from the trade in slaves—can hardly be a subject of international trade, and even with slavery can never give rise to a highly perfect market. The factual point to be made clear now is that the business-ethics principle of exchange of equal values is an obvious modification of primitive economic equity; the difference is that the value equivalence itself is subject to free adjustment in the market instead of being fixed by tradition at a specific figure.

But it is vitally important that, due largely to the survival of primitive notions of personal equity, modern civilization in general has never wholeheartedly accepted the dualism of "business *versus* charity" in business itself, or accepted its sharp dichotomy between standards of formally organized behavior and the ethic of personal human relations. The notion of "fair price" and even of a considerate or humane price has persisted with varying strength in different connections, depending in part on the actual effectiveness of competition, in greater part on the public's conception of its reality and effectiveness, and in large part on more subtle factors of "psychology."

In any case, one of the main factors in the present crisis is that the public has lost faith, such faith as it ever had, in the moral validity of market values. In large part, as suggested, this is due to the failure of even the educated public to understand the mechanics of exchange relations, and to the existence of monopoly and of friction in price and production adjustments. It is especially in the field of wages, the price of "labor," that the tendency to reject market standards is strongest. But the dualistic principle must be accepted whole-heartedly in relation to economic organization if the kind of civilization we call free is to exist.[7] Business must be separated from "charity," meaning all personal considerations. The principle of business-is-business is on a par with that of justice-is-blind, though both must be sometimes seasoned with mercy. Moral obligation to persons in consequence of special relationships is the general principle of feudalism, and is anachronistic and disruptive in a commercial or enterprise economy. Yet it persists; and not only in connection with the employer-employee relation; it, or its conflict with business principles and with wide areas of law as a whole, remains a fundamental aspect of the ethical problem-situation in modern society. The mixture of intellectual confusion with value judgments in the discussion of problems of economic ethics, as it takes place, baffles analysis, and is of course most sinister in import.

9. It must be kept in mind that the main, immediate driving force back of the liberal revolution in political thought was a technological revolution which could only work itself out, and yield the enormous increase in economic efficiency potentially available, through economic transactions between individuals spread over a vastly greater geographical and social area than that of the primary social group, or any natural community, an area within which "social" relations in the ordinary sense become physically impossible.[8] The natural result was "economic" conflict and the necessity of legal regulation of economic relationships in this larger area, where "social" problems inevitably take a "political" form. But the contrast between social and political is a vague one. These wide-area relationships involve just as much conflict of interest and opportunity for clash as, say, a card game or neighborhood social rivalry; but the conflicts take a special form, which we tend to call political because of the character of large-group psychology and behavior. It is, however, a fallacy to view them as economic, which is no more true

than it is of personal dislikes or family feuds. There always have been rivalries and wars between groups formed on every conceivable basis, local, political, or religious, or even purely artificial or partisan. In modern times the somewhat special form of nationalistic rivalry tends to predominate.

10. The next point has to do with the nature of political coercion, beyond its negative role, and with the nature of the state. It is of the essence of liberal doctrine that action by the state is not action by individuals, although of course it is carried out, in the concrete, by human beings, officials of some kind. The liberal state is essentially "The Law." [9] In the liberal view, the individuals who implement state action do not act as individuals, but are the agents of the law, and the law is the creation of society as a whole, of the "sovereign people," and not of individuals. The same principle applies to legislators as to other officials. Of course this is an ideal, which no conceivable machinery could realize at all perfectly; but it is an ideal of fairly definite and intelligible meaning, and surely is one of ethical character and import. Undoubtedly it received its purest and classical formulation in the eighteenth century, at the hands of the political theorists in the British colonies in North America, and in the United States as a nation during its formative period. It is embodied in the principle, or slogan (of older date), "a government of laws and not of men." Much, of course, might be said about this ideal, as regards its practical consequences, in relation to various circumstances and conditions—notably the contrast between the conditions of frontier settlements, on a virgin continent peculiarly rich in natural resources, and those which obtain in the United States (to say nothing of Europe) towards the middle of the twentieth century. But our concern here is with the ideal.

The primary difficulty with the notion of law as an ethical principle or norm is that the content of the law itself can never be taken as simply "given," or beyond dispute, even at a given moment. In the liberal doctrine in its original form, this problem did not seem serious, because of the limitation of law itself and of its functions to the negative role of suppressing coercion. But even under this restriction, there was always and inevitably occasion for "interpreting" the law in enforcing it, and also for making law outright, i.e., changing it, in consequence of changing conditions and standards.

11. We should next consider the meaning in liberalist thought of that coercion of individuals by individuals which it is the primary function of the state, i.e., of legal coercion, to prevent. To begin with, this was taken to mean simply "force and fraud," concepts which it was

assumed could be fairly easily defined, by legal process and in words, with sufficient definiteness and accuracy for practical purposes. This view now seems naive to the philosophic student of the problem; a very little perusal of a legal encyclopedia under the pertinent headings ("duress" and "fraud") will show that the problem admits of no definite solution.

In connection with private coercion we must also deal with the distinctively economic category of monopoly. For the liberals of the nineteenth century and even earlier (notably in England, and notably those classed as economists) clearly recognized that monopoly is a form of coercive power, and inadmissible in a "free" state. As is well known, at least among students of economics of the present day, the liberals, and specifically Adam Smith, tended to assume that monopoly would not require coercive repression, that it would not arise to an important degree in the absence of positive support, aid, and abetting, on the part of the state itself. This indeed is still a "moot" question, one on which the writer has no very positive opinions, but on the issue of which he is by no means so optimistic as, for example, Professor von Mises and Professor Robbins of the London School of Economics. However, it must be admitted that governments have never given the original liberal position any fair trial, and do not seem in a way to do so, in the visible future, even in the United States or Great Britain.

12. The observation next in order, as a sort of footnote, is that the "individualism" of liberal doctrine by no means excludes, but rather expressly includes, guidance of the activities of one individual by another, in the interest of increasing efficiency through more competent direction. It means only that the individual must be "free" to place himself under direction and guidance or not to do so, and hence to choose his own counselors, and to follow their advice or not to follow it in any particular case, and to discharge a counselor at will, with or without replacing him by another.

A peculiar and important consequence of the freedom to accept and to give advice or counsel (by free mutual consent) is that in many fields advice or counsel becomes a commodity in the market, subject to competitive purchase and sale. In fact the separation between direction and execution is one of the most important cases of the division of labor. Professions which tell others what to do include among many others the law, medicine, and business management. But expert counsel or leadership is a commodity unique in the absolute logical impossibility of standardizing it or even describing it objectively. This means that the market is peculiarly imperfect; and this fact helps to weaken popular faith in market values, and has wide ramifications.

13. We come now to consideration of certain elements of vagueness and ambiguity in the liberal principle of mutual free consent. Three examples call for notice. The first, and logically most puzzling, has to do with contract, the freedom of an individual to alienate his own freedom—for any consideration which appears satisfactory when the contract is made—for some specified period of time in the future and with respect to some specified scope of activity. Freedom to dispose of one's own freedom is evidently something of a paradox; it obviously has in practice to be allowed within limits but just as certainly has to be limited if freedom as a general condition is to be maintained.[10]

Liberal doctrine, according to my own impression, which is based on limited knowledge of Anglo-American law, has never had any clear position on this matter. In America, the problem receives a peculiar twist from the special emphasis of our founding fathers on "inalienable rights," from the fact that our government rests on a set of written constitutions, including national and state bills of rights—also from the circumstance that chattel slavery as an institution became established under peculiar conditions and was abolished only at a very late date in history, in consequence of a long and hard-fought civil war, the results of which, again, were incorporated in the federal and state constitutions. It is evident that freedom of contract, i.e., the extent to which the law will enforce a contract binding anyone for the future (or permit any other enforcement), must be restricted to narrow limits if anything like individual liberty, in a practical common-sense interpretation, is to be maintained (if it is not to run into "involuntary servitude"). But on the other hand, this inalienability of control over one's own person, meaning especially over its economic powers and capacities, though based on the peculiar sanctity of such control, results in placing in an especially weak position anyone who owns productive capacity only as embodied in his own person in the form of labor power. For what cannot be sold cannot be pledged; and the man without "property," in the usual meaning of the term, is dependent upon a practically continuous opportunity to market his services, as well as upon continuous possession of capacity to render service (for himself and dependents) to secure the means of livelihood. For these means must of course be had in almost completely continuous flow—"three meals a day," or some other number. This "would be" the case if "society" made no provision for "relief," outside the system of exchange relations; but of course some other provision is necessary for many categories of the population, who do not have "productive capacity" to sell of sufficient value to afford a socially acceptable scale of life, and this obligation on the part of the state has always been a feature of liberalism.

14. The second element of vagueness is of a different kind but of equally vital importance. It arises out of the fact that a large part of the goods and services which are subject to exchange cannot be effectively standardized, because their relevant qualities and characteristics are not a matter of common knowledge and direct observation, or of physical measurement, but are very largely a matter of judgment, and there is wide diversity of opinion. In such cases, market dealings inevitably become affected by *efforts to persuade* on the part of the seller, or buyer, or both. As it works out, also inevitably, it is ordinarily the seller who immediately sets the price, and marketing becomes a literally "competitive" endeavor or struggle on the part of sellers to influence buyers. (The Economic Man neither competes nor higgles—nor does he cooperate, psychologically speaking; he treats other human beings as if they were slot machines.) In a sense what is involved here is a coupling with physical goods and services of information about them, which the buyer purchases, and of course pays for, along with the physical entities themselves. The social problem involved theoretically comes under the head of fraud; but the field in which, and range over which, assertions about wares cannot be viewed as objectively true or false is so limited that, from the standpoint of common sense, what is involved is rather the exercise of a kind of coercive force, or at least a struggle between opposed "forces," and not an exchange. The problem ties up with the general fact of uncertainty as a limitation on rationality. This is an infinitely complex and subtle problem; uncertainty itself is subject to uncertainty; we do not know how much we know, or how accurately; there is no visible boundary between knowledge, opinion, and ignorance.

The crux of the matter, from the standpoint of the workings of an enterprise economy, is the fact that the machinery of law, the formulation and enforcement of criminal statutes or precedents, cannot deal satisfactorily with these phenomena in terms of either coercion or fraud or the two combined. To the extent that there is no objectivity in the matter at issue, there can be none in the law. At the same time and for the same reason, the machinery of the market also fails to evaluate as information or counsel the persuasive or "selling" activities of parties to transactions. The role of middlemen whose whole business it is to buy and to sell the same wares presents especially interesting features. The whole arena is one in which, *prima facie,* high ethical standards and sentiments might be expected to produce results beyond those possible for any formal social machinery; and, in fact, ethics plus certain considerations which tend to make honesty good business policy probably have more weight than legal action, though it remains necessary to treat as fraud and as criminal such persuasive efforts as go too far and fall "reasonably" within that category. The factor most neglected by critics of the enterprise economy is the irrationality and greed of the consumer himself; but outside the highly organized markets, the whole system is saturated with "sentiment," rivalry and suspicion, and "strategy"—a polite name for trickery.

15. The third of the qualifications referred to is that the primary principle of liberalism, free mutual relations, takes no account of inequality in economic position. The ability of one party to bring to the market a vastly greater quantity of saleable service value than another, coupled with imperfections in the market mechanism, may amount to the exercise of coercive power by the stronger party over the weaker. From the standpoint of pure theory, it is the market imperfection which is primarily in point, and this may operate in special circumstances to place arbitrary power in the hands of the "weaker" party, the party possessed of less economic power as measured from a long-run point of view. The outstanding case, in the popular mind, is of course the "bargaining" between employer and employee. But the popular notions regarding the intrinsic superiority in bargaining power of the employer are very largely false. This is true even apart from situations where there is effective monopoly in one form or another; and the monopoly factor itself may operate on either side.[11]

Freedom of accumulation not only carries with it the possibility of cumulative increase in the inequality of *economic* power and creates a strong tendency in that direction; in addition, economic power confers power in other forms, including the political. And freedom of association is equally important in the same connection, since association may be for the end of power as well as that of efficiency. Freedom of association also raises questions as to the meaning and limitations of mutual consent, questions which cannot be taken up here.

16. Before turning to considerations of a somewhat different kind, it may be well to consider the general meaning of the principle of freedom in the light of the points already made but from a somewhat different point of view. Politico-legal freedom, i.e., the restriction of organized social action to the prevention of force and fraud, means that within the

sphere of freedom, i.e., outside the sphere of legal control, social relations are left to the control of "social forces" other than law as deliberately enacted and enforced. That is, all relations not covered by the concepts of force and fraud, as defined in the terms of the law and in its
actual enforcement, are controlled by other, less formal and deliberate
modes of action or social processes. Further investigation and analysis
of what is involved in these other forces or control processes would have
to inquire into the philosophical problem of "free" activity, first in the
individual, in "private" action, and secondly in social behavior under
"free" mutual consent. Free activity would have to be compared and
contrasted with such other categories as *(a)* the exercise of control by
one free agent over another, by innumerable means and methods; *(b)*
control by society over individuals; and *(c)* "positive" cause and effect,
physical, mental, "moral," and cultural. In such an inquiry methodological and philosophical problems step into the foreground. Any pure
cause-and-effect relation means that the social-human unit is an incident
in an inevitable flow of cosmic process in some conception. All notion
of effective purpose is excluded, and all discussion—such as the present
effort and likewise the efforts of the advocates of natural or dialectical
cause-and-effect—is reduced to meaningless physical or metaphysical
process. But the main point is simply the fact that the hands-off policy
on the part of the state means leaving the course of events to such other
causes or controls as do and will actually operate under the conditions
present. Its opponents are right, as far as they go, in insisting that inaction is also a policy. These other forces or controls, apart from politico-
legal action, cry for classification and analysis, but the task, the main
problem of sociology and social philosophy, cannot be undertaken here.

17. It is to be emphasized that acts most freely assented to and actually advantageous to parties immediately and directly affected almost
always have effects for evil or good on others, whose consent is not obtained. The liberalism of the free market provides for the consent only
of parties to transactions. Where either good or ill effects accrue to
others, such a system cannot protect the interests of remote persons
in wider circles, or motivate action which "radiates" beneficial effects.
This, however, is rather a mechanical than an ethical weakness in the
mutual-consent system, and its detailed consideration is outside the
scope of the present article. As already noted, liberals have always believed both in political action for protection of important unrepresented
interests and for "public works." But theory must recognize that a most
intricate and subtle combination of public and private enterprise would

be required to secure anything like a maximum utilization of resources in terms of purely individual interests. And the problem of community interests would call for separate consideration.

18. These reflections naturally lead up to the most important single defect, amounting to a fallacy, in liberal individualism as a social philosophy. The most general and essential fact that makes such a position untenable as an exclusive principle of organization is that *liberalism takes the individual as given,* and views the social problem as one of right relations between given individuals. This is its fundamental error.[12] The assumption that this can be done runs counter to clear and unalterable facts of life. The individual cannot be a datum for the purposes of social policy, because he is largely formed in and by the social process, and the nature of the individual must be affected by any social action. Consequently, social policy must be judged by the kind of individuals that are produced by or under it, and not merely by the type of relations which subsist among individuals taken as they stand.

From the economic point of view, both this fact itself and its vital importance are especially obvious. The economic individual is a complex of three main sets of factors; namely, wants, physical capacities (of himself and all that he owns) usable in satisfying wants, and knowledge of the processes involved in the direct and indirect use of means in rendering want-satisfying services, i.e., in "production" and "consumption." It cannot require more than a reminder and a moment's reflection to make any person interested in the facts realize that all three elements in the individual are very largely built up in and molded by the social traditions, institutions, and processes of the culture in which the individual grows up. More specifically, they are largely the product of forces operating in primary-group life, in which the "primary" primary group, the family, is overwhelmingly important. It is chiefly from and through the family that the individual is formed and endowed in all these respects.

Indeed it is evident (as we have already remarked) that liberalism never really meant individualism, and could not do so, in view of unalterable facts of life. From the standpoint of social policy, as well as that of scientific history or sociology, the "individual" is an evanescent phenomenon; he comes into the world destitute and helpless, and necessarily remains a liability for a large fraction of his life-span, before he can become an asset to himself or an "individual" with capacity for membership in an organization of responsible units. In the nature of the case, liberalism is more "familism" than literal individualism. Some sort of family life, and far beyond that, some kind of wider primary-group and culture-group life, of a considerable degree of stability, must be taken as they are, as *data,* in free society at any time, until they change or are changed, by action in accord with policy, into other forms. This is true not only because primary groupings and institutions are in fact "there," but because no society could possibly exist without them; and to safeguard them where it is necessary, and improve them where it is possible, must be the first concern of any intelligent social policy—on a level with the preservation of physical life itself. "Man is a social animal." And the social philosophy of freedom and mutual consent is finally tenable only in so far as it can be shown that there is a natural harmony of interests between individuals and between the individual and society as free behavior affects the social structure at the level of primary-group life, as well as harmony of interest between individuals in their individual interests. For the most part, liberalism, in taking the individual as given, took society for granted also. It recognized, indeed, the right of "the people" to change their political constitution, and to make laws touching property and the family. But this could only mean the people of an existing political unit, or in fact, far more narrowly, the existing control system in such a unit. The revolutionary liberals were, as opponents have again pointed out, excessively rationalistic; they did not seriously consider the problems involved in the relationship between freedom of transactions and political freedom on one hand, and freedom of association in these wider institutional contexts of family and primary-community life on the other. Social policy in terms of action (beyond the merely preventive) means law-making, which is to say law-changing, and only to a very limited extent do individuals act independently in their efforts to bring about changes in the law. They act chiefly as members of groups, either previously existent, or spontaneous and *ad hoc,* or deliberately organized, or combining these characteristics in various ways and degrees.

19. From a practical point of view the naive faith in the power and benevolence of the non-political and non-legal social forces which is logically presupposed in *laissez-faire* individualism is questionable in connection with all three of our economic factors in the individual, but in connection with the third—his endowment with economic or "productive" capacity—it is palpably untenable. In free society, in the legal sense of a society which does not tolerate slavery, productive capacity falls into two main divisions—*(a)* the physical and mental qualities and

endowments of the individual himself, and *(b)* earning power embodied in the properties of external things "owned" by the individual.[13] In the popular mind and in the propaganda of reformers, there is a sharp ethical contrast between these two forms of earning power, between "property" and "human rights." It is very hard to find much foundation for this view in the facts. Both forms of earning ability are alike in being largely created and conferred on the individual by the social-cultural process, and primarily in and by the family. Both forms of capacity are partly inherited and partly built up by the individual. They are built up by "investment" in the individual himself or in external things, as the case may be. The investment in both cases is made partly by the individual himself and partly by others ("parents") or by society—on the basis of an inherited nucleus, or "start." Ethically considered, both forms or sources of income seem to be more or less equally affected by the same complex of factors—inheritance, intelligent and conscientious effort, fate, fraud, and "luck."

In a "free" social-economic system there is every presumption that movement will be away from and not towards fundamental human equality. It "tends," more or less effectively, to realize "commutative" justice, but "distributive" justice is completely ignored. And real human equity seems clearly to include a right to "be" equal as well as to "have" equal "rights." Freedom, again, means the right to do what one is able to do, i.e., to use power, and has content only in so far as one possesses power. Equal right to use unequal power is not equality but the opposite. The difference illustrates a fact which will concern us especially as we go on to a comparative consideration of ethical systems; namely, that social ethics must look to the distant future and take into account the unborn and the whole character of culture, and not merely relations between given individuals.

Moreover, even commutative justice or equity—quantitative equivalence between what the "individual" puts in and what he takes out—has meaning only for the independent recipients of income. The effective social unit in consumption is the family, and for other members of the family than the head, at least for all "dependents," there is little or no relation between reward and contribution, or desert in any form. The position of wives is quite anomalous—their economic status being a "reward" chiefly for their wisdom in choosing husbands—and the injustice to children cries out to heaven. But these matters for the most part go with the family as a social institution; and it is doubtful how far they can be altered by any change in the economic organization, particularly because the changes proposed mean substituting politics (competitive or monopolistic) for economics (property and the market).

In an economico-ethical or political view, property is simply power to render saleable service, in a form which is itself saleable or exchangeable outright. But purchase and sale of property is an incidental feature of economic life or economic organization. The essential thing is exchange of services, by whatever agency they are rendered. Nothing fundamental would be changed in economic society if all property except the most perishable consumption goods were "entailed" and could not be alienated. Investment and accumulation would persist, and the interest rate would have the same economic significance as "now." Moreover, none of these things would be substantially changed by establishing "socialism," with property ownership and the control of enterprise a monopoly of the government.

As suggested at the outset, the principle of *quid pro quo,* of equality in exchange, defines a power system as regards relations between individuals. It has moral significance only in so far as the individual's contribution, what he brings to market, has moral significance as a measure of desert. There is, indeed, a moral factor (universally regarded as such) in the mode of use of resources, though this "intelligent efficiency" in pursuit of one's own self-interest seems ethical in a rather "low" and even dubious sense. But the individual's economic status depends altogether on his *possession* of economic capacity, and this is justified in moral terms only in so far as it has come about through the intelligent use of pre-existing capacity, and of course only in so far as the efficient use of capacity in one's own interest is an ethical virtue.

The meaning of freedom is freedom to act so as to make changes in the course of events as it would be or occur in the absence of such action. That is, it is freedom to use power, possessed in some form, to this end. Any intelligent defense of freedom as a principle, or effort to discover its proper limits, must consider the long-run historical consequences and must be based upon knowledge of what men will do with freedom and what effects their acts will have on the social life as a whole. It is not merely a question of the conflicting individual interests of different individuals. Market dealings leave wide circles of contemporary individual interests unprotected and fail to give others effective expression in motives to action, and this fact alone calls for compulsory coordination of activities by some inclusive group organization. The individual cannot possibly know the effects of his acts or transactions even upon

living persons and their interests, and still less upon "civilization," beyond an extremely narrow segment of space and time, and even then
usually neither accurately nor at all completely. He does not "know"
their effects upon himself but always *takes chances* in various ways and
degrees.

20. We are not at the moment concerned with the question whether
or under what conditions some organ representing the group and acting
or ordering action on its behalf may be able to see farther or more correctly (and may be relied upon to act in the general interest). The point
at the moment is simply that society has strong reasons for maintaining
powerful brakes on departures from the "beaten path." Primitive society
was wise in its conservatism, for it knew at least that the group had
previously lived somehow, both as individuals and as a group. And liberal society, it now seems, has acted frivolously in switching over quite
suddenly to an extreme opposite set of assumptions, that the new is
better than the old, that the good consists in change, or at least in freedom of the individual to make changes, rather than in stability. This
emphasis on the necessity of an *onus probandi* in favor of conservatism,
and against change, must stand as our last word at this point.

II. Idealism and Marxism

In this section we shall consider, in their relation to the problem of economic reform, two of the three general ethical methods or approaches
which seem to be most important in Western civilization as bases for the
criticism of liberalism, and possible successors to it as the ethical basis of
a social order. The three viewpoints referred to are Idealism, Marxism,
and Christianity. For a discussion within the scope of an article, the
respective viewpoints or conceptions must naturally be taken in a rather
general interpretation, without any attempt at precise definition or references to the literature, or an adequate polemical defense of the view
presented as to what constitutes the essential and distinctive principle of
each. They will be considered more or less comparatively, in relation to
liberalism, which, as the accepted moral basis of social order hitherto in
our culture, seems to be entitled to the advantage of the *onus probandi.*

A. Idealism

In the academic and speculative ethical tradition of the modern world,
the most important view of ethical problems and principles alternative

to liberalism (utilitarianism, economism—and, we may add, pragmatism) in terms of which the latter has been criticized, is what may be referred to as rationalistic or idealistic ethics. It is represented philosophically by the Hegelian and neo-Hegelian school or tradition. The contrast between liberalism and idealism may be provisionally indicated by the terms "individualism" and "groupism." The task of the discussion is to show what these concepts really mean for the purposes of our problem. It will be recalled as the main thesis of the previous article that the crux of utilitarian liberalism did not lie in the theory of hedonism, or any theory of the content of the good, but simply in the doctrine of individual autonomy, with mutual consent—assumed to be in general a criterion of mutual advantage—as the ethical ideal in all dealings or relations between individuals.[14] The central tenet of idealism, in contrast, is that "society" is the real repository or locus of value, and the real choosing subject or moral agent. The idealist considers the individual as existing "for" society, much as an organ or cell exists for the organism, instead of the converse, or instead of viewing society as having no reality except as an association of individuals for mutual individual advantage. Of course both of these positions are untenable in any extreme version. Any simple either-or dichotomy of viewpoints in social philosophy is necessarily wrong. In this case it is especially clear that there is validity in both positions and that both are partial truths in various meanings, along with many other conceptions of society. (Among these other conceptions, that of a part of the members of society exploiting or using others must not be left out of account.)

From the standpoint of a critical survey of principles advocated for the guidance of social action or policy, the elementary difficulty of definition or clear formulation arises out of the relation between theories of what is, and theories of what ought to be—assuming that the word "theory" can properly be used in this second connection. As regards idealism in particular, the first point for emphasis is that in the statements of the position by its advocates it is primarily a metaphysical theory of the nature of society and derives most of its appeal as a program from its merit in this regard. Its implications, or the ostensible deductions from it, for the guidance of action are much less cogent, either logically or ethically. That is, the social policies advocated are open to question, both as to their actual relation to the premises from which they are ostensibly deduced, and as to whether they are valid on any grounds, either as axioms or as deductions from any axioms which are acceptable as such.

The philosophical problem as to the nature of the empirical social and political reality is properly in question here only or in so far as such truths or postulates can be validly used as premises for the inference of principles of a distinctly ethical sort. On this point, it seems necessary to take a negative position, with one important qualification. Moral ideals, in the strict sense, must be either axioms of moral common sense, or deductions from such axioms. This problem is almost purely one of "critical" thinking, and relative to norms rather than facts. Its relation to any question of fact in the meaning of sense observation is very indirect. The qualification is that there is not really much meaning to moral-political speculation in a vacuum, i.e., without reference to what is possible and practicable in the real world. (The human significance of descriptive essays on "Heaven" is a question about which the writer has puzzled a good deal, without reaching any very satisfactory conclusions!) From this practical point of view, it is certainly necessary to keep clearly in mind that the question is one of changing an existing situation, beginning with that situation as it is "here and now," and using means and procedures which are actually available as elements in that situation.[15]

In spite of their divergent metaphysical premises, both utilitarianism and idealism have a common general conception of social action, which is the real essence of each position from the point of view here in question, the discussion of policy.[16] In terms of a first approach, the difference seems to be, in short, purely metaphysical. Both systems conceive of society or the state in terms of law, and of law as the expression of a "general will." The difference has to do with the relation between the individual will and the general or social will. Idealism defines its concepts in such a way that the two are always identical, while utilitarianism, in the "moderate" version of liberalism, recognizes both harmony and conflict.[17] The essence of liberalism was, or is, the conception of a legal state with law or legality as a moral-religious concept—in spite of the pose of hard-boiled individualism—and with absolute and "sacred" equality of all individuals before the law. This equality, moreover, holds both in the passive sense of the treatment of individuals by the law, and in the active sense of their equal participation in "making" the laws (equality of voice or vote). Government officials in particular are supposed to have no "power" (and hardly any existence) as individuals, but to act exclusively as agents of the law, both when they enforce law and when they make (i.e., change) laws. This includes a theoretically equal voice in the selection of officials, and equal opportunity to be elected to office (both under the law) through the suffrage of all. Thus ideally all political decisions in a liberal state represent the best possible compromise between the (more or less conflicting) interests of individuals—a composite, or center of gravity, or "equilibrium of forces," force being the form under which interests are conceived as operating.[18]

Differences between this ideal result and the way things work out in practice need not be considered in detail here. The "worst" features of the reality are no doubt two: First, the general conception tends to get to be that the majority has the "right" to rule the minority, which is an utterly different matter than the conception of the general will with voting as the best method of ascertaining or expressing it. (Also the vote which decides a concrete issue need not in fact be a majority, or even a very large fraction of the total, and need not be cast with much reference to that issue.) Secondly, and perhaps worse still, the machinery operates through campaigning and partisan organization designed to influence the electorate, and in the nature of the case campaigners use any procedure or device which "works," which brings victory to the user. Public political discussion under actual conditions very frequently works in the opposite direction from that of forming a real intelligent general will or consensus, giving rise to hostility, bad blood, and partisanship for the sake of partisanship.

Mere competitive persuasion of the masses is not generally, if it is under any conditions, a good test of truth or of the real merits of a question. The saving grace of liberalism lay in the assumed moral and constitutional commitment to minimizing the functions of government and the sphere of its activity, i.e., to "freedom" as the fundamental ideal, and the use of coercion negatively for the most part, to prevent coercion by individuals and private groups. This means using it to enforce the ideal of mutual free consent as the basis of social relations, plus only such regulatory measures and "public works" as are not seriously questioned. Apart from this ideal, as an accepted constitutional principle, the notion of majority rule would probably never have been seriously defended by competent thinkers as essentially better than other forms of tyranny.

Turning to consider idealism as a contrasting political conception, with "society" as the unit instead of the "individual," we confront in the first place the rather mechanical but vital question of the definition of "society" in the concrete sense of physical boundaries. To this question there are two main possible answers. The first is to accept as "given, once for all, the existing political map of the world—divisions and subdivisions!—as it stands, at the moment when the question happens to be raised.[19] Now it is a glaring matter of fact, however unpleasant, that the political organization of the world, or lack of it, at any date in history is a product of the historical processes of the past, which present a mixture of "brute force and accident," lying and trickery—the "horrid tale of murder and spoil, etc.," of the poet. The result is satisfactory to no one who views it with any impartiality. As an ideal it would be accepted only by the furious partisan of some glutted imperialism which could not hope to get more and would be certain to lose rather than gain by any change.

The question of a possible redefinition of political units, a redrawing of the political map of the world, is usually discussed in terms of the unity and diversity of "culture," which is the second conceivably possible solution of the problem of definition of "society." But this solution is in practice hopelessly ambiguous, whether referred to populations themselves and their will to unity or separateness, or to "experts." In much of Europe, in particular, it would be physically impossible to draw the political map in such terms, by any interpretation. The European (and African-Islamic-Asiatic) settlement of 1919, after the First World War, with the aftermath, renders superfluous any detailed discussion of this topic. Besides the vagueness of the principle, in relation to the facts, we must also recognize that cultural unity and divergence are also, and nearly to the same extent as legal boundaries, the product of the same largely non-moral or immoral historical forces.

The position as to "real" or ideal boundaries of societies which is, quite naturally, taken in practice, for the most part, is one which mixes or combines the two possible solutions in such a way as largely to get the worst consequences of both. Most of the interpreters are partisans of some existing state, and draw the boundaries of that unit to include everything actually included at the moment and as much more as any plausible historical reason or justification can be found for doing. There are hardly any limits to the extension of most of the greater states on this principle, if one goes far enough back in history (and not too far). But in fact the process does not stop even here. The notion of "natural superiority," racial or cultural, is called in to support a "right" to include any strongly desired slice of the territory and population of the globe "inferior" in culture, either on the basis of incorporation or of permanent retention in a more or less servile status. (Nor is this a mere manifestation of wickedness; the problem of backward peoples is real.)

Thus the physical question of the boundaries and the inclusiveness of the state merges into the ethical question of the nature of the social end which is set over against the individual ends (individually judged) of liberalism. It is natural to assume that the end of political policy is itself political; and this runs naturally if not inevitably into the conception of the end as aggrandizement of the political and/or cultural unit as such. And again, political aggrandizement inevitably takes chiefly the concrete form of military power. A glance at modern history is enough to show that in particular the economic policy of states has aimed at military strength practically to the extent that it has been "socialized," i.e., has departed from the liberal ideal of allowing each individual to pursue his own well-being in his own way, subject only to the principle of mutual consent, enforced by law.[20]

The considerations just noticed have to do with the meaning of society in relation to other societies, or concretely with "international" affairs. With reference to the internal problems of any group, the fundamental issues may again be raised by the question "Who is the state?" but with a different interpretation. The crucial fact is that when a society has occasion to "speak" at all—to declare itself on any matter, internal or external—it necessarily speaks through some individual human being, or at most some very small group; and when a society acts, either on any of its own members or externally, it acts similarly through human agents. The tendency in philosophical formulations of the idealistic theory is to ignore the social-problem side of this whole matter, to explain what happens by assuming that a social group acts as a whole and spontaneously, either directly in dealing with concrete situations affecting group life, or at least in designating agents to act for it. That is, the theory tends to abstract altogether from power relations within a social group and the problems which these involve. (Or if there is a contest, one side is naively taken as representing the society, the other as subversive.)

Now this view is in accord with fact in some divisions or aspects of social life, such as language, and social usages, in so far as these do take care of themselves "automatically," without giving rise to any recognized problem. In a small primitive group, the activities of various kinds, economic, religious, and "social" in the narrow sense, may be reduced to a routine or ritualized to such a degree that this view is valid over most of the field of activity. It may even hold for the enforcement of the criminal law—if the concept of law is taken to apply under such conditions; that is, the "law" may either be enforced by "mob" action (as we should call it) or by functionaries selected by ritual and proceeding in strict accord with ritual. It is conceivable, at least, that in nearly any connection the general will may be a plain matter of fact and may present no "problem" of discovery, interpretation, or execution.[21]

The idealistic theory of society as an "organic" unity, or "whole," applies very well, in short, as long as there are no problems. A social problem arises out of difference of opinion, and/or clash of wills, within the membership of a group. A clash of wills, it should be observed, does not of itself give rise to a social problem; it does so only if there is a difference of opinion connected with it in some way—at least as to what "society" is to do about it. It is in connection with problem situations that the difference between liberalism and idealism comes to light. Such situations have arisen especially in connection with war, which resists ritualization, and with demands for *change* in the law. In the face of a real problem, idealism tends to advocate the "traditional" solution in so far as one can be found; first, in the literal sense of following tradition on the concrete issue; and second, when tradition gives no direct answer, it tends to emphasize the traditional distribution of authority in the group. Thus the whole bias and tendency of idealism is *conservative,* in both the natural meanings of the term, adherence to any established practice, and leaving all matters of social action or change to the decision of the parties actually established in positions of authority. And under conditions where the need for action is recognized, the latter tendency predominates, meaning that an extreme concentration of power in the hands of irresponsible persons as functionaries is favored; or, in everyday terms, it means aristocracy and monarchy.[22]

This view finds cogent argumentative support in the theory of division of labor. One thinks at once of the fable of the quarrel between the bodily members, hand, stomach, and brain. The doctrine of evolution has contributed to strengthen its appeal, especially as to the progressive centralization of control functions in the organism in the brain ("cephalization"). Philosophically, or analytically, speaking, the issue between aristocracy and democracy (idealism and liberalism) is largely a question of the relations between knowledge and will, or of their relative importance. The social interest is naturally thought of as pertaining to the population as a whole. But knowledge, both of the precise nature and content of that interest, and even more, of the technical means or procedures adapted to promote it, is naturally treated as a specialty of selected individuals or circles. In practical affairs, the question of the relation between individual interest and group interest tends to drop out or become "academic," the issue being joined on the *method* of determining the best interest of the group and its members, which both parties virtually (and ultimately no doubt quite properly) assume to be harmonious. There is no possible issue on the fact that a group of any size must act through agents, officials, including under modern conditions the activity of law-making (i.e., law-changing). Thus the concrete issue becomes that of the "responsibility," or irresponsibility, of officials, and of concrete means for getting officials really to act for the interests of society rather than in their own interests, as individuals or as a "class." On this point there is much to be said on both sides, but this essay is not the place to say it, except for one point.

Our concern is with ethics, and specifically with remedies for the basic ethical defect of liberalism or individualism. This defect, it will be recalled, has to do with the preservation and improvement of culture in those aspects which are not adequately taken care of by individual self-interest or the interest of the private family, or other private or voluntary associations. It is a question of fact and of factual analysis to determine what these are, since it is presumably admitted that there are moral and social interests of many sorts which will in practice be *better* promoted by "society as a whole," which means the state, or specifically the government, than they will be if left to voluntary action on the part of individuals and spontaneous free groups.

At bottom the problem is obviously twofold—assuming that we do not accept a rigid ruling-caste system in which the rulers either use the mass of the people for their own ends or treat them as little children. First, there must be provision for adequate *discussion* of questions of social policy from the standpoint of the ultimate long run or of fundamental values as distinct from individual interests, leading to the formation of a recognized general will. Second, provision must be made that the results of such discussion shall be carried into effect as fast as genuine results are reached. As regards the first issue, there is relatively little difference of opinion that leadership in discussion needs to be the work of specialists, of men of "leisure" in the sense of freedom from routine economic cares and ability to devote their entire energies to the "intellectual life." (The relation between this and "education," in the narrow sense, is a question.) In practice the question has to do with the selection of the individuals to perform the function of intellectual leadership, specifically whether they should be a hereditary class or caste, or a profession recruited from the whole population; and if the latter, what is to be the method of selection, and the method of their training and remuneration or support.

The final question of application or execution, perhaps most crucial of all, is whether the class or group of intellectual specialists should have *power* to effectuate their decisions, or should have to act by persuading either political officials entirely distinct from themselves or the masses. These questions cannot be discussed here. We may remark that the "commercialization of culture" is one of the most sinister phases of liberalism as it actually works. On the other hand, the idealistic alternative to liberalism, while, viewed in the abstract, it does seem to offer some solution for the weaknesses of the latter in the way of a more adequate consideration of those interests of the distant future which seem to form the content of the concept of group interest, yet presents equally fatal weaknesses in practice. In particular, as already pointed out, idealism means, in practice, first the deification of the state and the interpretation of the interests of the state in terms of political aggrandizement through military power rather than in terms of cultural values; and second, it means either traditionalism or authoritarianism in the constitution of the state.

A few words are called for in relation to the current historical development in the direction of social stratification and dictatorial leadership, or "corporativism." Superficially, this presents important differences as compared with a traditional-authoritarian system such as obtained in the later Middle Ages, the period of feudal monarchy. One detail, which will not be gone into here, is the tendency of the political state to absorb or even to replace "the church"; in reality, this is only a continuation of a tendency which has been going on in the national states throughout their history, and which, one must say, is a logical development, probably an inevitable one if national states were to survive and not give place to a world political order corresponding to the teachings of the accepted world religion. As to the corporative dictatorship itself, the essential fact may be stated in three words: it is new. This means, in the nature of the case, that it is not traditional. But this does not mean that, from the moment it becomes securely established and accepted, it will take the location of ultimate political power any less as "given" or a given basis for its further extension, than would be true in the oldest and most stable system under any ideology. It is also obvious that prior to the

establishment of any dictatorial regime, in so far as it appeals for popular support, its promoters are in essentially the same position as the candidates for office under any democratic regime. (In so far as a political
coterie is struggling to get or keep power through conspiracy and force,
this of course does not so fully apply.) The special feature of the position
of a group publicly campaigning for dictatorial powers is that they virtually announce in advance, to all who are intelligent enough to understand the simplest political situation, that once in power they will do as
they please, as far as they "can," that the people are being asked to write
a political "blank check" valid for all future time.

It is also in the nature of the case that any new power organization,
while it is organizing and stabilizing itself, will present much of the
appearance of co-option, on a "merit" basis. In this respect, the most
important question regarding the new dictatorships—"communism" in
Russia as well as "fascism" or national socialism, or whatever name any
ideological dictatorship may have given itself—cannot be answered for
a generation or two, at least. That is, we cannot tell to what extent, or in
what form, such a system will settle down into a "class" structure in the
only proper sense of the word, a stratification in which position is determined primarily by birth. On general grounds, such a stabilization is
what one would expect to happen—as feudal relations and guild privileges tended to become hereditary in the Middle Ages.

B. Marxism

During the better part of a century—since the publication of the *Communist Manifesto* in 1848—economic reformism in the European world
has been coming more and more to mean the philosophy and movement
known as Marxism, ostensibly a development from the Hegelian form
of philosophical idealism. As hardly needs to be said, it is impossible to
discuss it briefly without seeming both superficial and dogmatic. This
impression will undoubtedly be aggravated by the content of what the
present writer has to say. For the movement presents an especially aggravated case of a large part of the world being "out of step with me."
Especially interesting is its relation to Christianity. For where the latter
seems to involve romantic oversimplification of a sentimental or moralistic sort, Marxism seems romantically immoralistic, destructive, diabolical. Sombart has somewhere remarked that Marx was a man of two
souls, a thinker and a hater; I should say that as a hater he was undoubtedly entitled to a very high rank. If the gospel of love will not solve our

problems, we must admit the fact and turn from it in sorrow, but we can both confidently and joyfully reject the gospel of hate.[23] Marxism is not merely a romantic oversimplification; it is intellectually self-contradictory and ethically nihilistic and monstrous.

To intellectual analysis, Marxism presents two main elements or aspects, a philosophy of history and a social propaganda; and the two meet and fuse in the highly ambiguous doctrine of the class war.[24] It is hardly possible to take the class war seriously as a theory of history, or even to form a judgment as to how seriously it was "really" taken by Marx and Engels, or is taken by their followers. The essential meaning of the notion is obviously its pragmatic significance. The class war idea was put forward as a theoretical view of what happens; but the aim, conscious or unconscious, obviously was to use the theory to make it happen, to foment a class war—which of course had not previously existed, at least in the desired form and degree, or there would have been no occasion for the propaganda. What is ominously as well as profoundly significant is that human nature and human mentality are such that a theory of what does and must happen—and especially such a theory of "inevitable victory," annihilating all opposition—will tend to make people act in accord with it, and so to bring the facts into accord with it. But this is largely the case. The doctrine that social life has been and is a war between classes has proved so effective in promoting a class war that it begins to seem doubtful whether there is an effective preventive, i.e., any effective mode of resistance except war, in which other classes will take up the challenge of the "proletariat" and its sympathizers and fight the thing through to a finish. This is what current history seems to show; where the Marxists have shown serious strength but without being able to carry through their program for seizure of power, Marxism is being suppressed and all the liberties of the masses along with it.

At the time when the propaganda became active, in the later nineteenth century, the social situation clearly was not one of class war. But the propagandists hoped to develop a political movement of that form, by which they would in the first place, of course, ride to power; afterwards, they would (presumably) use their power to effect certain political objectives and social changes which they considered desirable. The nature of the ultimate program will be briefly noticed later. The interrelations and relative importance in the minds of the promoters of Marxism, as of any movement, of these two motives—getting power, and using power to achieve particular results—it is useless to attempt to unravel.[25]

Underlying the historical theory of the class war, the intellectual basis or content of Marxism is in the first place "dialectical materialism." This is a supposedly materialistic interpretation of social process, arrived at by inverting the Hegelian idealistic or dialectical world view. There would be no point to any extended examination into the meaning of "materialism." As every student knows, it dissolves under critical examination into phenomenalism, sensationalism, conceptualism, or field theory, or some sort of non-physical conception of the ultimate nature of matter itself. The essential fact is that Marx and Engels never gave the matter any competent or serious critical examination. What they seem to have meant by it can be best expressed by some such designation as naive empiricism, positivism, or sensationalistic phenomenalism, really involving an injunction against any effort at definition of content that would go beyond the common sense of the man in the street. The crucial matter for practical purposes, in line with the general standpoint of these articles, is that the position reduces all discussion to nonsense, all utterance to noise or physical configuration of some sort. The statements of the propagandist himself, like other utterance, are also social and historical phenomena. And to assert that they are merely the physical effects of physical causes amounts to saying that one is not saying anything, a self-contradiction which seems to surpass any other conceivable example of the species self-contradiction in self-contradictoriness.[26]

In the second place, the Marxian historical philosophy is called "economic." This concept is so ambiguous as to involve confusion of most of the irreconcilable conceptions of the nature of social reality which the human mind has recognized or invented. On one hand, it may refer to a doctrine or thesis that all individual behavior is economically motivated, meaning fully accounted for in terms of use of means, or effort to use means, with maximum efficiency in realizing given ends. But even this statement is ambiguous, since the assertion that men do act in such a way as to maximize something and the assertion that they attempt to do that, and nothing else, themselves belong in two incompatible philosophical systems. All treatment of motives on the analogy of mechanical forces, tending to establish equilibrium (or perpetual oscillations) involves abstracting from the factor of possible error, and consequently from that of effort, in human conduct and the elimination of any problem-solving character and denial of the reality of problems. If behavior is really economic, it cannot be "perfectly" economic. It is in fact and undeniably problem-solving, which is to say that it involves effort and the liability to error. Any other conception, excluding effort and error, destroys its economic character and is clearly untenable.

The third meaning which the concept of the economic has, or is assumed in Marxism to have, is a form of historical causality, or historical law, or cultural positivism. This is a conception of cause and effect in cultural phenomena as such, without reduction to physical terms on the one hand, or to psychological terms on the other—i.e., without ascribing human conduct to motivation of any sort. This third meaning forms the natural and best interpretation of historical dialectic. It is the sort of methodological assumption ordinarily made in the study of linguistic change, and of which linguistics furnishes the best example. Languages are supposed to change in accord with their own laws of change, and the changes are explained when the laws are discovered and stated. And the same interpretation can be applied to law and other social phenomena. Marxism applies it first to "economic" process—somehow defined, or left undefined; it then explains other phases of the historical process by treating the "economic" element or factor as an independent variable or cause, which proceeds thus in accord with its special laws and controls all other elements in the historical process as dependent variables or effects. As to the meaning or content of the economic element itself, it would seem that the best interpretation of the Marxian conception is to take it as meaning technology, in an inclusive sense, and to view the whole position as a technological interpretation of history. This view cannot be derived conclusively from the writings of Marx and Engels, which do not indicate any one view unambiguously. But it seems to be more defensible than any other interpretation. A technological interpretation, again, amounts to looking at history in "Darwinian" terms and accepting a theory of biological determinism. At the human level, biological efficiency as a variable may be considered to be a matter of technology, and historical change viewed as the "survival of the fittest" in a competition between groups on the basis of technical efficiency, taking account both of growth in numbers and of military superiority.[27]

Darwinism, in turn, is ordinarily thought of in terms of "natural selection" in a "struggle for existence"; and this struggle may verbally suggest the class struggle, or war, of Marxism, already referred to. But a little reflection will show that if Darwinism is made to support a culture-positivism interpretation of history, in the way just indicated, it cannot at the same time support, or even leave room for, a class-struggle theory. A criticism of the class-struggle concept requires consideration of the two notions, struggle and class. The first question is how far and in what sense human history is an affair of struggle at all, as opposed to cooperation, or some other form of motivation, or of unmotivated action. Now the concept of struggle is really a new theoretical category of behavior entirely distinct from all those hitherto mentioned, and in addition is itself a highly ambiguous notion. It clearly cannot be reduced to cultural positivism or "dialectic," although that is the meaning which must be given to it in the connection just considered. If it is a positive category, it is not struggle in the meaning of ordinary usage in connection with war or any contest between human beings, whether individuals or groups, for this is or involves purposive behavior, and at a very high level of complexity.

The notion of biological struggle, either against the environment or as "competition" with other species, is very difficult to interpret. We raise the whole question of the nature of biological phenomena and of evolution in particular. It seems to be impossible to think of the facts entirely apart from some idea of struggle and competition. But it is competitive in a sense in which competition is completely foreign to the behavior of the economic man, and which yet is essentially teleological, and not reducible to positive process. In any event, the class struggle, if it is to serve the purposes of the Marxian interpretation, must be taken in a sense categorically different from both. This must be a real fight. It is competitive in a far deeper sense than is, for example, a foot race. In the first place, it is like those games in which it is as much a part of the player's objective to impede and thwart the efforts of his opponent as it is to achieve his own positive aim of "scoring." But there is a third degree of difference from individual economic effort which itself, in so far as it is economic, is not competitive at all in the psychological sense. The Marxian class struggle is not merely a duel à outrance but is a duel without rules of any sort. There seems to be no intellectual bridge between such a notion and any form of historical determinism.

This brings us to the second element in the class struggle notion, that of classes, social or economic. But any effort to define the notion of class and to identify classes, as defined, in any actual historical situation will make one more than hesitant in treating historical conflict as a class struggle. In history, both individuals and groups in infinite variety of kinds, and changing in character almost from hour to hour, are constantly pitted against each other on an infinite variety of issues. And very largely there is no issue at all except the struggle for power for the love of power or even, in no small degree, for the love of struggle, or of victory.

For one thing, a matter of detail but fatal to the theory, if a class struggle or war is to be realistic, the lines must be drawn between two factions; even a three-cornered war is hardly thinkable. A final or crucial struggle must be between those who are "for" and those who are "against" something or other, some leader or program of action. On the political arena, to be sure, there may be maneuvering and jockeying for power among a number of conflicting parties or positions, apart from any issue except that of power itself. But the effort to interpret any important historical struggle, especially in modern history, in terms of classes and class interests seems to reduce the idea to absurdity. Political parties do not correspond to classes, and neither does the line-up on particular issues. And this is a most fortunate and praiseworthy circumstance. For if political divisions did take place on the lines of particular but conflicting economic interests, or of sharply conflicting social philosophies, it is hardly conceivable that free society would continue to exist. In other words, the result would be a real class war, in which some class would win and all others would cease to exist, politically at least, if not physically.

Before leaving the intellectual confusions of Marxism and turning to its ethical aspect, and particularly the ethics of the class struggle theory, we may repeat once more our main point in this whole discussion of the ethics of reform. It seems to be a first and "absolute" requirement for any ethical discussion that it rest on philosophical premises implicit if not explicit, which make discussion possible, meaningful. But all the interpretations of the economic interpretation which have been mentioned have the characteristic in common that they violate this elementary requirement; they all make all social discussion of social policy unreal. Every one of them embodies either some form of positivistic premise or some form of egoistic voluntarism. And if anything whatever is self-evident, it is surely self-evident that the members of a group cannot carry on a discussion of group policy using exclusively propositions beginning either with "in fact" or with "I want." There must be recognition of some "objective value judgment," recognition that questions of policy for the group are problems, and have better and worse solutions. In so far as any discussion on the basis of any of the philosophical positions so far considered is thinkable at all, it is thinkable only in and for an intellectual community completely segregated from the society whose phenomena are the subject of the discussion, and the phenomena must be regarded as presenting problems only in the sense of intellectual problems for the discussion group, not problems of action for the society itself. This hypothesis would raise the philosophical question whether it is possible to believe in the reality of a discussion group without believing that other societies, taken in relation to other phases of activity, have the same fundamental character to some extent, i.e., that in human society in general problems of action are to some extent settled by real discussion.

If discussion itself is mechanically or culturally determined, or if it can be adequately accounted for (causally) in terms of individual interests alone, whether these are thought of as being essentially economic or of whatever kind, then discussion simply ceases to be discussion. The completely candid Marxist would have to begin every statement with the observation that the noise he is about to make is to be regarded as the effect of appropriate causes, or (really also, at the same time) that the proposition he is about to utter is purely an expression of certain (economic) interests of his own ego. Even this is not the whole story. A slightly more persistent and penetrating philosophical critique would show that without both individual problem-solving and real discussion between individuals, it is impossible to believe in facts, in the plain man's sense, to say nothing of the facts and principles of science; utterance itself becomes unreal and illusion an illusion. Ultimately there is no categorical difference in intellectual status or objectivity, in the general sense of validity or verity, between judgments or statements of fact and judgments or statements of value. Truth itself is finally a value, and the will to believe the truth, rather than anything else that one might for any other reason wish to believe, is the foundation of all morality.

Before we can take up the ethics of the class struggle theory, we have further to note that the theory violates the premises of its general position by its conception of classes. These are taken as given, as real, but as purely self-seeking entities, though without moral principles of any sort. They are unified by pure individual self-interest or some purely unconscious force. The Marxian economic class carries to a higher power the inherent unreality of the economic man. In the first place, given such classes, if any one of them entered into negotiation of any sort with any other, the activity would necessarily be regarded as purely a technique of manipulation, or essentially of combat, to be employed only when and as it should seem likely to be more effective or "cheaper" than any other procedure, and to be categorically dropped, and all past results ignored, the moment these conditions ceased to apply. No agreement, commitment, or promise made by such a class would have the least validity, and no statement it might make would have any status as truth. As Kant pointed out, if assertions and promises are recognized as having this character, they cannot be either effective or meaningful; the very notion is a self-contradiction. Negotiation in such terms can be meaningful only as deception; but the Marxists make this impossible by openly declaring their position in advance. The clear implication is that the only rational procedure is a literal fight or war from the outset, one which recognizes no rules and gives no quarter. Any utterance is a pure inanity, unless possibly of the nature of a war-cry intended to terrorize and unnerve the enemy, or to heighten the courage and energy of the partisans by and for whom it is employed.

In the second place, it should be superfluous to elaborate upon the absurdity of the notion of an economic class. The historical unreality of the category, already pointed out, is no mystery. It is as impossible for a social class, containing a minimum of two individuals, to be perfectly homogeneous in interests as it is for a society in any sense whatever. That is, there are "class" distinctions within any class, different in degree at most from distinctions between classes. Any group which is able to hold together and to function in any way as a group must be unified either by moral ideals or by a possible predominance of a common interest in the attainment of some very specific objective over the conflicting interests of the members. It cannot be held together by literal force, unless it is composed of a single individual possessing sufficient power in some form to dominate all others, who must be weak enough and few enough to be so dominated, both individually and in any combination which they are able to effect. For any ruling group or power group is again a society, necessarily more or less heterogeneous and with its own conflicts of interests. Under realistic conditions, the only possible common interest which, apart from some ethical unifying force, is conceivably able to predominate over divergent individual interests, is the conflict interest, a "war" against some other group or groups. And this is in conformity with the Marxist conception itself. What is overlooked, or purposely not mentioned, is the obvious fact that if any such combat group succeeds in its objective of destroying the enemy power, it must either in turn be held together by the interest in keeping power and exploiting the defeated enemy or it will immediately disintegrate along some lines into new groups or "classes" of some form, struggling for power.

We come now to the ethical ideals of Marxism, its critique of existing society and its program of social change. Viewing it as a social phenomenon, and ignoring, as we have to do to consider it in that light, all its facade of philosophical hocus-pocus, we find an interesting variant on the not uncommon theme of romantic destructionism. Its philosophy of social action reduces to a variety of the doctrine popularized if not invented by Rousseau, that men are naturally good except as they have been corrupted by society and its institutions, but that these are entirely wicked, and consequently, the formula for the reform and regeneration of society is to destroy its institutions. The advocates of such a program are oblivious to the fact that to destroy social institutions would be to destroy society in any possible human sense. They are victims of a naive theory of social contract, according to which all social arrangements have been thought out, discussed and agreed upon, and consequently are subject to change, without limit as to extent or speed, by the same process. The view is completely unhistorical and essentially fantastic. There is no need to deny that men have any power at all to change their institutions; but it is certainly limited with respect both to the amount and the kind of change which is even "possible" for any society at any time, to say nothing of costs. To any competent mind, dissatisfaction with existing institutions should suggest as the first question the critical formulation of ideals, and then, and not really separable, the possibilities, methods, and costs of change.

The contribution of Marxism to this theme is its discovery and identification of a particular supposed source of social corruption. This of course is that some selfish "class," varying more or less in character through history, has taken possession by "force," in some form which is left unanalyzed, of the virtuous masses of society as a whole and is "exploiting" them for its own purposes. The recipe for salvation through destruction in our own day therefore takes the particular form of "liquidating" the class which is said to be performing the role of devil in modern European civilization, namely the "bourgeoisie." All political opposition to this program is assumed as a matter of course to derive from the bourgeois class itself, either directly or through paid agents or dupes. (Non-Marxist economists are allowed to hover more or less between these two classifications, paid agent and dupe.)

What is really significant about such a theory is the fact that it is taken seriously, and not only by its proponents and by the masses, but even by so many students of recognized competence and presumptive freedom from conscious and crude political bias. As already remarked, this acceptance of the class-struggle program is highly indicative as to the prospect of intelligent and moral political action by human beings. It not only does not seem to occur to the masses, or to the intelligentsia, who are taken in—to say nothing of the propagandists themselves—that the allegation of selfish interest which is glibly pinned on the opposition

applies even more obviously to the promoters of the class war themselves. They are assumed to be free from any taint of self-interest! They
are merely soliciting for themselves the role of absolute monarch over
their country and the world, or of some satisfactory position at court or
in the administration—the details to be worked out after the revolution. Their devotion to society and to humanity is so great that they offer
to serve in the highest capacity, up to the unconstitutional imperatorship
of the world.

The doctrine itself—that all that need be done in order to awake
the next morning in, or on the way towards, an idealistic Utopia is to
destroy the admittedly crude and imperfect civilization which the race
has developed through history thus far, by destroying its institutions
and power relations and turning over all power to the promoters of the
destruction for the purpose of reconstruction—has an evident if mysterious appeal to elemental human nature.[28] How such propaganda, and
the romantic appeal of destruction in general, is to be effectively combated, is perhaps the most serious of practical social problems. And the
most serious as well as most puzzling phase of this situation is that in
their manners and conscious intentions the promoters are for the most
part "nice people," and "honorable men," and will readily, and often
artistically, "with reasons answer you." Not only that; they are morally
earnest, even to a fault—in fact, to a degree which makes it a serious
ethical problem whether moral earnestness can be assumed to be a virtue at all. For in a plain factual appraisal, what they are doing is more
catastrophically evil than treason, or poisoning the wells, or other acts
commonly placed at the head of the list of crimes. The moralization of
destruction and of combat with a view to destruction, goes with the
kind of hero-worship that merges into devil-worship. Such phenomena
show that human nature has potentialities that are horrible, in full
match for all those which are noble and fine. Which qualities spring the
more from original nature and which from social institutions is a question of little meaning. Man is a social animal, a product of history. All
that is good in him is obviously a reflection of social discipline and the
product of the age-long travail through which has developed that civilization which our romantic destructionists propose to sweep away by
violent revolution.

As suggested above, Marx himself (or Marx-Engels) did not unambiguously expound any doctrine of an immediate and complete establishment of the ideal Utopia through a single revolutionary act. At least
as early as 1852, he began to make vague references to a "dictatorship

of the proletariat" as a transitional stage between capitalism and ideal socialism or communism. As the professed followers and interpreters of the highest recognized authority in the Marxist parties have never reached any agreement as to the concrete meaning either of this transitional state or of the perfected stages which follow it, or the process of transformation, there would be little point in the present writer setting forth any extensive speculation on these matters in the present essay. In fact he makes no pretense to extensive Marxian scholarship or to any of the qualifications required for achieving an authoritative position in this particular branch of exegetics. On the basis of an admittedly brief and unsympathetic study, it would appear that what is really meant by the revolution is simply the seizure of political power through a *coup d'état* on the part of the leadership of some working-class party. And the dictatorship of the proletariat would be the dictatorship—over the proletariat and not by it, as well as over anyone else whom they might choose to allow to continue to live—of these same people and their successors in the positions of power, however the latter might come to power, as long as they called their system by that name and were able to "get away with it." The ultimate "classless" society has never been described in the least detail. It is simply the bright vision of an anarchist Utopia, a society in which there are no problems or issues, especially economic issues, on which people at all seriously disagree. This is the only meaning which the writer can attach to such slogan-phrases as "the withering away of the state," "the administration of things without authoritative control over men," and "production for use and not for profit." Historically most notable is the fact that in Russia the dictatorship has not only become progressively more dictatorial over everybody, and more ruthless, and less equalitarian, but has obviously tended more and more to put off to the Greek Kalends the removal of the dictatorship and establishment of the classless communistic society.[29]

In extenuation for Marxists—though hardly for Marxism—it would be possible to bring forward a *tu quoque*. (This famous "argument" has an embarrassing way of seeming to provide a sort of defense for the advocates of any position, however bad morally or intellectually!) At least it should be understood that there is practically nothing in Marxism which is not either copied from or equivalent to older contemporary doctrines and widely regarded statements of position.[30] The Marxist ethical doctrine—meaning anti-ethics or ethical nihilism, absolute egoism or moral solipsism—is identical with the theoretical position of the early-nineteenth-century utilitarians, who were practically the classical economists under another name. For this purpose it does not matter whether we consider the utilitarian position to be that of psychological hedonism or give any other theory or interpretation of the actual content or "object" of individual desire. The other form of ethical nihilism which is represented in Marxism, namely, "dialectical determinism," has already been shown to be practically identical with positivism, in the sense of culture-historical positivism, which was the "first philosophy" of nineteenth-century liberalism, usually combined, to be sure, with egoistic voluntarism, in spite of the fact that the two are palpably contradictory.

Of course this line of argument "defends" Marxism at the cost of the complete sacrifice of his originality. If there is any main element in Marxism which is new, to any substantial degree, it is the class struggle theory. That also is well known to every student to have a long history prior to Marx, but the Marxian version of it may perhaps be defended as substantially different. In any case we are not concerned here with the details.

In a recent pamphlet entitled *Warning to Europe,* Thomas Mann refers to the bitter thought that to a degree the crisis in which European civilization finds itself is the consequence of the fact that the nineteenth century was too generous to the masses. Perhaps it might be said in defense, or extenuation, that the liberal reformers of the nineteenth century did not allow for the fact that members of the cultured class itself would make careers for themselves by preaching to the masses the annihilation of the cultured classes and their culture, as the way to a just, humane and more highly cultured order of things; or perhaps they did not allow for the readiness which the masses would show in listening to such preaching and following it. Proclaiming to the unfortunate and underprivileged that workers have no stake in civilization, "nothing to lose but their chains" and "a world to win" through "violent revolution sweeping away all former social order," was a political technique to which the naive Victorians perhaps did not think responsible men would stoop, or thought that, if one occasionally might do so, no considerable number of sane men, though uneducated, would listen receptively.

III. Christianity

The bearing of its most generally accepted religion upon problems of social-economic reorganization in a modern "Christian" nation is obviously a difficult subject to discuss objectively, or, especially, briefly. Not merely is it almost universally affected by emotional attitudes—"prejudices," religious or iconoclastic as the case may be—or by a more mundane, prudential regard for religion as a supposedly vital element in social order. Even from a strictly scientific point of view, we confront virtually unanswerable questions as to the causal relations between religion and morals, or *mores,* or other controlling social forces in culture and conduct. The two difficulties overlap; for there is no doubt that the belief in religion as the foundation of morality, and of social order and peace, is itself held as a prejudice or a tradition far beyond any possibility of justifying it by social-psychological analysis. Many earnest scholars and thinkers who both profess to be Christians and are recognized as such have considered the question whether modern civilization is Christian, or if so in what sense, and have admitted themselves puzzled as to the answer.

But it remains an important fact that a large majority of the people living under West-European civilization call themselves Christian in some sense of the word and at least profess to believe both that moral progress since ancient times has been chiefly due to the influence of Christianity and that the New Testament writings (and/or the teachings of "the Church" based thereon) afford an answer, in principle, and in large part, to all the moral and social problems faced by mankind. It is the purpose of this article to subject this idea, especially the second aspect of it, to a brief critical examination.

Our thesis will be twofold. First, we point out that the teachings of Christianity give little or no direct guidance for the change and improvement of social organization, and in fact give clear *prima facie* evidence of not having been formulated to that end. On this point there is relatively little disagreement, even on the part of Christian apologists. It is indeed common for the promoters of nearly any "reform" to lay claim to the support of these teachings. But this may be explained by a desire to capitalize upon the esteem in which they are held; and the wide divergence among movements for which such support is claimed is rather an argument against the view that the teachings really support any particular social change. Real differences of opinion—likely in fact to be more or less violent—arise in connection with the second part of the thesis; this is that even indirectly there is also little to be found in Christianity in the way of moral principles or ideals which can serve for the ethical guidance of deliberate political action. The question whether any proposed measure is in harmony with the "spirit" of Christianity commonly admits of no clear answer or at least none of a sort which will be accepted by Christians as a solution for practical political issues. Indeed, evil rather than good seems likely to result from any appeal to Christian religious or moral teaching in connection with problems of social action. Stated in positive form, our contention is that social problems require intellectual analysis in impersonal terms but that Christianity is exclusively an emotional and personal morality; and this, while unquestionably essential, does not go beyond providing or helping to provide the moral interest, motive, or "drive" towards finding solutions for problems. This is not only a very different thing from furnishing the solutions or even indicating the direction in which they are to be sought, but the teaching that it does furnish solutions has results which are positively evil and decidedly serious.

As already noted, the first thesis is generally accepted, and it need not be discussed at any considerable length. There is relatively little in the Gospels or other New Testament "Books"[31] which seems to refer directly to politics or the general structure of social relations. But there is enough to make it clear that the intent of the teachings was to have these conditions accepted and recognized as "given" factors in the world in which individuals and groups have to live their moral and religious lives.[32] Besides the much-quoted injunction to "render unto Caesar the things that are Caesar's," found in all three synoptic Gospels, there are even more pointed passages, such as the categorical command (in Matthew only) to obey the Scribes and Pharisees (though not to imitate their deeds!). The epistles repeatedly enjoin obedience and respect to political rulers, and command servants to be obedient and respectful to their recognized masters. This last injunction appears in at least a half-dozen places, in as many Books in the New Testament. The word for "servant" covers, if it does not specifically mean, slaves, and it is a familiar fact that the Church never condemned or officially opposed slavery. Slavery, and then serfdom (in numerous grades) gradually disappeared in Europe, for reasons various and obscure. Before the process was complete, the African slave trade, and the exploitation of slaves in European colonies (and in part in Europe itself) developed. The defenders of Negro (or Indian) slavery found no difficulty in justifying it from scripture.

We turn now to consider briefly the "spirit" of the Christian teachings and its possible implications in the way of providing ideals which might serve as a moral leaven and indirectly work for the transformation

of social institutions and relations, and ultimately furnish guidance
for conscious social action. Passing over the limitless problems of disagreement among the sources themselves or among authoritative interpretations, and looking only for agreement on some ultimate essence,
we undoubtedly find the latter (in so far as it is to be found) in the
acceptance by students and by popular opinion of the "gospel of love"
(caritas, agapé). This is embodied especially in the parallel passages on
the "greatest commandment" in Matthew and Mark, and in the answer
in Luke to the question what one must do to inherit eternal life. "Thou
shalt love the Lord thy God . . . and thy neighbor as thyself." Loving one
another is also the main theme of the teaching in the Gospel of John, and
there is the famous paean to love occupying I Corinthians 13, and further extensive documentation is familiar. If Christianity does not mean
this, there is nothing that it can be said to mean. It is no doubt justifiable to take as either interpretation of the Great Commandment or an
equivalent exhortation the "Golden Rule" of the Sermon on the Mount,
found in closely parallel wording in Matthew (7:12) and Luke (6:31).[33]

In connection with the two texts suggested, the question, What is
the spirit of Christianity? (leaving the application to social reform for
later consideration) becomes, What is the meaning of "love"? or what
do men want "others" to do to them?[34] The "love" doctrine, in the
abstract, is certainly an appealing idea. It seems natural to believe that if
people "liked" each other better, or enough, a large part of the problems
which occasion strife, hatred, and suffering in the world would not
arise, or would not be acute. Conflicts of material interest would perhaps not arise at all, or at least would not matter so much, and envy,
contumely, etc., could hardly exist. But the least critical examination in
the light of facts will show that this view cannot be maintained. Even
between friends in the narrowest and most ideal sense, conflicts of interest would by no means disappear; and while different in form, these
do not necessarily "hurt" less than in the case of strangers.

But the more serious question is how far ideal friendship intrinsically admits of generalization over, say, the population of a modern nation—and, of course, it must ultimately be over the world, since, for a
world religion, national boundaries have no moral significance. Considering love in terms of the Golden Rule, it is clear that men do not want
from many "love" in the special sense of ideal friendship. If it is not a
contradiction in thought that one might give the same quality and intensity of affection to all human beings, good, bad, and indifferent, to
the most callous criminal or the farthest Eskimo or Patagonian as well

as to one's "nearest," and still "love" any of them—if this idea can be formed, it is surely neither attractive nor helpful as a moral ideal. It would seem that a "Christian" who tried to practice such love would have no friends—being in that respect like the famous economic man. He would not be human. Hospitality as well as friendship would lose its meaning, to say nothing of "love" in any accepted interpretation.

Such universal love quite clearly is not the meaning of *agapé* in the New Testament writings. It evidently refers to some intimate association, not to human relations in general. In most cases, perhaps especially in the Gospel of John and the writings of Paul, the reference is clearly to the "brethren" in the religious group. The material as a whole strongly suggests the fraternity idea, which is such a familiar and important phenomenon virtually throughout history and anthropology. Any attempt to universalize this attitude is obviously contradictory to its nature. We have to keep in mind that Christianity was originally a gospel or cult of "brotherhood," in much this sense, and only gradually became a world religion. Moreover, its message was first addressed to the lowly, the weak, and especially the politically helpless, living in a world where they had no outlook, no future, no "hope." And the sex limitation of the concept, though not as extreme as in many other cults, can by no means be overlooked. In Paul's churches the women were distinctly silent partners. Again, an essential feature of the teaching was the conviction of the imminence of the "second coming" *(parousia)* and the establishment of the kingdom of God (or the Millennium). And even without this feature, the interpretation of Christianity as escapism, emphasized by Nietzsche, unquestionably has a large degree of validity for the early period.

That the existence of affection, in the sense of the most intimate and ideal friendship, still leaves problems to be solved, is obviously true where there is any disparity of circumstances between the parties. Perhaps it is true in rough proportion as such disparity exists. The romantic ideal of friendship seems to apply primarily to comrades in arms, or partners in adventure of some sort, hence almost exclusively to men, and men in the prime of life. Much of it is bound up with the concept of chivalry, which historically is neither Christian nor European. (But it was no more Mohammedan in the East than it was Christian in the West.) Chivalry is anything but democratic or equalitarian; it involves superiors as well as "brothers," and obedience as well as comradeship. The more prosaic but practically far more important modern conception of "live and let live," specifically as regards tolerance of differences, in religion and politics and in opinions and tastes, is for the most part the product of commercialism, of business, and not of religion. This is certainly more constructive with relation to social problems than the ideal romantic or mystical brotherhood, in the religious or any other form.

The general idea that love is no solvent of problems or reliable guide to conduct is perhaps best brought out by relations within the family. Certainly no amount (or kind) of "love" answers or removes the problems of conduct in the relations between husband and wife. And this is more poignantly true of the relation between parent and child—as the difference in "circumstances" is greater. Deficiency of love surely is not the most common or serious source of family problems. Loving one's children does not tell how to raise them properly. The problem is rather that of loving in the right way, or expressing affection in the "right," meaning "wise," conduct. Very commonly it appears that the presence of love complicates the concrete problems rather than contributes to their solution. Love may certainly clash with science in connections where the verdict rightly lies with the latter.

The family relation is also the best illustration of the undoubted fact that we are under a moral obligation to treat in different ways persons who stand in different social relations to ourselves. We seem even to be bound to feel differently towards them, though an obligation to have a feeling also appears dubious under critical scrutiny. Passing over the whole question of the ideal emotional relations between husband and wife, we consider only the relation of parents to children. The command to love one's neighbor as one's self may seem like a "hard saying"; but it is "nothing" in comparison with the obligation to love other people's children as one's own, as would be required by universal and undifferentiated or impartial love. This is not conceivably possible without destroying the private family and going over to some Platonic communism as the basis of social order—than which nothing could be more antagonistic to the accepted teachings of Christianity. And even if this were done, likes and dislikes within some kind of primary group appear to be quite inevitable. And in any case it is physically impossible to have organized social life with obligations diffused uniformly over the whole race without regard to nearness either of personal ties or functional connection.[35] It is clear that personal obligations depend on and presuppose some form of social organization and that ideals of personal relations and feelings cannot be used as premises from which to deduce norms of change in the social order. Conditions of effective action in daily life and of material progress conflict with any idealistic dream of universal freedom and brotherhood—even if that were really ideal in itself. Universal love or friendliness is only one aspect, one value, in the formulation of the ideal society towards which we must try to move.

We turn for a moment to consideration of the Golden Rule ideal of doing as one would be done by. In most real situations, intelligent people know that the "other" not merely does not want what we would want in his place, but also that what he wants is not what is good for him, or for the world, and that to give it is not the right course of action. And this is true even in the case of face-to-face personal relations, before we get to the problem-field of how to organize society. The solemn fact is that what people most commonly want for themselves is their "own way," as such, or especially *power*. And the question whether anyone ought to have power must be answered with very little reference to his desire for it or his own (honest) opinion as to his fitness to have it. Indeed fitness seems to bear rather an inverse relation to desire—as Plato taught. The question of whom to love, and how, or specifically how to express love in action, under infinitely various conditions, is certainly not to be answered exclusively in terms of the desires or wishes of the "beloved," though these are data which must be carefully considered. Love must be wise, and often stern. The New Testament scripture itself says that "whom the Lord loveth he chasteneth" (Hebrews 12:6).

What men want of others, as a matter of fact, is a question somewhat difficult to discuss without seeming to be cynical or satirical. What most of us actually want from most of the rest of mankind is pretty largely to "mind their own business and let us alone." And on examination, this is found to be by no means a mere manifestation of original sin. It is in fact very largely the moral ideal! But it is not love. On the other hand, it is like love in that it answers no questions as to the social organization; for the whole content of minding one's own business also depends on the social organization, and takes this as given. Yet it helps towards a correct statement of the ethical problem. It helps to make it clear that the ethical side of the problem of social reform is not a matter of personal feelings, but that on the contrary, as we shall further emphasize later, positive effort is necessary to keep moral emotion out of the discussion or keep it from playing a direct role. The social problem is a matter, first, of attitude towards the law or the rules of the social game as they stand at any place and time, and second, of attitude towards higher general cultural and human values as a basis for changing such an existing setup. It is the second which is the social problem in the strict sense.

Before coming to that, however, a few remarks seem to be in order on the subject of personal feelings or emotions towards others. In the first place, the type of personal contacts and relationships which an individual naturally has, or as a matter of choice may have or avoid having, itself depends on the character of the social organization. In any functioning social order, an individual undoubtedly has in some sense an "obligation" to be friendly towards others with whom he comes in any contact, and also to show special sympathy, compassion, and material helpfulness on "appropriate" occasions. This is not the place for a detailed homily on that subject, but one or two further observations seem to be called for on the content which is to be read into the Golden Rule injunction to do as you would be done by, and presumably to feel correspondingly.

What we ought to wish for others is clearly what they ought to wish for themselves—with "due" regard for their actual opinions and feelings, of course. In this connection, the first general observation in order is in line with the principle of Puritanism—which is hardly suggested by the wording of the Gospels. Each person ought to want, and very largely does want, to stand on his own feet, to play his own hand, in accord with the rules of the game.[36] In this regard, it is clear that much of what is commonly said about "helpfulness" and "service," etc., is "mush," or worse. Not only does love, as concession to the other's wishes, often conflict with respect for the person himself, or with intelligent desire for his well-being; in addition, love of persons often conflicts with love of the higher values of civilized life. It is in this connection that the really subtle and difficult problems of moral conduct arise, and the great tragedies of life. Not all the persons whom society has to treat as enemies and whom individuals have to shun or oppose are morally odious.[37] It seems to be not merely impossible, but actually undesirable and unthinkable, that living should not to a large extent take the form of contest relations and be impelled by the competitive or emulative interest. This is overwhelmingly the nature of play, recreation, or "free" activity, and it is clearly a large factor in the ideal social order to convert work into play, or give to it the psychology of play as far as possible. This side of life seems not to be recognized in the New Testament at all, even in the Pauline and other letters, which are much more realistic and disposed to emphasize purposive action than are the reported teachings of Jesus. It is hard to think of sport or sportsmanship in connection with New Testament personalities or teachings. But sportsmanship seems to be the best that modern civilization has produced as a practical and effective moral ideal or sentiment. In a contest, what each one is trying to do and wanting to do is to win. (This *means* to win in accord with the rules, though many are often willing to win by breaking them, by "cheating"!) Moral goodness towards an opponent in a game certainly does not mean "letting" him win, either openly or secretly (with possible exceptions of course).

Moreover, it seems that helpfulness in "material" or economic activities should ideally be mutual, as far as possible. Now mutual helpfulness is precisely the ideal result of economic organization on the basis of free exchange. Yet the formal, and enforced, mutuality of the market is only a short first step towards the ideal society and, as must be emphasized on every occasion, it leads to ideal results only under ideal conditions, i.e., under the condition that the whole framework of economic relations is ideal, as well as the individuals who enter into these relations.

Viewed in the large and in ethical terms, what each and all should primarily help each other to do is to realize sound ideals of personality, which inseparably involves realization of ideal social relations and institutions. But this again can only be done in the main by helping them to help themselves, together with striving cooperatively to provide the most favorable possible conditions of self-realization. In this connection, as already suggested, the most difficult of all the concrete problems is undoubtedly that of the "right" kind and degree of impartiality, and of partiality, to those who stand to "me" in any special relationship. It is evident that love of one's friends, and especially one's own children, is not unselfish and that the conceptions of selfishness and altruism admit of no simple definition. Even devotion to a cause, even a good cause, is often more or less selfish.[38]

A general view of the whole problem situation in society may be secured by adopting the standpoint of our earlier observation that in the context of reality and of relevance to reality, all discussion of moral values and conduct in the larger social relations must take place in two main stages. The first step in moral behavior in organized society is to obey and to support the existing legal order. The first and presumptive definition of what is right in any doubtful case is the answer to the question What is the law? And the law must be interpreted to include all generally accepted customs or standards which create "legitimate expectations" on the part of others.[39]

But the duty of conformity with law is only a presumption, and is valid only within limits. Often there is no law which clearly applies, or there is a serious question as to how far the law itself is "right." In so far as the individual feels compelled to pronounce that the law does not apply, or is wrong, the question of what is right behavior becomes exceedingly complex and difficult. It is not simply a question of what the law ought to be. It may be one's duty to disregard and break the law, because the particular case is clearly exceptional for some reason, a situation which law could not practically be made to cover. (This, of course does not militate against the theoretical validity of Kant's principle of generality as the criterion of rightness.) To the question how far one should give the law the benefit of the doubt, because of modesty of belief or of the value of maintaining the legal order inviolate, there is no general answer. And whether the decision is to obey the law or to break it, one confronts the separate question whether to try to get the law changed. In general, the social problem is that of changing the law, including both tradition and the public and constitutional law, which is the legal machinery for changing the law itself.

Thus our discussion brings us to the social problem as such, i.e., the problem of law-making, which always means law-changing, and in general means *legally* changing an existing law.[40] Society itself is properly defined as the legal order under which any group of people live. Any society is bounded by the area (along various "dimensions" of size and of kind and degree of sociality) within which people are actually subject to the same law. The area is not necessarily spatial or geographic, though this is now typically true for law in the formal or political sense. But any accepted rules of relationship among persons define a society as to extent, and as to the sense and the degree in which it is a society. Social problems, then, root in the brute fact that all organized relationships, or relationships of any degree of permanence whatever, imply a common recognition of rules, or an accepted pattern of action. It is an axiom of sociology that *human* beings, especially beings capable of discussion, could not possibly come into existence or continue to exist apart from a culture, or set of institutions.[41]

The point here, and the main point of this discussion of Christianity as a whole, is the negative one, that the Christian teaching not only has nothing to say about this whole problem-field of change in social organization, i.e., about law-making and constitution-making, which involve institutional change, but that it positively diverts attention both from a correct view of the problem and from the fundamental facts of social life out of which the problem arises.[42] The spirit of New Testament Christianity (passing over the politico-legal activities of organized churches in later times—for which, incidentally, there is no scriptural foundation whatever) points definitely away from all matters of positive social action, whether thought of as compulsion exercised upon individuals, or merely as the rational adaptation of means to ends. As already noted, it has little if any bearing on the rational adaptive side of even the purely individual life.

Since all organization involves more or less compulsion, Christianity may be said to point towards an ideal world in which all organized activity would be absent, a society of antinomian anarchism. Even the type of constraint involved in public esteem and disesteem in relation to "good manners" can hardly be admitted into the picture. And it is surely beyond argument that such a social situation implies the complete absence of even individual economic problems and activities, to say nothing of organized economic life.[43] Possibly it may be useful, in some very attenuated sense, to have such an ideal held up before the world for contemplation, with no indication of the character of organized action required to move towards the ideal, and with the apparent implication that it can be realized merely by admiring it or by acting as if it already existed. This seems very doubtful to the present writer, but the question may be arguable. Such an ideal, we must observe, would involve not merely material conditions of life categorically different from any that are possible for any biological species living on this earth, but also a race of "men"—if they should be called men rather than gods—having uniformly very different characteristics from any known or any possible human beings, the differences reaching far down into their biological endowment. The kind of "goodness" that would be involved is certainly not "good" for actual human beings living either in the actual world, or in the world as it can be imagined to become, as the result of any reasonably possible process of transformation, however long, by human agency. The social value of the role of parasitic saintliness in the real world is a question too long to argue, but the amount of it which can be defended as valuable, or which the world can afford, is certainly limited, and its value is highly indirect. It would seem that the situation is picturable in imagination only for disembodied spirits very different even from the "gods" of which we have anything like a concrete picture in any extant religion or theodicy. Certainly the deities of either the Greek or the Teutonic mythology would not fit into the picture.

The intellectual problem underlying any project of social reform or transformation, i.e., the "scientific" sociological problem, is in the first place the relation between good men and good institutions or laws. Within some limits, undoubtedly, the one implies the other, and either may result from the other; better men will make better institutions, and better institutions will make better men. That is, the problem of action centers in the order of priority, or of emphasis on the two lines of action, preaching or educating, and legislating. Perhaps the first phase of the question to be distinguished, approaching it from the standpoint of Christianity itself, is that of how far it is possible to perfect human nature simply by preaching good will, by "converting" individuals.

Logically prior, however, to the problem of action in the concrete sense is always the problem of deciding upon the results to be achieved by action. This is the problem of formulating ideals, the particular problem which these essays are written to emphasize as an intellectual problem. It is not even seriously discussed in most of the talk and writing about social reform, and it is no wonder that utter confusion reigns with respect to it. Recognition of the problem of ideals as logically prior to the problem of action does not in the least imply that it is necessary to have a detailed picture of the ideal society, the ultimate goal of action, agreed upon and blue-printed in advance. On the contrary; in the writer's view, all activity is more or less explorative. Perhaps no proposition about purposive behavior needs more emphasis than the fact that goals of action are probably never completely foreseen when the action is begun or decided upon. A certain element of uncertainty as to the result of action, a certain amount of curiosity as to what the result is to be, seems to be a necessary factor in motivation. The end is always more or less redefined in the course of the action itself, and an interest in this process of redefinition is inherent in the interest in action. The end or ideal which functions in advance of action is rather a sense of direction than an end in the concrete sense. Moreover, there seem to be no ends which are really final (no *summum bonum* in the classical sense) or which are not more or less consciously recognized in advance as means to further ends, and as becoming means to the extent that they are realized.

But on the other hand, ends, even in the proper limited sense of a direction of change, are not simply fabricated by creative thought. They arise out of the criticism of what is, and rational reflection on the possibilities of improvement. This means that the question of ideals takes the form of "sound" criticism of the existing situation, and hence that a logically still prior requisite is knowledge, including understanding, of what the existing situation is. This is especially important not merely because all activities looking to change begin "here and now," but because they must operate entirely on the basis of means (in the most general sense) which themselves exist as a part of the existing situation. All these knowledge data are rather a part of the process of formulating ideals than temporally prior or prerequisite.

In Western culture in our own day, the criticism of what is and the proposals for change of a reconstructive sort have come to center very largely on the economic organization of society. From the standpoint of the intelligent student of the problem of reform, this fact is itself one of the essential features of the existing situation. And it becomes in a sense the "very first" step to inquire into the validity of this belief. This is particularly important because relatively little objective examination is necessary to show that the belief that life is to be transformed for the better by changing the economic system has only a very limited amount of truth.

This fallacy is a feature in the confusion of prevalent "common-sense" assumptions about the social problem. It is at least closely related to the doctrine of the "economic interpretation," the falsity of which has received brief consideration previously.[44] It could be argued along several lines that the Christian teaching is more or less responsible for the spread of this idea, especially in the sense that it is undoubtedly in part a reaction from the indefensible notion that economic facts and interests are of no real or moral importance.

In the present connection we can only sum up the situation very briefly by pointing out that a rational attack upon the problem of social change is to be envisaged under three main heads or topics which in a sense are largely steps to be taken in the order indicated, but in a deeper sense are aspects of one process. The first topic, or step, must be the understanding of the "existing" economic situation, especially the mechanics of organization of the enterprise economy (usually miscalled "capitalism"). As pointed out in part I, on liberalism, this inquiry itself again necessarily falls into two steps or stages, the understanding respectively of the general theory of such an economy and of the divergences between the concrete reality and the theoretical picture, with the reasons for these divergences. As was also previously emphasized, this analytical order of attack is practically necessary because the first question of policy looking towards change is whether the undesirable features of reality are inherent in the general principles of the system or are primarily due to the divergences, and consequently whether the main principle of policy must be to make the system "work" more in accord with the analytical theory, or to replace this general type of organization machinery with another type embodying different principles.

The second "stage" in the analysis is the formulation of ideals, and in the first instance ideals of economic relations and choice of directions of change, though this process cannot be carried very far ahead of the exploration of possibilities. The real difficulty is that the notion of possibility cannot be taken relevantly, if at all, in a strict yes-or-no sense. It is rather a matter of costs, and costs again are measured by values, or ideals. Thus we are plunged at once into the third aspect of the problem, or stage in the analysis, the problem of the means or processes of social change, meaning conscious (social) self-change or self-determination. Change must obviously be taken in a transitive and active sense or the discussion has no meaning at all. There is literally no "sense" in arguing purely in terms of causal analysis, either that changes in one phase of culture are treated as independent variables and regarded as "causing" changes in other phases, or more generally that an antecedent state or condition of culture as a whole causes or determines its subsequent state or character as a whole, from moment to moment.[45] We have to assume that there is real action, initiative, on the part of "individual minds." Moreover, all action has to be pitted against a resistance of some sort to be thinkable. As already suggested, a social problem originates either in a difference of opinion—not merely of interest—between different members, or groups of members of the society itself (either as to the end of the change or as to some detail in the process) or at least in an opinion on the part of some member or members that change is desirable (not a mere desire for change); and the effort to effect the change must be resisted at least by "inertia."

If we consider the economic aspect of society as the main field in which problems arise and change is called for, we face two main questions. The first has to do with the way in which the individuals who advocate change can act upon economic relationships. This suggests the alternatives already mentioned, that they may act either directly as individuals—in their own economic conduct, and by influencing the economic conduct of other individuals through moral and intellectual persuasion—or they may act through the politico-legal organization of society by changing the laws and/or the methods of enforcement. For the most part it is, of course, the latter method which is chiefly in point (whatever ought ideally to be the case). The immediate question then is one of the efficacy of law in changing men's economic behavior, either by its very existence or through the machinery and process of enforcement. This refers chiefly to the "criminological" machinery of punishment, though the use of rewards may also be an important possibility.[46]

More generally, the problem of culture mechanics is that of the possibility of acting—meaning the ability of the proponents of action to act—either by preaching or by legislation, upon the economic side of life without at the same time affecting other phases or elements in the social and cultural life. More accurately, it is a question of social action that will effect a *net* improvement, an excess of good over evil in the economic sphere considered by itself, and either without affecting other social-cultural values, or without producing in other spheres a net damage which equals or exceeds the gain in that of economics. Even a summary outline of the main items of probable gain and loss through various possible measures of social action, in the economic sphere itself and in other spheres, would far exceed our space limits here. It should hardly need to be emphasized that as Bentham perpetually urged, there is a heavy *onus probandi* against legislative action, which is an intrinsic evil, because it involves compulsion, and also entails moral as well as material costs and uncertainties in enforcement. This is particularly true because the compulsion must always be administered by human beings politically selected and operating in a political setting, and—perhaps practically most important of all—because it tends in numerous ways to strain the resources of government, which are limited, particularly those of free government, and need to be conserved for indubitably necessary and possible tasks.

Perhaps the feature of the situation which most calls for emphasis, because it is certain to be inadequately considered, is the general fact that any economic legislation—even if it were wise from its own point of view, which experience gives little ground to hope for!—inevitably has widely ramifying and serious effects on other phases of culture and social relations. This is particularly vital in connection with the family as an institution. On one hand, it is in the family system that the problems very largely arise, because, as merits constant reiteration, it is through the family that the "individual" comes into being and acquires most of his economic endowments and characteristics—because, in short, an individualistic system is necessarily very largely familistic and not individualistic in a literal sense. But at the same time, it is also through the family that the individual becomes what he is in all other respects and that culture in general is perpetuated. The economic individual is not really an individual, for the purpose of any social action, not even the administration of the crudest and most essential features of the criminal law. Any possible action by political society upon its members as economic units involves some transfer of functions and of responsibility from the family to the state and tends to aggrandize the latter at the expense of the former, and morally to weaken both. As already suggested, what we carelessly call egoism is in reality as much family egoism as it is individual; the basic conflicts of interest lie as much between families as between individual persons.

One of the most appealing economic reforms is the reduction of the "artificial" advantage or disadvantage in the competitive struggle which individuals receive through the "accident" of birth. (And, we should add, through either the "accident" of marriage, or the influence upon marriage of economic status and prospects of prospective or possible partners in that relation.) Inherited handicaps can be dealt with to some extent by such measures as inheritance taxation on one hand and by the provisions at "social" expense of educational opportunity—and conceivably also other elements of a fair start in life—on the other. But all such measures are subject to limits and to grave dangers if carried to extremes, unless we are prepared to contemplate the abolition of the private family altogether and the establishment of some kind of Platonic or ultra-Platonic communism. (This idea is no less un-Christian because Plato is supposed to have intended his proposal of property and family communism only for the governing classes of a society stratified almost to the ideal of caste.)

The teachings of Christianity, as a basis for the discussion of ideals for the guidance of economic reform, present in the first place the same general and essential weakness or defect that was emphasized in the discussion of liberalism. They look at morality as a matter of ideal relations between individuals who are taken as given. But from the standpoint of any discussion of organization, individuals are not given, and in fact are not really individuals at all. For the purposes of any formal or legal action directed towards rational change (in contrast with preaching), society is a thing of institutions far more than of men. And at the head of the list of institutions, transcending in importance all others combined, is the institution of the private family—or whatever institutions might take the place of the private family in any other type of social order.

It is to be kept in mind, too, that there are fairly narrow limits to the theoretical possibilities of replacing the family by any large-scale political unit. There seems to be no way of preventing any administrative group from being more or less of a "clique," and indeed, the matter of personal harmony in the staff is one of the primary features of effective administration or management in any enterprise. How far it is conceivable for the teaching of Christianity and/or any possible educational system (whether itself based on the spirit of Christianity or on compulsory discipline, as the Marxists seem to contemplate) to reduce the importance of this factor is an open question, as indeed is that of how far it is abstractly desirable to do so.

But the heart of the difficulty of Christianity as an approach is not merely in the fact that it ignores the concrete problems of the moral-legal order in any possible world of social relations conceivably realizable by any biological species living on the earth. It lies not even in the fact that the Christian type of moralistic teaching tends to distract attention from the real problem by clearly implying or actually saying that "love" would solve all these problems, or what is still worse, that it is practically possible to solve them by preaching love. The concrete effects of envisaging the problem in terms of any sort of individual rights or individual obligations to any other individuals are positively evil in a more concrete sense. It implies—and as far as it is effective at all, tends to bring about—a social order which is definitely contrary to fundamental moral ideals, and not merely to our ideals but to the general character of moral ideals which is necessarily implied in the fact that they are discussed at all. The direct effects of "preaching" about economic relations and obligations are in general bad; and the kind of legislation which results from the clamor of idealistic preachers—and from the public attitude which such preaching at once expresses and tends to generate or aggravate—is especially bad. All this is the natural consequence of exhortation without knowledge and understanding—of well-meaning people attempting to meddle with the workings of extremely complicated and sensitive machinery which they do not understand.

The paradoxical results in real life can be sufficiently indicated by a little consideration of the worst concrete cases, namely, religious-moralistic pronouncements about the obligations of employers to employees, particularly in the matter of wage-rates. An adequate example is at hand in the doctrines of the papal encyclical *Quadragesimo Anno* of Pius XI in 1931. And the Report on Christianity and the Economic Order of the Oxford Conference of World Protestantism (non–Roman Catholic Christianity) of 1936, is similar; it is better, or not so bad, in that there is less of it in content and less self-confidence and authoritative dogmatism in the expression. The least familiarity with the "laws" of economics—a much-abused term which properly means only the general *facts*—will show that any general pressure on the employers to pay wages appreciably above the market value of the service rendered is in the first place certain to be injurious to the interests of wage-workers— but more especially to those wage-workers who are already in the weakest position. The argument in proof cannot be elaborated here.[47]

But even this is by no means the end of the evil that naturally follows from such ignorant if well-intentioned tinkering with the machinery of economic organization. A very little, and very elementary, analysis would again show that the general implication and natural result of making the payment of wages in excess of the value of the service a moral or legal obligation of the individual employer is in the first place to establish a feudal or quasi-feudal relationship between employer and employee generally. But under modern conditions of technology and other factors involving (ultimately worldwide) economic relationships in production, exchange, and distribution, such a feudalism is itself not generally or permanently possible. The natural political consequence of such interference must be either to segregate whatever elements in the population are not economically worth the wage set, and make them permanently wards of society, or else to cause the reorganization of society itself under some kind of all-inclusive bureaucratic despotism. In the long run, the latter is much the more probable, or some combination of the two, involving much of the evil of both.

In conclusion: We come back to our initial contention that Christianity affords no concrete guidance for social action, beyond an urge to "do good and avoid evil"; and this is not Christian in distinction from any other religion, or from secular morality. The problem is, What is good, and what is evil, in political activity? In the first centuries of its history, the appeal of Christianity was to the lowly strata of society, not to persons holding any sort of power. The lowly were clearly exhorted to accept the existing structure of status and power relations, to obey constituted authorities, and not to try to "do anything about it." When persons in positions of power, and particularly rulers of states, came to be Christianized, they found little if anything in Christian teaching to guide them in the use of power. There was no doubt an implication that they should be gentle and humane in the performance of their "duties"; but as to the content of these duties, it could only be inferred that they consisted in enforcing the laws, and perhaps gradually "humanizing" them—whatever that might mean. Surely it was not their function to introduce any important changes into the political or social constitution.

By that time, however, the Christian movement itself had become highly organized along authoritarian lines, and the official interpreters of Christian doctrine regarded it as the first and main duty of the political authorities to support, and defer to the authority and power of "the Church," i.e., of these officials themselves. And in performing this duty, political functionaries were by no means supposed to be either gentle or humane. At least, it was made very clear that heretics and blasphemers who did not promptly yield to admonition faced the most cruel punishments that could be devised, culminating in death by torture. In fact, the Church more and more demanded political power in its own right, to be exercised by its own administrative and judicial appointees.

In consequence, down to the time when the power and unity of the Western Church were broken by forces partly religious but largely secular, the meaning of Christianity for political action would be read less out of any moral pronouncements than out of the acts of the Church itself, in its courts low and high, and in its political and even military struggle for power. The general verdict of history is that, where its own power was not at issue, the policy of the Church as a political system was simply utilitarian, in accord with highly conservative standards. It may be argued that—again, where its own power was not in question—it was a humanizing force, in some degree. But it certainly cannot be shown that the humanizing of political power and of ordinary morals and manners went on more rapidly than would have happened under different religious conditions. It is not implied that the contrary can be shown; we do not know.

If we turn to the "scriptures," the one recognized source of Christian teaching now generally recognized as authoritative, it seems impossible to read into the text any exhortation to, or ideal of, rational efficiency, or progress, in any form. On the contrary, we find quite definite statements that such things do not matter. But we know, if we know anything, that if they do not matter, civilized or human life does not. For civilized life under mundane conditions simply cannot be pictured without quite extensive power relations between human beings, in addition to power over nature. A defensible ethic doubtless condemns overemphasis on power; but it must include both the right use of power and the quest of power—by right methods—for right uses. The concrete relation between amount and kind of power in both these senses and its various uses, and the quality of culture and of human life, measured in moral terms, is indeed a problem; but it is merely one of the most important phases of the general problem of social action on which the teachings of Christianity shed no light, or even tend to be definitely misleading. Indeed, with the possible exception of some aspects of face-to-face personal relations, scriptural Christianity gives no more guidance for individual action in fields where power plays a minimum role than it does for individual or social policy in relation to power itself. It makes no place for either the intellectual or the aesthetic side of life, or for either the appreciative or the creative aspect of either of these realms of value. By implication it condemns all these interests. The Church has indeed found a place for intellectual speculation and for art,—but only in the service of the religious life and of the Church itself, as an organization, a power system.

Moreover, the practical result of the teaching, in connection with the material and cultural progress which modern history has exhibited, is paradoxical, morally disconcerting, and largely evil. In large part, religion seems merely to sublimate any moral urge which people have, giving it expression and release in more or less aesthetic ritual, and leaving them entirely free, except for an hour or so in the week, to pursue worldly objectives by worldly methods. And when the urge to action persists, and the "Gospel of love" ceases to mean merely a mystical, almost cabalistic, emotion among the lowly, a consolation for the lack of more substantial life advantages, a mental-spiritual escape from its evils and deprivations—and perhaps a formula for salvation in a future world—and when it comes to mean active love for the lowly and down-trodden on the part of more fortunately situated persons, it quite naturally tends to become both a gospel of hate towards the "privileged classes," and a conspiracy to seize and use powers to effect a social revolution in which these classes will be "liquidated." Thus, in good Hegelian style, extremes meet and antitheses blend. Not only does love turn into hate as the effective social attitude, and submissive renunciation of power into resort to violence, but the gospel of peace turns into a call to arms for the proverbially most brutal sort of war, civil war, class war. The tendency of Christianity to join hands with revolutionary Marxism is one of the conspicuous trends of the times, in countries where all social movements and public discussion of social problems have not been suppressed by a dictatorship, either of the (self-appointed spokesmen for the) exploited proletariat, or of the (self-appointed leaders of the) advocates of preserving civilization—as the case may be. And in any event, as we have emphasized, the approach to problems of economic inequality and unfreedom (or what appears to be such) in terms of "moralistic" judgments of personal rights and duties, in the absence of careful economic and politico-legal analysis, is virtually certain to have consequences utterly different from the intentions of the reformers, and predominantly evil.

But it is usually easy for the Christian apologist to escape from any unpleasant implications, by alleging wrong interpretation of the meaning of the doctrine. It is perhaps better to leave this problem-field with the observation made at the outset that the actual role of religious professions and beliefs, to say nothing of religious "practices," in the working lives of men is one of the profound mysteries of history and of social life. Indeed, mystery—or plain ignorance—seems to be the last word in the discussion of all the main elements in the political-economic problem. We do not know, either what are right ideals, or how the social-economic process works and what it can be expected to bring forth in the absence of interference, or how to interfere "intelligently" with its "natural" operation and development. At least there is little evidence of a consensus of the competent or unanimity in the mass on any of these main elements of the problem of reform. Only on that part of the second and third problems which is the subject matter of price-theory economics can it be said that any great headway towards satisfactory treatment has been made, and that is but a limited aspect of the total problem of action. Without an adequate ethics and sociology in the broad sense, economics has little to say about policy.

Notes

1. Much of our "philosophic" thought carries the first, or reducing, process another step, holding that all felt motives "really" are "merely" incidents in world mechanics or positive natural law somehow conceived. Idealism in the Hegelian sense is not practically different from mechanism in this regard.

2. In a rough way the sphere of coercion is that of law, but this needs qualification. For law may be taken to include recognized rules of social behavior which are not "coercively" enforced, and, on the other hand, political coercion may take the form of administrative action which only indirectly if at all comes under the rubric of law enforcement. Law-making, or legislation, presumably does not ordinarily refer to promulgations not meant to be enforced by penalties intended to be adequate.

3. Notably Jeremy Bentham.

4. One senses a certain hollowness, for instance, in Spencer's exhortations to and praise of charity, so strong is the balance of emphasis on the repudiation of any properly legal obligation.

5. Cf. a paper by John Sherman, "Some Observations on Custom in Price Phenomena," *American Economic Review* 18 (1928): pp. 663 ff. It may be noted

that at times of catastrophic change, either in the direction of shortage or demoralizing superabundance, the price system tends to give way even in our own culture and be replaced by rationing, price-fixing, governmental absorption of "surpluses," and the like.

6. See Brentano, *Die Wandlungen der wirtschaftlichen Einheit*; Hoyt, *Primitive Trade*.

7. Business must be allowed to operate on business principles in relation to its given and legally defined conditions, and these must be clear and reasonably stable. Undesirable features and results of the economic order can be modified through taxation and public expenditure, and perhaps changes in the laws of inheritance, but only within the very narrowest limits through price fixing and other arbitrary interference with the workings of the markets. In these fields general laws mean a straitjacket and administrative discretion an intolerable fog of arbitrariness and uncertainty.

8. And they still are for the most part. Development of instantaneous communication has changed this somewhat and may change it more if television develops sufficiently. But there is another and especially sinister aspect to mechanico-electrical intercommunication itself. Mechanism may make it possible for any number of individuals, even the whole population of the world, to listen or attend at the same time to the words and perhaps the facial expression and gestures of any one individual. But no invention can ever increase the efficiency of communication in the converse sense in the least degree. In spite of all science and technology it will remain impossible for one person to listen or attend at the same time to more than one! The whole tendency is to increase the effectiveness and power of "leadership" and to multiply mob-mindedness.

9. This was not true genetically; the state was originally the military system, and law was a social phenomenon of a non-political sort. The state gradually assumed legal functions, and at first only on the side of law enforcement; conscious law-making, or legislation, came much later.

10. The problem is somewhat akin to that of free exchange in dangerous drugs, weapons, etc., and it is still more closely related to the problem of lending and borrowing at interest, which are universally prohibited in primitive society—though gambling is usually less stringently dealt with!

11. It seems necessary to refer in various connections to the failure of economic teaching to give even the educated public any conception of the actual workings of competition as a mechanism of control, which failure and lack are one of the most serious causes of the failure of the system to work effectively.

12. We reserve for later and extended consideration the fact that the other commonly accepted systems of social ethics make the same mistake, notably the Christian ethic.

13. Under the individualism of pure theory one individual has no power or control over the productive capacities of another otherwise than through purchase from moment to moment in a free market. In reality there are considerable exceptions. The case of minor children is perhaps the largest; but the serious imperfections of the market for "labor" (really markets for innumer-

able kinds of labor) give rise to more political discontent. It should be noted that all intangible property, including "goodwill," represents claims against or control over the productive power of persons or of things owned by them.

14. The main difficulty in this whole field of discussion is the vagueness in the meaning of terms, which is partly due to the efforts of the advocates of every position to treat some compact verbal designation of it as a slogan and to interpret it in a question-begging way to include as much as possible of all that is accepted as good by ethical common sense (especially that of the particular culture to which the discussion is addressed). This is particularly true in connection with the pleasure principle, which can be used to interpret and to defend practically any ethical position. It is a familiar fact that its advocates have never found it inconsistent with ascetic ideals and practices, and indeed have not found suicide a serious intellectual difficulty for their doctrine. To the present writer, it seems to be an essentially meaningless idea, a dogmatic psychological verbalism. If the term "pleasure" is used by definition as a general designation of all motive, the hedonistic principle is true by definition. And if this is not done, if it is admitted to be possible for men to desire anything else than pleasure, then the principle is axiomatically false, or incomplete. It is possible to argue that what men desire is always a mental state, and to call "desired mental state" by the name of "pleasure." But it is as certain to common sense as anything can be that men rarely if at all think they are desiring pleasure, until they are asked (by themselves or someone else) to give a "reason why" they desire something which they do immediately desire. And when this issue is raised, the form which the answer takes seems to be chiefly a matter of the cultural traditions or education, including self-education, and habits of verbal usage, of the individual in question.

15. The negative proposition that statements about facts do not contribute to the solution of the problem of the end or ideal really contains but half the truth about the philosophical difficulties of the relation between facts and values. There is a sharp contradiction between the world views involved in approaching human data from the standpoints respectively of the intellectual or explanatory interest and of the practical interest, the interest in action. (This is true whether the interest in action is taken in the form of personal desire or objective value judgment.) The conception in modern thought of a "theory" of any subject matter is descriptive or positivistic. Positive science excludes any notion of "real cause," which is to say any notion of activity or initiative on the part of the subject matter treated as cause. But in human phenomena, a subject is always in some sense and to some degree being acted upon by itself. And for social phenomena we have also to recognize group self-action in the degree to which the society is "democratic," in contrast with a dictatorship, taken in the "absolute" sense that a single individual would own all the rest of society and treat his subjects as things. Thus the difficulty becomes twofold; for even individual freedom is to the scientific intelligence "transcendental," mystical, and unintelligible or simply illusory, but group freedom or self-determination is far worse in this respect.

In addition, liberal social thought has tried to straddle the world views of positivism and of individualistic voluntarism, utilitarianism, economism, or pragmatism. These are inherently contradictory even between themselves, while both reduce to nonsense any conception of intelligent group decision in belief or action, because they make discussion or meaningful utterance unreal. And Hegelian idealism reaches by a different route essentially the same impasse for thought, as far as human interests and activities are concerned. Its preservation of some kind of freedom or initiative for the "Absolute" (if it does preserve any) is of interest only to the speculative philosopher. (In fact, as far as this writer can see, the role of speculative thought itself, as a real activity, as "problem-solving," is just as effectively excluded by the notion of the Absolute as it is by that of universal mechanism.)

16. This refers to one interpretation of utilitarianism, i.e., the ethical interpretation, which is just as contradictory to the psychological interpretation as it is to positivism, mechanistic or culture-historical. The psychological interpretation, whether in the form of hedonism or any purely individualistic conception of motive or interest, lands one in solipsism.

17. In the more extreme versions of utilitarianism, such as that of Hobbes, the notion of primitive antagonism, as a feature of "human nature," is carried so far that there is not much left of the unity, or the social nature of man, *à la* Aristotle, or *à la* Hegel. Yet even Hobbes's notion of the primitive contract with a "dictator" (dynasty) for the purely negative purpose of preventing the "war of all against all" may be said to preserve some vestige of it.

18. The relation between interests in a purely individual, egoistic or selfish interpretation, and "opinions" as to what is "right" in some objective sense is a question to be mentioned here as of the heart of the problem, but one which cannot be discussed at the moment.

19. We take for granted the definition of political units primarily in terms of territory, and omit any discussion of the exceptions, which are by no means unimportant. The difference between the treatment, by states, of citizens by birth and of resident aliens and of travelers, and the claims of states over citizens abroad, and their descendants, and everything having to do with freedom of movement of men between states,—all these things are rapidly growing in importance under our eyes.

20. The essential ethical and historical-psychological problem or problems brought to mind is (or are) why men wish to preserve and to propagate their culture and political institutions, and what is the human right and wrong of culture differences and their preservation, propagation or extinction, by various processes in both cases. It is not clear what are the actual desires back of the urge to cultural expansion beyond "material self-interest" on the part of individuals and groups whose power-status will be improved; and that, while important, is certainly not the main factor. The facts of culture rivalry are especially puzzling, because the basis or nucleus of it all is so largely language, and linguistically educated people do not think of one language as being sub-

stantially superior to another in a utilitarian or aesthetic sense, to say nothing of moral value. Latin-American nationalism is especially puzzling. But such topics would lead far afield.

21. The close connection between the idealistic social philosophy and the historical jurisprudence and the *Kultur-Historismus* in general is well known; also its relation to the Romantic Movement, with the latter's idealization of mediaeval conditions. The sociology of the "social organism" should also be mentioned, especially because it was promoted, in a very different sense, by the individualists (and positivists) Spencer and Comte.

22. An undemocratic, traditional, and authoritarian organization of religion naturally goes along with a similar conception of the state, the two being supposed to work together, but with one or the other predominating, depending on the "school" of idealism which is speaking.

23. There is a natural causal connection between these two positions in spite of the superficial antithesis. Love for the downtrodden plus superficiality in diagnosis takes the form of hatred of the privileged, and belief that their wickedness is the cause of poverty and their destruction its cure. There are many Christian Marxists.

24. This sketch will not go into questions of critical interpretation. Marxism, which is like a religion in many respects, is so also in this, that the problem of what it means is a question of orthodoxy, the "party line." We shall discuss the materialistic or economic interpretation of history and the class struggle as a version of that doctrine, and as an ethical position. If Marxism does not mean that, there is nothing that it can be said to mean. For a survey, the reader may consult M. M. Bober, *Karl Marx's Interpretation of History* (Harvard University Press, 1927); Sidney Hook, *Towards the Understanding of Karl Marx* (John Day, 1933); Henri Sée, *The Economic Interpretation of History* (Adelphi Co., 1929); E. R. A. Seligman, *The Economic Interpretation of History* (Columbia University Press, 1902; reprint, 1924); on Christianity and Marxism, see John Lewis, ed., *Christianity and the Social Revolution* (Gollancz, London, 1935, 1937).

25. But it would be impossible to overemphasize the fact that such an analysis of the relations between individual motive and social purpose, and between both and action, individual or social, would be necessary as a foundation for any significant or genuine social philosophy. In these essays, there is no effort to go very far beyond demonstrating the necessity of such a philosophical viewpoint, through exposure of the self-stultification involved in any theory either of positive causality or of purely individualistic voluntarism—which two positions, though contradictory between themselves, have both been assumed in the social-philosophical literature of modern liberalism.

The connection in which the psychology of motivation most requires careful consideration, but is most neglected, is the motivation of social reformers themselves. Much light could undoubtedly be thrown on this psychology by an investigation of the mentality of inventors of perpetual motion machines. They usually "know" that they can produce the general result striven for, but are not committed to any particular method to a degree that causes any inclination to give up their project when it fails experimentally.

26. In spite of the absurdity involved in using any form of historical determinism as the basis of a propaganda for action, it is obvious to the most superficial student of history and politics that the device has proved effective in many hands and in many connections. Confident insistence that a course of events is inevitable is typically an excellent procedure for securing wide and active support in bringing it about. The election theory of salvation in Calvinistic theology is a conspicuous case in point and is especially interesting as an interpretation of Christianity widely accepted by the best people and the greatest minds of the "Christian" world. And they have been perhaps the most effective as well as the most active Christianisers, from the apostle Paul to Calvin and Knox. Moslem and other Oriental fatalism, with its effect upon soldiers, is another case in point.

In interpreting all these facts, the objective student must keep in mind the ambiguity of his own role, or at least face the question whether he really means to be purely objective, or thinks also of influencing social change by his own activity as a student. If he wishes merely to achieve intellectual clarity—presumably for other members of some intellectual community as well as for himself, since otherwise he would not publish his analysis or give any utterance to it—he must make conscious and careful provision against exerting such influence, by keeping his work a secret outside the circle of "intellectuals" for which it is intended. Publication in any society of any discussion of that society and its activities must be expected to have some effect on the future course of events.

27. This interpretation seems to be advocated, for example, by the American Marxist A. W. Calhoun. See his review of M. M. Bober, *Karl Marx's Interpretation of History* in *American Economic Review* 18 (1928): pp. 275–76.

28. Marx probably did not teach exactly this extreme form of revolutionism, and his followers have tended away from it to a considerably different position, especially with the rise of modern communism, as will be noted presently; but the fact does not invalidate the substance of this paragraph.

29. The main texts from Marx and Engels (and Lenin) bearing on the topics mentioned in this paragraph are to be found in Lenin's *State and Revolution* and *Critique of the Gotha Programme by Karl Marx,* ed. C. P. Dutt (New York: International Publishers, 1932 and 1938).

30. In this essay, we have had no occasion to refer particularly to the "economic theory" of Marx, because it seems to have—or to be especially conspicuous for having—nothing at all to do with the problems of social action or change. Of course, it does pretend to afford a "proof" that all income except wages (at some level) represents "exploitation" of the workers. But since Marxism itself makes no pretense of defining exploitation, and cannot possibly give it any meaning which is at all consistent with the other features of its general philosophical position in any of their possible interpretations, this may be

passed over as a detail. In any event, practically all the elements of Marxist pseudo-economic analysis, and especially those which are most screamingly absurd, could have been copied out of Ricardo or other acknowledged authorities on the Ricardian economics who wrote before the publication of the "Critique of Political Economy," in 1859, in which Marx's system may be said to have taken on something like its final form.

31. Christianity is, of course, a "scriptural," or "book" religion. It goes without saying that some Churches or spokesmen for Churches claim divine authority to "interpret" the sacred writings, and that, in this case as in all similar cases, interpretation requires no long time to change fundamentally or even to reverse an original pronouncement. But since theologians rarely hold explicitly that the New Testament Scriptures have been superseded outright by the dicta of later authorities, we are justified, in a brief sketch, in limiting our attention to these. Moreover, consideration of the Catholic Fathers and Saints or of the great Protestant leaders would only enforce and intensify what is said as to the indifference or positive conservatism of the Christian doctrine on political and social questions.

32. In this respect the political environment was placed on the same footing as the physical-natural; there is no more suggestion of transforming the former in the interest of greater fitness for a higher type of human life than there is of the desirability of transforming the latter through promoting science and technology or medicine. And it is superfluous to note that the numbers and qualities of human beings were similarly taken for granted, as well as the general framework of non-political social institutions. Indeed, it is clear not only that to change these given conditions of social life is no part of the Christian's duty, but that he is enjoined against such activities and the critical attitudes which would prompt them. Such interests would distract attention from the real or "spiritual" values. Except for purely moral-spiritual attitudes and sentiments, "the world" expresses the will of God, or natural law; and if conditions are hard, this is presumably deserved punishment or at least useful discipline for the soul. As to political or economic revolution, the mention of such a thing is hardly less than sacrilegious.

The position of Christianity on all these matters is roughly that of the contemporary stoicism, particularly Roman stoicism, of the first Christian centuries. It is not asceticism, but rather supreme indifference, plus, perhaps, and to an uncertain degree, "faith" that "God will provide," that "all these things will be added unto" those who diligently seek "the kingdom of God and his righteousness." It should be noted that the whole spirit of the Sermon on the Mount is very different in the two versions we have, in Matthew and Luke. And in general, there is the greatest diversity in the spirit of the teachings as between the different Gospels and the other Books of the New Testament (chiefly Pauline writings); but such questions cannot be taken up here.

33. The wording in the King James version of Matthew is, "Therefore, all things whatsoever ye would that men should do to you, do ye even so to them:

for this is the law and the prophets." It is worth noting that the final comment-
ing clause which ends the verse is closely parallel to the verse in Matthew which
follows the Great Commandment: "On these two commandments hang all the
law and the Prophets" (Matt. 22:40). We are naturally concerned here only
with the second part of the Great Commandment, which indeed Matthew tells
is "like unto" the first.

34. In Luke, the question, Who is my neighbor? is asked and is answered
by the parable of the Good Samaritan. This may be briefly dismissed. In the
context, the significance is uncertain, and any general implication is doubtful.
Taken as an injunction to render humanitarian assistance to the helpless victim
of a calamity on the part of anyone in a special position to give aid, there is
nothing distinctively Christian about it, to say nothing of any indication as to
how laws ought to be made or society organized.

35. The question of obligations bound up in the relation between employer and employee as individuals is of course particularly important in our
world. One aspect of it will be mentioned later.

36. In this respect, the "Pauline" letters are often much more to the point.
See Gal. 6:4,5: "But let every man prove his own work and then he shall have
rejoicing in himself alone. and not in another. For every man shall bear his
own burden." It is true that verse 2 in the same chapter reads, "Bear ye one
another's burdens, and so fulfil the law of Christ." There is, of course, no necessary contradiction. Even the Pauline writings which explicitly command men
to work (even as a condition of eating! 2 Thess. 3:10) stop short of any clear
injunction to economic efficiency or recognition of economic progress as a
real good.

37. "Love for the unborn" only partly removes such conflicts, even in an
abstract logical sense; and it cannot be identified with personal love, and is
more of a rationalization than a reality. This meets the contention of those
theologians who try to defend the Christian Ethic by *defining* love as identical
with morality. It is fantastic to extend the concept to cover the moral urge or
emotion as such; but even if that be done, the whole intellectual problem of
conduct is still left out of account. The facts may be brought out by asking any
chance group of Christians—say ministers—what should be done in regard
to any public question. There will typically be no more agreement than in any
other group from the same social and culture strata, or if there is, it can usually
be accounted for in terms of specific idols of the tribe; and where economic
analysis is involved, the preachers and reformers or religious cast can be
counted upon to advocate easy and pleasant-looking or romantically appealing
solutions for hard problems. In practice, they are particularly given to advocating the program of taking away (by force) from those who have and giving it
to those who have not; and the pleasantness of this line of action is not at all
necessarily a matter of pure love for the beneficiaries.

38. When both are reduced to intelligible meaning, the principle of the
Golden Rule and the Great Commandment is substantially identical with that

of utilitarianism. In the latter the only doctrine which was either intelligible or effective was that "each should count for one and none for more than one." (As we have already shown—in our discussion of idealism—the pleasure principle is either nonsensical or anti-ethical, and the same applies to the notion of "the greatest good of the greatest number.") When we ask in what *respect* each is to count for one or what is the content of the good, Bentham—especially in his economic writings—interprets pleasure to mean freedom, and this is also the best concrete interpretation of doing as one would be done by. Yet, interpreted in an absolute sense, it yields the social philosophy of Herbert Spencer! The limitations of this have been pointed out in our first essay (*Economica,* February, 1939) on liberalism. Freedom is relative to actual wishes, which may be wrong, and also to actual endowment with power in every form, which may be inequitable, or wrong in other ways. Extreme individualism has no place at all for the "helpless" except through their moral or romantic appeal to the strong as individuals.

39. This seems to be the practical lesson to be derived from Rev. Reinhold Niebuhr's strenuous preaching. See especially *Moral Man and Immoral Society* (New York: Scribner's, 1932). For example there may be no moral gain from the liberation of slaves by an individual master in a slave-holding society. The act might both make worse the condition of the individual slaves affected and strengthen the hold of the institution. It might well be more intelligent and more ethical to treat one's own slaves as humanely as possible and to work for gradual rather than sudden improvement in the status of slaves as a class.— But this is not often the way moral sentiments work in history! They tend rather to generate strife and war, as happened in America over the slavery issue—in contrast with Europe, however, where slavery was not tied up with conspicuous racial differences.

40. Revolution, and even violent revolution, is not absolutely excluded. But there is an "almost" overwhelming presumption against it. (Cf. above on the consequences of the American in contrast with the European process of abolishing slavery.) And it is to be noted that "real" revolution, a profound and sudden change in the legal system of a country, is a thing which practically does not and cannot occur.

41. Historically, beyond doubt, societies, which is to say groups of men living under some common institutional or legal order, "grew"; they were not "made." No doubt there was a gradual transition from association by animal instinct, physically inherited, to culture, transmitted by unconscious imitation ("ritual" in the broad sense) and then to conscious ordering of relations through law-making. But in the long stages of unconscious evolution there were no social problems in our sense. Whether the institutional pattern under which a group lived before becoming critically conscious of its institutions, as a system of constraint, should be called legal or not is purely a matter of convenience in verbal usage. Our point is simply that social problems come into existence when this critical consciousness develops to a certain point. And their content

is institutional or legal change, advocated as desirable (not merely desired) and opposed as undesirable, in more or less rational discussion—or at least advocated as desirable by some part of the group, against resistance, perhaps through mere unthinking inertia, on the part of the rest of its membership.

42. Categorical negations are not only undemonstrable in the nature of the case, in the field of social phenomena, but they are rarely if ever entirely valid. In this case, one certainly could not say that the teachings of Christianity have had absolutely no influence on the development of law in "Christian" countries. No doubt, moral judgments and principles which the law-makers and judges have supposed to be Christian teaching, or implications of Christian teaching, have played an appreciable role in guiding the activities of legislators and of judges in courts of record. Whether the sources were really and distinctly Christian, or are to be found in stoicism and natural-law philosophy, would be another question, and the main historical problem. It would be extremely valuable to have a careful study of the problem by competent theological and legal historians, particularly from the standpoint of the influence, first of the Roman Catholic canon law, and later of the Chancery and Equity courts, in the formation of our Anglo-American jurisprudence.

43. On the other hand, it would be wrong to assume that if all economic problems (in the ordinary meaning) ceased from troubling, a "Christian" social order would become easy. A little reflection will show that any group activity—in play or the pursuit of culture, as well as in "work" (even in psalm-singing!)—involves power relations and differences in status. The "politics" of organizations in these other fields, and specifically in churches, do not actually differ significantly from the politics which relate to economic relations and problems—or they seem to be worse as often as better.

44. See "The Ethics of Liberalism," *Economica,* February, 1939.

45. It is doubly nonsensical, proceeding from the standpoint of economic problems, however defined, to adopt the economic interpretation of history, i.e., to take the economic phase of social life (defined in the same way) as the independent variable which causes or determines everything else.

46. The working of reward and punishment is formally equivalent to exchange and a notion of equality or equity obtains in both. But we do not think of the imposition of a specified fine for being drunk and disorderly as an offer to sell the privilege for that amount! The psychology of exchange is very different from that of punishment even when both are in the hands of the state.

47. The writer happened to be invited to speak to a conference of liberal ministers in the early days of the New Deal, and specifically of the N.R.A. One of the items on the program of the meeting was an almost hysterical protest by a Negro minister on the way in which the wicked employers were tending to replace Negro workers with white as a consequence, or by them pretended consequence of the legal fixation of minimum wages. It was, of course, entirely useless for an economist to point out to the assembled highly intelligent and liberal brethren that such results are in fact the inevitable consequence of such

action, that in fact given the action, replacement of inferior by superior employees is actually desirable; for if there is to be unemployment, it is better to have it concentrated on the least efficient. This is in the interest both of increased production and of reducing both the public burden and the amount of avoidable suffering and discomfort in connection with relief. All that they could see or imagine was that here were some unexpected, detailed effects of the nature of evasion, to be met by further restrictions and more punitive measures of enforcement. They could not be envisaged as indicating anything wrong with the general policy.

2

Socialism: The Nature of the Problem

I

The discussion of socialism affords an opportunity to kill two birds, or indeed several, with one stone. Apart from the importance of the subject in itself, socialism and prevalent thinking about it present an especially interesting case study in the nature of social problems and social thinking, and hence in the methodology of a social science relevant to social action.[1] The writer, at least, is more interested in the character of economic and political thinking as illustrated by the discussion of socialism than in socialistic schemes or even the general concept; for the nature of most of the thinking about the problem seems to be the most important datum in connection with the problem itself. The present sketch, written from the standpoint of economic theory, will attempt no more than a partial analytical indication of the character of the problems and the methods of attack. Its content will lie entirely within the field of the obvious, not to say the trite.

We start from the vague conception of socialism as a proposal to replace the organization of economic life through markets or to replace the enterprise economy (which socialists and others miscall "capitalism")[2] with a political system for the organization and control of economic life. The revolution and transition would also be worked out through political process. Intelligent discussion of the problems involved obviously calls for clarity of conception as to the character and mode of operation of the enterprise economy itself and also as to the nature of political

Reprinted with permission from *Ethics* 50 (April 1940): pp. 253–89.

phenomena and processes. The question or problem of socialism as a policy is one of comparison between two social-economic patterns, plus the question of the feasibility, and costs, of the change from one to the other—if the comparison results in a judgment in favor of socialism. Thus any solution of the problem involves use of facts and principles from the two social sciences of economics and politics—and beyond these of the more fundamental disciplines of history, sociology, etc., and also, in particular, of ethics, from which all final criteria of judgment are to be derived.

At the outset we encounter an interesting contrast between economic and political thought. Economic thought runs almost entirely in terms of the obvious and commonplace, while political thought is almost as exclusively inchoate, indefinite, and inconclusive, and in consequence political opinion is a matter of wish-thinking and romanticism in overwhelming variety. The most interesting feature of economic theory is that its larger and more important questions are generally self-answering when explicitly and correctly stated—in so far as they can be answered at all. Indeed, the problem of social action, from the economic standpoint, is chiefly that of getting people—those in control of social policy, which in a democracy ultimately means the electorate—to act in accord with principles which when stated in simple and set terms are trite even to the man in the street.

A hoary illustration of this methodological dictum is the problem of international trade. Everyone understands—or at least admits without question—the economic advantage of geographical division of labor. And no one contends that the economic gain is reduced, or the situation affected in any way, by the existence of boundaries between political divisions. (We abstract here from political interests based on political antagonism, and also from the possible effects of war, even on a country not a party to it; for the most part, these qualifications are not in question in the actual political discussion.) Yet the overwhelming mass of civilized and educated mankind today insist on social-political action which is rational only in terms of the precise antitheses of these truisms. And the same general situation confronts us in connection with problems of internal economy, where emotions such as patriotism and antipathy to foreigners cannot be called upon to explain the irrationality. No one who is not definitely *non compos mentis* thinks that the economic prosperity of a country is increased by reducing the production of goods and services. Yet leading features of the policy of the most advanced nations today aim precisely at that result, under the leadership of their most eminent statesmen and with the overwhelming approval of the people at large and the enthusiastic cooperation of practically every important economic group. That raising the price of a commodity will decrease its sale is one of the least disputed laws of economics; but to apply it to the labor market is likely to brand one as an enemy of the workingman. And more generally it is assumed both in passionate propaganda and in action that the way to improve business is forcibly to raise wages, the main element in its costs; this is called creating purchasing power. The reasons for such paradoxes in the relation between thought and action in the field of social-economic problems seem to the writer to constitute much the most important subject for investigation for social science at large, in so far as it aspires to illuminate practical social questions or to be of service in bringing about any improvement through political action.

The situation in the field of politics is similarly paradoxical though the superficial character of the paradox is strikingly different. In connection with political problems there is disappointingly little scientific basis for believing in one principle in preference to any other or for formulating any communicable principles which can serve as a basis for prediction, even in the hypothetical, or "if-then," sense in which sciences in general do predict—to say nothing of absolute or historical prediction, such as is achieved by a few sciences, exemplified by astronomy. The natural result is, as already suggested, that even the most intelligent people—perhaps these especially!—typically hold and advocate political opinions (if they should be so called) which have no discoverable basis in fact and reasoning and even run sharply against historical experience. This is undoubtedly the most important general observation to be made in connection with socialism. There being no way of effectively disproving any political proposition which does not palpably violate recognized laws of physical nature, men first imagine and then believe in political processes of any character, and working in any way, which appeals to any individual's particular variety of romantic fancy.

Two examples of this romanticism really must be mentioned. One is the belief, expressed on every hand by the "best minds," in the unlimited possibility of changing human nature through passing laws or remodeling the political constitution. This possibility is supposed to be proved by the fact that human nature has changed. Now, whether human nature has changed in historical time is still a matter of dispute even among the most competent students and is very largely a matter of the definition of words. One might say that it is changing human nature to teach men to read or to ride a bicycle! In any case, the fact that human nature had changed, even in its fundamental features, even if true, would certainly not prove that it could be changed—i.e., that anyone could produce changes according to plan. And it is a still more glaring truth that no one would want any human being or group to have any such power—no one with a minimum of modesty or good sense would want to have it himself. The other example, equally pertinent in connection with the problem of socialism, is the facility with which so many people explain anything that seems to them wrong in the world by finding an enemy and then find the simple cure in liquidating somebody. The reference here is of course to the idea of the class war. The essential fact seems to be that political man is a religious animal and that the most fundamental principle of his logic is *credo quia impossibile,* or at least *credo quia mirabilis*. It is a striking fact that the outstanding feature of the gods worshiped by men in all times has been power joined with caprice, or at least with enormous and unpredictable partiality. The conception of a God who could reason with anybody—even with himself—is so foreign to human thinking as to seem quite absurd.

It is not implied that political beliefs really stop with what there is no good reason against believing. They are in fact, even in the case of the same individual, largely a tissue of contradictions as palpable and demonstrable as any propositions can be in a problem-field in which both the data and the objectives of action are so resistant to clear definition and classification. Regarding socialism specifically, perhaps the most important fact is that no definition of it can be given which combines any degree of definiteness or concreteness with internal consistency. The conception actually lies in the realm of prophecy as well as in that of vague ideals or wishes well designated as "cloud-cuckoo land." In the absence of any real science to serve as an adequate basis of prediction, and in disregard of such science as does exist, men exercise their freedom to believe almost anything and to promote almost any line of action. They even advocate ideals which have neither conceptual content, self-consistency, critical defensibility in themselves, nor any visible connection with any line of action sufficiently concrete and definite to make sense. In particular, it is easy to imagine and to believe (as shown by the fact that intelligent people regularly do so imagine and believe) that the (supposed) evils in the world or in any particular society *(a)* are economic in basis, *(b)* more specifically, that they are consequences of the form of economic organization, and *(c)* can without serious difficulty be corrected by replacing the economic organization with a system of control by politicians. The combination of these beliefs is the essential content of socialism, defined in accord with the beliefs and propaganda of most of its proponents. It is imagined that the state, i.e., the government, conceived in the abstract as a benevolent and all-powerful agency—essentially as God rather than realistically as a group of politicians—could order economic affairs rightly without generating new evils or incurring serious social costs; that humanity would with approximate unanimity approve and like the result; that no other serious problems would remain; and, finally, that everybody—or nearly everybody, apart, perhaps, from a few criminally minded recalcitrants—would "live happily ever after."

But we hasten to add, with all emphasis, that what has been said involves no condemnation of socialism. The reasoning on the basis of which it is condemned is commonly no better than that by which it is supported. It would be as irrational to condemn it as it is to advocate it in the absence of any intelligible definition. The main intellectual task of a discussion of socialism is that of investigating the possibility of definition and of what can really be said for or against it after such a definition (or definitions) is formulated.

One common misconception in particular must be corrected at the outset. Economic theory, as such, involves no disproof or rejection of socialism. Rather the contrary. Theoretical analysis of the mechanism of economic organization as worked out through free exchange and free contract, operating under the control of market competition, reveals many indisputable weaknesses which could, in theory, be remedied or avoided by an all-powerful, wise, and benevolent political authority. The problem of socialism is the practical one already suggested. It has to do first, with the possibility and probability of such an authority, or some approximation to it, being created on earth and among human beings, by political process, and the means and cost; and, second, with the question whether, in view of human interests and values other than those of economics, the citizens or subjects would really approve or like this consummation if it could be realized. The problem is in the first place political, not economic at all; and, in the second place it is a problem of what human beings really want and/or of ideal values in relation to desires. The economist, as economist, has nothing to say about any of these questions. Only within fairly narrow limits, and subject to explicit hypothetical postulates, can economic science make any pronouncement as to conditions as they would exist under socialism or give any picture of the socialistic state or world. And economics has even less to say on the questions as to whether human beings would approve or like the pattern of social life according to any hypothetical picture or whether it would be good or better than the world as it is, was, or would be under capitalism at any place and time.

With reference to the first question, as to what society would be like under socialism, it is easy to show that the change in the form of economic organization might involve no substantial change whatever in the concrete character of economic life. Under socialistic forms every human being might be doing the same thing, in an economic sense, and reaping the same remuneration or reward as before. Socialism presupposes an all-powerful government enforcing its will on its subjects or at least an authority whose edicts are enforced on those who do not obey them without enforcement.[3] In consequence, the problem of prediction, or prophecy, as to what socialism would be sets the question of what the state, however constituted, would actually (a) wish to do, (b) try to do, and (c) succeed in doing, either on the basis of the will of the people or more or less in opposition to this will, and of what the will of the people itself would be after socialism became established in any country or area. The main fact is, to repeat, that socialists themselves have made little effort to put any intelligible concrete content into the picture or ideal. It is in order to suggest that this may be one of the main sources of strength in their propaganda (though this is another question on which the economist, as economist, has nothing to say).

One thing economic analysis can do: it can show the character of the economic problems with which socialism proposes to deal. And if these are not at all of the sort which socialists assume or represent them to be, no special political competence is required to reject the socialists' appeal for supreme power (and the perquisites thereof).[4] We do not turn our bodies over for major surgery and hygienic management to persons who in place of knowledge of anatomy and physiology have ingenious theories, even though they profess the best of intentions. Very recently—since the World War, and chiefly in the past few years—very few socialists have made a beginning in the way of discussing the concrete problems of a strictly economic sort which would confront the socialistic state and the organizational policies which would be appropriate for dealing with them.[5] The assumptions made by socialists in general, and by these socialists in particular, as to the character of economic problems, and specifically the problems of economic organization, afford the only concrete basis for discussing socialism at all. Since the practical proposal is one of substituting socialism for a pre-existing capitalistic organization, the concrete question to be considered takes the form of what are or would be the main similarities, and the

important differences, between the two systems? In this connection it is
the similarities which especially call for emphasis. In order to define any
problem which can be discussed at all, it is necessary to begin with the
economic problem; and limits of space, as well as the intrinsic difficulties
of political discussion, already mentioned, will force us to confine ourselves chiefly to that phase of the issue as a whole. As already emphasized, it is not at all the main problem which lies in the field of politics
and social psychology and ethics. But it is at once the aspect of the general issue which can be treated by an economist (or at all definitely by
anyone) and the first aspect to be considered in a logical order of analysis. A summary examination of the economic problem will carry its own
implications as to the more general aspects of the broader and really
fundamental issues. We begin by noting briefly some of the main similarities, features of social-economic life which would be the same under
socialism as under capitalism.[6]

II

The first major characteristic of socialism, in the conception of its proponents, in which it would be identical with capitalism—say as the latter existed in the nineteenth century in England and in the United
States—has to do with the character of the ends to be realized by the
organized use of means. Socialists accept the social philosophy in accord
with which ends are individual rather than social. This is really expressed in saying that society is viewed as an organization rather than as
an organism.[7] Socialists (in our sense) have agreed with the proponents
of liberalistic individualism in viewing society as essentially an organization of individuals for mutual aid, or cooperation, and specifically for
economic cooperation in the interest of increased efficiency in the use of
means (to realize individual ends). In both systems or philosophies,
moreover, ends or values inhere in the individual rather than in society—or some transcendental realm to which society itself may be a
means; and in addition, ends are defined, in both cases, by the free
choices of individuals. Ends are individual, and each individual is accepted as the best judge of his own ends.[8]

A detailed examination, impossible here, would show that, in fact,
socialists have typically been more individualistic in the philosophical
sense than have their liberal opponents, whose position is often distinguished as individualistic. Economic socialism, socialized production, or
planned economy, has often been advocated, in opposition to free enterprise or economic individualism, as a means for the more perfect real-

ization of the ideal of social and ethical individualism. And in the abstract, this is entirely defensible. This might be both the aim and the result of socialism. The question raised is twofold: First, is economic socialism itself feasible? and, second, could or would a state which socialized economic production be individualistic or free in the economic and other fields of activity or aspects of life? It will also be seen that liberalism—a synonym for individualism, in so far as the latter includes the second element noted above (that the individual is the judge of his own ends)—is subject to the same ambiguity. Socialism may claim to present the conditions of maximum individual liberty, even true economic liberty, and hence to be the true liberalism.[9]

More particularly—and the fact is vitally significant—socialists have gone much farther than liberals (or than other liberals) in treating the problems of individual and social life as essentially economic. This is perhaps ultimately the most serious of the gross oversimplifications, amounting to an evasion of the main difficulties of the program from which socialistic propaganda derives its plausibility and its appeal. The truth seems rather to be that in the ultimate and essential problem the economic factor is relatively superficial and unimportant. If we imagine all individual economic problems solved once for all—say by giving to every adult the power to satisfy all his economic wants by magical procedure (say, again, by rubbing a copper lamp and wishing, or merely by wishing)—it seems probable that the conflicts which cause strife and unhappiness among men and give rise to problems of social policy would be intensified rather than ameliorated, and even that they would not be essentially changed in form. The deeper motives back of human activity and struggle center to a minor extent in concrete results to be achieved because of any inherent significance which they possess. They center rather in the desire for freedom and power for their own sake, associated with the more fundamental want for interesting activity. It is true that rational activity always seems to aim at some results, in play as well as in work. But it is not necessarily instrumental to the result or dependent upon the value of a result for its own value or interest. Rather, the situation in play seems to be the ultimate nature of most economic activity also; the result is set up to make the activity interesting and, in the deeper view, is instrumental to the latter.[10]

Acceptance of the individual's choices as the final criterion of economic value has as its first concrete consequence or meaning for economic organization freedom of consumption. Each individual—really each family or some equivalent primary social unit—must be allowed to choose freely among final products the particular goods and services to be used to satisfy his (its) own wants. The only possible way of granting people this freedom is to give them their total economic income in the form of abstract purchasing power, i.e., money of some sort, to make final products available at prices uniform for all, and to allow each purchaser to select products at will as to kind and amount. Thus the socialistic economy will necessarily be a pecuniary organization in this sense. And since the prices of products will have to be set, or the relation between price and supply in each case adjusted, so as to clear the market, it follows that in the whole field of the final distribution of products the mechanism of socialism must be identical with that of capitalism. And in fact this has not been questioned by socialists or any other arrangement adopted or attempted in any of the quasi-socialistic economies, whether communistic or totalitarian, which have been set up in recent years.[11]

But the essential and necessary similarity by no means ceases at this point. Socialists also accept the view that the individualistic criterion of values also includes freedom of choice of the role to be played in production by the individual, i.e., his occupation. The clear implication of this freedom is that the money income of the individual must be received in the form of payment for services, at a level measuring the economic value of the service rendered, which is the amount which other persons as consumers are willing (freely) to pay for the contribution made to production by the services of the individual in question. It may not be apparent that it is necessary under socialism for wages to be equal to the service rendered. But a fairly simple economic analysis suffices to prove that no other rate of remuneration will apportion the laborers most economically among different occupations, that is, will apportion them in such a way as to secure at the same time the best relation between income and sacrifice for the worker and the maximum output as measured by consumers' choices.[12] In any case, payment at any other level than that of productive contribution is equivalent to payment of all at this level, modified by taxation and subsidy to produce any other distribution desired; and it would be much easier to carry out rationally the second policy—if indeed the first is possible at all. The effect on efficiency of either mode of distorting payment away from the productivity level is the same. Thus only at a cost in loss of output can a socialistic government redistribute income toward greater equality or according to any criterion of need as between individuals of divergent earning power.[13]

It is now evident that the general pattern of organization in a socialistic economy, if it operates efficiently and in accord with individual choices as the norm of value, must be essentially the same as that of capitalism. It should go without saying that production is assumed to be carried on on the basis of modern technology. That is, there would be production units of the familiar types—factories, farms, railways and ships, stores, and even banks or some equivalent financial agency. A large proportion of such units would involve the organized cooperation of a large number of human beings and would presumably have managers. Each production unit would, as a unit (whatever its mechanism of control or management), buy productive services and make and sell a product or products of some sort; and in its buying and its selling operations each would compete, in the economic sense, with all other production units in the same industry and in different industries. Prices of products would measure marginal utility and prices of productive services their marginal productivity. All production units would be organized and managed on the basis of profit-seeking, just as under private capitalism.

The only important difference in this respect arises in connection with monopoly. Natural monopolies would in theory be conducted so as not to earn monopoly profit; but this has also been the aim of public policy under private enterprise, achieved or attempted either through regulation or through public ownership. In theory, socialism would not allow the existence of artificial or predatory monopolies. Space limits exclude any adequate discussion of monopoly. It would show that socialists and the general public have both a much-exaggerated conception of the magnitude of the monopoly evil and a gross misconception of the character of the problem. (It is largely the problem of profit in a particular aspect, since in terms of correct analysis all profit is monopoly gain; the role of profit will be considered later in connection with progressive chance, and it will be found to be inevitable under socialism also.) The further course of the argument should at least suggest that the establishment of socialism would in itself afford no solution of the monopoly problem, where it is a real problem, and that it is problematical how much difference the changed form of organization would make.[14]

The discussion of the necessary similarities between socialism (if it is to be an efficient organization) and capitalism leaves, up to this point, two major questions unanswered. The first has to do with the internal organization of the productive units or enterprises. The general theory of socialism requires that management be in the hands of salaried appointees of the government. That is, socialism would prohibit the specialization of risk-taking, which is the essence of the entrepreneur function under private enterprise. It should hardly be necessary to point out that this would involve a restriction of individual freedom. Under the laws of modern liberal states the participants in enterprise can have any form of organization they prefer. Specifically, it might be that of a producers' cooperative, with the fruits of operations apportioned among the participants in any manner whatever upon which the parties might come to agreement. As between management and labor, the familiar relationship in distribution might even be reversed, management receiving a fixed share and the workers, the contingent share; and any functionary or arbitrarily chosen group might also be the legal owner of the business, with the others in a position of employees. Ownership of an enterprise has no necessary connection with ownership of wealth, which may be borrowed or leased for use, and this is typically the case, in large part, in business enterprises.

Any serious attempt to answer the question as to why the managerial function and the receipt of a contingent remuneration or residual have been associated in the manner actually familiar would have to start out from the fact that this is the arrangement which has in general seemed most satisfactory to the parties concerned. The main reason for this satisfactoriness, in turn, is that it is the arrangement which has been found to involve greatest efficiency and the larger returns all around. (More harmonious and agreeable conditions of work are undoubtedly another reason, partly distinct from the factor of efficiency.) No reason has ever been suggested, to the knowledge of this writer, why any of these facts would be different under socialism. The contention that the owning entrepreneur, individually subject to loss or the recipient of gain, according to the success of the enterprise, can be replaced by the government, *assumed* to have no such interest, without loss of managerial efficiency, surely rests more on the will to believe than it does on inference from experience. But this is not impossible; it *might* work out in that way! It is a political or psychological question, not one of economics. And the main problem will only be reached at a later point in the essay when we come to discuss changes in conditions.

The second unanswered question is essentially a different aspect of the first, just considered. It is the question of the disposition of the profits—or losses, negative profits—i.e., of the margin of contingency in the fruits of operations, the excess or deficiency of the earnings of an enterprise above what can be safely predicted in advance. It is one of the familiar and essential principles of the competitive economy that in so far as the magnitude of the result from any productive activity can be positively foreseen, it will be imputed to the productive services participating; that is, these will be valued and priced so as to exhaust the product, and there will be no profit. Of course, the participating productive services include non-human agencies or property, and the participants in distribution include the owners of these; and that would also be the case under socialism. Socialists, and the public generally, almost universally confuse the earnings of property with profit; but correct analysis, and rational policy, actually require their separation. The nature and role of property—what socialists regularly call the means of production, in contrast with human beings or their services—will come up for consideration presently. But it should hardly be necessary to point out that, for the purposes of the rational management of production, human beings (or their services, i.e., labor) are also a means of production in essentially the same sense, economically speaking, as any other useful agencies or services.

Unless it is assumed that under socialism both the managers and everyone else concerned will have perfect foresight of the future, there will be profit, including loss, in connection with most enterprises. It would be impossible to organize and control production without making a separation between the amount of productive result which can be anticipated with reasonable certainty, and with reference to which fairly definite plans can be made, and both an excess of uncertain magnitude to be hoped for and a deficiency which may arise. The amount of the contingent share will depend on the accuracy of the foreknowledge on which plans are based. Its distribution between positive profit and negative profit or loss will depend on the degree of conservatism with which expectations are formulated and definite plans made for the distribution and use of the product. The more conservative the plans, the more likely it will be that the departure of the actual results from expectations will be favorable—a profit in the ordinary sense rather than a loss. All this, again is identical with conditions under private enterprise.

The question of what would really happen under socialism—i.e., what the authorities in power would actually do—carries us at once, and obviously, into the field of political prophecy, where, as sufficiently explained at the outset, objective discussion is practically hopeless. We may take it as obvious, if any assertion in this field can be made at all, that on one hand, the individual participants in production in any situation will desire, and strive in any way in their power to get, an income which is (a) as large and (b) as certain as possible; while, on the other hand, mere prudence on the part of management (in a particular enterprise or in society) would call for conservatism, i.e., for not guaranteeing or assuring to anyone a larger income, or to any use a larger allotment, than the planners can reasonably count on realizing. The political conflict generated and its probable results are again matters on which most students will form opinions on grounds too vague for discussion. But since some assumption has to be made, if the discussion is to proceed any farther, we shall assume that the management is prudent, i.e., conservative, at least to the extent that the profits earned in some enterprises—above distributive commitments in one form or another involved in the social-economic plan—would be at least sufficient to cover the losses incurred in others. Under this assumption the first use to be made of profit, where it occurs, must be to cover losses which occur elsewhere. That is, the profit made by any production unit must necessarily go to the state; it cannot be retained in the enterprise where it is made. If there is a profit in the aggregate, in excess of aggregate losses in the system as a whole, it will be available to the government for any use which it may choose to make of it.

III

It should be obvious that all management is largely a matter of prediction and that the accuracy of prediction in economic affairs and hence the possibility of planning and acting in accord with any plan depends upon the amount of change in the conditions of economic life as a whole. Change may be deliberately produced or accepted as desirable or tolerated as unpreventable. And the relation between change and accuracy of prediction is not simple. If conditions were unchanging, and known to be so, prediction could be accurate and presumably would be. On the other hand, it is not theoretically impossible to predict the future when it is expected to involve change. And change deliberately brought about will presumably be foreknown, in so far as it is under control, and other changes may be more or less accurately predicted. But it will hardly be disputed that in practice the accuracy of prediction will be correlated directly and closely with the amount of change expected or recognized as probable.

It is also self-evident that any problem of action is a problem of making some change in a natural course of events—a course which events would take in the absence of action or interference. Intelligent action accordingly requires knowledge of two general kinds. The actor and planner of action must know (a) what the course of events would be in the absence of any action and (b) what changes will result from the various possible lines of action or interference. Knowledge on the second point includes knowledge of the means or power in any form at the disposal of the planner and director of action and of his actual control over available means of action.

These observations really bring us finally, and for the first time, to the heart of the problem of socialism. Relevant discussion calls for analysis of the natural course of events in economic life, how far it involves change, and what kinds of change, and how far changes of the various kinds are predictable in the absence of action; and consideration of possible lines of action for preventing undesirable, and bringing about desirable, changes, and how far the results of the various kinds of possible action can be predicted. Beyond all this lie the political problems: how far the hypothetical planning agency, which would be the central feature of the socialistic state, could be expected to possess or to acquire all these different kinds of knowledge and what it would actually do about it and with what actual results. And before any final judgment could be passed on the desirability of socialism we should have to have and to apply correct criteria for comparing and judging all the differences which the analysis would show between the course of events under socialistic planning and the course of events as it would be in the absence of planned action, i.e., under competitive individualism. The utter hopelessness of any such a task and the futility of attempting it in any detail—and hence the unfathomable presumption (if it is not sheer ignorance and simplicity) involved in passing any judgment about socialism in general—is the main point which this article is attempting to drive home. It may be noted, too, that the problem of socialism as a conceivably real or practical issue, is purely one of degree, with respect to every detail in the complex of changes proposed. No one has attempted or proposed, or conceivably will seriously propose, anything approaching absolute economic individualism or absolute socialization of production or of any feature of economic life.

It is possible, however, to carry the investigation a few steps farther, to give some further indication of the character of the problems. To do this we turn from consideration of the principles and facts which are necessarily identical for the two systems—i.e., for all systems of organization which accept individual judgment as the final criterion of value and which aim at maximum efficiency in the use of means to create or produce such values—and inquire briefly into the differences between private enterprise and socialism. In this connection also the content of the discussion must, to the writer's regret, chiefly take the form of pointing out palpable errors, and especially vital omissions, in the theory of socialism as propounded by socialists.

The proposal of socialists is, in brief, to transfer from individuals acting in their own interest (individually or in voluntary groups) to society as a whole, meaning to the government, and concretely to politicians of some type, the management of production and the ownership of the chief means of production. By means of production, as already indicated, the socialist understands the nonhuman means or property; human beings themselves (as workers) are to remain each under his own private ownership. Socialists lump together and treat as a unit, as essentially identical, the ownership of property and the management of production; and the identity is assumed to hold under socialism as well as under capitalism. The fallacies must be indicated in brief outline, without the extensive discussion which would be necessary to prevent our own statement from seeming merely dogmatic at many points.

As a beginning it is necessary to note explicitly a few of the essential facts as to the nature of economic organization and the problem of its direction or control on a social scale. We have seen that the general form of the twofold system of markets and prices is largely inevitable under any form of economic organization, and it is entirely inevitable, in so far as the result to be achieved is efficiency in the use of resources in terms of individual choices. The general pattern of organized production must be that of enterprises buying productive services, using them to make products, and selling the products at prices determined in both cases by competition over the whole field of production.

In such a system it is a sheer fallacy, in contradiction with the postulates, to speak of any individual or human agency exercising any considerable amount of control at all. Every individual in the economy exercises an infinitesimal amount of control over production in making his choices as a consumer in expending whatever money income he has to spend, i.e., in allocating his expenditures among products at the prices which he finds marked upon them. And the prices of products must be set at the level which will clear the market of the actual supplies brought to the market in any short period of time. (In a competitive market all the talk about bargaining power is sheer nonsense; bargaining is possible only where both buyer and seller are monopolists.) In the second place, if production is to be directed in accord with the choices of consumers, productive services must be allocated to the industries making the various products by setting prices of productive services in every case to measure the value of the productive contribution of each. The only alternative is direct coercion, through the machinery of the criminal law or through process without law. The owner of any productive resource (whoever he may be and whatever the resource in question) can only choose between modes of use on the terms set by prices of productive services determined in this way. Each resource owner, including explicitly free laborers as owners of their own labor power, also exercises an infinitesimal amount of control in so far as he has any preference, on other grounds than the money return, between different occupations or modes of employment. The rest of the organization process follows automatically under socialism as under private enterprise. There is room for social control or planning only in so far as the market machinery may fail for one reason or another to work ideally and without friction; and under the assumed conditions, the only action which is desirable is to facilitate the achievement of the results of theoretically perfect competition. Natural monopoly may be mentioned again as one of the important situations calling for action in the social interest. It is worthy of note also that the main cause of imperfection in the working of the market mechanism is error in productive adjustments due to the fact that individuals will not plan and adhere to announced plans but expect the machinery of organization to make provision far in advance for their possible wants while they reserve decision until the last moment.

The entrepreneur function, identified by socialists with the ownership of a particular kind of productive resources, not only has no connection with ownership of resources but has no real existence, except in the limited sense indicated. It disappears entirely in so far as the market machinery works effectively; managerial decisions can only be in accord with the choices of consumers and resource owners, or fail to be in accord with them, which involves a loss of social efficiency. The essential feature of the enterprise economy is that it theoretically and to a reasonable degree in fact places managerial decisions, i.e., production planning, in anticipation of consumers' choices, in the hands of functionaries so situated that the major loss consequent upon any failure to make correct decisions impinges primarily upon the individuals responsible for them—those who make them, either directly or through agents whom they appoint and control.

In the second place, the categorical distinction made by socialists— derived as usual from the fallacious notions of common sense—between the ownership of property and the personal freedom of the individual as a laborer is fallacious economic analysis. The substance of the matter is that any individual "owns" whatever productive capacity he does actually own! This is a matter of brute fact in any society at any time. The kind of resources owned, and specifically whether they happen to be located "inside the individual's skin" or outside of it, is merely a technical matter and of limited importance for economic organization.

Personal productive capacity or labor power is in the same position as earning power embodied in external things, in all respects which are important for economic theory or economic policy. There is no general difference in relation to economic mechanics of cause and effect except for certain consequences of the laws affecting the two kinds of property and the individual's freedom of choice with respect to them, which will be noted presently. In general, both personal capacity and property in the usual narrow sense are simply forms, or congeries of forms, of economic power; any property effectively possessed is properly regarded as an attribute of the personality of its owner, along with his personal qualities; or, alternatively, an individual may properly be said to own himself, his person with all its attributes, viewed as a productive instrument.

More interesting and important still, the categorical distinction in ethical terms between property and labor (power) which in popular thinking is universally accepted as axiomatic, and which is a cornerstone of socialistic propaganda, will not stand critical examination either and turns out to be equally untenable. The ethical questions as to whether an individual deserves to receive and enjoy the income produced by any productive capacity in his possession may be divided into two parts. The first has to do with the source of the economic power in question, or how the individual comes into possession of it, and the second with the manner or conditions of its use. In both cases—property in the narrow sense and personal capacities—possession originates in a similar list of facts and processes. These include in both cases, first, inheritance, and, second, the working of social-cultural and legal processes over which the individual has no control. Beyond this causally given basis or nucleus, productive power is created in the individual by a process of investment—in education and training in the inclusive sense—which is neither economically nor ethically different in any important respect from the investment which gives rise to any other productive agency. All these factors are affected to a large if not overwhelming extent by all sorts of imponderables and contingencies which may be lumped together under the head of "luck."

There is no visible reason why anyone is more or less entitled to the earnings of inherited personal capacities than to those of inherited property in any other form; and similarly as to capacity resulting from impersonal social processes and accidents, which affect both classes of capacity indifferently. And in so far as the creation of either form of capacity is due to motivated human activity on the part of the individual concerned or of his parents, or to anyone else, the motives may in either case be ethical or unethical in any possible sense or degree. And, finally, the use of productive capacity of either type may similarly be more or less intelligently motivated in accord with ends or ideals which are ethical or unethical in any degree and in any meaning. The grounds for the distinction generally drawn so sharply and so confidently seem to present a major problem in social psychology. The "labor theory of value," which has been the most important source of corruption in economic thinking through most of its history, is an unanalyzable mixture of fallacious causal analysis and false ethics.

A part of the reason for the idea commonly held is, no doubt, that the poor usually get what income they do get chiefly from the sale of personal services. But there is no close correspondence between the size of income and the character of the source.

The major difference between incomes from the two types of source is, as suggested above, a consequence of social institutions and law. The individual who is dependent upon the sale of personal services for his living is subject to a peculiar disadvantage in the way of security, which is a paradoxical result of the legal sanctity of freedom. Since an approximately continuous flow of some economic goods and services is practically necessary, such a person becomes dependent upon access to a continuous market. This does not apply to owners of property. The latter may derive an income for a time (though it is not really income) from the sale of assets or from a loan based on these as security. But the sanctity of personal freedom in Western legal systems, the doctrine of inalienable rights, makes it impossible for a person effectively to pledge his future earning power in exchange for present resources. This weakness, again, exists irrespective, in principle, of the magnitude or value of the earning power itself.[15]

The most important question in connection with the socialization of property is that of what would be gained from the change. Critical investigation of this question in terms of the statistical magnitudes the general order of which is known will show that the results would certainly be disappointing. In the United States, under the relatively normal conditions of the middle twenties, about three-fourths of the national income represented the value of personal services and one-fourth represented the yield of property. This fourth was about equal to the sum of the costs of government (all units) plus the annual saving added to capital. (Under the depression, governmental expenditure has soared and property incomes have shrunk far more than those derived from labor.) The maximum amount which a socialist government would have found it possible to seize out of property income would never have been as much as 10 per cent of the total labor income. Out of this it would have to pay the greatly increased expenses of government involved in administering the economic life of the country. (Some of this might conceivably be saved by cutting down high salaries paid to executives by private enterprise, but detailed analysis would show that this is very doubtful). Moreover, in any sweeping process of income equalization much income would simply disappear through the downward revaluation of rare luxury products. The ultimate resources which produce a thousand dollars' worth of champagne or diamonds, or the services of a highly exceptional medical genius or portrait painter, would not yield a comparable value in products in demand from persons of average income, at prices which such persons could pay. In general, the "choice cuts" would fall in value much more than the ordinary ones would rise.

The discussion has come around again to the point we had reached a while ago. Under the accepted postulates as to the general objectives of economic life, and under any set of given conditions—wants, resources, and technology—as they stand at any given time, the changes or differences that would be made in the concrete nature of economic life could not be great and would be highly problematical as to both magnitude and favorable character. (In saying that they are problematical we mean to reiterate that within the physically possible limits they are a matter of political prophecy.) In other words, the power of a government committed to socialism to make any considerable difference in the economic lives of its citizens or subjects, i.e., in the production and distribution of goods, would depend upon its bringing about some fundamental change in the given conditions (wants or resources or technology) or upon its employing coercion or substituting some altogether different objective of economic activity, replacing individual want, satisfaction, and freedom of choice. We have seen that the "expropriation" of the "more important means of production" from their previous private owners involves no very important exception to this general statement, even with respect to distribution and even considering only the state of affairs immediately following such a confiscation of wealth, accumulated under a different system—i.e., without raising the question as to the probability of a socialistic administration effecting its revolution and "taking over" without extensive destruction and dislocation. Mere change in the form of organization, without sweeping changes in the given conditions, holds great potentialities for loss and quite limited potentialities for improvement, even taking the latter in accord with the estimates of the proponents of socialism in so far as they can be reconciled with objective facts.

Considering in positive terms the differences between socialism and free enterprise, the establishment of socialism would involve two general changes. The first is the appointment of the managers of business enterprises by political process and the second, the socialization, expropriation, or confiscation of private property, or whatever portion of it the socialist regime might actually think it expedient to take over. All objective inquiry into the effects of either or both these changes tends to minimize their importance—except for the possibility of catastrophic loss in case the political administrations should behave more in accord with the expectations of the gloomier prophets than with those of the optimistic votaries.

The chief statement which can be made objectively is that if the new administration seriously attempted to fulfill the expectations suggested by socialists themselves—and on the basis of which they would probably come into power, if at all—the consequences would certainly be disastrous. We should note in particular that the realization of the theoretical possibilities of socialism in the way of equalizing the distribution of income—if extensive change in that direction were seriously attempted—would call for a sweeping reorganization of the productive system from top to bottom. For, as just noted in another connection, no great redistribution could be effected without changing the character of the physical output. Any attempt to replace at all rapidly the production of luxury goods with the production of things that would be demanded by persons of something near average income would create a task for any organization machinery which it could not be expected to perform without producing large derangement and loss; it would be comparable to the task of shifting national production from an ordinary peace footing to what would be required for total war, or the converse change. (Again, both the ultimate limitations—the sheer disappearance of a large part of the value of luxury items consequent upon specificity of ultimate resources, and the serious political consequences to be expected as a result of impossible promises made for campaign purposes—should be kept in mind.)

Socialists commonly believe in the possibility of a great increase in the efficiency of production, merely through the change in administration. But it is quite certain that such beliefs rarely if ever rest either on any quantitative study of the facts or on any objective analysis of the organization problem. The judgment of students who emotionally are entirely sympathetic with socialism has generally been that the political administration at best would be doing extremely well if it maintained approximately the general level of efficiency achieved under capitalism, without estimating this standard very near the ideal. A feature of the whole discussion situation is the fact that even educated people inclined to radical criticism—and the disposition is a trait of human nature closely related to moral idealism—have wild ideas as to the amount of loss and inefficiency in the modern economic organization. The best-known study of facts is that made by Nourse and Associates of the Brookings Institution for the United States in the 1920s.[16] Their results, estimating achievement under normal conditions at about 80 per cent of what could reasonably be regarded as possible, are in the opinion of the writer a fair estimate, though the statistical quantities involved have no definite meaning, to say nothing of accuracy.

The point for emphasis is that socialists grossly oversimplify the organization problem which would confront the political order under their system by treating it as one of routine administration. In fact, it would necessarily be one of revolutionary reorganization. It is merely absurd to think of socialism being established in any visible future for the purpose of freezing a pre-existing state of life and preventing change.[17]

Thus the third major confusion involved in socialist theory has to do with the nature of the problem of management. In the few brief remarks which are possible here on this topic we shall continue to assume that the general objective of maximum individual want-satisfaction remains unchanged—as far as possible.[18]

The fundamental changes in the given conditions of economic life which the socialistic state must make to bring about any important change at all fall under the three heads of wants, resources, and technology. These are the three classes of conditions which, in the nature of economic activity, are actually given at any time and place and which determine everything else. For our purposes these may be reduced to two, resources and technology being combined under the head of productive capacity, over against the wants to be satisfied, as the two more elementary sets of economic data. Inventions and technical improvements of other sorts, whether patentable or not, are in fact private property under the law of modern industrial nations, or they certainly are such for the purposes of economic analysis as long as the person who makes an innovation is in a position to derive any income from it in excess of the necessary remuneration of the productive agencies employed in putting it into effect. (As already suggested, the major fraction of the profit in an economic system consists of this inherently temporary monopoly gain in connection with innovations, the prospect of which is the chief economic motive leading to economic progress.) In addition, inventions and other forms of property are genetically similar in that they all (including personal capacity—see above) result from investment, mixed with natural process and "brute force and accident."[19]

In consequence of these facts, all the different elements in productive capacity would present similar problems to the overhead control system, the government of the socialistic state. Productive capacity has traditionally been classified into three divisions or kinds: the "holy trinity" of labor, capital, and land. The classification is open to fatal objections from the standpoint of any accurate and thoroughgoing analysis, but the reasons cannot be elaborated here, and it may be followed for the purpose of a topical survey.[20]

Only one or two major facts or principles can be touched upon by way of characterizing the problems which would confront the government of a socialistic state. In connection with the given conditions of economic life—wants or other ends, resources of all kinds (and however classified), and technical knowledge (if that is separated from resources)—two facts stand out as overwhelmingly important for general social theory. The first is that in the absence of change or the possibility of producing changes no problem can arise, while any activity directed to change involves uncertainty as to its results and is inherently a gamble. It is in connection with initiative that management has meaning. An obvious consequence of the uncertainty of results is that managerial activities cannot be evaluated until after they are performed— and often a very long time afterward, and most vaguely and doubtfully even then. This is the fundamental reason for the specialization of entrepreneurship or risk-taking, which is the central principle of the enterprise economy and the real meaning of the profit motive or principle. The socialistic state would have no objective or rational basis for fixing the remuneration of managers, the indeterminacy of their value being proportional to the degree in which they exercised initiative.[21] To secure a moderate degree of efficiency, along with adaptive flexibility, the socialistic state might well find itself compelled to revert to the

enterprise principle of leaving the remuneration of all final management—i.e., of innovators—to be determined by results actually realized. If so, the last important economic difference between socialism and
capitalism would disappear, and with it all chance for any approximation to economic equality. Making innovations is a gamble, and a lottery
cannot function without large prizes. In any case, it is certain that the
problem of selecting, motivating, and rewarding real management or
planners with power to make substantial changes is one which has no
solution. Such matters can only be ruled either by the pull and haul of
free individual bargaining or by that of political and social forces.

The second fact referred to is that under the economy of free enterprise, the primary agency for perpetuating the various given elements
or factors and for bringing about changes in them is the institution of
the family. This proposition surely does not need defense or elaboration.
In practically all forms of society known to history it is primarily
through the family that the individuals of each new generation receive
their equipment in all these respects—and the statement applies to the
group as a whole in so far as the phenomena pertain to society as a
whole rather than to individuals. No society can possibly be really individualistic. In a world in which individuals go through the biological
life-cycle, and especially where they do not inherit acquired knowledge,
training, and habits, the minimum ultimate unit is the natural family;
what is called individualism would be far more descriptively designated
as "familism." It really makes little practical difference whether the ultimate mechanics of continuity be that of biological heredity or culture
inheritance, i.e., tradition perpetuated by some mixture of unconscious
imitation and more or less deliberate education. It is true that in modern
Western civilization the biological and subjective individual has come to
play a much larger role in culture continuity, and especially in culture
change, than was true in primitive society or earlier civilizations. But
there are fairly narrow limits even to the possibilities in this regard. The
individual cannot possibly be other than a social product, a social or
domesticated animal. The more important peculiarity of what is called
individualism is the greater role assigned to the private family, meaning
to parents; and "parental individualism" might be a still better designation for the most important distinguishing characteristic of modern free
or competitive society.[22]

The general conclusion which follows from the type of consideration suggested, and which is important for the purpose in hand, is that
the effective changes which are possible under socialism and which

would make up any important difference consist overwhelmingly in the transfer of functions from the private family, or from individuals as parents, to the political state. Reflection will show that, in addition, both voluntary groupings of all kinds, and also of the smaller political divisions, must very largely lose their functions and their very existence in favor of the nation. Whatever socialists may wish or intend, and whatever they may think, effective socialism must largely mean, in practice, "the omnipotent state."[23]

The importance of this for the ultimate problem of social control is twofold. First, the selfishness or self-interest of the family, as against other families, is far greater than that of the individual against other individuals. Or, the selfishness of parents for their children is greater than that for themselves. The ethical injunction to "love one's neighbor as one's self" does not get to the heart of the problem at all, either as to what is important or as to what is really difficult—as an obstacle to equalitarianism. The crux is rather the necessity for loving one's neighbor's children as one's own. In the second place, it is not merely the sanctity of the family relation and family institution which is at stake. If the family were consigned to limbo—as some socialists have been quite willing to do—its place would inevitably be taken by some other primary group in connection with which essentially the same problems would arise.

The abolition of inheritance of wealth would tend both to weaken the family and to shift the family interest into other modes of creating and passing on to heirs a favored position, a position of power. The abolition of ownership of productive property would by no means close all opportunity for families to strive to give their heirs a preferred position as a start in life. Many channels for such activity would remain open, but the most important would be that of politics. Indeed, the program of socialism seems to consist primarily in transferring from business to politics the whole competitive struggle for power and the fruits of power—the things which men want and for which they scheme and struggle in life. To ask whether the results of such a change would be desirable or what the concrete results would actually be would merely carry our discussion into fields where, as sufficiently pointed out before, and for reasons sufficiently indicated, discussion cannot be expected to establish any conclusion.

The most important general result with regard to the ethical aspect of the social problem which should follow from the foregoing exposition is, stated in negative terms, that it is a fallacy to think of the problems of large-scale social organization—and specifically of large-scale economic organization—in terms of the relations between given individuals. Stating it in positive form, the problem is rather that of creating or producing the right kinds of individuals. Given individuals with the requisite endowment of capacity and disposition, the general principle that freedom is the only basis of ethically defensible relationships among men and the essential condition of all moral or personal life calls for leaving such individuals to work out and establish such relations as they themselves deem most conducive to economic efficiency, to personal and cultural well-being, and in general to their mutual advantage in their pursuit of the good life. Sound policies of social improvement must be based on a sound analysis and appraisal of personal and cultural values, taken in relation to a sound objective comprehension of the mechanics of economic organization and of cultural phenomena, as studied in the various social disciplines. Moralizing about the problems, in terms of the sentimental values and obligations appropriate to intercourse in small face-to-face groups, can lead to no good results and is certain to do harm rather than good.[24]

Notes

1. This paper contains the substance of one of a series of four lectures on "Collectivism," given at the London School of Economics and Political Science in May, 1938. The content of another lecture in the same series, on "Ethics and Economic Reform," has appeared as three articles in *Economica* for February, August, and November, 1939.

2. The word was popularized, if not invented, by Marx, to characterize modern free enterprise economy on the ground that the capitalists as a social class are in power and in a position to exploit the workers in a sense formally but not fundamentally different from that which fitted the hereditary aristocracies of slaveowners and feudal lords of earlier economic civilizations.

3. Socialists of the nineteenth-century liberal stamp have tended to assume an ideal democracy, with a unanimity of public opinion bordering on the ideal of anarchism. This is one of the important romantic simplifications of reality and of the problem involved in the position as a whole. This view has of course tended to be replaced by the communistic theory of a proletarian dictatorship, as a transitional stage, to re-educate humanity for the ultimate classless society, the nature of which is anarchism pure and simple.

4. There is another aspect of socialism which is patent to any person of good sense (including economists) but which strangely enough is so generally overlooked that it may be mentioned. This is that in promoting socialism, its devotees are seeking political power for themselves. In view of this fact, their

contention that opposition is based on economic self-interest and is to be over-come by revolution through class war and the fact that the contention is taken seriously by others are interesting phenomena of social psychology.

5. Most notable in this connection are undoubtedly Professor Oskar Lange and Mr. A. P. Lerner. See especially Lange's two articles, "On the Economic Theory of Socialism," in the *Review of Economic Studies* 4, with a critical note by Lerner (ibid.) and reply by Lange (ibid.). The Lange articles, somewhat revised, are republished in the volume *On the Economic Theory of Socialism,* by O. Lange and F. M. Taylor (University of Minnesota Press, 1938). Mr. Lerner has given a penetrating analysis of the problem of natural monopoly under socialism in his article "Statics and Dynamics in Socialist Economics" (*Economic Journal,* June, 1937), though he fails to recognize the limited character of the problem to which his treatment is actually relevant. Several books and articles by Mr. Maurice Dobb might also be mentioned, but they are not so notable for rigorous economic analysis. But even these writers seem oblivious of the main problems. They treat management as mere administrative routine, ignoring innovations and substantive changes, where the real problem of con-trol lies. And they also ignore the fact that any important change in economic life must be based on transformation of its given conditions, which means a revolution in social institutions, beginning with the family.

6. The more general principles of economic theory would be valid under any conditions possible on earth, regardless of the form of society as a whole and of the social philosophy accepted in it. They would be valid in a Pharaonic dictatorship, a society in which all people, outside the personnel of the ultimate governing class, would be the property as well as the subjects of the latter, i.e., would be slaves in the ultimate sense of beasts of burden, and where conse-quently the only ends or values considered at all would be those of the ruler, regardless of what possible character or content these ends might have. (Much of the body of theory is also valid for a Crusoe economy or a society made up of individuals or families purely self-sufficient in their economic life, i.e., with no economic organization whatever.) In any possible human life, limited re-sources must be utilized to realize a plurality of ends and must be apportioned among different modes of use. Hence there is always a problem of so appor-tioning means as to realize to the maximum extent, with the means available, the abstract end or common denominator of all concrete ends recognized and pursued. Moreover, a large part of the resources in any possible society must necessarily be employed in meeting the economic needs of individuals and must be apportioned among the various needs. Thus there must be some ap-portionment of resources between meeting individual needs and other pur-poses treated as social. It makes relatively little difference for the problems of abstract economic theory what the concrete ends are or who estimates their relative importance or makes the decisions through which the apportionment and use of means is carried out. That is, the general character of economic theory is not dependent on social forms or institutions or on any historical accidents. This fact reinforces the observation already repeatedly made that

economic theory as such has nothing to do, one way or the other, with the problem of choice by a society as a whole, either of the ends to be realized or of the general principles of the organization of the use of means in realizing them. More concrete problems of economics do, indeed, call for solution in terms of theoretical principles of less general applicability relative to more specifically defined conditions. Economic theory is a generalized description, first, of economic behavior, which means the principles of economically correct apportionment of limited means used to realize ends and used in accord with some given body of technological knowledge. And, second, it states certain principles of economic organization, in a social sense, of the use of means. It is not a description of actual behavior or organization and has nothing to say as to how far either is economic, or would conform to economic principles, under any hypothetical set of social conditions. Its main content has nothing to do with the actual machinery of organization or with the character of either the ends recognized or the means or the technology employed in any particular situation.

7. Thus the socialism which we are considering is distinguished, more or less sharply and completely, from totalitarianism (secular or theocratic-ecclesiastical), in which the individual is treated as a means to social ends, on the general analogy of the position of the cell in the human body or other biological organism. Totalitarianism might be said to be socialistic in a categorically higher sense.

8. It should be noted that this conception of ends is a theory or form of social ethics. Contrary to many common statements, no system of ends which forms the basis of any social policy is or can be mechanical or objective, or merely quantitative, in a sense which does not involve social, ethical evaluation. And society is necessarily ethical, in so far as it has any consciously accepted social policy whatever. Under capitalism or liberalism, as under socialism, realization of individual ends is conceived and treated as right.

9. In order to have the record straight and complete, it is in order for the writer to record his positive conviction to the contrary. It seems to me certain: *(a)* that the governing personnel in a socialistic state would be in a position to perpetuate themselves in power if they wished to do so; *(b)* that they would be compelled to assume permanence of tenure and freedom from the necessity of seeking frequent re-election, as a condition of administering the economic life of a modern nation, even if they did not wish to do so; and *(c)* that they would wish to do so—that we cannot reasonably imagine political power on the scale involved falling into the hands of persons of whom this would not be true.

10. The utilitarian rationalization of freedom—the theory that freedom is good because, in general, individuals will manage their own affairs better than they will be managed for them by the government—seems to be but a small part of the story even so far as it is true. The liberal social philosophy itself seems to rest not merely on recognition that men want freedom for other reasons than because it is a condition of economic efficiency, but also on the view that, within limits they ought to be free, whether they may wish to be or

not. This is clearly the meaning of the doctrine of inalienable rights, a moral-philosophical belief that it pertains to the dignity of man to lead his own life as a responsible person, even to making his own mistakes. Considered objectively, the type of society advocated by Utopians and radical reformers usually bears a striking resemblance to a model penitentiary or asylum of some sort. One must question both whether that is a mode of life which men would like (or pronounce good) and the likelihood that under the conditions of the real world the asylum would be or would continue to be a model one.

11. Some exception should be made for the use of ration cards or equivalent devices. But these have been treated as exceptional and temporary by the authorities. (The effective difference between rationing and accomplishing the same result through setting appropriate prices is important but cannot be taken up here.) It is not abstractly necessary that prices be uniform to all—say to those with large and those with small incomes. But the effects of differentiation could be much more simply achieved by taxation and subsidy.

12. On this point see Lerner and Lange, op. cit.

13. This does not imply that it should not be done. It is a question of how far efficiency is to be sacrificed to other values. It is unquestionably necessary, in any society, to bring about distribution with some regard to need, in contrast with the strict value of services rendered. Every society must have some provision for the relief of the destitute and incapacitated and of persons normally dependent upon others who fall into this class. The question whether the difference between consumption and economic earnings should be called wage or charity where it is positive, and wages or taxation where it is negative, raises serious ethical and social-psychological problems and, hence, serious political problems. Any rational formulation of policy must face this issue, and this is not usually done in socialistic or popular thinking. A socialistic state would have of necessity to keep its account and manage its business in terms of productivity, i.e., for labor, wages actually earned. If it were democratic, its accounts would almost necessarily be open to public inspection, with the consequence that the individuals taxed or given bounties of any sort, and other individuals concerned, would know of the difference between remuneration and productivity. The situation calls to mind one of the most fundamental conflicts in popular common-sense conceptions, as to whether one deserves and ought to receive what he earns or a share fixed on some other standard.

14. Socialists themselves generally assume that there will be very much more monopoly under socialism, even in particular industries, to say nothing of the fact that all production would in the nature of the case be one gigantic monopoly in the hands of the government—but of course all are assumed to be managed purely in the public interest. The idea that large-scale production is more efficient than small-scale, beyond fairly narrow limits, is another fallacy taken over into socialistic theory from popular thinking.

15. One ground which might be given for socializing the more important nonhuman means of production, while leaving the laborer his freedom or ownership of himself, is that, even if there is no theoretical difference, it is easier or

more practicable to socialize property. A very little critical reflection would show that this is not the case, when we think in terms of economic value, which is the only significant point of view. It is undoubtedly true that the government could not very well separate the labor power or any part of it from the individual in which it is embodied, while it could readily seize physical things and retain control over them. But what is relevant in both cases is the earnings, and with reference to these no such difference exists. And far more important is the fact that the development of earning capacity in an individual depends on investment in him, and the conditions determining the amount and character of this investment in any case are social facts and theoretically subject to political control.

16. *America's Capacity to Produce* (Washington, D.C.: Brookings Institution, 1934).

17. It is true that the original theory of Marxism involved an apparently more logical evasion of this difficulty. It is assumed that the socialist state would come into being through a fairly simple process of taking over a ripe economic society, one in which the problems of organization would have been worked out to an approximately final solution by the dialectical processes inherent in the evolution of capitalism itself before the revolution. The difficulties of that view are two: First, that the dialectical processes, in the two or three generations which have followed since the publication of the *Communist Manifesto,* did not work in close conformity with the Marxian prediction, to say nothing of the speed of change in comparison with the expectations of the early scientific socialists. In particular socialism came, where it came at all, not in a ripe industrial economy but in the economically backward country, Russia—following upon disastrously destructive wars, foreign and civil. And, in the second place, Marx and his followers overlooked the fact which we have emphasized, that the redistribution of income cannot be viewed as a simple matter of taking money away from some recipients and giving it to others, but itself involves a fundamental reorganization of production (in which a large fraction of the distributed would disappear and most of the famous surplus would prove illusory).

18. In fact, this seems extremely improbable. The course of recent world history indicates rather that socialism is much more likely to establish and maintain itself on the basis of some transcendental or totalitarian conception of the character and ends of social life, most likely military power and conquest, and abstract considerations of social psychology derived from history as a whole point in the same direction. These indicate that man is a religious animal and that the prospects of individualistic utilitarianism establishing itself as a religion are remote indeed. But we must follow the conceptions of socialist propagandists as to the nature of socialism if we are not to get clear off the earth into idle speculation.

19. It is true that the results of activities—i.e., the use of resources—in making innovations are less predictable than some other kinds of economic activities. But the importance of the gambling or the aleatory element in differ-

ent kinds of economic activity is a matter of degree, and no simple classification in this respect is possible. In particular, the results of exploration and development, which are the real source out of which natural resources (so miscalled) come into economic existence, are similarly unpredictable (as the activities are similar in other respects), and the investment which results in the productive capacity of human beings—rearing and education—is almost as much of a gamble. In fact, technology might very logically be treated as an attribute of human beings, and the social and individual problems connected with it, as a detail of education in the broad sense.

20. The essence of the confusion involved lies in the fact that all these forms of productive capacity, and inventions as well, theoretically result from the same elementary causes or processes, i.e., more or less rationally and more or less ethically directed investment, superposed on the processes of physical nature, human biology, and social culture—as we have already had occasion to observe.

21. Thus the contention of Professor von Mises, and other opponents of socialism, that there would be no objective rationale for the organization of production under socialism, while adequately refuted by Professor Lange (and others) for the routine operations of a stationary economy, is after all essentially correct for the really serious problem of organization. This is the problem of anticipating substantial changes in the given conditions of economic life and in making necessary adaptations and/or of bringing about such changes.

22. It will be evident that any real discussion of the problems under consideration would call for a sociological and historical analysis of the relations between the individual and society, which in turn is an almost infinitely complex system of groups—political, traditional, and voluntary. Perhaps the most important feature of all in modern liberal civilization has been the greater freedom of individuals to form voluntary groups, including the much more free and voluntary character of marriage, as against the control of tradition and authority (meaning largely control by religion).

23. The form of the state itself is a political problem, and especially of a sort to be solved by wish-thinking rather than by rational discussion. Liberal socialists, of course, believe that it is realistic to think of their state as being democratic and to advocate socialism on this assumption, especially because it is thought to mean the preservation of individual liberty. On this point the main comment which it is pertinent to offer has already been made, but we may add the suggestions that the difficulties of any real democracy are increased in large ratio with increasing size of the contemplated unit and also that even if theoretical democracy could be realized, its meaning to the individual becomes correspondingly attenuated. To the writer, both recent history and general considerations point strongly toward the conclusion that not only would the socialistic government necessarily be of the authoritarian type, but that to maintain the social-psychological unity necessary for effective functioning it would have to substitute some totalitarian ideal for individual freedom and individual liberty.

24. The most important aspect of socialism, which it has been impossible to consider at all in this overlong essay, is the problem of business depression. It is probably in this connection that the most plausible case for the centralization of the control of production can be made out. Indeed, it is quite easy to prove that in a socialistic economy, under able, wise, and benevolent government, assumed all-powerful or without serious opposition (or disharmony within its own personnel), cycles and depression and unemployment would altogether cease from troubling. The difficulty with this argument is that it can about as easily be proved that a capitalist government could also abolish these evils, without the need of any legal or constitutional powers beyond those already unquestionably possessed, even under the eighteenth-century written Constitution of the United States—if only it had sufficient wisdom, internal harmony, and support from the public in taking the necessary measures. Economic depression is a phenomenon of the mechanics of money and presents an especially interesting and significant problem—a sort of test case on governmental action—in that it does not rest upon or involve conflict of interest. Practically everyone loses by depression and would gain from its abolition. The problem is merely one of knowledge of causes and appropriate remedies and of administrative competence on the part of the political organization. The import of these facts for the discussion of socialism can hardly need underlining.

3

Anthropology and Economics

It should be said at once that this reviewer discusses this book from the standpoint of his own specialty—economic theory, including economic methodology and pedagogy.[1] Those interested in a review from the standpoint of the author's own specialty will naturally consult the appropriate anthropological mediums. It should also be said that the discussion will be frankly critical in tone. This is justified, in the writer's mind, by the importance of the book itself, as an able pioneer effort in a field which has long been crying for cultivation. That field, in general terms, is the interrelations of the different social science disciplines, and the objectives clearly in the mind of the author are more effective collaboration, and less mutual misunderstanding and criticism, between the workers in the different branches of social science. It is the reviewer's hope, by a critical examination of this work, and specifically by pointing out what seem to be errors and shortcomings, in nowise to "blame" the author but to contribute something to the promotion of the cause in the interest of which the book itself was written.

By way of introduction, we may make use of the first aid to reviewers kindly provided by the publisher, in accord with time-honored custom, on the dust jacket; and, first of all, of some parts of a statement from the anthropologist Professor Ralph Linton of Columbia University. Says Professor Linton, "This book is the first general survey of the field of primitive economics to appear since the development of adequate techniques for the study of primitive institutions." So far, there can be no

Reprinted with permission from the *Journal of Political Economy* 49 (April 1941): 247-68.

disagreement; and he might have added that it is unquestionably a book which deserves characterization as a "monumental" as well as path-breaking achievement. When Professor Linton goes on to say that "the findings of modern ethnological work" are "presented in a form which makes them intelligible to economists," one is not quite sure of his meaning or of his right to speak exactly as he does. Finally, when Professor Linton says: "It is made clear that the economic problems of 'primitive' man are essentially the same as our own and that many of them can be studied even better in 'primitive' societies, because they manifest themselves in simpler form"—a theoretical economist who has read the book with care may be tempted to remark that he simply does not know what he is talking about, and, in so far as he is speaking the mind of the author, the same observation applies to him also.

On the other hand, Professor Herskovits himself places in the fore-ground of emphasis "the *differences*[2] between our economic system and the economics of primitive peoples. He analyzes production, exchange, and distribution in non-literate societies . . . searches out the nature of the property concept [and considers how] a surplus [is] produced," etc.—all, inferentially, with the emphasis on the differences (quoted from jacket flap). He explicitly says, "In short, capitalism as we have come to know it since the advent of power machinery, is foreign to primitive economies" (p. 12). And again, "Yet another distinction be-tween machine and non-machine societies lies in the development of that tradition that may be subsumed under the heading of business en-terprise, as we know it" (p. 17). But, on the other hand, again, he tells us that "except for the business cycle itself, practically every economic mechanism and institution known to us is found somewhere in the primitive world"; and also that "the distinctions to be drawn between primitive and literate economies are consequently those of degree rather than kind" (p. 448). Since to most philosophers all differences in kind are ultimately differences in degree, neither set of statements can be disputed! And it is hardly necessary to emphasize either the difficulty confronted by Professor Herskovits in making a satisfactory general statement about the similarities and differences between primitive (non-literate) economies and our own, or the similar difficulty confronted by a reviewer in making general statements by way of criticizing the book.

However, as must be said, the book as a whole makes it clear that in using the terms "capitalism" and "free enterprise," Professor Hersko-vits shows little comprehension of what they mean in an economy such as that of the United States in the era of liberalism, and to a competent analytical economist. By way of definition of "business enterprise," our author continues (p. 17): "As will be demonstrated, practically no present day human group is self-supporting, and there is good reason to believe that trade existed in quite early prehistorical times. Where the localization of natural resources decrees tribal specialization, . . ." etc.—proceeding with a discussion of intratribal commerce. And the next paragraph deals with "sparring between primitive traders for advantage," in contrast with the fixation of prices in exchange by "traditional usage," and the contrast between modern and primitive "traditions of trading" in terms of personal versus impersonal attitudes. And in connection with the earlier citation above (pp. 11–12), "business enterprise as we know it" is defined first in terms of "buying to sell at a profit" and then as "exploitation of labor" and the existence of a "labor market." Such phenomena in primitive society are characterized as "of some importance," and "not inconsiderable," and then as never attaining "a place in any measure comparable to [their] importance in our own economic order." These last phrases are quoted to show the difficulty of generalization, already mentioned, rather than in criticism of the author. In fact, neither (foreign) trade, nor buying to sell at a profit, nor sparring for advantage is a distinctive feature of "free enterprise as we know it," while the impersonal attitude (which excludes bargaining!) and a labor market are really distinctive.

The opportunity for usefulness of this review essay is that of considering what contribution to the solution of general economic problems might be derived from a study of anthropological data, presented in such a way as to bring out their relevance. It is to be admitted, and even emphasized at the outset, that there is no great clarity, to say nothing of unanimity, among economists themselves, as to the nature of the problems. Consequently, no severe criticism of Professor Herskovits is involved in saying that he did not achieve such clarity through the study of economic writings, which he obviously undertook, at some length, as preparation for writing his book. He may well even have been confused by it. He can hardly be "blamed," either, for leaning heavily upon the definition of economics given by the outstanding authority in the past generation among economists themselves, namely, Alfred Marshall, or for taking toward economics and its methodology the general position of numerous members of economics faculties—the "institutional economists" (but cf. pp. 41, 275). Marshall's is quoted as "probably the best known definition" (p. 29): "Political Economy or economics is a study of mankind in the ordinary business of life; it examines that part of the individual and social action which is most closely connected with the attainment and with the use of material requisites of well-being." The author proceeds to comment on the generality and inclusiveness of the definition and to remark that the promise of Marshall's definition is by no means realized, that his actual treatment is centered upon price phenomena and the activities of the market, and that "Marshall is concerned in everything but his definition with just those aspects of our economic system that are seldom encountered in other societies" (pp. 29–30). True enough; but the question is, in the first place, whether it is Marshall's definition or his treatment which correctly represents the modern science of economics. Herskovits assumes that it is the definition; the verdict of a critical appraisal from a standpoint of economics itself must certainly be the opposite. But the most careful study of Marshall will hardly yield any clear conception of the nature and objectives of economics as an analytical science.

When we turn to Professor Herskovits's specific criticisms, we find the statement: "That economic theorists have based their definitions and principles solely on data from one culture means that from the point of view of the comparative study of culture their 'laws' are the equivalent of a statistical average based on a single case" (p. 28). Since a comparative study of cultures was the farthest thing from Marshall's intention, this is sheer nonsense; and our author's own further discussion is a tissue of contradictions. The beginning of any rational approach to the problems must be recognition that there are universal principles of "economy"— as indeed our author recognizes in his next sentence, which contrasts "the general principle of maximizing satisfaction, which is valid" and "everywhere works in practice" with "more particular and less general propositions," the validity of which in cultures other than our own remains in question. It also goes without saying that there are such less general propositions, such as those relating to markets, enterprise, etc., which apply where they do apply; and the habit among economists of making the bulk of the content of their treatises deal with those which apply in our own culture misleads no one and hardly calls for defense.

As already suggested, the error, in so far as there is an error, on the part of an economist like Marshall is primarily in his definition, but the use of such an all-inclusive definition has no doubt helped to obscure the argument itself. A satisfactory definition should certainly indicate something of the hierarchy, as to generality, of the "principles" to be developed and the vast range of subject matter to be excluded in arriving at the actual content of the main field to be considered in detail. A definition like that of Marshall would, on the face of it, include the whole of technology and all the empirical details of "economic" activity, meaning virtually all activity, over the whole world, and over all time, as far as any data exist for such "study" and "examination." Marshall's main error is failure to conform to the title of his book itself which (in all editions from the very first—in 1890) reads *Principles of Economics*. It is too universally understood to require encumbering the title of a book on the subject by specification that a treatise with such a title deals with the principles of economics, distinctively as exemplified in "modern" culture. Undoubtedly the concept of "economy" in general usage includes technology; but in our culture no one would think of reading a book or attending a course on "economics," without a modifier, for the purpose of learning either about any technical, concrete, or descriptive aspect of our own economic life, or about the way in which the "principles" are exemplified in any other culture.

The first essential weakness of Professor Herskovits's opus is that it explicitly sets out to make anthropological data "intelligible to economists" in the absence of any clear grasp on his part of *any* of the principles in which economists are interested and with which they deal, whether the most general principles involved in "maximizing satisfaction" or the "more particular and less general propositions" applicable to organized competitive markets or to "business enterprise as we know it." Naturally, these less general principles do not apply where the phenomena to which they relate are absent; and, on the other hand, the most general principles are not different in different culture situations—exactly as the principles of mathematics are not different.

It is the last point which needs emphasis, particularly in the present connection. Economics, in the usual meaning, as a science of principles, is not, primarily, a descriptive science in the empirical sense at all. It "describes" *economic* behavior and uses the concept to explain the working of our modern economic organization and also to criticize and suggest changes. It is, of course, of some interest, in connection with the description, to point out contrasts between economic behavior and actual behavior, in our own and other culture settings, which does not conform to the principles as stated. But the interest in this contrast itself arises primarily out of the fact that the conceptual ideal of economic behavior is assumed to be, at least within limits, also a normative ideal, that men in general, and within limits, wish to behave economically, to make their activities and their organization "efficient" rather than wasteful. This fact does deserve the utmost emphasis; and an adequate definition of the science of economics, as treated in modern textbooks, might well make it explicit that the main relevance of the discussion is found in its relation to social policy, assumed to be directed toward the end indicated of increasing economic efficiency, of reducing waste. This practical objective requires that the discussion deal with principles as they operate in the setting of our own institutions. But an adequate definition of economics would require at least a long chapter in a book, if not a volume, and the task cannot be further pursued in the scope of a review article.

It is interesting to compare with Marshall's definition of economics one cited from an anthropologist and presenting the anthropological point of view. Professor Herskovits quotes (p. 39) from an especially authoritative recent volume[3] the definition of Dr. Ruth Bunzel: "The total organization of behavior with reference to the problems of physical survival." Such a conception can produce nothing but confusion, and, as further matter quoted by Herskovits shows, the author herself is immediately involved in contradiction by referring to "material needs" and especially by stating as one of three "complementary principles which are to be discerned in the functioning economics that satisfy wants" a "psychological principle" which is "concerned largely with the general question of value in the widest sense, the structure of the personality that determines choice and the attitudes that animate institutions." The confusion here is surely too obvious to call for detailed comment. Economic activity in the inclusive meaning certainly must include an activity which involves the economy of means, quite regardless of the end or purpose which is in view and motivates the action. The cost of living, even in the narrowest sense of the term "cost," always depends on the "standard" of living, which is chiefly an aesthetic category, and in a sense in which aesthetics includes all values; but discussion of these problems is not the task of economics.

The very first "crying need" of social science in general, at the present juncture in history, is clarification on the old, old question of the relations between induction and deduction. The point of this observation just here is that to no small extent this means in practice the relation between other social sciences and economic theory. For the latter is the

one social science which effectively uses inference from clear and stat-
able abstract principles, and especially intuitive knowledge, as a method.
In contrast with it, all other social sciences are empirical, including those
which use the word "economics" (or "economic") in their designation—
though it should go without saying that no science can be at once social
in any proper sense and empirical in at all the sense of the physical
sciences. This relationship between observation, induction from observations, and inference from *a priori* principles forms the very pivot of
the problem of collaboration between the social sciences, and specifically
of collaboration between economic theory and the "quasi-empirical" sciences of history, sociology, and anthropology, including institutional—
one might say anthropological—economics. An essential feature of the
situation is that all these sciences are distinguished primarily not by differences in the subject matter, in a designative sense, with which they
deal, but rather by centering upon different features or aspects of the
same phenomena. The principles of economy are known intuitively; it
is not possible to discriminate the economic character of behavior by
sense observation; and the anthropologist, sociologist, or historian seeking to discover or validate economic laws by inductive investigation has
embarked on a "wild goose chase." Economic principles cannot even be
approximately verified—as those of mathematics can be, by counting
and measuring.

One of the main obstacles to effective cooperation is the hostility to
principles, and specifically to economic principles, which is a universal
bias on the part of those who work with the more empirical aspects of
social phenomenon. This bias appears in Professor Herskovits's book in
the form (among others) of several rather scornful animadversions to
the "economic man" (pp. 33, 37, 57, etc.; and note index!). Now the
concept of the economic man is merely an analytical, essentially termi-
nological, device for referring to the economic aspect of behavior, an
aspect universal to all behavior in so far as it is purposive (or even unconsciously telic, since we can speak of plant economy). The convenience of the concept amounts to necessity, if economists and other social scientists are to avoid the sort of confusions in their thinking that
are here pointed out. Yet the scientific and logical "morals" of theoretical
economists themselves, not to speak of divergent and more or less antagonistic "schools," have been so corrupted by the bias for empiricism
in our intellectual mores that the term, which was current in the literature a century ago, has virtually disappeared from usage even in that
speciality.

The philosophical problem of the distinction of categories, or interpretive aspects of social phenomena, cannot be developed at length here.
But it may be useful to observe briefly that at least four or five quite
"fundamental" categories have to be recognized. The first is physical
mechanism, though the fact that man is first of all such a machine is no
doubt rather to be taken for granted as a substratum than explicitly
brought into the discussion of social phenomena. And the same is partly
true of the second category, the biological view of man, the distinctive
notion in which is unconscious teleology. In a critical-philosophical
sense, this category includes a considerable range, from the features
which man has in common with the lowest plant life, through the "instinctive" behavior (individual and social) of animals and the "institutional" aspects of human social life itself. But a workable classification
should probably separate at least the last, as a third evolutionary and
logical level of existence, because it is virtually distinctive of human
phenomena.

But what is finally, and almost uniquely, distinctive of human phenomena is the aspect of conscious purpose, or rationality. However,
clarification of notions, even at an elementary level, requires emphasis
upon a sharp differentiation between two main aspects of rationality
itself. At a lower level (fourth in our series) rationality means economic
rationality, which again means the deliberate, problem-solving, designed, or planned use of means to realize *given* ends. But human behavior or conduct also involves a "higher" form of rationality, namely,
deliberation about ends. This is also a virtually or quite universal aspect
of conduct, along with the economic. Purely economic behavior, in
which ends are given and only the use of means in realizing them is
"problematic," is rather an analytic abstraction, a "limiting case" hardly
exemplified in reality, though indispensable for discussion, because discussion must proceed analytically. Deliberation about ends as problematic takes many forms, but they do not call for analysis here.

Another vital consideration in connection with cooperation between
social sciences is the "human equation" in the scientists themselves. Any
social scientist should early learn to recognize the fact that "man" (in
our culture, if not universally), including himself and his fellow scientists, is a competitive, contentious, and combative animal, given to
self-aggrandizement, and inclined to make this end justify nearly any
means. We are all anxious to cooperate, provided it means having others
cooperate with us and learn from us! This human trait is copiously exemplified in most social science writing, especially that which comes in

contact with methodological problems in any way, and Professor Herskovits's chapters dealing with general problems are no exception. A conspicuous example is his quotation of economic generalizations from fellow-anthropologists (e.g., on p. 29) and from such "economists" as Karl Bücher (see references in the index—incomplete as usual), who, if he was either an anthropologist or an economist, was decidedly the former, with the evident motive of putting "economists" in the wrong. And this same "human, all too human" motive is also the natural explanation of many confused, contradictory, and absurd general statements in the author's constructive argument.

Naturally enough, the same type of argumentation, *ad hominem,* is also used against fellow-anthropologists as such. Early in the book, as would be expected, we encounter the characteristic scorn of the modern "enlightened" anthropologist for the notion of evolutionary "stages" in economic life and systems, which is extended to the distinction between "types" of economy (e.g., pp. 61, 457). The author cites, as a bad example, the use of the term "preliterate" instead of "non-literate" (p. 35). Does he really think that serious scientific error will result from implying that men were nonliterate *before* they were literate? Similarly, in a late chapter (p. 357, also p. 399), he insists upon using the notion of "degree of complexity of economic organization" instead of "evolutionary stage," and the same question applies. Of course, such notions must be used "intelligently," as in general they probably have been, though doubtless not always. But surely no serious student needs to be warned against the implication that human development has proceeded by a uniform, linear, serial sequence, with exact uniformity over the whole earth at a particular date in evolution or history. Rather, what he does need to be warned against is the disposition, already hinted at, of imputing stupidity to other writers, when at least a moderate degree of intelligence would be a more reasonable assumption. It is, however, important to emphasize that practically all "early" features of human nature and social organization persist in the modern, most highly civilized peoples. Evolution, prehistoric and historic, has for the most part taken the form now familiarly referred to as "emergent" in which new developments are superposed upon and incorporated into the older pattern, adding cumulatively to the degree of complexity and pluralism.

The list of kinds of emotional bias which corrupt scientific study and exposition, and which are exemplified in this book, cannot be left without mentioning one in particular, which is perhaps the most serious of all. The author illustrates traditionalism and unwillingness to change in our own economic organization by referring to "the vitality of the concept of *laissez-faire* in the face of changes in the mechanical phases of our economy that have deprived this point of view of all but that justification which psychologically, is the strongest of all, the appeal to traditional usage" (p. 61). As a matter of fact, this statement illustrates at the same time two fundamental forms of bias. On the one hand, it exhibits a *political* position, or attitude, not to say a prejudice; and, on the other hand, it is surely questionable to bring such evaluations into descriptive exposition without considering *(a)* the conceivable alternatives of the institution condemned, *(b)* their merits and demerits in terms of all that would be involved in any hypothetical substitution, and *(c)* the concrete possibilities and costs of change.

Another example of the corruption of scientific morals by political romanticism is found in our author's repeated statement that "planned scarcity on the scale on which it exists among ourselves is indeed unique" (p. 448, also p. 10). The merit of the political position exhibited or insinuated in these statements is not a subject for discussion in this review; the question of fact involved will call for notice later. But it is interesting to note the emotional appeal which the conception of a well-managed penitentiary or orphan asylum as a social ideal (the meaning of a planned or regulated economy) so commonly exercises upon the minds of writers about society from any point of view other than serious and competent study of the problems of social betterment through social self-transformation by political action along economic lines. The second romantic bias illustrated (if it is not a form of the same one) is perhaps even more interesting, since it is the precise antithesis of the one which the author's statement is intended to illustrate; it is the emotional disposition to *iconoclasm*. This is perhaps as common and perhaps also as serious as the prejudice in favor of conservatism, or the rationalizing adulation of the institutions and usages of a writer's own culture.

Discussion in further detail of the anthropologist's failure to understand the meaning of economic concepts must be omitted here because of limitations of space. It can only be set down as a dictum, from the point of view of the special student of economic theory, that Professor Herskovits, in constantly making use (as he must) of such general concepts as production, wealth, capital, money—and especially the treacherous notion of an economic surplus, which constantly recurs—shows a conspicuous lack of understanding of what such terms have to mean if they are to be fruitfully employed in economic discussion or if their use is to result in clarity rather than confusion. To be sure, it should again be noted, by way of extenuation, that a writer from any other field would find the greatest difficulty in getting adequate light on these matters from any sampling of the writings of economists such as he could readily make, or without intensive study of carefully selected recent literature. The notion of "labor" as a measurable magnitude (intrinsically an aspect of the general economic problem of value) should be added to the list, as an especially egregious case, from both points of view, i.e., the confusion in this book and also in a large proportion of the recognized authorities in the main tradition of economic theory itself.

It would be natural and proper to ask which, if any, of the "errors" referred to really make a serious difference for the argument as a whole, for such conclusions as may be said to follow from it, and for its general usefulness. To some extent, certainly, they are relatively "harmless," at least to economists. Their significance, as confirming belief in man-in-the-street economic prejudices in the minds of non-economic social scientists, is more important. Similar observations no doubt apply, *mutatis mutandis,* to the errors of economists in making use of references to "primitive society" in economic exposition, on which anthropologists are fond of dilating. Such discussion of this problem as is allowable here can best be given by discussing the more general question as to "what use" anthropology can be to the economist, either in his own thinking and investigation or especially in the teaching of his subject.

The first observation under this head must be to emphasize the point as to harmlessness just mentioned in the opposite relationship. One thinks immediately of Adam Smith, whose "romantic" archeology has been satirized in particular by Veblen, posing as an anthropological specialist (with what justification is not in question here; the question would raise large issues as to the relation between science and satire in Veblen's work as a whole). As to the significance of such allusions in economic exposition, the answer must be that it usually makes little or no difference whether the comparisons are anthropologically authentic or not. Indeed, we probably should not stop here; it would seem to be definitely requisite in the teaching of economics to bring out principles affecting our own institutions by means of comparisons between our own and "simpler" societies and at the same time out of the question to make the comparison refer to any particular society or social type as reported by anthropological investigation. The reform which would be in order from this pedagogical point of view would be to make it clear in all such comparisons that the situation used for contrast *is* a hypothetical one, and to describe it clearly as such, in the points actually significant for the purpose in view. In fact, all that is really called for is a "reasonable" interpretation of the literature as it stands, in line with the suggestion already made. But teachers and writers in economics might be admonished to make it explicit, perhaps by the use of some such phraseology as a "*hypothetical* primitive society," what they are doing—in so far as they consider it important to avoid contributing to the entertainment of anthropologist-critics or nourishing their "superiority complexes."

The chief requisite for better mutual understanding between economists and anthropologists is that the latter should have some grasp of the categorical difference emphasized above between economics as an exposition of principles—which have little more relation to empirical data of any sort than do those of elementary mathematics—and as a descriptive exposition of facts. From the opposite point of view, there is this important difference—that any intelligent or useful exposition of facts imperatively requires an understanding of principles, while the need for facts in connection with the exposition of principles is far more tenuous, and the "facts" which are really in question need not be facts at all in the sense of actuality for any particular point in time or space, provided they are realistically illustrative.

Beyond the admonition mentioned, it would be highly desirable on general grounds for economists to know more about the facts of economies other than their own. Even if no direct use is made of it, such knowledge would be fertile in suggestion of facts, relations, and principles in one's own economic system which might otherwise escape observation because of the well-known psychological principle that what is too familiar is very likely to be overlooked. From this point of view, again, "authentic" facts are not necessarily more useful than travelers' tales based on superficial and largely false impressions—the bane of modern anthropological science—or even outright fiction or poetry. A good economist certainly needs both the proverbial "broadening" effect of actual travel and a wide range of reading in history and all branches of literature; and knowledge of scientific anthropology will be useful in much the same way.

It is undoubtedly true that, *if* economists are going to teach anthropology, they should know something about it and not teach too much that "isn't so." But, again, the main sin of this sort calling for expiation and reformation is on the other side. The teaching of utterly false and misleading economics (and putting economists in their place) is a favorite practice in the classrooms and textbooks of the other social sciences. Moreover, until such time as a sweeping reformation shall be accomplished in the understanding and use of economic principles by historians, sociologists, and anthropologists in the presentation of their own subjects, it will be difficult to the point of impossibility for the economist to make much use of "authentic" data from these other fields. For, in the absence of such understanding—and of much more caution in making statements whose meaning depends upon it—the economist cannot trust the statements of fact and can, after all, use them only as hypothetical or imaginative and suggestive.

One important fact which the economist can really learn from even a cursory perusal of the volume before us is the virtually infinite variety in the ideas and institutions of primitive peoples which are connected in one way or another with the economic side of their lives and problems. Even a moderate dose of this material should suffice for the admonition already mentioned—that the economist should distinguish between authenticity and the hypothetical character of primitive or simpler social situations used for purposes of comparison and contrast. He should at least realize that practically any simple generalization in this field, which would be significant for his purposes, is probably indefensible as a descriptive statement in the absence of an understanding of the culture context as a whole. He would then avoid any appearance of teaching anthropology as such, unless he uses, in its entirety, some actual and full report of a particular society at a particular date by an anthropologist accepted in his own profession as reliable.

The need of the economist (as pedagogue) for simpler conditions to contrast with those of our own culture suggests the question as to what general contrasts, if any, can be made between the economic life and organization of "non-literate" peoples and our own, beyond such commonplaces as the fact that they did not have modern machinery and technology. Professor Herskovits discusses this topic of differences in his introductory chapter, entitled "Before the Machine" (already referred to). Perhaps the most important specific question has to do with stability versus change and progress and with the closely related contrast between the individual liberty in economic matters which is a characteristic of modern Western civilization and the commonly reported and accepted prevalence of a fairly rigid control by *custom* in "early" economic life. On this point, Professor Herskovits has a good deal to say, but it is difficult to interpret. In his general chapter on production

(chap. 3, "Getting a Living") he makes the following categorical statement (p. 60): "As a matter of fact, the brief history of these peoples in
contact with those who could write of them, has given us quite sufficient
grounds for holding that as regards both their willingness to accept
inner change and outer borrowing they are no different from other
people." And this is the view which is chiefly emphasized whenever the
question comes up explicitly—notably in chapter 10, "Consumption
and Capital Formation," and chapter 11, "The Nature of Primitive
Property." (This last and the three following chapters, dealing with
various forms of property, are the most informative and illuminating of
any in the book for the student of economics and particularly of "institutional" economics.) The emphasis is on the fact that in different societies, including our own, "taboos" differ chiefly in being effective in
connection with different activities or aspects of social life.

But the general argument is largely contradicted by specific data;
and, in particular, it is rendered dubious by statements regarding taboos
in our own society which clearly cannot be taken at their face value,
which at best might be defended as literary exaggeration for the sake of
emphasis. For example, in the paragraph following the citation just
given (in connection with the reference to the institution of *laissez-faire,*
already cited in another connection), the statement that our culture is
receptive to technological innovations but not to those of an organizational sort can only be characterized as false to the facts and based on
political prejudice. It is enough to mention the proliferation of corporate
and other forms of business enterprise, revolutionary reorganization of
market institutions, etc. And at the level of social-political action there
has been a corresponding growth of public enterprise, while the volume
of regulatory legislation and case law is such that, as legal authorities tell
us, it would tax the utmost capacity of any human being to read it all.
The outstanding fact of the history of the past two generations is not the
dominance of taboos against change but, on the contrary, the growth of
a general and uncritical clamor for revolutionary change in our fundamental economic institutions and organization as a whole. This situation goes back to and overlaps in time the preceding revolutionary period in which the doctrine and system of economic freedom called
laissez-faire became established. On the issue as to primitive society, a
smatterer in the literature cannot help noting a radical change in the
tone in recent years in the direction of Professor Herskovits's position,
i.e., indicating that the degree to which primitive society is custom-
bound and in consequence problem-free was previously exaggerated.

Common-sense reasoning leads one to suspect a tendency now to swing to exaggeration in the opposite direction.

In relation to the same problems we are also brought back to the question of fact raised by Professor Herskovits's references to planned scarcity as a unique feature of our own economic civilization. As to conditions in the United States specifically (and other countries are different only in detail and in degree), it is a commonplace among competent economic analysts that the great bulk of the planned scarcity which is real is either the direct and intended effect of governmental policy (the "New Deal") or is a consequence which any such economist would have predicted of economically indefensible policies intended to alleviate the condition of depression during the past decade (hence going back of our New Deal administration). That such policies were advocated by economists of repute merely points to the sad state of economics as a science and incidentally to what is perhaps the major problem of free society; we mean the problem of any intellectual leadership being effective or getting attention which stands for ideas or policies very different from the conceptions and prejudices of the man in the street. Apparently Mr. Herskovits regards the N. R. A. and the A. A. A., and the wages-and-hours law, as exemplifying the prevalence in our society of taboo against any departure from the policy of *laissez-faire!*

The only economic meaning which planned scarcity can have in private business is monopoly. Data scattered through Professor Herskovits's book itself, as well as "common knowledge" about conditions in pre-industrial society, above the most primitive level at least, make it fairly clear that, in relation to totality of economic life, monopoly is more important in such societies than it is or has ever been in our own. This is surely true if we except monopolies created or fostered by governmental action and "natural" monopolies which have always been recognized and treated as calling for public action of some sort. The writer does not need to be reminded that this is not the view of the man in the street, or even of many "economists," and he takes it for granted that his own statement will be imputed to political prejudice by those who do not agree with it. It is not, indeed, implied that planned monopoly does not present a significant problem, actually and potentially. But unquestionably the most serious phase of this problem itself is the kind of action to which it moves the public mind in the effort to do something about it—on the basis of a wildly exaggerated opinion of the amount of monopoly power possessed and exercised by producers and a gross misconception of the nature of the real evils of monopoly and of the problems raised. The real, root problem is again found in a well-recognized trait of human nature, the urge to explain any supposed evil by finding an "enemy" and to deal with it by "liquidating" somebody.

The problem of change versus stability presents a major issue of policy on which the study of primitive society might conceivably throw some light. This is the question of the gains and losses involved in individual economic liberty, in comparison with a greater stability which, in theory at least, might be had through a greater emphasis on the folk wisdom presumptively embodied in the traditions of the past, enforced by authority. Perhaps we ought educationally and in our laws to emphasize the sanctity of tradition as such—including the authority of functionaries whose authority rests upon tradition or upon religious grounds. Obviously, this is a political rather than a distinctively economic problem, and beyond that is one of social psychology and the mechanics of institutional permanence and change. The present writer has no opinion to put forward here in this field; he merely suggests the possibility of drawing some "inductions" from the widest possible view of the experience of the race as to the nature of man and institutions (or the absence of any such "nature") for ascertaining the given conditions of the problem of change, including the prevention of undesirable changes.

As a last observation, we return again in a sense to the meaning of the "economic category" as an element in individual and social life and specifically to the fact that it is an element or aspect of varying meaning and importance in all conscious activity whatever. Professor Herskovits repeatedly and almost constantly convicts himself of accepting another naive conception of the man in the street as to the meaning of "utilitarian" considerations. Of all the fallacious and absurd misconceptions which so largely vitiate economic and social discussion, perhaps the very worst is the notion—exemplified in extreme form in the citation from Dr. Bunzel given above (but later, as pointed out, contradicted in the same passage)—that all interpretation of utility, or usefulness, in biological or physical survival terms has any considerable significance at the human level. A discussion of human society, even if restricted to "economic" life in the narrowest meaningful interpretation, must unquestionably relate as much or more to what may be called the "higher values" as to "subsistence" in the sense of physical nutrition and protection from the elements. As all anthropological data themselves clearly show, such a conception of "subsistence" in connection with man is meaningless to the extent that man is human. One thing that must strike the attention of any critical reader of this book is the absence of any consideration of the economic side of the distinctively human aspects of life, such as the universal craving for beauty and for play or recreative activity.

Indeed, the general impression given is rather worse than this statement indicates. The author (following Veblen!) virtually treats all interests and activities above the purely animal level as wasteful and as expressing an immoral struggle for domination and display. He devotes a full-length chapter (chap. 18) to "Wealth, Display, and Status," and it is the main theme of another chapter (15) on "Population Size, Economic Surplus, and Social Leisure." In the latter chapter we read the following remarkable statement: "From all parts of the world, materials are thus on hand to make clear that primitive societies everywhere, producing more goods than the minimum requirement for the support of life, translate their economic surpluses into the social leisure which is only afforded some members of the community—persons of privilege supported by this excess wealth" (pp. 369–70). And the same thought pervades two further chapters—chapter 16 on "Cost of Government," and chapter 17 on "The Service of the Supernatural."

To be sure, a writer of intelligence could hardly be so blinded by a theoretical prepossession as to be quite so consistently wrong as we have indicated. Near the end of chapter 15, we do find the following: "Nor is it intended to suggest that members of the leisure class [two groups, those who govern and those who command techniques for placating and manipulating the supernatural forces of the universe] occupy their time purposelessly, or that they are not often hard-driven by the cares and preoccupations of their obligations toward the groups from which they derive their support" (pp. 371–72). But surely the statement is primarily interesting for the ambiguity of its implications! Incidentally, what is meant by population size in chapter 15 is the size of the social or political unit; this is rather incidentally treated in two paragraphs, and there is no consideration anywhere of population density or of the relation between population and resources, hence none of the vital question as to how population comes to be limited so that there is an "economic surplus." We are certainly justified in saying that politics and religion, as well as art and recreation are practically viewed in Veblenian terms, as non-utilitarian and "invidious" activities.

As to the aesthetic side of life, we have noticed the word "art" just once in the book. This is in the concluding chapter (p. 465), where social organization, religion, and art are contrasted with economics as aspects of primitive life about which our knowledge is already relatively satisfactory. (Neither this word, nor any close synonym appears in the index.) As to recreation, there are two references to sport (pp. 389, 483), in both cases as a leisure-class activity in Polynesia.

In conclusion, it is in order to repeat and re-emphasize the statement that this review has been written with the exclusive aim of making some constructive contribution to the problem of collaboration between social science disciplines in a particular case—economics and anthropology— where the opportunity and perhaps the need for collaboration is especially obvious. If apologies are in order for making the discussion excessively critical in a negative sense, they are offered unstintingly. But however unconventional, and quite possibly wrong, the view may be, the writer does not consider the main usefulness of a book review to consist in the dispensing of praise and blame. Our strictures, in so far as they are such, would apply as well to a similar discussion as it would be written from the point of view of any social science other than economics (and in part including economics, *mutatis mutandis*). Indeed, much more damage is actually done in the way of lending scientific and scholarly sanction to economic fallacies and popular prejudices by sociologists, and especially by historians, than is done or threatened from the direction of anthropology. Professor Herskovits himself has not been sparing of criticism; but, while his language often borders on the scornful tone, it is all in good temper, read in the total context.

As already stated, the book is a pioneer effort in its field, and as such has the merits and the shortcomings to be expected in a "path-breaking" work. Moreover, a perusal of it will prove of great value to economists in many ways. As also suggested, the damage it is likely to do, if any, is rather to readers from the other social sciences, notably anthropology itself; but the danger is probably not very great of making the situation worse than it was before. Moreover, let us also repeat that the errors which we think we have found, and which we have endeavored to point out, solely in the hope that doing so in the clearest terms may contribute to their correction or mitigation in later work (we may hope especially in a later re-working of the material by the same author) are not at all original with Professor Herskovits or peculiar to him. And we have also tried to emphasize that, if they are to be blamed upon anyone, it should be, above all, on economists as a group. As is well known, this profession is largely a shambles in consequence of the activities of men of the cloth who clamor for the substitution of history, or sociology, or anthropology—or "most anything"—for economics. The tragic failure of social scientists in all branches to see that the disciplines and "approaches" are complementary and that the problem is more effective cooperation, not mutual destruction, is merely an aspect of the naive positivism consequent upon the triumphal march of physical science in the modern age.

Thus the errors and prejudices of this book are an integral part of the prevalent mores of social discussion, which social scientists have made little headway in overcoming. It is a sobering commentary that they have largely grown out of the development of "science" itself. By a false analogy the spectacular success of the natural sciences has inspired a misdirected endeavor to apply the same empirical categories in the field of social phenomena, where the relevant data and the problems are of an entirely different character. The resulting prejudice against intuitive knowledge and against deductive reasoning and the recourse to interpretation is the root of the main difficulties in the way of social science in general becoming either true or useful. There will be little hope of overcoming them until they are clearly brought to attention; and a review of Professor Herskovits's notable volume seemed to present an appropriate occasion for making an effort in that direction.

Notes

1. A review of *The Economic Life of Primitive Peoples,* by Melville J. Herskovits (New York: Alfred A. Knopf, 1940). The title above is that of chap. 2 of the book itself. This chapter has also appeared as an article in the *Journal of Social Philosophy* 5, no. 2 (January 1940).

2. Italics mine.

3. *General Anthropology,* edited and partly written by Professor Franz Boas (New York, 1938).

4

The Business Cycle, Interest, and Money:
A Methodological Approach

One of the most important criticisms of a mechanical sort[1] which is
urged against the "capitalist system" (as it is familiarly misnamed) by its
attackers centers in the phenomenon of unemployment and, specifically,
in business depression. In serious economic discussion, depression is of
course the correlate of "boom" conditions, and the real underlying phenomenon is the tendency for the control of economic life by market
competition to give rise to oscillations, or fluctuations, of a more or less
rhythmical or cyclical character. An argument frequently urged against
economic theory, in its aspect of apologetic for free enterprise (which a
functional description inevitably gives the impression of being), is that
it has overlooked or ignored the existence of cycles and depression
which the critics assert is inherent in such a system.

The question of theory, the nature and causes of economic cycles,
will be our chief concern in this paper, which will refer to the problem
of policy only briefly, in conclusion, for the purpose of clarifying the
explanatory argument. Economic theory, as expounded in the orthodox tradition, down until very recent times has been criticized validly
because it failed to recognize the business cycle as a reality, and to inquire into the causality of the cycle. However, this criticism does not, as
frequently contended, involve repudiation of the deductive-theoretical
method of attack upon economic problems if correctly used, as the
following argument will make clear. On the contrary, in the present
state of economic analysis, little argument should be required to show

Reprinted with permission from *The Review of Economics and Statistics* 23 (May 1941): 53–
67. © 1941 by the President and Fellows of Harvard College.

that purely abstract theorizing about the free market system of economic organization should long ago have led students to expect cyclical changes as a matter of course, even if the occurrence of these changes and the evils which they involve did not force them upon the attention of students.

The issues go back to methodological considerations. Economic theory, as an abstract logical system and as a functional and hence more or less apologetic account of the free market economy, has always pictured the free market economy as an "automatic" mechanism—assuming voluntary exchange, or the absence of force and fraud. Its nature is that of a machine self-regulated by a governor. A little reflection about the workings of any mechanical governor suffices to show that such a device always controls the regulated phenomenon—the speed of an engine, the temperature of a room, etc.—within some limits, between which it oscillates in a more or less regular or rhythmic cycle. This follows from the inevitable presence of "lag" in the working of the mechanism. The shape, amplitude, and periodicity of the oscillations to be expected depend on the nature and amount of the lag in the response of the mechanism. In fact, under conditions which are both quite simple and fairly common, the first response of a governor may be "perverse." The analogy of a thermostat regulating the temperature of a house by controlling the flow of fuel onto a coal fire has long since been suggested in connection with economic cycles. The immediate effect of the thermostatic call for more heat will be to cool off the fire appreciably; and conversely, the fire will burn more intensely for a time after a rise in temperature lessens the flow of fuel.

Application of such simple mechanical principles to the price system, with recognition of its obvious factual characteristics, should have led economists to recognize the inevitability of a tendency to oscillations in practically every economic adjustment or response. Consequently, they should have recognized not merely the unreality of the notion of a tendency to establish *stationary* equilibrium, but also a limitation amounting to a degree of falsity in the logical method of simultaneous equations. In the presence of a lag between cause and effect, the function-and-variable conception of cause and effect itself is valid only for long-run tendencies; it applies to the equilibrium situation only, giving no information as to the quantitative relation between the cause and the effect (the independent and the dependent variable) at any moment of time.

Variations in an economic cause can never be expected to produce

strictly simultaneous variations in its effect. The functional relation between, say, the price of a particular commodity and the quantity consumed, as depicted by a demand curve (the simplest and most reliable
case of economic causality), tells us nothing about the relation in time or
even in magnitude between *changes* in the one and the responsive
changes in the other (assuming such relation is accurately known). The
response may be delayed by an indeterminate interval, and may at a
given moment have a magnitude indeterminately divergent in either
direction from that of the new position of equilibrium.

Two special cases of economic cause and effect are particularly important. On the one hand, even when the causal relation at equilibrium
is simple and monotonic, *perpetual* oscillation of the dependent magnitude may be the natural reaction to a constant value of the independent
variable. A perfectly constant air pressure in an organ pipe sets it into
vibration. On the other hand, changes in one variable may produce
changes, which may or may not include oscillations, in another, in situations in which at equilibrium the magnitude of the second is completely independent of the magnitude of the first. This phenomenon of
"disturbance" is especially important in monetary theory, which will
presently be our main concern. A monetary change may be expected to
produce a *temporary* change in any price ratio—to be followed, after a
varying course of events, by a return to the original value.

For a simple mechanical example of the phenomenon of disturbance in the absence of any long-run causal relation, we may think of a
dam across a stream, with control works of any sort, backing up a substantial quantity of water on the upper side, and we may consider the
relation between, say, the amount of opening in a spillway and the flow
of water at the dam and in the stream below it. Any opening or closing
of sluices will produce a temporary change which may be of very great
magnitude in the level and the rate of flow of the stream below the dam,
but no permanent change. After a period of adjustment, the flow below
the dam will be the same as the flow above it, which is not affected at
all by the control exercised at the dam itself. The flow below the dam is
not a "function" of the size of opening in the obstruction, or of the
height of the latter, whether at equilibrium or at any moment during
readjustment to a change in the effective height of the dam.[2]

It should be emphasized that none of these special considerations
invalidate the concept of equilibrium, or the necessity of using the concept in causal analysis. Even in a simple mechanical situation, where the
result to be expected from a constant cause would be perpetual oscilla-

tion in the effect, as in an organ pipe or other vibrating systems, the notion of equilibrium is necessary for analysis and explanation. This is also true of a system which does not convert energy, such as a pendulum oscillating without friction in a vacuum. The attraction toward a position of equilibrium is the vital point in the theoretical explanation.[3] And in practice, the problem of action is to construct or modify the mechanism—in so far as steadiness in operation is desired—so that oscillations will be held down to whatever extent is justified by the cost involved. A thermostatic regulator or speed governor can be built so as to operate with a degree of accuracy to which no definite limit can be assigned, short of absolute perfection.

Main "Cases" of Economic Oscillation

In practically every economic adjustment or cause-and-effect relation, conditions are present which clearly involve a tendency to oscillation. Three main cases must be briefly considered.

First Case: The Demand Relation

The first and simplest case is the demand relation, the adjustment of price in a speculative market for a product, under the assumption of an approximately constant flow into the market on the supply side.[4] We may think of a commodity such as wheat. Price is assumed to be unaffected by monetary changes, to be an ideal relative price, measured in "neutral" money or any ideal *numéraire*. At any moment of time, such a product exists in some quantity held in stocks which are more or less constantly drawn down by consumption and replaced from production. The effect of, say, a reported prospective increase in demand or reduction in the supply (whether the report is true or not) is an upward movement in the price, in accord (here) with general demand theory. The next step called for by general theory is a reduction of purchases and stimulation of sales, and the establishment of equilibrium at the "correct" level. But in the first place, if there is an appreciable lag in the response of consumption to price change, the response will be "overdone" and will reverse itself, since in the meantime the rise in price will go beyond the point at which it would have stopped if the decline of consumption had simultaneously kept pace with it.

The tendency of such a change to be overdone is accentuated by another factor. A well-recognized psychological phenomenon is that an upward movement in price tends to create a belief in an upward *trend,* and the effect of this belief is to stimulate purchases and retard sales, leading to a cumulative rise in price. This effect, of course, is the opposite of the theoretical effect of the price movement. But this cumulative tendency can operate only within fairly narrow limits. The buying which is stimulated by the rise in price will be speculative buying to hold, not buying for consumption even if it is done by consumers. Its effect is to hold more "wheat" out of consumption, and so to increase the stocks speculatively carried. In a well-organized market, this situation must soon be recognized by professional speculators and will lead to a reversal in the direction of movement, which will then similarly tend to go to an extreme in the opposite direction. Thus the general result to be anticipated is more or less regular oscillation within more or less definite and fairly narrow limits.[5]

The question arises whether, even in the absence of any definite change in either supply or demand conditions, price in a speculative market could be expected to remain constant. The answer would seem to be in the negative. It is a case of *unstable equilibrium*, and any small, accidental change will upset it and start oscillations. Such phenomena are not explained in terms of what happens at the turning points. If a cone is balanced on its point, we do not inquire as to what particular "cause" makes it tip over. The situation of a market is far more complex than that of the balanced cone, due to the time dimension and the role of energy flow. A closer analogy is the flow of water through a channel. However smooth the surface over which the water flows, there will always be ripples of some amplitude, their detailed character depending on conditions which, as in the case of the cone, could not be accurately determined. In the case of a market, however, psychological factors create vastly greater complexity, sensitiveness, and uncertainty in the result.

Second Case: The Supply Relation

The second case is that of supply, the regulation of production by the price of the product, this time assuming an approximately invariable demand function. Price, as before, is assumed to mean relative price in terms of an ideal measure of exchange value. Here the natural tendency to oscillation is enormously aggravated, since the lag of productive adjustment behind a price change is typically much greater than that of consumption. The technical reasons for delay in the adjustment of production to prices need not be developed; and to simplify the analysis, we assume "constant cost" in the long run. The fact that cycles occur in particular industries and the reasons for their occurrence are well known. During some interval before an increase in price becomes reflected in an increased flow of the good into consumption, commitments in the direction of increased production may go forward without producing any effect in the way of reducing price—and reciprocally for a decline.

The situation may be illustrated by an aggravated case, a product with a very long "production period," such as apples. If at a particular time the production of apples is profitable, a period of some ten years— the time required to plant trees and bring them to the age of bearing— may elapse before an increased flow of the product into the consumption market acts to reduce the price. In the meantime, the extent to which the development of productive capacity may be overdone might go virtually beyond any assignable limit. The production of apples has been chosen for illustration because the construction period for the chief item of specialized productive equipment used—the growth period for orchards—is especially familiar and definite. But the same argument applies to any product whose production calls for specialized equipment which itself requires a considerable time for production, so that a corresponding interval is required to expand the output of the final product in response to an increase in the demand.[6] It should be emphasized, again, that the situation is likely to embody unstable equilibrium to such a degree that fluctuations in production, of a more or less rhythmical sort, are to be expected, even apart from any such change as would attract attention in the demand or the supply. Where this is the case, the productive fluctuation or cycle does not call for any concrete causal explanation beyond the fact of unstable equilibrium itself—as, similarly, we do not need a specific explanation of why an object resting on a point does not remain balanced.

These phenomena also are due to speculative conditions, to the absence or imperfection of foresight. The development of an active and well-organized market would contribute substantially to the stabilization of the industry. The existence of such a market would stimulate investigation and the dissemination of information. (If the product can be standardized, sale for future delivery is possible, even beyond the period for which storage is feasible.) Even an active market for the specialized capital goods (orchards) should contribute to stabilization if it is not too much influenced by the "sucker" mentality. But we should always keep in mind in economic reasoning that perfect foresight is theoretically as well as practically impossible, unless all the parties plan collusively in advance all details of their procedure and adhere to the agreed plan. The resulting situation would be the antithesis of individualism—the ultimate communistic-anarchistic collectivism, as impossible as a perfectly competitive system. But lack of knowledge by one individual (or unit) as to what others are doing and planning is mentioned as one form of uncertainty in economic life.

In this case also, the first effect of a primary change, such as an accidental shortage or an increase in the effective consumption demand for the product, may be perverse. This result appears in such a case as livestock, where a rise in the price may cause a withholding of animals (females) from the market for breeding purposes, and so may lead to a temporary reduction instead of an increase in the flow of the product into consumption. The "corn-hog" cycle is a familiar illustration of an oscillation which is no doubt aggravated by this factor. Similar effects might arise with a grain like wheat in a poor region where the yield was a small multiple of the seed. In this general case, also, as in the first, we should no doubt expect oscillations of appreciable magnitude even in the absence of noticeable changes in the underlying conditions.[7]

Third Case: The Theory of the "Business Cycle"

The third case is the main phenomenon mentioned at the outset, the tendency to oscillation of production and of general prices in an economy as a whole, i.e., the phenomenon of the business cycle. Discussion within the limits allowable here must be considerably oversimplified. The position to be argued is that the cause of fluctuation or oscillation in an economy (in contrast with a particular industry) is found in a combination of the two general principles already considered—the first reinforced by the second. In the argument for the economy as a whole, general product prices and cost prices, in money, take the place of relative price and cost for a particular product in some ideal *numéraire*. That is, we are concerned with general prices, or the price level, which is another way of referring to the "value of money." The basic phenomenon of the cycle is, then, speculation in money, combined with lags in the actual output of final products behind planned changes or commitments in production. This third case, however, is further complicated not merely by the heterogeneity in the "commodity" and the conditions of production, but especially by the behavior of money costs of production in relation to product prices, as a consequence of induced changes in stocks and flows of money.

Cycle analysis properly begins with the fact that the general price level, the reciprocal of the value or purchasing power of money, is subject to the same psychological tendency already pointed out in connection with the price of a particular product such as wheat. An incipient tendency of prices (of products in general) to rise creates the impression of an upward trend (a downward trend in the value of money). The root of the phenomenon in this case is the fact that money, while not literally consumed, is in part effectively "used"—i.e., employed in a real, technical, or quasi-technical role in organized production and distribution—and in part it is held "idle." The motive for holding money idle, or especially the main variable motive, is speculation for a rise in its future value. The fact that men commonly do not think of the activity in these terms operates as an aggravating condition. Since cash holdings yield no return in any other form, any cash held longer than necessary to bridge over the regular non-coincidence of receipts and disbursements must be expected to increase in value (relative to other wealth) at a rate equal to the yield of any property to be had in exchange for the money, at existing prices—with allowance for the uncertainty in both alternatives.

The economic process in a pecuniary economy involves the holding or owning, by somebody, of wealth—all the wealth of the economy— and also the entire stock of money. Hence every property owner has the alternative either of holding money up to the amount of his fortune or of choosing the concrete kind of wealth other than money that he will hold. The existence of claims against wealth, bearing "interest," specified as a periodic amount of money, and (usually) promising redemption at a specified money value at a specified future date, is a further complication which will be dealt with later. Any belief that the value of money will rise in the future, relative to real wealth, tends to lead men to hold money (or such "bonds") instead of real wealth, the natural effect of which is a fall in the money value of wealth (and a rise in the value of bonds), which tends to confirm the belief and aggravate the tendency, and so on cumulatively. (And conversely, of course, for the opposite movement if it is once started.)

For reasons which are fairly obvious, the tendency to accumulation of idle money held speculatively, thus lowering the price of wealth (and raising the price of "bonds"), does not reverse itself before the movement gets far from the equilibrium position, as does the similar movement in the case of a particular product. On the one hand, the "real" demand for money, for use in effecting transactions, is not of a comparably definite character. This real demand depends on two factors, the price level and the volume of trade, and both factors are largely

dependent upon changes in the demand for money for speculative holding. Thus the concept of an equilibrium value of money is extremely
vague at best. But it is none the less necessary for analysis, and none the
less real: and the knowledge of its reality as a center of oscillatory tendencies is an essential factor in the situation at any point in the cycle. To
this vagueness must be added the absence of any basis for accurate knowledge, or any general consensus in the minds of wealth owners as to what
the "true" value of money, the "natural" price level, is in any momentary
situation, even in so far as such magnitudes exist and or are believed to
exist. This aspect of things is further aggravated by the peculiar psychology of money already mentioned, the tendency of men generally to
think of it as "absolute" in value and to believe that other values are
changing, instead of realizing that they are speculating in money when
they are actually doing so. (The exigencies of accounting probably have
much to do with this attitude.) In short, in the case of money, the speculative demand predominates over the real demand, while in the case of
a commodity the opposite relation holds. Thus the tendency for increase
or decrease in speculative holding of money (i.e., disposition to hold
which reflects itself in general prices, the quantity of money being constant) to feed upon itself cumulatively is subject to no such effective check
as results from the accumulation of a consumable commodity with a
fairly definite demand curve, which is fairly well known, as is the stock
held speculatively. Indeed, in the case of money, just what does set a
boundary to a movement of general prices in either direction, and especially the downward movement, becomes something of a mystery.

The general condition of instability is further accentuated by the
role played in economic society by the banks, which function as central
depositories or storehouses for idle money, or lending power. Two facts
are important. The first is that in real life the banks are the primary
agencies through which "money," including circulating deposits, is "created" or put into and withdrawn from active circulation. The second is
that these changes are effected mainly through the making and cancel-
lation of loans for production purposes, i.e., for investment in productive
equipment (or for holding such assets, including all inventories). For
reasons which are familiar, the consequences of short-period lending are
peculiarly serious.

This discussion brings us to consideration of the role of the second
of our two primary tendencies to oscillation, namely oscillation in production, which has already been noticed in connection with a particular
industry but is now to be considered for production as a whole. Even in

the simpler case, the relation between the demand price for a product and its output was noted to be one of unstable equilibrium, so that cyclical fluctuations in production will be the rule, quite apart from periodic changes (or any notable changes) in demand. The relation between changes in production plans and actual output placed on the market may, as was also noted, be inverse instead of direct for a time after a turning point in the cycle.

When we turn to production in an economy as a whole, these factors may be expected to be present and operative, but operative in a somewhat different way. Producers' decisions are, of course, based on the relations between money prices and money costs. In connection with a single product, we could assume that variations in the price would not appreciably affect the prices (rent) of *ultimate* productive capacity — labor and fluid capital — i.e., that the incentive and the resistance to expansion or contraction would be a matter of mobility, meaning conversion into and out of specialized forms.[8] In relation to production as a whole, this principle of price constancy for ultimate productive capacity cannot be assumed; or more accurately, like the mobility of "capacity" between industries, it now has meaning only with reference to the different "stages" of industry in general. These stages may be simplified into two, the creation of new productive equipment and the operation of equipment already existing in the creation of the final product for consumption. The essential fact now is that the prices of final products are more responsive to those *monetary* changes which fundamentally operate upon general prices and manifest themselves in changes in the price level.

Speaking in concrete terms, the ultimate cost of production, for industry as a whole, consists largely of wages — excluding agriculture, which plays an extremely small role, and probably on the whole an inverse or stabilizing role, in the cycle. Especially with reference to moderately short-run changes, the *variable* costs of productive enterprises, as they are actually organized and financed, consist overwhelmingly of wages.[9] Wages are notoriously sticky, especially with respect to any downward change in hourly wage-rates, which is the important fact in the unit cost or marginal cost of products.

Behavior of Money

To sketch in an explanatory way the course of events to be expected in the competitive adjustment of production to demand, we require a simplified picture, or "theory," of the behavior of money. For present purposes the following assumptions seem justifiable: *(a)* The total quantity of money (*M* in the Fisher equation) is constant, including both "cash" and the lending (deposit-creating) power in the hands of the banking system. *(b)* The transactions-velocity of circulation of money in effective use (we may call it "active *V*") is also constant. This means that changes in "total *V*" reflect transfers from idle reserves or hoards (where $V = 0$) to active use, or in the opposite direction (hoards including idle lending power of the banks). In consequence, finally, *(c)* changes in general prices *(P)* reflect changes in "active *M*." That the division between active and idle funds is not definite or determinate goes without saying, and the other assumptions are more or less unrealistic, but the whole group of assumptions seems to be a close enough approximation to the facts to function as a hypothesis for a general explanation of the cycle.

Sequence of Events in the Business Cycle

With respect to production, the course of events expected will be virtually the same in principle as in the corn-hog cycle, or the apple cycle, but will rest upon a tendency of general prices to fluctuate and will be aggravated by the concentration of this effect upon final products while cost-prices are sticky. Let us begin our discussion with a condition of depression, involving unemployment of labor and equipment, especially in the production-goods industries. Any incipient upward tendency in business conditions—or even a belief that such a tendency is in prospect—naturally tends to act cumulatively as a stimulant to operations. Re-employment will result in increased disbursements, especially to labor, which will increase the demand for consumption goods, with a further reaction upon production-goods industries, and so on cumulatively. The increased disbursements are assumed to come out of idle money, either cash (or deposits) in the hands of enterprises, or deposits newly created through loans or perhaps resulting from governmental action.

As unemployment of heavy-industry equipment is absorbed, a wave of investment in these industries will naturally follow, with a still greater increase in disbursements but, during some period of lag, without any increase in the output of consumption goods. Hence the investment tends to be "overdone" and/or to be made at "excessive" cost. This last feature is connected with the absorption of unemployed labor, and perhaps with a drawing in of "inferior" workers, but especially with a rise in wages, probably gaining upon the rise in prices of consumption goods.[10] The interval of "inflation" may continue until idle funds (including lending power) are exhausted. This situation will certainly lead to a "crisis" and the reversal of the whole process. But reversal may come about from other causes, such as the overtaking of prices by costs, a crop failure or any calamity in the business world, or mere "psychology." Too much attention has been given to this problem of the cause of the collapse. The essential fact is merely the unstable equilibrium. As already noted, we do not try to find out what particular cause upsets an object balanced upon a sharp point or knife-edge.

For reasons which are not very mysterious, the declining phase of the cycle tends to be relatively precipitous and catastrophic, in comparison with the ascending phase. And the turning point at the "bottom" is also a more obscure phenomenon than that at the peak. The essence of the matter presumably is that investment reaches an effective minimum, actually with a substantial amount of undermaintenance or disinvestment, for a time.[11]

Behavior of Interest Rates

In the argument so far we have said nothing about the course or the role of the interest rate, or rates. This topic involves two questions: first, the effects of interest rates on the course of the cycle itself, and second, conversely, the effects of the course of events in the cycle on interest rates. To the first question, as to what interest rates have to do in an effective causal sense with the course of events of the cycle, the answer undoubtedly is "very little"! To be sure, interest is an element in cost of production, and interest rates, as well as wages, show an important lag. But clearly, in view of the way in which enterprises are commonly organized and financed, the borrowing rate on money, including the rate of yield at which bonds can be sold and the bank rate, is relatively quite unimportant, in comparison either with the effects of wage changes or with the role of speculative considerations. Its effects are important "in the long run" but not for the periods for which businessmen can or do make plans *in a depression*.

It is no doubt hypothetically or theoretically true that if interest rates were to rise high enough, and soon enough, on the upswing, they might put a check to the boom before it reached a point involving the inevitability of collapse. But in fact they do not rise to any such level or at any such speed.[12] In the other direction, an effective stimulus to recovery might occur if money could be made available at rates low enough (or at negative rates "high" enough) in the time of depression. This situation, however, would probably require either enormously high negative rates for the short term or lending on long term at very low rates and without critical scrutiny of the security of the loan. Negative rates can hardly prevail naturally, because of the negligible cost of storing money, and the second possibility is also excluded for private lenders. Thus, apparently, any action operating through interest rates can only be effective for moderate fluctuations (cf. Mr. Hawtrey's earlier views) or as a detail in connection with those of major proportions.

We turn now to the second question, concerning the effect of the events of the cycle on the interest rate, which is a more interesting question for general economic theory. The first fact to be noted is another way of stating what was commented on above, i.e., that a relatively moderate decline in speculative conditions may suffice virtually to kill all demand for loans for new real investment (at rates above zero) or even for the maintenance of existing investment, beyond that which may be loosely designated as "necessary." Such a situation, reducing the effective demand for capital for real investment to zero, completely changes the ordinary meaning of the interest rate, and the causality affecting it. As already noted, capitalistic economy is "normally" progressive, in the sense that total investment is growing at a substantial rate. This point deserves the utmost emphasis. We do not know whether a free-enterprise economy is permanently possible under any other conditions. Under the assumptions of rational behavior and foresight, a stationary condition or even retrogression should not interfere with efficiency. But growth is clearly required for a high degree of effective mobility. For other reasons—of a psychological and institutional character—and in the absence of historical experience, speculation as to what would actually happen under an established expectation of stagnation or decadence becomes unrealistic. (The concept of a stationary society is none the less necessary for analytical purposes.) In any case, under "normal" conditions, with a substantial amount of net real investment going forward, the loan rate on money must approximate the expected rate of yield on such investment. Allowance must of course be made for "risk," and also, in connection with long-term loan contracts, for foreseen changes in the "value of money" and for this particular form of risk, since loan contracts usually call for payment of interest and repayment of principal in lawful money.

The contract for a loan of money is always equivalent to a sale of an interest or equity in some assets owned (or to be created or acquired and owned) by the borrower, plus a lease of this equity interest to the lender, plus, usually, a contract for the repurchase of the equity at the terminal date, for a money sum (usually) equal to the principal of the original loan. Any typical loan contract could be replaced by such a combination of contracts, effecting exactly the same result. It could also be replaced by "co-partnership" arrangements of various forms. Under ideally perfect competition and perfect foresight, all these forms of contractual arrangement would be a matter of complete indifference to all parties. In fact, under these ideal conditions there would be no occasion for "contracts" at all! Choice among the possible arrangements by the parties in question is purely a matter of the specialization of the bearing of risk or uncertainty in various forms. In fact, all contracts, or commitments over future time, are essentially of this sort; the typical contract relates especially to the uncertainties due to market imperfections.

While the rate of interest stipulated in long-term loan contracts will naturally be affected by any anticipated change in the value of money over the period of the loan (the loan being made in money), monetary phenomena have absolutely nothing to do with the theoretical nature or causality of the rate of return on real investment. A Robinson Crusoe would have to calculate this rate of return as a condition of making rationally any plan for the future. In the same way, in all essentials, the rate of return is involved in the plans and decisions of individuals or enterprises in the most complex, organized, enterprise economy using a money unit of value in any form whatever. All plans involving any commitment for the future include, or essentially are, plans for investment or disinvestment, or for both together (i.e., for the transfer of investment from one field to another). This would be true even in a Crusoe economy using no "goods" other than those which were superabundant and free. In all essentials, the training or re-training of a laborer—of a Crusoe or a worker for wages in contemporary society—is a matter of investment or the transfer of investment; and the economically rational management of such activity involves the same kind of investment-yield calculation as the production of any material instrument or the replacement of one such instrument by another—presumably in response to a change in the form of consumption demand.[13]

In a capital-using economy, with effective freedom to invest (and specifically with new investment going forward in substantial volume), it is (to repeat) self-evident that if loans of money are made, the effective rate must tend to be approximately equal to the rate of return on investment, regardless of the value unit in terms of which computations are made. In long-term contracts involving any stipulated exchange ratio, this contractual price will of course be influenced, in a mathematically simple way, by the general market anticipation of future price changes and the prevalent attitude toward any recognized risk of such changes. And if any contract calls for payments of "money" at future dates, the amounts will be affected in the same way by any expected change in the value of the money unit. The loan of money at interest is such a contract.

If loans are made for some entirely different purpose than that of constructive investment, they will be made at the same rate, if men act "sensibly," since no one need pay more or take less. The only "other purpose" which comes to mind is that of the consumption loan. A little reflection will show that only a net change in the whole volume of such loans outstanding can be counted, either as demand or as supply in the loan market, and then it must be counted on both the demand and the supply sides. The logically correct procedure in loan-market analysis is to take account of consumption loans only by allowing for any increase or decrease in the flow of capital into investment which may result from a change in the total demand for and volume of such loans. That is, if the actual net saving in any period is correctly stated, borrowing for consumption need not be explicitly mentioned at all. Where there is an effective investment market, the rate on other loans is set exclusively in the competition for real capital for real investment.

Speculation as to what the rate of interest would be in a society or world with its stock of productive capacity fixed, and with consumption loans the only ones being made, is practically pointless. Assuming an ideally perfect market, the rate would undoubtedly fluctuate "wildly" over a wide range of positive and negative values between winter and summer and over holidays, etc. This is the situation in which the interest rate would be determined (à la Fetter and one of Böhm-Bawerk's theories) by the general market comparison between present and future consumption. In the actual world, the comparison between present and future is reflected in the volume of saving—or eventually of dissaving—and not to any extent in the rate of return. The rate of return can be affected only indirectly, and very slowly at best (and under *ceteris paribus* conditions which are contrary to the facts). Also, a change in the rate of saving may produce a disturbance in the market rate of interest, followed by re-establishment of the original rate after the period of time required to adjust the speed of new capital creation to the changed flow of saving into the capital market (or eventually, to adjust the rate of obsolescence to the planned rate of dissaving).

Correctly interpreted and applied, this hypothesis of a world in which no investment is taking place is of the greatest importance for understanding the behavior of the loan rate during a depression. In a severe depression that formal situation is approximately realized, because, as already noted, only a relatively moderate decline in business prospects is required to stop the growth of investment. However, the differences between the real world in a depression and the world of our hypothesis are fully as important as the common characteristic of the two, the bare fact that net investment is absent, total investment stationary.

Under depression conditions, everyone concerned knows, or normally assumes, that the suspension of investment is not due to physical conditions (no possibility of productive investment). Nor yet is it due to any unwillingness of savers to offer a considerable supply of new capital at a real rate equal to what the investment would yield, correctly measured in value units, if economic equilibrium could be restored and freedom and flexibility reestablished, along with ordinary foresight and confidence. Finally, everyone knows that the situation is not caused by any lack of persons able and willing to function as entrepreneurs. The condition is known to be one of "accidental" disorganization of price relations and foresight of the future. Men know, in a general way at least, how such a condition came about; or at least they know that the economic system has gotten into such a state many times before and has gotten out again, in a fairly short time compared with the human lifespan. Hence they naturally assume that the state of suspension of net growth of capital and of investment demand is temporary.

There is another vital difference between the real condition during a depression and the hypothetical one of a world in which all productive agents are physically given ("original and indestructible," and without any possibility or adding to supply—like the mythical Ricardian land). This difference lies in the fact that, as a survival from the preceding relatively normal condition of affairs, a very considerable volume of long-term "gilt-edged" bonds exists—and a few such issues may also be floated during the depression itself, especially by governments.[14]

The course of events under these conditions is what would be expected from simple, general considerations. The loan rate for very short periods falls to "zero," i.e., to a figure which in any instance is a measure of the estimated risk and the cost of making a loan, without any actual interest. The rate as reflected in the price of long-term evidences of debt substantially free from risk does not, however, fall to anything like this level, for the simple reason that men do not expect the depression to last forever. This rate on long-term and highly safe loans measures the speculative anticipations in the economy as a whole as to the future course of events in the depression and especially the course of the rate of return obtainable on loans for real investment after recovery is expected to set in, reviving effective opportunity for such investment. This speculation is also, as goes without saying, affected to an important degree by speculative anticipations of a "fall in the value of money" in connection with recovery, which is a very important factor in offsetting the plethora of idle funds as a force that raises the price of bonds and reduces the long-term rate of interest.

If for some special reason, men should come to expect an indefinite duration of depression conditions, the absence of real investment opportunity, present or prospective, would become the predominant condition, and ultimately society would approach the condition mentioned above, in which saving and borrowing and lending would be purely a comparison of present and future consumption. The form taken by any accumulations made would then be a pure speculation in future values of the various forms of (non-productive) wealth, for storage, including money. In the conditions of our own real world of today, such a state of expectations is hardly so remote as to be summarily dismissed from serious consideration; but the more probable eventuality is a salting over of the investment and entrepreneur functions by government, i.e., the establishment of some kind of collectivism.

Keynesian Theory of Interest

The considerations just set forth indicate the amount of validity or weight which is to be attributed to a "monetary" theory of interest. It is possible for a monetary disturbance to bring investment to a stop for a time and for anticipated change in the value of money to be so great as largely to predominate over the real forces which "normally" determine the interest rate—i.e., the productivity of investment. The effects of such factors on the terms of contracts of known duration is easily calculable. But the primary datum in interest contracts is the expected real rate of yield on investment, even during severe depression—as long as this condition is not expected to be permanent. Monetary and other derangements act only as distorting forces. It ought to be unnecessary to expound to competent students of economics the general relations between these various factors affecting the loan rate, or particularly to point out the necessity of considering all of them and of separating them. The stipulated rate in loan contracts becomes a monetary phenomenon precisely to the extent that prospective changes in the value of the unit in which such contracts are drawn is the predominant (eventually the only) factor in the calculations of borrowers and lenders. It goes without saying that the price of bonds must equalize the attractiveness of bonds and of money for holding. As to the first part, the grammatically positive part, of the liquidity-preference theory of interest—with an important emendation—there can be no argument: "[T]he rate of interest at any time, being the reward for parting with liquidity, is a measure of the unwillingness of those who possess money to part with their liquid control over it"—in exchange for bonds. In other words, the rate of interest is the premium on present money over future money. The substance of the theory is in the negative part of the statement, the denial that other things need be considered, making the positive statement an *explanation*. By the same reasoning the price of eggs—of hens or of dodoes—would be explained by the relative preference for the commodity and for money, or "liquidity." But there is a vital difference in the application; a change in the quantity of money would in fact tend to change the price of a "good" in the same ratio; but it would *not* change the price of bonds—future money—beyond a possible temporary disturbance.[15]

In a discussion of the influence of speculation in the future value of money on the rate of interest on loans—under any possible conditions—the most essential fact is that there is no *functional relation* between the price-level and any rate of interest. Consequently, no monetary change has any direct and permanent effect on the rate. On this point such writers as Keynes and Hicks fall into the simple methodological fallacy dealt with in the early part of this paper—confusion of the power to "disturb" another value magnitude with a real functional connection of causality. Mr. Keynes bases his whole argument for the monetary theory of interest on the familiar fact that open market operations can be effective.[16] Mr. Hicks makes the error more palpable by saying explicitly that new currency injected into an economy "at first" and "in the first instance" lowers the rate of interest, or discount, but afterwards raises prices and "*therefore* tends to increase discount."[17] But in his entire subsequent argument, Mr. Hicks assumes without qualification or reservation a definite (inverse) functional relation between the quantity of money and the interest rate.

It is a depressing fact that at the present date in history there should be any occasion to point out to students that this position is mere man-in-the-street economics. The position is analytically absurd, and any respectable textbook in economics explains why. The rate of interest in its normal aspect as the rate of return on investment is the ratio between two value magnitudes, income and wealth. A change in the unit of value can affect this ratio only as it affects one of its terms *more* than it affects the other. There may (or may not) be such a differential effect for a time, after a monetary change. Of course if created currency is used exclusively to buy bonds, or even to construct new equipment, it can temporarily raise the relative price which the principal, or source, will yield. Such an occurrence is a temporary disturbance only. As a monetary change diffuses through the economy, it comes to affect all classes of prices in the same way, and at equilibrium any relative price will be the same as before the monetary change occurred—except in so far as in the meantime changes may have occurred in the factors which really control the price relation in question. For the interest rate, the controlling cause is the income-cost of producing capital goods per unit of expected income-yield. Beyond the phenomenon of disturbance, any expected change in the future value of the unit in which payments (of interest and/or of principal) are made will affect the nominal rate in long-term contracts in the same way for loans as for any contract to make any payment (in the same unit) in the future.

That a monetary theory of interest should be defended by economists of repute is especially mysterious in view of the facts, which are directly contrary to what the theory calls for. There seems to be no defensible way of defining or measuring the esteem value of money for holding ("liquidity preference") such that its magnitude is not *high* in depression (relative to anything but monetary obligations) when interest rates—by any possible definition—are *low*, and vice-versa. But as we have seen, the facts accord with common-sense. Short-term rates are low or zero in a depression because opportunity for real investment is temporarily cut off, and such loans do not require the lender to part with his money, or his command over money, for a period significant for changes in its value. The decline in the rate of long-term loans (bond values) is much less and is easily accounted for in terms of an expected recovery of opportunity for investment on the one hand and of the value of the unit in terms of real wealth on the other.

The Question of Policy

We turn now to a very brief consideration of the problem of action in connection with the business cycle. The sketch of the theory which has been given is sufficient to indicate the general character of the problem of action set by the phenomenon. Some means must be found for preventing individuals, business units, and banks, acting separately or in conjunction, from behaving in such a way as to change drastically and rapidly the amount of effective money in active use—or the velocity of circulation of the total stock of monetary medium, actual and potential. Such a change causes not merely a movement in general prices (*ceteris paribus*) but more especially differential changes in the prices of (*a*) consumption goods, (*b*) capital goods, and (*c*) productive services, especially wages, which are the entrepreneur's costs of production. In a free market these differential changes would be temporary, but even then they might be serious: and with important markets as unfree as they actually are—and prices as sticky, and labor and capital as unmobile—the results take on the proportions of a social disaster. Hence it is "necessary" to prevent speculation in money, or hoarding, i.e., important changes in the amount of money held idle. General prices and the more sensitive prices of final products and regularly marketed capital goods must be maintained at a relatively stable level, and the public must be given confidence that this action will be taken.

Such action can be accomplished only by positive monetary control. Up to a point socialistic critics have been right in regarding cycles and depressions as an inherent feature of "capitalism." Such a system must use money, and the circulation of money is not a phenomenon which naturally tends to establish and maintain an equilibrium level. Its equilibrium is vague and highly unstable. Its natural tendency is to oscillate over a fairly long period and a wide range, between limits which are rather indeterminate. Turning for illustration to the field of mechanical analogy, we may think provisionally of the difference between the behavior of a balloon in the air and any object whatever which is released in water as a surrounding medium. The balloon, lighter than the air at the ground level, will find its position of equilibrium at a height where its specific gravity is the same as that of the displaced air, and will remain at that level. But any object released in water (which is practically incompressible) will go either to the bottom or to the top. It will never remain naturally stable at any intermediate position between the two. Consequently, either a fish, or a submarine boat built by man, must constantly expend energy to keep from rising to the surface or sinking to the bottom, and cannot maintain a stable position at any point. The best that is possible is to keep correcting the tendency to move in one direction or the other, upward or downward.

This analogy is oversimplified, particularly in that the movement of the fish or boat will not ordinarily reverse itself and give rise to oscillations; but it does indicate the nature of the problem involved in monetary control. The monetary system can never be made automatic. An approximate constancy in general prices, or in the relation between product prices and wages, can in the nature of the case be achieved only by deliberate action, based on constant attention, correcting or offsetting incipient tendencies to expansion or contraction. More detailed analysis must be left to the study of monetary theory as a special branch of economic analysis. Serious problems are involved in finding a reliable indicator of the actual monetary position and its changes, in devising a prompt and effective mode of action on the monetary situation, and especially in the political and administrative field, in safely delegating the necessary authority to any human political agency for exercise on behalf of society.

With reference to the use of the cyclical tendency as an argument for collectivism, however—or any sweeping action by government outside the monetary field—two very important sets of facts should be pointed out. In the first place, with negligible exceptions, the business cycle does not work to the advantage of any significant group or interest in "capitalistic" society. On the contrary, practically everyone suffers heavily from it. incurring serious economic loss, if not privation. Hence the problem of cycle analysis does not arise out of and does not involve conflict of interest. This means that remedial action is a matter of economic understanding and of political intelligence and administrative competence in matters of an essentially technical character. The situation would hardly seem to call for solution along lines which would involve the most intense conflicts of interest and would raise the most serious political problems in that regard, while, in addition, the technical organization problems in connection with establishing and operating a collectivist economy would presumably be of infinitely greater magnitude than those involved in the control of one detail of it, the monetary system.

The second set of facts relates to the nature of the problem as it would present itself to the government of a collectivist society. If a collectivistic, or socialistic, state is to preserve any of the traditional economic liberties of individuals, it also must operate on the basis of money and market transactions, with prices of products and of productive services controlled by competition, in essentially the same manner as in the enterprise system. The fact that the government would be the chief owner of productive wealth, and the "entrepreneur" in the great bulk of economic activity, would not change things in that regard. The totalitarian communistic regime in Russia, if it ever seriously tried to get away from the pecuniary market structure as the general framework of economic organization, certainly did not succeed, but ran into disastrous consequences and soon gave up the attempt. Serious realistic contemplation of the problem of administering the economic life of a modern nation, using modern technology, surely makes it clear that effective administration would be impossible by any other method, even if the government possessed unlimited power and took no interest whatever in the liberties of citizens. In particular, the lending and borrowing of money (or credit) would have to be the chief medium of control between the government and the managers of concrete enterprises.

In short, the monetary situation in a collectivist economy would have the same character that it has in an individualistic or free-enterprise system, and in particular, the same tendency to cyclical oscillation would manifest itself and would present essentially the same problem of control. Though private individuals would not own productive wealth, productive enterprises would in effect do so and, at any rate, would have to decide when and in what volume to borrow and invest, or to disinvest and pay off loans. Both would be free to accumulate and decumulate money—unless prevented by measures designed and implemented for the purpose. It does not seem that the technical and administrative problem would be substantially simplified under collectivism, or that there is any ground for assuming that government would be much more likely to be successful in solving the problem. Certain kinds of remedial action would be carried out more easily in a collectivist state, under the conditions which would have to be present for the state to exist at all, but on examination these conditions will be found to root in arbitrary power over the activities and lives of individuals. As has been remarked before, there is no problem of unemployment in a penitentiary. In any other sense, the argument for collectivism from the standpoint of the problem of the business cycle does not seem to have much force. The general presumption is that, as already suggested, the control of all features of a national economy by a central authority would present much greater difficulty than the control of one feature.

Notes

1. Mechanical criticisms are to be distinguished from ethical. The former allege that the enterprise organization is bad because it does not work in accord

with the "theory"; the latter, that it is inherently vicious even if competition were always perfect, etc.

2. In this case the effect-magnitude would not be thrown into oscillation to any important extent, but mechanical situations in which the result would be of this character can be invented without difficulty. It is to be noted that in relation to such a situation there is no meaningful short-period equilibrium. Most of what is said in economic literature about what happens "in the short run" involves some confused reference to some phenomenon of disturbance, but further inquiry into the topic is not called for here.

3. Incidentally, it is interesting to note that economic theory has generally treated the absence of friction as the condition requisite for establishing and maintaining equilibrium. Pure mechanical theory generally has the opposite implication, that only the presence of friction will put an end to oscillations, and only a particular kind of friction (fluid viscosity) will result in a position of rest coincident with the position of theoretical equilibrium.

4. All markets are speculative and, in fact, approach the character of an ideal market more or less in proportion to the degree that they are explicitly and effectively speculative, i.e., to the degree in which there is organized speculation. Of course, direct, explicit speculation is possible only in connection with a commodity which can be stored and which regularly exists in stocks; but the reasoning will apply in a more complicated form to the prices of most services. For services which do not become embodied in products and get marketed as products are in practically every case the services of things or agents (including human beings) which can be accumulated and "produced" by services of previously existing agents.

5. The range will be fairly narrow, except in so far as the completely irrational psychology of a "boom" may become operative, in which traders bet on the behavior of other traders rather than act on estimates of the economic facts.

6. The time required for contraction, it will be noted, depends on the *durability* of the specialized equipment—within the limits beyond which the plethora of capacity may justify outright destruction. Hence the expansion and contraction phases need not be approximately equal in time length; the histogram of the cycle may be quite unsymmetrical. But there probably is in fact a general correspondence between the time required to produce specialized equipment and its service life.

7. Discussion of oscillations in the production of a single commodity seems to call for some mention of the so-called acceleration principle. But the reasoning underlying this principle, or relation, seems to the writer to be interesting chiefly for the confusion which it involves, specifically with reference to that notorious source of difficulty, the "time dimension." It is argued that if a new demand for a product equal to a certain fraction of the replacement demand is added to the latter (in an industry in equilibrium), the effective demand may be increased in a much greater ratio, in consequence of the durability of the product. For illustration, if the service life of a product is ten years, the replacement demand at equilibrium will be ten units per year for

each hundred units in service. Then satisfaction of a new demand for ten units within one year would call for production of twenty (for each hundred previously in use) instead of ten units, an increase of 100 percent instead of 10 percent.

Such reasoning rests in the first place on the selection of an arbitrary period of time. If the latter is assumed to be sufficiently short, the multiplication of demand can be raised to any ratio, while after the "year" is ended the number required for replacement goes back to the old figure for the rest of the ten-year period. The tenth "year" again, and every tenth year, would see a demand for double production. Enough has been said to show the unreality of the reasoning. That "demand" is also taken as an absolute quantity, as well as a quantity for an arbitrary period, is evident. As soon as the correct view of it as a function is substituted, the argument seems to become practically meaningless. But a change in the rate of growth of demand for a product may cause an absolute decline in the "apparent demand" for a durable means of production (new curve at a lower level), if there is a sufficient lack of foresight back of the apparent, or empirically actual, demand. The subject is important and cries for thorough and careful investigation as to both the theory and the facts.

8. In the case of labor, this means re-training or different training of the youth coming into the ranks of labor, and involves no real substantial difference in principle in comparison with other forms of capital.

9. Stickiness of the prices of intermediate products at various stages in production, or of dealers' margins, and the role of ownership, would have to be considered as important in an exhaustive analysis.

10. If there is a notable "perverse" reaction, it is because of diversion of productive capacity, specifically labor, from the consumption-goods field to that of investment, so that the flow of final products is actually reduced until the new "crop" of capital goods comes into bearing.

11. The most serious problem in the cycle is undoubtedly the occurrence of a condition of relatively stabilized depression, after recovery has proceeded to approximately the point where heavy industry is being maintained at a level which will permanently supply the existing consumption demand, but without the growth in total investment which must be regarded as a normal feature of "capitalist" economy. (And for obscure reasons a considerable growth of investment may be necessary to make a free-enterprise economy operate at a level near its capacity.) We have seen in England in the twenties and in the United States in the thirties such a relative stabilization, with a considerable amount of unemployed labor, some excess plant capacity in industry, and a great plethora of idle funds. In the writer's opinion, this may be explained by political conditions. In view of these conditions—notably the aftermath of one world war and preparation for another, and, perhaps worse, the reformist activities and especially the reformist talk of governments which have worked directly against recovery—the phenomenon is not really very mysterious.

12. The momentary "crisis" rates, for funds to meet payments for which commitments have already been made, are not really in point.

13. A logically simpler way of looking at the problem of the rate of return

on invested capital under ideal conditions—in a Crusoe economy or an organized economy, considered as a unit—is to think of the present worth of a future income stream. The decisive fact is that "sources" of future income can be produced at a cost which (apart from disorganization and blockage) consists of the sacrifice of a consumption-income stream during the interval required to make the investment, i.e., to construct the source in question. If the new source will be productive at a known and uniform income rate for a very long period, and if the construction period is very short, the calculation of the cost as a multiple of the perpetual annual yield (assumed to be known in advance) is a matter of simple arithmetical division. Under more realistic conditions, the interest rate itself is a factor both in the calculation of the cost and in the conversion of the time-limited yield-stream into a perpetual one. The problem becomes mathematically more complicated, but still not difficult, and the principles are identically the same.

14. These are referred to as "securities" by the currently popular romantic school of interest theorists (Mr. Keynes and his followers), making use of a "metonomy" convenient for their argumentative purposes.

15. The quotation is from J. M. Keynes, *The General Theory of Employment, Interest, and Money* (New York, 1936), p. 167. Beyond reasonable doubt, if the conventional monetary unit became too uncertain, but other features of a free-contract economy were maintained, and the disposition to save and invest and to make loans for this purpose also continued to prevail, men would cast about for some other value unit in which to make loan contracts.

16. Ibid., p. 197.

17. See *Econometrica,* 5(1937): p. 151. All this is quoted by Hicks from Marshall. I have italicized the word "therefore" but will not discuss here the question raised. Without more explanation than is given by Mr. Hicks, or by Marshall, the statement is fallacious; only the expectation of a future rise in prices, during the term of any loan, will operate to raise the contractual loan rate. Mr. Hicks's *Value and Capital* (Oxford University Press, 1939) does not seem to give a quotable statement of a liquidity-preference-function theory of interest. His "imperfect moneyness (p. 166)" theory involves an even more palpable fallacy, since if all wealth were "ideally" money, the price level would approach infinity, but at equilibrium the rate of interest would still be the productive yield of wealth-creating investment. But present purposes do not call for an examination of the manifold confusions of which unfortunately this book largely consists.

5

Some Notes on the Economic Interpretation of History

It has already long been recognized that one of the intellectual vices of that far-off age, the nineteenth century, was the excessive "rationalization" of human behavior and human nature. The economic interpretation of history was a phase or product of this error. The modern rationalistic world view may be said to have come in with the European Enlightenment; but it was given a special twist by the empirical-practical English mind in utilitarianism, of which the classical economics, the science of the economic man, was essentially an application, after considerable logical purification. Marry this to the German romantic rationalism, or rationalistic romanticism, of Hegel, and the Marxian interpretation of history is the natural, reasonably predictable, offspring.[1] The doctrine of our title is already well on its way to the discard and might before now have become a topic of historical interest only, if it had not got into politics. In that field, almost as in religion, a theory retains its truth, and even a degree of untouchable sanctity as long as a large number of people will abide by an agreement once made to believe in it.

A convenient approach to the issues raised by our topic is afforded by a well-known small volume of lectures by Professor G. N. Clark of Oxford University, entitled *Science and Social Welfare in the Age of Newton*. The third chapter, on "Social and Economic Aspects of Science," is explicitly a reply to an essay on "The Social and Economic Roots of Newton's Principia" by the Russian Professor B. Hessen, which is a

Reprinted with permission of the American Council of Learned Societies from *Studies in the History of Culture: The Disciplines of the Humanities* (Menasha, WI: George Banta Publishing, 1942), pp. 217–31.

polemical interpretation of the English seventeenth-century movement in terms of orthodox Marxism.[2]

Professor Clark's work is also suited to bring out other relations between history and economics, and to illustrate the type of reasoning one may expect to encounter in this field of discussion. Writing as a historian, the author on one hand rather adequately demolishes the Marxist error but on the other hand himself falls into economic fallacies of equal magnitude, in addition to missing the main point (according to this writer) of the subject he is discussing. His economic reasoning is of a kind which is characteristic of historians and of educated people generally, a fact which is at once the main practical reason for teaching economics, and the despair of those whose profession it is to do it. It would hardly be possible to imagine a "better bad example" than is afforded by a couple of sentences taken from near the end of Professor Clark's second chapter: "Again, technological improvement was most active . . . in those industries in which there was international competition . . . the export industries, which each state now tried to foster in order that its dependence on imports might be lessened, and its exporting power increased." Obviously, the fostering of export industries would *increase* a country's dependence on imports—unless the exports were given away to foreigners, which is not customary. And importation is the only intelligible motive for fostering exports, as well as its natural consequence. There are other hardly less "flagrant" sins against facts and logic, such as the observation that a labor-saving invention is a "synonym for unemployment," but we must turn to the main subject of the present essay.

In arguing against Professor Hessen's economic interpretation of the scientific movement in which Newton was the most dramatic figure, Professor Clark admits that the economic interest plays an important role in the activities of men, and hence in social change. But he argues that five other types of interest, distinct from the economic, have also to be recognized as playing roles which are of comparable importance. The first of these is the *health* interest, underlying medical science. He admits that this is "utilitarian," but distinguishes it from the category of economics. Clark's second non-economic interest, he says, is not even utilitarian, unless "everything is utilitarian"; this is the interest in the *fine arts,* particularly painting and music. The third is *war*. The fourth is the *religious* interest, to which the discussion centering around the life work of Max Weber has drawn so much attention. The fifth is the pure *intellectual* interest in science, the desire for knowledge for its own sake. The validity of the distinction between the scientific and utilitarian interests is explicitly argued in connection with mathematics and the motives and personalities of the leaders in that field; but a reasonable person must surely admit its reality in connection with any branch of inquiry.[3]

In attempting to build upon this analysis, and to get beyond it, we may start from the question which will undoubtedly be raised by any-one disposed to advocate the economic interpretation—the question whether these various interests or motives are really distinct from the economic. The thesis of this paper is that this question itself rests on a fallacy, so that no answer to it can be correct. Properly speaking, there is no distinctively economic motive, or end, or value. We may speak of an economic *interest,* but only if we are careful to understand that what we mean by it is not an interest in doing any particular thing or kind of thing, or in achieving any particular kind of end; it is merely the interest in doing "economically" anything that one does at all, i.e., in acting efficiently or effectively. These terms, "economic" and "efficient," which are closely synonymous, refer to the use of means, or resources, or "power" in any form in the pursuit of any given end, regardless of its nature. Any activity or problem is, then, "economic," or is affected by the economic interest, in so far, first, as it involves the use of resources or power, and second, in so far as the problem is actually and realistically one of "economizing" the available means or power.

No yes-or-no answer can be given to the question whether any problem is economic or not; at most it is a matter of degree, and at bottom even this form of the question embodies a misconception. Every human activity involves the use of means or power, and the degree of satisfactoriness of any activity is always in some sense a matter of success in achieving what is attempted, and hence a matter of the efficiency or effectiveness with which means are used. All human capacities, and time itself, a dimension of all activity, are, formally speaking, means or "resources." And all activity involves economizing human capacity or time, as well as more tangible means and resources which are practically always involved to a greater or less extent in any project or problem of action. This is clearly true of all the activities which are contrasted with the economic by Professor Clark. All of them involve the use of what we call material means, in the loose general sense of the word "material." This is apparent if one goes through the list: doctors, artists, soldiers, ministers of religion, and scientists have their economic problems, and so do institutions concerned with these fields of activity. Professor Clark must be aware that universities have them, and by all reports it is as true of armies, hospitals, art schools and museums, and "even" of churches.

To begin with, "one must live," as a familiar aphorism says, as a condition of pursuing any of these "higher" activities; and "living" is universally recognized as an economic problem. But this undisputed fact glosses over the deeper issues. Some of these are uncovered by asking what is included in a living, and attempting to relate that category in turn to the activities to which it is alleged to be prerequisite, such as health, art, war, religion, and the pursuit of truth—and others which, as will be noted presently, might be added to this list. The complexity of these issues may also be suggested by an aphoristic question regarding the means-and-end relations of eating: Do men eat to live or live to eat? It is obvious that they universally do both, and in a multiplicity of senses. And the same is true in every conceivable degree of curing disease, searching for truth, and of all the higher activities; they are both ends and means.

The question whether any activity is economic or not is, to repeat, the question whether, or how far, it makes sense to regard the *problem* involved as one of economizing means in realizing some end, given in advance. Living, in the large, does not seem to fit the means-end relation to any specific activity, but rather to *consist* of an indefinite aggregate of activities and interests, which are mutually means and ends to each other. In particular, it needs to be emphasized that that "living" which is prerequisite to any of the so-called higher activities cannot possibly be defined in biological terms. Human living is always a complex mixture of the higher activities themselves. Living, at the human level, means living in some way, according to some standard. This is clear if we reflect that in our own culture a relatively small fraction of what is nominally spent for "food" even by people classed as poor, really represents the cost of physiological nourishment, while a still smaller part of the cost of clothing, shelter, and other budget items ministers to animal needs, to physical life and health, or to "comfort." The human value even of "subsistence" is esthetics and social.

It is possible however, to make some headway in the analysis of the general problem of what is meant by the economic as a category, as a more or less distinct form of motivation. To begin with, there are two aspects of economic activity, or of economizing, in ordinary common-sense usage. The first aspect is "technical" or technological; there are various concrete, manipulative ways of using any means to any end, which are "effective" in various degrees. But economics, as a recognized special science or subdivision of knowledge, is not concerned with technological problems. These belong to the various branches of technology as such, including the fine arts and the crafts. Every art or craft has its technique—not merely the fine arts and the professions, engineering, etc., but also agriculture, business management, cookery, and the most menial occupations, in the home and outside of it. Economics is not concerned with these techniques. It deals with another aspect of economic activity, which—putting the matter in crude, common-sense terms to begin with—is that of employing means or resources for more important rather than less important uses or immediate ends.

Refining the conception somewhat, economics deals with the *apportionment* of resources among various modes of use. The science takes its rise from the empirical fact that (in consequence of the principle of "diminishing utility") the effective use of resources commonly involves such apportionment. Hence there is a problem of "correct" apportionment, in order to secure the "best" results, or what is called in economic jargon, "maximum satisfaction of wants." Much of the difficulty of economic theory as a science inheres in this conception of a generalized end of activity, called "want-satisfaction." It means simply the common denominator of the more specific and concrete ends of action, the perfectly abstract general end to which all concrete ends are means.[4] We do compare these prospective results as quantities, insofar as we choose "rationally," in deciding how much of our total expenditure, in money or productive capacity, is to be allocated to each. "Want-satisfaction" commits one to no theory of motive or the good; it is merely the term which has become conventionalized to refer to *that which* any individual is trying to "maximize," to get more of in preference to less, in choices between different ways of using means.

It will now be clear that it is at best a vague question of degree how far any problem of action, or the effective motivation in any human activity, is "economic." It is a matter of judgment, of one's feeling as to how far it is good sense, or is realistic, to view any type of action problem as one of economizing means. Of the five interests discussed by Professor Clark, religion and the fine arts are perhaps least realistically described as economic, in the problem they present; war and medicine would surely be "more" economic, with scientific activity somewhere between. Writing poetry surely is not primarily a matter of economizing paper, ink, and "labor," and neither is religious worship. The need is first to understand what statements about economy mean, and then to realize the vagueness and subtlety, amounting to sheer paradox, in the means-end relation. When we say, for example, that the ministry of religion, or musical composition, is not primarily an economic activity, we mean only that we do not ordinarily think of the problems involved as problems of the allocation or effective use of means. Under critical scrutiny, it is evident that we "could" do so; and sometimes and within limits we do. Thus the validity of usage or of our thought habits as a test of the nature of things becomes questionable. Worship and the creative arts certainly involve the use of means, and specifically of what are unquestionably classed as economic resources; and these can be used more or less "effectively." Moreover, economic resources certainly are apportioned between these activities and other (competing) uses, and a "margin of indifference" is determined upon. The apportionment of resources between "higher" and "lower" uses is presumably made, or people try to make it, in such a way that at the indifference margin all the different uses are "equally important." This makes the meaning of importance itself something of a paradox. But there is no escaping the logic which makes this equalization of the importance of all alternative uses of any means, "at the margin," the *meaning* of economy (in the aspect of apportionment; technical efficiency is another meaning).

Before leaving Professor Clark and his list of five interests, it must be emphasized that while undoubtedly useful for the author's purpose in making it clear—as against Hessen and naive or dogmatic economic interpreters generally—that other interests than the economic must be recognized, this list itself will not stand scrutiny as an analysis or classification of the ends, motives, or interests which must be taken into account by the historian or other student of social life. It seems doubtful whether anyone can make a clear analysis of human motives, or one which will stand much critical scrutiny. It must suffice here to point out that this list has nothing to say about such fundamental interests as play, self-expression, and self-development; of activity and achievement for their own sake; or of social interests, including emulation and personal and group likes and dislikes, as well as sociability as such—all in highly various forms.

The play interest seems to be especially important, and seriously neglected in discussion. It seems to stand at the opposite pole from the economic interest, however defined, and is indeed largely anti-economic in principle; and yet it also contains its economic element. In play as well as in "work," one is always trying to do something, to achieve some objective, and to do it effectively. And yet, as someone has remarked, the first step in organizing a football game according to the ideal of economic efficiency would be to put all men on the same side; it is wasteful and absurd to have half of them struggling with all their might in opposition to the other half. Moreover, an element of the play interest is probably universal in all voluntary activity. Reflection upon the meaning of these facts is sufficient in itself to reduce any economic interpretation of conduct as a universal principle literally to "foolishness."[5] In addition, all interests are suffused with a desire for *power,* dominion over men and over things. But power as an end, apart from any desirable result to be obtained by its use, is outside the concept of economy or economic rationality.

In sum: Economic thinking deals with the problem of using given means to realize given ends. Its scope is limited in one direction by critical reflection about ends, in contrast with the problem of getting things wanted, and in the other by the unconscious or mechanical cause-and-effect aspect of behavior. The means available to any individual (or to any group, considered as an economic subject) are at any time "really" given; but the end is not given or is given only in a partial and provisional sense. There is no final end in conduct, in any concrete and intelligible meaning. Such terms as want-satisfaction, or "happiness," or self-realization, as general ends, are little more than names for the fact that, for our thinking, activity is at any moment directed to some purpose beyond the concrete end immediately in view. All concrete ends are really means, as one realizes the moment any end is questioned; and the ultimate end is simply "the good life!" And "the good" must include many species, which resist analytical differentiation. Moreover, the means-and-end relationship is complicated by the indisputable fact that means—or more properly the procedures by which means are used, i.e., activities as such—may evidently be good or bad *per se;* they are subject to value judgments about as much as are ends themselves.

Again, even the immediate, concrete end or objective, in a particular limited problem or project, never is fully given at the beginning. It is always subject to re-definition during the process of its realization. This is true in all degrees. In the limiting case at the opposite extreme from the concept of economic behavior, the end is not given at all; the essential motive of the action is "curiosity"; it is to find out what the result will be. Such activity is *explorative.* And all activity seems to involve this motive as a factor. For example, we would never read a book or listen to a lecture if we knew in advance exactly what book we are going to read—its content—or what we should hear the speaker say, though to be moved to action we must have some idea of what is to be expected. And all creative activity above absolute drudgery is more or less explorative and creative. Worse still, reflection about play makes it clear that in a very large measure the end is really instrumental to the activity, rather than the converse. We deliberately set up an end for the purpose of making the activity interesting. This is also true in all degrees of "economic" life in the empirical sense, both in production, or "business," and in consumption. Activity in either of these fields may have as much the character of a competitive sport as that of satisfying wants, as a specific and final consequence of the use of means. Or the motivation may be that of play in games of solitaire. There is no clear distinction between work and play, and the concept of economic activity has no clear relation to either. All economic activity is affected by the creative and explorative interests, which have much in common with play, and by numerous social and individual motives which do not enter into the make-up of the hypothetical "economic man." In short, the economic interest is an aspect of conduct in general, varying widely in importance relative to other aspects. It does not pertain to any distinct field of action or class of activities.

It is a particularly serious fallacy, associated with the economic interpretation, to think of economic activity as the only field in which conflicts of interest occur, between individuals or between groups, or as the only field in which conflicts reach the proportions of a major problem. Candid reflection will rather make it seem doubtful whether the abolition of all economic problems—say by a fairy gift to every adult of the power to work physical miracles—would ameliorate social conflict, or would even change its form in any important respect. All the "higher" activities are both competitive and cooperative, including religion and pure sociability, as well as science and philosophy, and it is doubtful whether the competition and power relations in other fields, and particularly in politics, are morally better or tend less to conflict than those of the business world, or whether they are essentially different.

The application of this brief and sketchy theoretical analysis must be briefer still. The quest of the historian, as a philosopher, or as methodology-conscious, is for causes, forces, laws, uniformities of sequence, or elementary concepts in some form, which will serve to make historical writing intelligible, to "explain" the past, and in some degree, as he fondly hopes, give an inkling as to what may be expected in the future.

A classification of the possibilities in this direction should undoubtedly begin with a dichotomy. The first question is to decide as to the relative importance in historical process of motivated and unmotivated behavior, or deliberate action as against unconscious "social forces." Surely, this is a matter of degree; neither sort of causality can be excluded, or have fundamental importance denied to it. And the same will be true of numerous subheads under each of these general categories; especially on the side of motivated action, one must recognize many kinds of ends, good and bad, rational and irrational.

In teaching economics, and writing for economists, who are notoriously afflicted with a naively utilitarian, rationalistic, and individualistic bias, it is the unconscious and social element which needs emphasis. The writer's favorite procedure has been to insist upon some reflection on the part of students about language and the scientific study of language. Linguistics is recognized as perhaps the most "scientific" and intellectually satisfactory of the "*Geisteswissenschaften.*" The outstanding fact in the study of linguistics is that no one proposes to explain or interpret the evolution of language in terms of conscious or rational individual motivation. Indeed, it is something of a paradox that, although language is evidently one of the most important instrumentalities or tools of social life—and hence of all human life—and is consciously and purposively used as a tool, effort to increase the functional efficiency of language is found to play a relatively small part in linguistic change. Even the struggle for existence and selective survival among variations hardly seems to work toward the "improvement" of language.

In the respect indicated, language is only a somewhat extreme example of features in which all social-cultural phenomena share in greater or less degree. Next to language in this respect would doubtless come the law. In fact the same statements made about language would apply literally to the law through most of its history. It is only in fairly advanced civilizations that laws are "made," or changed, by "taking thought," or that they even become subject to conscious observation and criticism on the part of the mass of the people who live under them; and even here the historical school of jurisprudence denies or minimizes the effective reality of legislation.

We might go through any working list of departments or forms of social behavior and show that tradition, subject to slow, unconscious modification, is the basic element in all of them, though this is decreasingly so, in most fields, as we approach the conditions of today. Language still obstinately remains exceptional; we do indeed see efforts made to improve language or make it more "scientific," but they do not get far. In primitive society, conscious motivation seems to function almost exclusively in a conservative sense, in all fields; it acts to resist change, to enforce conformity to tradition.

It would seem that this unconscious and highly conservative form of change, called "drift" by the linguists, and custom or tradition by sociologists, is the proper meaning of the "historical," as a distinct type of causality or process, and as a category of interpretation. Thus it is largely antithetical to the category of the "economic," as understood by economic theorists, for the latter refers to behavior of a conscious, highly deliberative and "rational" type.[6] In this usage, a "historical" interpretation of history is the antithesis of the "great man" interpretation, to which the "economic" interpretation would be closely related.

But this is not the way in which the terms are commonly used; and surely the supreme need is for the removal of ambiguity in usage, and establishment of some consistent terminology. Most history, as actually written, is primarily biographical; its main problems and its method of explanation run in terms of individual motivation, though not, for the most part, of "economic" motivation, as defined by the economist. The chief motive recognized by historians is the desire for political power.[7] On the other hand, what *historians* (and Marxists, in the dialectical aspect of Marxism) mean by the *economic* interpretation is a species of what we have called the "historical" category *per se*. The economic interpretation, commonly so-called, consists in selecting a particular field of activity, and thread of change, called the economic, but defined vaguely or not at all, and making that, conceived as a drift, the "independent variable" in historical process, and treating other types of behavior and threads of change as causally dependent upon it.[8]

In the field of economics, it is important to note, we find a situation which may be regarded as either parallel, in a sense, with that found in history, or inverse, according to taste. That is, we find a succession of "historical schools" of economics, beginning especially in Germany about the middle of the nineteenth century, and with the *"Neo-Historismus"* of Weber, Sombart, et al., in Germany, and "institutional economics" in America, as current or recent phases. Thus, while historians have been running to an economic interpretation of history, many economists have been advocating an historical interpretation of economics. It would be interesting, if space limits allowed, to subject this situation to philosophical scrutiny. A combination of these two opposite views or approaches would make a good starting point for a real discussion of the general subject of social and historical interpretation.

Finally, there is space for only the briefest indication of the lines along which it would be interesting to develop a critical analysis of the economic interpretation of history as itself a phenomenon of intellectual and cultural history. We mean, of course, the theory—not really originated by Marx and Engels (who ever originated anything?!)—but which at least was forced upon the attention of scholars and of the public chiefly by their writings and the work of their followers. Marx and Engels, and the "scientific" socialists, shifted somewhat recklessly between the expressions "materialistic" and "economic" interpretation or conception *(Auffassung)*. The background is of course Marx's "flirtation" with the Hegelian dialectic, in which he more or less playfully, as he said, stood the dialectic on its head, or, in his own view, on its feet. "Dialectical materialism," is another stock designation of the position. It would be easy to show—in fact it hardly seems to need demonstration—that the three concepts—materialistic, dialectical, and economic—if clearly defined, are mutually exclusive, that they belong in different universes of discourse, with no intellectual bridge between any two of them.[9] All three undoubtedly have reality, and all three are valuable, even necessary, in the discussion of historical process, stability, and change. But in so far as a phenomenon belongs in any one of these categories, it does not belong in either of the other two. This means that a highly pluralistic conception of history is inescapable, at least until philosophy and metaphysics have made enormous progress, beyond anything either yet achieved or in sight for the future, in the way of unifying the ultimate concepts used in our thinking.

But this is by no means the end of the confusion in Marxism. For the Marxian Scientific Socialists, all three of the categories mentioned are intellectual preliminaries to their real interests—one might even say a kind of smokescreen. What they have been trying to promote is, in the first place, a "class struggle" theory of history. But it is evident, first, that in "struggle" and "class" struggle we have two more categories, irreconcilable as principles, either between themselves or with any of the prior three. And second, even these theories of history are still preliminary, a part of the propaganda for the real objective, which is the practical political one of fomenting a conscious class struggle, which did not exist or predominate before, or it would not need to be promoted.

Incidentally, critical examination would show the notion of an economic class to be so vague and shifting that it can hardly be used in any scientific discussion of *political* struggles.

The vital fact is that any single scientific or positive theory of motivation is self-stultifying, especially in connection with any sort of propaganda. For any general theoretical explanation of behavior or motive must apply to the activities of the (explainer and) propagandist himself, and any intellectually satisfactory explanation reduces his propaganda to nonsense, to selling talk, if not to mere noise. The suggestion of an economic interpretation of the economic interpretation is all that should be needed as an answer to it, if taken in a thorough-going and inclusive sense. The "victims" of the propaganda must be kept from thinking of that possibility—which in fact has an embarrassing amount of validity! For the real motive back of any political propaganda is largely the quest of power on the part of those who are carrying it on. The propagandist can usually see this clearly in connection with every propaganda except his own. To the Marxists, as to most reformers, it has been only their opponents who have been actuated by selfish or "class" interests. *They* are asking nothing for themselves—except supreme power and the perquisites thereof! From an impartial or objective historical and political point of view, perhaps the most interesting fact in connection with the Marxist theory of history is the paradox that, human nature—and specifically human political intelligence—being what it is, one of the most effective ways of securing active support for a cause is to "prove" that it will "inevitably" triumph, that in fact there is nothing that anyone can do about it. Predestinationism in religion (Islamic fatalism) is an earlier conspicuous illustration of the same psychological principle.

What seems most philosophically significant about Marxism is its bearing upon the problem of ethics. For what it primarily means in practice is the complete futility and even the unreality of any intellectual-moral discussion, especially of group policy. It teaches that economic self-interest is the exclusive principle of human action (except that of the teacher?) that all human conduct is to be understood in terms of such interests, backed up by force. It is essentially the repudiation of real discussion and of reason (except in so far as dialectical process means the will of the Absolute, really expressed in "my" will), and a direct appeal to violence in behalf of group self-interests. Since the same phenomena of class division and struggle would undoubtedly reappear within any "class," however composed, as soon as it became dominant (by "liquidating" its opponents), the doctrine finally spells the *bellum omnium contra omnes,* or complete social chaos.

In conclusion: Any unique or monistic interpretation of history is a delusion and a snare. But the "economic interpretation" particularly needs to be combated, above others, because, while it contains a large portion of truth, this is so obvious, and so much in line with the dominant trend of oversimplification in modern thought, that it naturally tends to receive too much recognition and emphasis. The "economic factor" is both assumed to have a much more definite meaning than can properly be given to it, and is also assigned a far greater role in comparison with other principles than is possible, if it is separated from other principles in any defensible way. It is the limitations in favor of other principles and the danger of oversimplification in historical analysis in general which call for emphasis.

Notes

1. It is notorious among critical students of economics that Marx and Engels got the main points in their position, and especially their most palpable economic fallacies, by copying from the Ricardian economics but paraphrasing in a somewhat more rigorous, and "consequent" or thorough-going presentation.

2. Clark, op. cit. (Oxford University Press, 1937). Hessen's paper is published in the volume *Science at the Crossroads* (Kniga [England] Ltd., London, 1932—see pp. 151–212) with other items presented by members of the Russian delegation at an international scientific congress held at London in 1931. (The fullest and best discussion in English of our subject as a whole is probably the volume of M. M. Bober, *Karl Marx's Interpretation of History* (Cambridge: Harvard University Press, 1927). See also E. R. A. Seligman, *The Economic Interpretation of History,* 2nd ed., rev. 1924; and Henri Sée, same title (trans. M. M. Knight; New York, 1929). This last, as well as Bober's work, has extensive bibliographic notes.

3. The story is often told that the great mathematician K. F. Gauss once closed a paper before a public meeting by giving vocal thanks to God that no one could possibly make any use of the theorem he had demonstrated.

Professor Clark recognizes a kinship between the scientific and esthetics interests, but still holds that they are different. He quotes Arbuthnot, a writer contemporary with Newton: "Truth is the same thing to the understanding, as music to the ear, and beauty to the eye."

4. Want-satisfaction is not really the *summum bonum* of the moral philosophers, since ethical or other critical evaluation is excluded from economic comparison, which is quantitative only. But logical definition runs in much the

same terms, and utilitarianism and pragmatism virtually reduce all ethics to economics.

5. Sociability, of course, combines with more concretely directed activities, in which the play and work interests on one hand, and cooperation and conflict interests on the other, stand out as two sets of polarities.

6. But as we have seen, the economic is by no means the extreme antithesis to tradition or historical causality. The economic view of behavior assumes that the end of action is given, as well as the means and knowledge of procedure; i.e., it abstracts from deliberation about ends, and consequently does not apply to behavior as affected by problems of evaluation—"truth, beauty, or good-ness." Thus scientific, esthetic, and moral activities, in which ends are not given but problematic, are rational in a higher sense than the economic. The latter, as already noted, is bounded in an upper direction on a scale by critical eval-uative action, on the lower side by unconscious or non-deliberative behavior.

7. It is true that in the "new" or "social" history this is less true than in the older and more exclusively political history. But it is perhaps still predomi-nately true, even in these newer writings, at least that the motives of action are conscious interests, though a broader range of such interests is taken into account.

The relation between political and economic power is an important topic, but must be passed over; it is obvious that each is in varying degrees a means to the other, with economic power growing in importance in modern times.

8. The best meaning for the expression "economic interpretation of his-tory"—if one were given the task of finding a definite, particular meaning for it—is surely to take it (as the American Marxist Calhoun has argued) as the application to human history of the Darwinian principle of selective survival on the basis of biological efficiency. This gives in effect a technological inter-pretation, which is the evident meaning of Marx and Engels in many passages, and undoubtedly has much truth in it. It also has limitations, among them its incapacity to explain decadence, which is a historical fact as real and as impor-tant as progress. The important but puzzling pretensions of Veblen to be the apostle of the Darwinian method in economics come to mind in this connec-tion, but can only be mentioned.

9. A dialectical interpretation of history is "practically" equivalent to a mechanistic view, the difference being purely a matter of metaphysical theory. The "rationality" referred to at the outset has become in Hegel "absolute" rea-son, which is so far from human reason that they are antithetical. The same paradox is found in connection with economic process; "absolutely" economic behavior is conceptually identical with mechanical sequence; without liability to error, purposiveness is unthinkable.

The Meaning of Freedom *and* The Ideal
of Freedom: Conditions for Its Realization

Our task of defining freedom is itself to be interpreted in relation to the subject of the second part of this chapter, to which this one is introductory. That is, freedom is to be defined as a social ideal, and considered from the point of view of its realization by appropriate social action. The aim of this section will be to survey the ambiguity and confusion which affect the concept of freedom in political and philosophical discourse and which consequently stand in the way of intelligent discussion of social policies aimed at progressive realization of the ideal.

It follows that we shall not be concerned with various meanings of "free" and "freedom" in general usage, where there is no fairly direct connection with our central problem. Examples are the use of the word "free" as a synonym for "gratuitous" or "costless," and as a synonym for "pure"—i.e., free from admixture or contamination, in a wide variety of connections, including morals. Even in the field of political discourse, freedom has become, in the context of modern culture, an "honorific" word (in Veblen's term), and one far more often used to arouse emotion, and to beg a question, than to communicate any objective meaning, of denotation or connotation. One need only think of "the land of the free and the home of the brave," or "When Freedom from her mountain height, Unfurled her standard to the air, . . ." and similar poetry and rhetoric in the literature of other modern nations. In this section we shall discuss the meaning only of internal political freedom, without reference to the particular situation of not being ruled by foreigners.

Reprinted with permission of The University of Chicago Press from *The Philosophy of American Democracy* (Chicago: University of Chicago Press, 1943), pp. 59–86 and 87–118.

Before taking up the problem of human and social freedom, how-ever, we must call attention to the use of the term in physical science, and also colloquially, in connection with the behavior of inert objects; for this usage sheds an important light on our special problem. The physi-cist or engineer speaks as a matter of course of "free" motion, "free" flow, etc., and of degrees of such freedom. In everyday usage, also, the situation of an object released from the hand, or of a stone or an icicle released by natural causes from its point of attachment, would be de-scribed by saying that it is "free" to fall. Moreover, if we think of a falling object encountering an obstacle on its way to the ground, it would surely be correct to say that it is not "free" to fall farther. But we should hardly use this language of an object lying upon the ground! The difference clearly has to do with the notion of a "normal" position of rest and stability. We shall come back to this notion in connection with human freedom.

In relation to human beings and their conduct, we shall have to consider freedom at the three major levels or categories of intelligible discourse: as a fact, as a desideratum, and as an ideal or a value which is in some sense objective—i.e., as valued in a higher sense than "merely" being desired by someone. This third meaning of freedom, a right in contrast with a wish, is the most important for our subject, but it seems to be relatively modern. Discussion of freedom as a fact—i.e., the meta-physical problem of freedom—is surely much older, and the notion of freedom as a desideratum, in a particular sense, is perhaps the oldest of all. Since long before history, men have known what it meant to be bound or imprisoned or enslaved, and have considered this condition undesirable in comparison with freedom as its opposite. This is the common meaning of the term, for example, in the standard version of the English Bible, especially the Old Testament. In earlier times, such unfreedom was recognized as a great misfortune and aroused sympathy, even pity, but freedom was not classed as a "right" nor was slavery re-garded as "wrong."

In the New Testament, we encounter the term in several varieties and shades of meaning within a quite different field. For example: "Ye shall know the truth and the truth shall make you free" (John 4:32); and "who shall deliver [i.e., free] me from the body of this death?" (Rom. 7:24). Such "mystical" conceptions of freedom are important for understanding the complex which men of today also crave or idealize as freedom. From the beginning of serious reflection about the issues of life, a craving for release or liberation from life as such, or from actual or possible earthly human life, became a conspicuous note in recorded utterances. It is especially characteristic of Hindu thought, both Brahmin and Buddhist, where it found expression in the Nirvana ideal. But a similar idea and craving are familiar in Greek and Roman literature, in early and later Christian mysticism, and even in modern English authors. One thinks of Shakespeare's Hamlet, in the familiar soliloquy, and in the description of the world as a goodly prison, "in which there are many confines, wards, and dungeons, of which Denmark's one o' the worst." Also the lines of Swinburne:

> From too much love of living
> From hope and care set free . . .

And Tennyson, the poet of evolution and progress, also wrote "The Lotus Eaters"; and even Browning, the romanticist and poet of action and struggle par excellence, says on one occasion,

> There remaineth a rest for the people of God
> And I have had trouble enough for one.

Other variations of what is ultimately the same theme are the fascination with magic, supernatural or unlimited power, so conspicuous in the Faust story as well as in the *Arabian Nights,* and the praise of intoxication—literal, as in *Omar,* or figurative, as in the lines from our own Walt Whitman,

> One hour to madness and joy. . . .
> O, to drink deeper of the deliria than any other man!

To all these ideals, however (but most especially to quietism), is antithetically opposed the modern view of life, and the concept of freedom which goes with it. In contrast with the religious-mystical yearning for freedom from freedom, from life itself, we moderns view life as action, adventure, and achievement, and our moral idealism centers in responsible behavior. Yet something akin to the other note is prominent in the current attitude of uncritical elevation of "security" to the position of a supreme desideratum and social ideal. We cannot here stop to treat in detail the characteristic modern view of life, with its fascinating combination of and compromise between romanticism and rationality, but it must always be remembered that in his more profoundly reflective moods modern man may also incline to regard as a higher rationality

the "escape" from rationality ("me this unchartered freedom tires"—
and "Tintern Abbey," also by Wordsworth). Moreover, some compromise between achievement and appreciation, and between action and
repose is necessary if one is to live at all, whichever extreme is philosophically embraced. It is literally impossible to be completely rational
in either of the antithetical meanings, the contemplative or the practical,
the mystical or the romantic. We cannot think entirely without acting,
even in parasitic monasticism, nor can we act entirely without thinking—or "think with our blood." It is an interesting fact that those who
have held and advocated the "escapist" ideal have had doubts about effective methods, particularly about the effectiveness of suicide (as with
Shakespeare's Hamlet) or about natural death as a solution.

Turning to our main problem, the meaning of human freedom in modern thought, it is appropriate to proceed from the simple to the complex,
hence to begin with the notion of freedom in purely individual conduct,
apart from social relations. For the purpose of analysis, it is necessary to
employ the hypothesis of a "Crusoe," a device long since recognized as
indispensable in economic theory. (We shall find later that economic
freedom is the most important aspect of our practical problem.) The
Crusoe hypothesis enables us to separate the three meanings of freedom
already mentioned: freedom as a fact, as a desideratum, and as an ideal.
    Let us suppose that our Crusoe, in wandering about his island, ac-
cidentally becomes entangled in jungle growth, or falls into an unobserved pit. Usage certainly justifies describing his situation as one of being
"unfree," and his subsequent behavior as an effort to "free" himself. But
if the situation is intensified, if Crusoe encounters a smooth perpendicular cliff upward or downward from his path, we should hardly think of
him as unfree to proceed farther in that direction, but rather as simply
"unable" to do so. The notion of individual unfreedom is clearly related
to that of the unfreedom to fall of an inert object lying, say, upon a table,
particularly in the abnormality of the situation, previously pointed out.
Yet it is very different in that it presupposes the possession by the human
being, Crusoe, of *desires* or interests, of some limited *power* to act, which
is under his volitional control, and of "will," the power or capacity of
choice. We may consider these three factors, beginning with the second,
power (or "ability"), where the main source of confusion lies, as just
suggested.
    We do not think of a Crusoe as unfree to pass an obstacle when he

knows beyond doubt that he does not control the power to do so, and consequently would not make the attempt, or even will the act. Moreover, if we modify the hypothesis by assuming that our man is completely disabled by the accident, we should again say that he has become unable rather than unfree to proceed. The problem of defining freedom is found to be that of clarifying the relationship between the desire to act and the power to act, in some desired way and against some obstacle or resistance. An ordinary person would not say that he or another is unfree to do anything which he "obviously" has not the power to do. We do not think of men as being unfree to lift mountains, or to fly (in the absence of suitable mechanical equipment), or to perform any feat calling for natural or acquired capacity or skill which they do not possess, nor do we think of a paralytic or a hopeless cripple as being unfree to engage in an athletic contest. Freedom, in its primary, common-sense meaning, refers negatively to the absence of some more or less abnormal interference with acting in some normal way in which the individual would otherwise be able, would possess the power, to act.

A philosophical difficulty at once calls for notice here, in the relation between freedom and power (for an individual in a purely physical environment). It appears self-contradictory to say that a person has power and is not free to use it. Unfreedom must be due to the presence of some obstacle which he really does not have the power to overcome. The idea clearly is that he normally would be able to act but for some special obstacle; and it seems to be further implied that the relation between the obstacle or resistance and the power is in some way problematic or uncertain. Even if the situation is abnormal, with respect either to the resistance or to the "incapacitation" of the subject, we hardly describe him as unfree, or consider it rational for him to feel unfree, if the action is unquestionably impossible. If an individual wishes to perform an act which he thinks is within his power, and attempts it and fails, while he might feel unfree, an impartial observer to whom the impossibility was patent would undoubtedly disagree.

The freedom-and-power relation in action is also clearly relative to the wish to act. It would be nonsensical to say that a person is not free to do anything which he does not have, and under no realistically imaginable conditions would have, any desire to do, and it would be irrational for the person himself to feel unfree. Real freedom is rather increased by barriers to harmful or dangerous acts, such as the practice of having fences along the edge of ravines. In short, it seems that logically speaking an individual is free to do anything he both has power to do and wishes to do, and is not free to do anything else. We shall return to this point later.

I shall pass very briefly over the venerable question of the fact of freedom in the sense of the reality of choice, the metaphysical problem of the freedom of the will. This question is certainly answered in the affirmative by the very act of raising it as a question, or that of answering it either negatively or affirmatively. Machines do not raise the question with respect to themselves, and "we" do not raise or argue it with them. To deny freedom is to deny the reality of denying and to assert that error itself, as well as all effort, is an error, an illusion, and illusion itself an illusion. Beyond this, self-contradiction cannot go. It is literally impossible to assert that one is not asserting, or that there is no difference between making a statement and making a noise. Freedom is an ultimate datum of experience and a condition prerequisite to all discourse, even to all thinking.

Certain aspects of individual freedom of choice call, however, for further brief analysis. The ultimate fact of freedom is freedom of thought, the power or capacity to control one's own mental content— or not to control it. The deepest meaning of freedom is the power of choosing between choosing and not choosing, the fact that the rational, self-conscious being "can" or is free to "set his fancy free." The meaning of the word "free" in this phrase should be noted. The free, or freed, fancy presumably follows some kind of natural or positive causality, analogous to the behavior of an inert object falling "freely" under the force of gravity. Yet the subject retains more or less continuously the power to "resume control." Again, choice, when it is made, may be either "arbitrary" or "rational," within some limits, but is always finally arbitrary. One must finally stop the deliberative process at some point and make an absolute decision on an intuitive basis. The alternative is to go on thinking forever, and "that way madness lies." Too much thinking is as bad as too little, even none at all. One must decide where to stop. Furthermore, in choosing to choose, one must select somehow, among an infinite number of questions which might be raised, subjects in connection with any one of which it would be possible to exercise control over thinking.

When one has chosen to choose, to control his thinking, he directs the activity in terms of "norms" of either an intellectual or an aesthetic character. He either solves problems or chooses between different idea patterns (and/or feeling patterns) on the basis of some kind of immediate appeal or distaste, which is of the nature of beauty and ugliness. The question whether individual choice necessarily involves objective "norms" beyond a personal preference need not be argued here. It is relatively more difficult to avoid imputing this normative quality to intellectual than to aesthetic judgments, harder to reduce truth to individual opinion than to think of preference in other matters as based on "pure" taste, without any question of "good" taste.

The second main aspect of freedom is freedom of overt action, a similar ultimate inscrutable power of choice over the translation of thinking into action, where the thinking itself involves some kind of imagined overt activity of the person. This is the psychological fact of activity or "innervation." Overt action, of course, begins with movements of the subject's "body," but an act includes any causal sequence of change in the external world which is intentionally initiated by bodily movements. It is, of course, in this field that all practical problems lie. Our problem of freedom lies in the narrower field of social action, including communication, which involves relations with other subjects; such individual choices and their consequences are to be interpreted in terms very different from those of the mechanical sequence of events in physical nature, but these must be considered first.

It may be said—it is commonly said, and seems admissible to say— that, in choosing some mode of overt action, one is ultimately choosing between patterns of future subjective experience, with some manipulation of the body and the external world as intermediary in such control. This seems to be contrary to the immediate facts of experience itself, a rationalization of the actual procedure. Rather, one chooses between courses of outside events. That is, the ultimate premise of choice in action (in a purely physical environment) is an intellectual or aesthetic interest in the external world. However, in considering the grounds of choice, we must take account of subjective factors, beginning with bodily pain and pleasure. Pain and pleasure are, in fact, inseparable from intellectual and aesthetic experience—with the exception, perhaps, of the cruder forms of pain (and, more doubtfully, a few very crude pleasures)—and this is one of the most important results of any realistic analysis of motivation. In connection with social relations, which in reality are always involved to an important degree in human choice (the Crusoe hypothesis being fundamentally unrealistic, though necessary for analysis), we encounter serious complications, and the grounds of preference consequently become vastly more difficult to describe or classify.

This analysis eliminates any valid and distinctive notion of freedom as a desideratum, for the isolated individual. Apart from social relations, freedom reduces to power to act (perhaps plus will power) in relation to desire and to the obstacle or resistance to be overcome in achieving any desired objective. Metaphysically, a solitary subject is as "free" in one situation as in another. He is always free to choose, in thought and action, between the "possible" alternatives; possibility is a matter of power, and power is what freedom as a desideratum really means. It is to be remembered that one has more or less control over one's desires, and in particular has some ability to choose desires which are more rather than less in harmony with one's power of action. It seems to be admissible to call attainable desires "rational," in comparison with those which are not attainable, as already observed. By carrying this principle far enough, and suppressing desire more or less completely, one may approach the ultimate freedom—freedom from freedom, annihilation, or mystical rapture, considered in our introductory section.

We should note that the rationality of having realizable rather than unrealizable desires is a very different matter from that of cultivating "better" desires. As a matter of fact, the consequences are rather in the opposite direction; for, in spite of the common romantic assumption to the contrary, the "higher" tastes are far more expensive than the lower. It seems reasonable to assume that a purely individualistic individual, such as we have taken our Crusoe to be, would not make critical judgments of any kind about his ends, but would deliberate and choose only in connection with the procedures for satisfying given desires. However we may think about a Crusoe, an unrealistic hypothesis at best, this is the assumption necessary for analysis—namely, that apart from social interests and influences, the individual would choose in action entirely in terms of actual preferences, of "mere" taste, in contrast with any form of "good" taste, or an interest in truth. To say the same thing in other words, all choices, as conscious and rational, would be economic choices; the isolated individual is an "economic man," or a pragmatist; all of his thinking is instrumental, about means and their use in achieving given or found ends, not about the high or low quality of ends. In the second part of this chapter we shall be much concerned with freedom in economic activity, and its relation to ethical ideals, but we need not here go into more detail with regard to its meaning.

By way of approach to the problem of the meaning of freedom in society, it will be analytically useful to consider briefly another hypothetical situation, a modification of the Crusoe idea, and quite as unrealistic. Let us suppose, briefly, that instead of a single Crusoe there have all along been two shipwrecked men on the same island, but unaware of one another's existence, and that one suddenly discovers the other's presence in some accidental way. Leaving realistic details to your imagination (the hopes and fears aroused by a footprint in the sand!), and disregarding the innumerable interesting questions raised, let us further assume, in order to minimize the factor of interindividual relationships as a first step to our real problem, that both men—we might call them Crusoe and Drusoe, or simply C. and D.—are misanthropic, or lovers of solitude, and wish to continue their previous type of life. It is impossible. Their worlds will be utterly changed.

Even in this rather fanciful situation, C. and D. will confront the condition or high probability of conflicting interests, and must make arrangements of a new kind. It will be necessary for them to arrive in some way at an agreement delimiting their domains and spheres of interest. The alternative would be conflict, to the extent of an effort at mutual extermination. In the nature of men as purposive beings, it is strictly impossible for one human being to regard another as a mere fact in his own environment, to be dealt with in the same way as any other given condition. It is impossible even for one to subdue the other, and use him strictly as an instrument for his own purposes, without some "social" relationships of a very different sort. Such a purely instrumental attitude and relationship is, in fact, impossible for one of a pair, even if the other should consent to it and "cooperate" to the utmost extent of any human capacity to do so. Apart from the fact that conflict itself is a social relationship, and one which it is reasonable to assume is especially abhorrent to an antisocial individual, no permanent relationship is even theoretically possible for two individuals living in the same "world" without some agreement, explicitly or tacitly accepted by both parties, delimiting spheres of action where interests do or may conflict. The agreement must be accepted as right—altogether or within the limits worth fighting for, a judgment in which power relations play a large role. And the judgment of rightness is arrived at by thinking which is very different in kind from the instrumental or economic thinking of the hypothetical isolated individual.

Thus at the ultimate minimum, if any two persons are to live in the same world—each being a recognized fact in the environment of the other—they must agree by rational ethical discussion on a body of "law." The alternative is that one must exterminate the other, to avoid being exterminated by him or must establish some impenetrable boundary, of distance or in some other form, so that the two no longer inhabit the same world. In other words, any two persons confronted with the problem of "living together" in any manner or degree must establish a society (or accept one in which they find themselves). And, even in our ultra-simplified hypothetical situation of two shipwrecked men, the society established will be found to involve in principle all that is essential to any human society. The essence of society is a body of rules defining a boundary between spheres of action of its members and preventing violent or destructive clash in consequence of conflicting interests. Addition of any or all details of the largest and most complicated social order—("economic") cooperation, sociability, cultural intercourse, political machinery for making and enforcing the law, or any that may be thought of—does not change the essential principle. Men who live in the same world cannot be "free" in the sense in which a Crusoe is free. They become subject to a new and categorically different type of limitation or restriction on their activities, and freedom in society must be defined in entirely different terms. The task of the remainder of this section—in fact, the main task of the section as a whole, to which all that has gone before may be regarded as introductory—is to explore this field of meaning, to indicate in outline the content of the notion of freedom in society, which in turn defines the problem of organized social action.

The essential fact about human society, in consequence of which it presents social problems to its members, individually and as a group, is that human beings have both conflicting and common interests. In the absence of common interests (at a minimum the common interest of living in proximity) they would not associate at all; and in the absence of conflicting interests association would present no problems. This, of course, assumes as a prior fact that human beings have interests, which they strive to realize through action directed by thinking. If they were automata there would, of course, be no problems of any kind. Human life contrasts in this respect with that of animals, or with hypothetical animals, whose behavior is assumed to be instinctive, which is assumed to mean that it is mechanical. Such creatures might live either individual or social lives, and we recognize an approximation to the ideal of mechanistic social life in the elaborate organization found among the colonial insects, such as the ants and termites. We assume that they have neither individual nor social interests.

The essential category, the substance, of human society is law. But it is law in a distinctive meaning of the term, in which in turn the meaning and conditions of social freedom are to be sought. All life exemplifies law, as does also the behavior of inanimate things. The "activities," or more accurately the course of events, in a termite colony, in so far as this is really based upon instinct and in so far as instinct is really mechanical, are based upon law in the same meaning as inanimate behavior. To elucidate the nature of human society and its distinctive type of law, it is necessary to return for a moment to the hypothesis of a rational individual living in isolation, and to consider the meaning of law in relation to freedom in that connection.

The great bulk of the conduct of a free human being is unquestionably in accord with law in a meaning which must be described as ultimately physical or mechanical. Without going into detailed analysis, it is a mixture of instinct and habit, both of which are automatic types of response. The freedom of the individual is "marginal," and in fact quite narrowly limited. To some extent various "situations" in which an individual finds himself raise questions which call for deliberation and choice, and to some extent he has the mysterious power to raise questions even in situations in which his established behavior patterns (instinct plus habit) "might" automatically go into action. The range of freedom of choice is partly a matter of choosing in given situations, *ad hoc,* but far more largely a matter of reflectively modifying established patterns of response, or changing his "character." This is accomplished chiefly through deliberation and "self-legislation" carried on in the "calm cool hour," rather than in situations presenting immediate problems calling for solution, where there is little time for thinking.

With reference to human social life, we have first to stress the unreality of the hypothesis used above of previously isolated individuals coming together and establishing a society, a body of law, by "contract" in the literal interpretation. It should be obvious that, even more than in the case of an isolated individual, the conduct of individuals in social relations must be based upon "established" patterns; *ad hoc* decisions are infinitely more difficult. And in the great bulk of social behavior these established patterns have become habitual, and even unconscious. Presumably, again, they involve an ultimate core of instinct, but this has certainly receded in importance as the social unit has become larger and more complex, and as the action patterns themselves have taken on more of the "artificial" character of civilization or culture. This is necessarily the case as society becomes more progressive or "dynamic."

Relatively little is known about the evolutionary development of culture, and it is not in place here to attempt to go at any length into that problem. The socially inherited habits or established ways of doing of men in civilized society are referred to in their social aspect by the distinctive names of "customs" or "institutions." Presumably their original development was partly a phenomenon of unconscious and automatic processes, through an indefinitely long initial stage, and partly a product of conflict and domination, such as seems to prevail in the herd life of gregarious animals. In any case, human society is distinguished from animal societies, of either the insect-colony or the gregarious type, first of all by the phenomenon of cultural inheritance in contrast with biologically inherited instincts; and custom remains the primary meaning of law in human society. Language is the basic law. Custom is still ultimately mechanical. But man as we know him, who is always highly "civilized" in comparison with any known animals, is characterized not merely by the fact of custom, but by a strong disposition against passive conformity, reflecting individual and conflicting interests; and human society is characterized by deliberate, organized control.

Law in its distinctive meaning in human society has gradually approached a form which may be called "contractual," as men have come to be conscious of their customs, to accept them, to enforce them upon recalcitrant individuals, and finally—much later, after an intervening stage of authoritarian organization—to change them deliberately by conscious social action. A society which has evolved to the point where it makes its laws by inclusive group deliberation is a "free" society, or a "democracy." The infinite variety of structures and procedures by which any group directly or indirectly makes or formulates its laws, including public and constitutional law, and by which, at need, it enforces them, need not be considered here. Our concern is with the twofold concept of freedom under law and free law-making, or (internal) political freedom. In the ideal or perfect democracy there would, of course, be no literal enforcement of law. The ideal is anarchy. It would mean complete agreement by "rational" process (ethical, not economic, rationality) on all the concrete content of the law. Short of that, the members of a society may still agree on "fair" procedures for making the law, and may voluntarily and rationally accept the results, even while holding divergent opinions as to the rightness or ideal character of the law as made, so that there is still no need for coercion. This second ideal is approximated in modern democracies; literal enforcement through punishment (as a threat) is restricted to a small "criminal" or incompetent element in the adult population, and to "infants." There is, of course, no clear line between conformity to custom through mere suggestion and habit, conformity for rationally ethical reasons of either sort described, informal quasi-enforcement by social sanctions, and literally coercive enforcement by punitive procedure. This complex mixture of categories, none of which can be clearly defined, makes the problem of defining freedom, for practical purposes, an extremely difficult one.

The primary meaning of freedom in society is twofold—individual freedom in one's own defined sphere and "free association" in contrast with coercion. It is always a negative concept (the absence of coercion), and "coercion" is the term which must really be defined. Freedom as absence of coercion is freedom not to associate, either without consultation or on any terms openly offered, together with freedom to offer terms of association to others. Or freedom may be viewed positively as voluntary agreement on the terms of association, but it must be "rational" agreement, and the terms must be "right." Persuasion is clearly a form of coercion—it is the use of a kind of force to control the action of another by controlling his thought. Coercion itself, it is to be noted, is a negative idea, consisting of prevention or deprivation. One being does not coerce another directly, but only by closing some alternative of action which would otherwise be open, or by threatening to do so, or by depriving or threatening to deprive the coerced subject of some benefit which he would otherwise enjoy.

The elementary meaning and function of law, as we have seen, is to prevent coercion, or clash, by drawing boundaries, defining spheres of action within which individuals are literally free, in the sense in which a Crusoe is free when he is the only individual in his "world." Law increases freedom when it is negatively coercive, preventing coercion and conflict. The ultimate limit of social freedom is realized when all the members of any social aggregate, who would otherwise infringe upon one another's spheres of individually free action, and so come into conflict, "freely" agree in the formulation of such boundaries. The boundaries still exist, and have essentially the same meaning, when individuals associate with any degree of intimacy in any way or for any purpose. In short, coercion arises or exists whenever one person associates with another or affects him in any way, and the terms of the relationship are not "voluntarily" and rationally accepted by the latter. Within a sphere of action defined by right law (in either of the meanings already distinguished), an individual is free in the purely individualistic or Crusoe sense. He is free to perform any acts which do not affect others at all, or affect them only in a way which they do not feel to be an infringement upon their own individualistic freedom—and which he wants to do and has the power to do. The individual himself is taken as given, as he stands, with respect to his desires and his endowment with power to act.

However, two important qualifications must be made for life in society, viewed as a "going concern." The first is that promises freely made must be kept; they must limit the freedom of the promisor in the future according to their tenor. The second qualification is similar but more sweeping. In social life, the established patterns of behavior involving relations between individuals come to involve a kind of quasi-contract or legitimate expectation, so that action by one party affecting the freedom of another includes any change in the pattern of action, even a mere failure to act in the expected way. It is this principle which gives rise in large measure to the empirical and practical problems of a free society, particularly where individual relationships have become widespread yet intimate and complex, as in the modern economic order. The typical individual tends to feel, and hence to believe, that he has a right to make nearly any change in his own course of action and that any restriction is an infringement on his freedom; but at the same time he claims the right, as a part of his own freedom, to have his own conditions of action exempt from injurious disturbance through changes by others in their routine. The contradiction is obvious; this combination of claims is virtually on a level with demanding the right to eat one's cake and still have it. It sets the main problem of the second part of this chapter.

It follows from what has been said that freedom vs. coercion in social relations is an ethical concept and an ethical problem. In ordinary usage, indeed, freedom covers all ethics; it reduces to the notion of right and wrong, of justice and injustice, where in the case of a Crusoe it reduces to the notion of power. Coercion is any act or failure to act which "wrongs" another. The philosophical problem of defining freedom and coercion becomes that of defining right and wrong, in a society made up of given individuals, meaning "real" right and wrong, specifically in contrast with individual judgments and feelings. The latter are the primary data for the social psychologist and for "that insidious and crafty animal vulgarly called a statesman or politician" (in the words of Adam Smith). The task for the remainder of our inquiry is to point out two main facts about the problem of social right and wrong. First, we shall briefly contrast the notion of freedom and coercion, or right and wrong, under the assumption stated above that the individual is taken as given, with the problem raised by dropping this assumption, and inquiring into its validity. That is, we must consider the "rights" of an individual as he is in relation to his "right" to "be what he is," to have the power and the desires which he may actually have. (The right to act in terms of given desires and power involves the right to change both; the right to be what one is carries with it the right to become what one wishes to become, to the extent of one's "ability" to do so.) The second remaining problem, or topic, covers certain matters of expediency, where the practical exigencies of workaday social life set limits to freedom and other personal rights and make compromise necessary— and in that sense right.

A little attention to the assumption involved in taking the individual as given will reveal at once that, in comparison with actual usage, our definition of freedom as the absence of coercion, or even of wrongful coercion, is only a partial one. The term "freedom" as regularly used in political controversy covers a much wider scope than merely the absence of coercion. It is used, and in the highest of high places, as we shall point out, to refer even to the vague right of the individual to "freedom from" want and fear, a right to support and protection, without reference to possibilities or conditions. Even with this layer of spurious meaning "peeled off," as it were, and discarded, the term is still excessively broad and ambiguous. The conception of unfreedom is applied to a position of disadvantage or limitations upon an individual's range of action due to the absence of power to act, to his "poverty" in means of action, apart from interference by any other agent, whether rightful or wrong. It has become common in discussions of freedom to draw a distinction between these two conceptions, under the designation of negative and positive freedom. In fact, usage typically refers to the former in contemptuous terms as "merely" negative freedom, implying that real freedom requires possession of power to act. This is certainly a wasteful and confusing use of language. The word "freedom" ought to be restricted to some definite meaning and not used as a general designation for an ideal society—to say nothing of implying that every individual is unconditionally entitled to anything he seriously wants and to protection from anything he regards as a serious evil (both at the hands of democratic government), as is done in Mr. Roosevelt's "Four Freedoms."

Unquestionably, the sphere of activity open to an individual depends just as much on his endowment with power, means, or capacity (always relative to some resistance to be overcome in acting or enjoying as he would like to do) as it does on the absence of interference (or, more generally, of resistance to action). While it may seem futile to quarrel about usage, and the more so where usage is backed up by a strong prejudice, such as the urge to capitalize upon the emotional meaning of a word, it is difficult to see how reasonably accurate communication is possible unless such independent variables as freedom and power are kept separate by different names. As a minimum departure from usage it may at least be suggested that such terms as "formal freedom" and "effective freedom" would be less question-begging and misleading than "positive" and "negative" freedom. Unquestionably, again, the individual's right to a rightful share in the distribution of means of action in society—whatever that may include, and where a reasonable possibility of social action exists as a basis for the social obligation—is a real ethical right. And the problem of having "society," however bounded, so organized and conducted, and having individuals so act, that all its members will come into adult life as individuals with a maximum proper endowment of the power to act which makes freedom effective in general and civilization possible is fully as important as the problem of formal freedom. In the second part of this chapter we shall find that the central problem of economic life centers in these facts as to power, which in popular thinking are grossly misconceived in vital respects.

This brings us again to the fact that freedom, in the formal meaning of noninterference, takes for granted as a datum individual will, desire, or taste as well as power or means. This twofold assumption as to the given individual has always pervaded our traditional, "British-American" social philosophy of utilitarianism, which is weak, not to say fallacious, in this respect. But the current "neo-liberal" reaction against this view, in the direction of statism as a remedy for inequality, is political romanticism and even more dangerous. It must also be emphasized that the "rights of man," by whatever name they may be called, must include a rightful share in the entire cultural inheritance from the past. The right to the possession and free use of power must be conditioned by a corresponding assumption of responsibility on the part of the individual, who must have a cultivated outlook on life in general, "right" wants and tastes, knowledge of what are the worthwhile things, the true goods of life; and he must also know and recognize the limited possibilities of their realization.

To ignore this condition would mean, on the one hand, that society may be wrecked and civilization destroyed through insistence on impossible standards of equality; while, on the other hand, ignoring right wants as a condition necessary to freedom would mean that the slave— of another individual, of some group, or of the state (which would then consist exclusively of a superior caste)—would be as free as anyone, provided only that he were effectively "conditioned" to accept his lot and be satisfied with it. That this latter notion is by no means fantastic will be clear if we merely recall that in all culture prior to modern Western civilization the conception of freedom embodied in both secular and religious-ethical thought has accepted and justified slavery and other caste, class, or status differences. Even the author of our Declaration of Independence was a slaveholder, and a large proportion of those who fought for freedom in the Revolutionary armies regarded slavery as necessary and as divinely ordained. In recognizing as beyond question the necessity of both freedom and power, absolute and relative, to the good life, our modern world view inverts the axioms of our inherited religious-ethical tradition. The latter has always repudiated wealth, and all forms of power and capacity, practical intelligence, and taste, as obstacles rather than instruments to moral value, which it also verbally identifies with freedom. If this modern view of life is wrong, then all the main objectives which are set up or taken for granted in current social discussion and the struggle for betterment should be re-inverted; the general objective of social action would be to set the clock back to the medievalism of the Dark Ages, or to some kindred type of primitive life.

But the point here is that, in the long view, the social problem is not so much freedom—liberation—as it is the creation of individuals fit for membership in a free society. Civilized life requires that "man" wield power over nature, and progress rests on the growth of this power. But ethical idealism requires that individual men do not have final or irresponsible power over other individuals. Free society is largely a matter of the diffusion of the power which is necessary to effective freedom; and this diffusion, or fundamental equality, is dependent also upon a generalized disposition on the part of individuals to use power "rightly." In the short view, the social task of individuals is to live their lives within a framework of institutions; but, looking ahead, institutions must both be maintained and improved in the light of the type of citizen they will produce. Neglect of this long view of the problem may be charged to both our traditional religious (Judeo-Christian) ethics and to utilitarian liberalism. Both tended to treat ethics as a problem of right relations between given individuals, though utilitarianism emphasized freedom and progress, and power in the sense of productive capacity as a prerequisite, while the religious ethic ignored these factors, and even condemned efforts directed to their achievement.

On our last subtopic, which has been referred to under the head of "expediency," what needs saying is closely related to what has just been said in relation to the place of institutions in the social-ethical problem. Anyone who has studied history or reflected about the problems of life must be impressed by two facts. The first is that, in the long view, which is primarily the standpoint of social policy, society is a complex of institutions in a sense even more fundamental than that in which it is an organization of individuals and relationships between individuals. And the second fact is that institutions are highly resistant to change, and likely to be destructively disorganized by any effort to change them sweepingly or rapidly. Order, and an order which is generally understood, and even taken for granted, is after all the first requisite of civilized life and is also a primary condition for its improvement. This means that stability and gradualness, or conservatism in the true meaning of the word, must be the first objective in efforts directed to maintaining and improving the quality of life on the whole. Social institutions are embodied in customs and laws, which must be relatively stable in order to enable the individual to form expectations and to act intelligently, hence freely, in the significant meaning of the word, in relation to his social environment.

It is clearly a natural craving, deeply embedded in human nature, and especially characteristic of "superior" individuals, to yearn to be "free" from the institutional order in which one finds one's self at a given time and place in history. The craving may, of course, take either of two forms—mere negative destructionism, or an urge to radical reconstruction. One thinks of the quatrain in Fitzgerald's *Omar* about grasping "this sorry scheme of things," and remolding it "nearer to the heart's desire." But the least critical examination must show that the second urge is practically equivalent to the first, and that both are aspects of the fundamental romanticism of human nature. This is undoubtedly a noble quality—provided its promptings are not taken at all literally and seriously as a guide to action. The wish of a man to be free from institutions is much like the wish of the fabled bird to be free from the existence of air, so as to be able to fly with unlimited speed. Human life in solitude is unthinkable and self-contradictory, and society without institutions is practically as much so. In fact, individual freedom even in relation to nature must be narrowly limited to be real or conceivable. Ultimately, freedom consists in the ability to change one's self, and must be an activity of a self with substantial existence; and it also means the freedom, and the power, to change one's world, which must similarly have substantial reality, hence stability. Thus, incidentally, the notion of omnipotence is doubly a self-contradiction. With respect to change, candid introspection will reveal to anyone that he has very little capacity to imagine either a different self, a different society, or a different physical world, which he would really expect to like better than those he already has to deal with. Certainly, no one would want to live in a society composed of people made to his own order and subject to remaking at will.

Moreover, it is obvious that the members of any society must agree with respect to its institutional structure, which means the kind of society it is and is to be, and they must agree freely if it is to be a free society, and this fact imposes even narrower bounds upon the possibilities of change. In a rational view, individual freedom in group life involves an antinomy. To behave rationally, in any activity involving others, the individual must know what behavior to expect of others; that is, for one to be rationally free, all others involved in any relationship to his activity must be mechanistically determined. The possibility of social freedom is therefore limited to rational consensus, which, as we have seen, requires agreement upon values. But, happily, the freedom of the good life is not strictly a matter of rationality in any sense, still less of instrumental rationality.

The restricting and constraining power of institutions is a fact of wide ramifications. The most literal freedom of anarchy is possible or can be approximated in associative life only in groups of extremely small size and of the most casual nature and aims. And even the most casual association—aimless sociability, conversation, and play—is seen on reflection to be far from acting in a moral vacuum. Every association is rather highly organized, with an implicit code of rules or law which must be available. This is even more the case with intellectual discussion—i.e., "serious" social intercourse—and in more formal play. And even in the freest intercourse, problems constantly arise due to conflicts of interest and the need to resolve these without disrupting the group and sacrificing its common interests. In intellectual discussion, for example, it is constantly necessary to compromise between the interests of those who want to be heard and of those who wish to listen to those with something to say which is in some way worth attention.

Any group or association of substantial size will necessarily be organized around interests which call for some degree of stability in the association, and such a group necessarily involves much coercion of its members. There must always be a large measure of compromise between individual freedom and other values functioning as ends in group life. For actual human beings hold opinions and cherish aims in action which are more or less individual in content and more or less conflicting and competitive. Such men do not spontaneously agree on the objectives or the rules and conditions of association. The burning questions which confront modern society and threaten its destruction arise in political and economic organization. The principles involved are not essentially different from those involved in play and culture, and even in religion in the noneconomic aspects (however, these may be defined) of these activities. It should be evident that the conditions of modern life set fairly narrow limits to the possibility of freedom for the individual either to depart from or to change the established patterns of activity, for most of these involve relationships with others, whom he cannot know personally and can with great difficulty consult, but who will be vitally affected.

The supreme concrete example of permanent, and stable, and large-scale grouping is, of course, the "sovereign state," defined in modern times by territorial boundaries. Living together, under the conditions of modern civilization, requires association—in particular economic cooperation—under stable forms. The cooperation is more intimate and complex between geographic neighbors, but is still "essential" between individuals and groups over an area which practically includes the world. And this also effectively applies to cultural relationships, partly because these are inseparable from those classed as economic, but also for larger reasons. It is inevitable that the world be divided up into a complex hierarchy of territorial jurisdictions, and the accidents of history and the facts of human nature have given us a political world map which few people would defend as ideal but which it is practically impossible to change extensively or rapidly without ruinously destructive war. For reasons which need not be considered here, the individual actually has very little effective freedom even to choose his place of residence and his citizenship among the limited number of national states into which the earth is divided.

Moreover, within each state there is an unlimited number and variety of more or less voluntary associations along lines of special economic, and cultural, and other interests, to which the individual is virtually "forced" to belong, as a condition of participating in the benefits of civilization. Of paramount importance for vast numbers has come to be his inclusion in some large-scale productive enterprise. Within his state, and other associations or societies, the individual is "bound" by the existing law and by the limitations of his power to secure the consent of the other members of the group to change the law, where he does not like it as it is, and he frequently does not. In large groups the difficulty of effective intercommunication increases at an increasing rate and soon makes any close approximation to literal democracy a mathematical impossibility. These facts, particularly the conflict between freedom and concrete substantive values and ends of action, set the social problems which must be surveyed in the second part of this chapter on the conditions necessary for realizing the ideal of freedom.

The Ideal of Freedom: Conditions for Its Realization

This section will naturally be a continuation of the preceding one. The meaning of an ideal or objective cannot be sharply separated from the conditions and the modes of action relevant to its realization. The previous section should have made it clear that, in our present culture situation, the problem of action under the guidance of freedom as an ideal cannot be discussed without constant and careful regard to wide differences in the meanings which the word bears, both in popular discussion and in the writings of social theorists and philosophers. We pointed out in particular that the term "freedom" has become a symbol for nearly everything that human beings think they want and do not have, and which, consequently, as they infer, it must be somebody's obligation to supply. Of course, people demand only what they claim a right to have, but the difference they make between this and what they regard as needful, or even what they strongly desire, is commonly less than would be made by an impartial spectator.

A fine illustration of the intellectual confusion with respect to the meaning of freedom which reigns in current social discussion is at hand in the enumeration of the "Four Freedoms," recently promulgated by President Roosevelt as the goal to be achieved in national and world reorganization after the present war. The list undoubtedly sums up, with the author's usual political astuteness, the things of which the great mass of the people feel themselves unjustly deprived in the social-psychological situation of prolonged economic crisis, followed by a war between "democracy" and "dictatorship" as types or principles of social order. Mr. Roosevelt's list, as you will recall, includes freedom of expression, freedom of worship, freedom from want, and freedom from fear.

The statement is so naive that it smacks of unkindness to ask what any of these freedoms has to do with freedom, or what it means, or what are the conditions or possibilities of its realization—specifically by democratic political agencies. One of its most conspicuous features, in the light of quite recent history, is the absence of any reference to most of the traditional freedoms of economic and political liberalism. There is nothing to suggest freedom in the consumption, exchange, or production of goods or services, or freedom of the individual to make provision for the future, his own or that of his family—and, in fact, no reference is made to any aspect of freedom in family life. Nor is there any mention of the concrete freedoms of democracy, the right to vote in the selection of the personnel of government and to hold political office.

Doubtless all these rights are taken for granted. But the more serious criticism is that nothing is said about the corresponding obligations, or the limitations or necessary conditions, which are obviously present, and in which all the real problems lie. Even freedom of expression is meaningless apart from a right to be listened to, and is likely to be taken to mean the right of an individual to be heard and heeded by his fellow-citizens as a body, a freedom which is mathematically impossible for any considerable number. Similar strictures apply to freedom of worship, which is hardly at issue with respect to private worship (the form originally enjoined on Christians), or apart from the right of some to prescribe and enforce forms of religious service for others. Freedom to organize worship may easily cloak an assumed right to build up a political machine or "party," with a view to controlling the state. There is no boundary between religious and other interests, and we are reminded that in American history, not so remote, the Latter Day Saints were prohibited by federal action from practicing a fundamental tenet of their religion, even in a sovereign state which they had founded and politically controlled. Freedom from want, again, is without content unless it means a right to be taken care of by someone with the necessary means, and whose freedom is surely affected by this obligation. And it is assumed without question that someone will have the means to take care of everybody, when such an obligation is attached to the fruits of production and accumulation. Throughout modern history, the right of anyone in acute want to relief has been unquestioned, subject to limits and conditions believed to be necessary, and the only possible issue has to do with these limits and conditions. Finally, freedom from fear suggests even more obvious questions as to what obligations are to be imposed, and how, and at what sacrifice of other freedoms or rights.[1]

As a preliminary to the main argument, it will be well to summarize briefly the main distinctions in the meaning of freedom in connection with our purposes, which were developed in the preceding section. We distinguished first between three ultimate general conceptions, corresponding to the religious or mystical (or quietistic), the romantic, and the modern liberal views of life. Both the first and the second of these mean essentially freedom from responsibility in thinking and action. In the religious view, this state is to be achieved by "accepting the universe"—either suppressing all desire, or bringing it into harmony with what God or fate or the Absolute in some meaning may send, and so achieving serenity and peace. In a thorough-going form, this means annihilation, at least as far as earthly life is concerned. At the practicable limit at which individual and social life could go on, it means the contemplative life, thinking without acting, which is possible only for a limited number of individuals living parasitically within a society pursuing a more or less antithetical ideal, or perhaps realizing this one vicariously. At the opposite extreme, romanticism means acting without thinking—"thinking with the blood." In this direction, also, some compromise is necessary to avoid destruction. Acceptance of some responsibility is a condition of life itself. The conception of freedom in the modern view of life allows the individual the widest range of choice in compromising between the two extremes but inculcates quite definitely a middle ground. Spiritual freedom is to be achieved through knowing and accepting the limiting conditions of activity and choosing intelligently among the alternatives open, while the substance of reasonable romanticism, an interesting life, is to be realized through free constructive activity within the possible limits. The ultimate end or purpose is worthwhile achievement in the form of individual growth and social progress. Our discussion of the conditions necessary for realizing freedom will run entirely in terms of this third conception, defined by the modern ethical world view.

We pointed out that in social relations freedom is necessarily restricted and largely defined by moral responsibility, and especially by law, customary and juridic, as a condition necessary for orderly social life. The free individual must live in a free society, in which his sphere of literally free activity is defined by such law, itself made by the free and equal participation of all members of society, and representing an intellectual-moral consensus as to the content of rights and obligations. Social freedom, under law, is essentially a negative concept; it means freedom from interference in individual activity, except for the limitations of law of the character stated. Ideally, it means free association, based on rational mutual consent in all relationships—i.e., freedom not to associate unless the terms are acceptable. The practical problem centers in the necessary legal restrictions, or the right scope and content of law, and in the democratic character of the state as the agency by which a society makes and enforces law. In general usage, the concept of freedom has been illogically extended to include the right to possess and control the means or power without which action is of course impossible. We suggested, as a compromise, calling this right "effective freedom." In a defensible use of terms, it is the right to power and not to freedom. Ideal social relations undoubtedly include also some right to assistance, to relief of want or suffering, and to security, subject to reasonable conditions; but it is merely confusing to bring all such rights under the conception of freedom.

Turning now to the subject of the present lecture, it should be obvious that, ideally, the conditions requisite for realizing the ideal of freedom in any society are intellectual and moral qualities in its members. The ultimate ideal (in an absolute, not a realistic, sense) is anarchy, in which the only law is the moral law, recognized—i.e., rationally agreed upon— by every individual, and needing no enforcement. Progress toward this ideal, from the present undeveloped and "sinful" state of man, as well as the maintenance of such civilization as the race has achieved, is possible only through social action involving compulsion. Ideally, again, at a first remove from the ultimate ideal, social action would doubtless take the form of intellectual and moral education, chiefly if not exclusively in childhood. This statement, however, leaves the conception of freedom ambiguous. The content of law might still be such as to realize freedom—in the sense that men would feel free—through conditioning the will, eliminating desire, or bringing it into conformity with actuality, rather than by providing the conditions of free activity. And we must constantly keep in mind the fact that from the standpoint of social peace—which is always a primary consideration, and a necessity within limits—it is this feeling of freedom, based on acceptance of things as they are, to the extent of eliminating destructive expression of discontent, which is in question. If men are to be free, they must be educated and habituated to self-discipline, at least to the extent of not struggling to achieve the impossible or to have benefits without paying the necessary cost; and this is just as obviously a condition of their being reasonably "happy." In our cultural situation, the danger lies in the direction of romanticism, of demanding the impossible, which actually threatens catastrophe and destruction, specifically through war. Excessive quietism would finally be equally destructive, but in an entirely different way, and human nature as we see it around us is not inclined toward that extreme.

Thus the immediate practical problem is in fact primarily one of intellectual and moral education. The public must be made to understand vastly better than it does the possibilities and limitations of life, particularly of life in organized society, and the possibilities and limitations of action directed toward its improvement. But the requirement of moral education is in a sense even prior to that of intellectual. Men must first of all have the disposition to act in the light of knowledge and to acquire the necessary knowledge and understanding. They must be cured of the age-old inveterate romanticism, which has found expression in the practices of magic, and especially of witchcraft—the disposition to explain all supposed evils by finding some malevolent agent, preferably some human being or group, and to resort to punishment or "liquidation" as a remedy. This disposition doubtless finds its primary exemplification in the history of "medicine," the treatment of disease. Even in the most civilized societies the development of a really objective scientific attitude toward these problems, in the mass of the population, is still largely to be achieved. Actual witchcraft has, to be sure, been largely eliminated, but beliefs and practices essentially at the level of superstition undoubtedly still predominate over science, except as the latter is directly enforced by law.

The natural man is still a romantic, disposed to act without much regard for rational knowledge and thought. He is still what has been called a "Gawdsaker"; his maxim is "for God's sake, do something!" Apart from witchcraft, what men have always typically done when they were ill is to take some poison; if they recovered, it was attributed to the treatment, and if they did not, it was held to be because they did not take enough, or because some detail was wrong. In the field of social maladies, the progress made toward superseding this attitude with action based upon rational investigation is small, in comparison even with the field of individual medicine. We must assume as the basis of any discussion that the masses of men are potentially intelligent enough not to strike out blindly against the inevitable, not to act rashly and therefore destructively, or even to make themselves acutely unhappy about what demonstrably cannot be helped. Otherwise, we must admit in advance that free society is an impossibility, and give up the problem as hopeless. No cure for the ills of society is to be found in blind resort to conflict against some supposed enemy, until he can be shown to be really to blame, or in the equally romantic impulse to take the machinery of social organization to pieces and rebuild it, without an understanding of the mechanism and of the functions to be performed by the social order and the problems which are involved.

By way of approach to the problem of freedom in and through social organization under law, it will be useful to classify individual and social interests and activities along psychological lines, under the three heads of work, play, and culture. With specific reference to our topic, play and work are commonly thought of as virtually synonymous, respectively, with free and unfree or compulsory activity, while cultural pursuits are more or less intermediate, combining the features of work and play. However, examination somewhat surprisingly shows that all these activities are structurally much alike, and that even the psychological contrast in men's feelings toward them hardly stands up under critical examination. All three involve the use of means and the economy of means, in realizing ends which the acting subject "wants" to achieve. The reasons why he wants to achieve them also analyze into the same list of basic human desires, urges, or interests—a vague mixture of "needs" for life and comfort and for satisfactory growth or development, merging into desires for things or types of experience viewed as less important. All are very largely socially conditioned; their content is a matter of social psychology and culture history. As already noted, the scientific problem of analyzing these desires and dispositions, and the social problem of giving them the right content, are very difficult to discuss, and we must here take them as given, until near the close of the chapter.

The meaning of work and play is a strangely neglected subject, and some comparison will be necessary to bring out the facts which are essential for understanding the feeling of unfreedom. As will be shown presently, the notion of work must be extended to cover all economic endeavor, regardless of the relation between labor and external means used in the activity. The least inspection of what is superficially classed as work shows that physical subsistence and comfort play a minor role in the motivation, while recreation is also necessary to comfort and even to health, and shows also that no sharp contrast exists even in terms of enjoyment. The real motive in both production and consumption is largely competition, emulation, or rivalry, which is also the characteristic source of interest in play. Work and play are clearly instrumental to each other, as is true of all the elements in "the good life," whatever elements may be distinguished. The psychological motivation of all activities must be provisionally described in some such terms as the famous "four wishes" of W. I. Thomas—adventure, security, recognition, and response—which tell us nothing about concrete content. In particular, all are competitive or involve emulation. To the list should undoubtedly be added the quest for power—as an end, not as a means—and "development," along right or approved lines, will be found to be the ultimate end in all cases, in so far as the activity is rational. But the concrete meaning of all these terms depends almost entirely on the social-cultural or historical situation.

The most important fact is that all three kinds of activity—work, play, and culture—present the combination of harmony and conflict of interests which we emphasized in the previous section as the basis and presupposition of the existence of any social or group problem, and of the need for law. Moreover, the problem of law in relation to freedom arises in essentially the same form in all our three fields of associative action. Play as well as work must have its law, the rules of the game, especially if socially organized, as it usually is, though there is no ultimate or profound distinction between social play and solitaire. In all cases, laws can be discussed only in intellectual terms, not those of mere individual desire. The social-ethical problem of "fair" play may easily be viewed in the same terms as that of economic life—i.e., "justice" in the assignment of roles and the distribution of the fruits of activity in relation to the effort and "capacity" employed in the game.

The psychological difference between play and work, the feeling of freedom versus compulsion, seems to lie in conditions which in the case of work bring about a relatively sharp separation between the activity and the result aimed at, a separation between "production" and "consumption." These conditions will be taken up presently. In play the activity and the achievement run closer together, and the interest seems to center more in the activity; the result seems to be arbitrarily set up as an end, in order to make the activity interesting, whereas the feeling about work involves the converse relation, the activity is instrumental to the result. (The means-end relationship in general is elusive, and this has been too much emphasized in recent thought to call for development here, even if space allowed.)

The psychology of work—specifically, the feeling of compulsion in the mind of the "free" worker—seems to be largely a peculiar product of advanced civilization. Among primitive peoples the contrast between work and play is certainly far less developed, if they have it at all. And the higher animals almost certainly do not have it to any extent, though we distinguish some of their activities, chiefly in infancy (in the wild state), as play. Incidentally, the economically rational man, all of whose ends were given, not problematic (the "economic man"), would not work and would hardly play, as he would be interested only in tangible results, and in particular would not experience competitive motivation. It is the work attitude which is especially distinctive of man, and more especially of modern civilized man, and this peculiar feeling of unfreedom in economic life sets our main social problem. But the philosophically more important fact is the tendency of work interests to dissolve under critical scrutiny into those of play, and specifically into competitive emulation—"keeping up with the Joneses," or getting ahead of them. The weakness of the economic view of activity is precisely in the fact that it takes ends as given, while for critical thought the immediate ends always resolve themselves into means, and the interest in ends in turn largely dissolves into unreality or into a play interest.

However, there are also "real" ends in economic activity. The "standard of living," which is for the most part aesthetic in content, represents the content of civilization and the difference between human and animal life. It is the combination of these real ends or values with the play interest and other activity interests which makes the social-economic problem at once difficult and interesting. If we inquire further into the ultimate ends, the values of civilized life, we shall find culture and cultural growth in the individual, and progress in society, the provisional answer to the question in the case of both work and play. It is more natural to raise the question of ends with respect to work, but we do ask it about play also, especially in ranking and choosing games. Culture, again, analyzes into the familiar triad of values, truth, beauty, and goodness, or intellectual, aesthetic, and moral experience and progress, while recreative enjoyment is as much a part of the good life as are its "serious" ends. In order to carry further the investigation into the purposive free life, we must consider in more detail the relation between means and ends, in connection with work, and the meaning of economic activity, which we have been taking for granted.

All the primary aspects of freedom as a defensible ideal—freedom to act, but to act responsibly (meaning the right use of power), and "effective" freedom as the right to have power—point directly to the concept of economic freedom as the central problem in the politico-legal order. The meaning of that concept must now be indicated more precisely than was done in the previous section. In a broad, logical sense it includes all freedom, since economy is a universal aspect of rational behavior or conduct. And even in the narrow definition in terms of monetary activities—buying and selling, which is virtually the meaning in popular usage—it is in the economic field that the feeling of unfreedom has given rise to serious problems in our society in recent times. It is in relation to the aspect of the state as an instrument in connection with economic relations that our problems center in politics and political action. Intelligent purposive behavior always involves the more or less effective use of power, or means, to realize ends. Economy is merely a synonym for efficiency, or effectiveness, and the effort to be effective makes every problem to some extent an economic problem. This is only one part of the problem of conduct, its "economic aspect"; the other part is selection among concrete ends in terms of final or noninstrumental values. The economic view takes the ends as given—i.e., as already decided upon. But the social problem as it arises in political life centers in the individual provision and use of means, and that phase of it will logically be considered first and primarily. In modern society men do not feel unfree in the selection of ends, except as this choice is conditioned by the available means and restrictions upon their use.

To avoid confusion as to the nature of the problem of economic freedom, one must be on guard against two major fallacies which pervade popular thinking and political agitation. The first is the notion that there is a distinct class of economic ends—specifically, that provision for the "higher" wants is not just as much an economic problem as provision for the "lower" or for the "animal" needs. As every literate adult really knows, what we call the necessaries or subsistence requirements in any social-cultural setting are overwhelmingly a matter of conformity to "standards" of "decency," which are aesthetic and social in content. In fact, it is the higher wants which are the more expensive, as pointed out in our first chapter. The second fallacy is that of thinking of economic means in terms of physical materials and implements, or "property" in the ordinary meaning of the term, in contrast with human beings themselves. In fact, some three-fourths of the productive capacity used in the United States, measured in money value, consists of human abilities. Analytically speaking, the human being himself, the individual's own person, is a "means of production" in much the same sense as any external material or instrument. Useful human capacities are also "artificial"; they are the product of previous economic activity, as completely as any machine or device more typically called a "capital good." And the same is true of what are called "natural resources." These three traditional "factors of production," as they exist and are used at any time, are all the result of the previous transformation of materials ultimately derived from nature, but which in their natural state would not be useful for the purposes of civilized life and would have no economic value. They present no differences in essential principle; all are "capital" in the correct definition of that concept. The human being in particular, as he comes into the world from the hands of "nature," is an economic liability, not an asset. He becomes a useful agent through a process of investment, made in him by others and by himself, which is not different in principle from that involved in the construction of a manufacturing plant, or of any tool or instrument.

From the economic point of view, the really distinctive feature of human life—which is to say civilized life—is not that men rationally use means; this is also true of the higher animals, in varying degrees and ways. What is distinctive of man is that the means used (human and material) exist in a highly transformed state, and that if such life is to continue, this artificial "equipment" must constantly be maintained and replaced, through rationally planned activity involving all the means already at hand. Human society uses a stock or fund of "productive capacity" embodied in human beings and external physical things— which has been accumulated through historical time from the dim evolutionary beginnings of human life. This stock has been maintained and increased (of course with notable recessions, as civilizations have developed and decayed) through the use of the stock in existence at any time in such a way as to increase the total, in addition to yielding its primary "product," a flow of consumable services. The social stock of productive capacity must not only be maintained if civilized life is to continue, but must be further increased if civilization is to be progressive—and it will almost certainly decay if it does not progress. Economic conduct and the problem of economic freedom refer simply to the economic aspect of life—activity, the economic or economically rational use of means, regardless of kind, for the realization of ends, also regardless of kind, but taken as given or already decided upon. But the end must include the maintenance and increase of the means, or there will be no sense in thinking about the future at all. This provision for maintenance and growth must, of course, be socially continuous. If it is to be effected by individuals, their interests in action must look beyond their individual lives.

Economic activity, as free, consequently has three "dimensions": It involves *(a)* choice, based on purely quantitative comparison, among partial or provisional ends for which means are to be used, the different given "wants" to be satisfied in consumption; *(b)* choice among concrete modes of using means, the technique or technology to be employed; and *(c)* decision as to the amount of means to be used in maintaining or increasing the stock of means itself, the human and material capital of the individual and of society. In all of these fields of activity all kinds of means, human and nonhuman, function in a complementary way and constitute an integral or organic unit, the social capital. It should now be clear why the concept of work must be extended to include all conduct in its economic, or economically rational, aspect.

The ultimate unity of all forms of purposive action—work, play, and culture—with reference to the problem of social organization may be visualized by imagining the conditions of life so changed that the economic problem would no longer exist. The result is somewhat disturbing, in the face of the fact that work is primitively (and religiously) thought of as the primal curse of human life. If we imagine that men were granted the ability to perform physical miracles, say by some supernatural power, or by the discovery of a magical process which would work, so that all economic production could be carried out simply by wishing, the social problem would not be solved and probably not alleviated or even changed in form. In the abstract, it is at least as arguable that it would be greatly intensified, and destructive conflict made correspondingly more difficult to avoid—unless play and culture (and social and religious) interests were at the same time so transformed that men themselves would cease to be recognizable as human.

The reasons for the work feeling, so characteristic of economic production in modern life—and which as irksome effort is not very different between property-owners and those who live by labor—are connected with the choice both of ends and of means. The roots of the compulsive power of the urge to maintain a relatively expensive standard of living have already been suggested; it is partly a matter of the awakening of taste in the masses, and partly one of psychological competition, emulation, and rivalry, and it cannot be probed more deeply here. In any case, the feeling of unfreedom undoubtedly arises to a greater extent on the side of means, as a consequence of obvious features of the production process. This has become at the same time highly mechanized on a vast scale and relatively precarious in its operation. It involves a large and intricate human organization based on impersonal relations, with the necessity of operating continuously. An individual, or a personal group, has little ability to make changes without disastrous consequences to itself and others. It is an obvious feature of organized relations that changes made by one member disrupt the plans and conditions of life of the others, unless all changes are worked out and preconcerted in advance on the basis of the explicit consent of all.

In any case, the fact remains that the social problem in our civilization centers very largely in what people call "economic unfreedom." The bulk of our substantive law has to do with economic life, and economic problems and relationships form the subject matter of most of our political discussion, by the general public and in our legislatures. The task of the philosophic analyst becomes that of explaining this fact, and of indicating to the statesman or politician the true nature of the problem, so that he may work intelligently at his practical task of finding appropriate measures for dealing with it. To attack the former task we must start with two facts as given. The first is that men have individual interests which take the form of realizing ends, achievement of which is narrowly restricted by scarcity of the means available, so that they are impelled to the economy of means, and also to efforts to increase the available total stock of means, the productive capacity or economic power under their control. The second fact is that the efficiency of these "economic" endeavors can be almost infinitely increased by entering into mutually instrumental social relationships of cooperation or organization, which at the same time involve direct conflicts of interest. The practically unlimited increase in efficiency involved is undoubtedly a main factor in causing organized activity to be felt as compulsory. In the present stage of civilization, unorganized or self-sufficient economic life would at best mean a standard of living which would be felt to be intolerable, even for a greatly reduced population.

In fact, of course, no one proposes that. The sense of unfreedom, and the discontent and protest, express themselves rather in a clamor for radical change in the *form* of economic organization. Consequently, our first main inquiry should center in a study of the existent form, from the standpoint of freedom and unfreedom. It should attempt to learn why the individual has so much the feeling of being coerced, how far this feeling corresponds with facts, how far proposed changes in the economic system, or any feasible changes, offer a substantial opportunity for increasing real freedom—or the real values which are called by that name—without intolerable loss of effectiveness, or how far the problem is one of dispelling illusion and mere romantic discontent, as already suggested. Such an inquiry must lead to the conclusion that the discontent with the form of economic organization is in fact based almost entirely on misconception and wishful or prejudiced thinking, or feeling rather than thinking—what I am calling romanticism. But this does not mean that there is no basis for action, that the solution of the social problem is merely to teach men to accept things as they are and be content. The true conclusion, indeed, is partly that expectations and demands commonly have little relation to possibilities, but, further, that the treatment advocated is wrong because the diagnosis is wrong—if, indeed, it should be dignified by the name of diagnosis at all. The inquiry itself cannot be carried out in the compass of a chapter; obviously it would call for a treatise on economics, as a first step. All that we can do is very briefly to run over the ground, list a few of the main results to which the investigation would lead—with a brevity which must make our statements seem dogmatic—and contrast them with the fallacious and romantic notions commonly held by the public.

In a liberal economic order, such as was approximated in this country in the latter part of the nineteenth century, the terms of association are defined by the prices of goods and services, determined by purchase and sale in markets described as "freely" competitive. The first "romantic misconception" which calls for notice centers in the use of this term "competition" to describe the market and the market organization of economic life. Transactions in an effective market involve no psychological competition whatever, and on this point the facts are very largely in conformity with the theory, as every literate adult really knows. The meaning of a market is simply that a plurality of individuals are in a relationship of effective intercommunication, in which each is "free" to offer terms of exchange to any other and to accept or refuse the terms offered by any other. As soon as a market is established as a going concern, it results in fixing a system of prices which are virtually objective, as far as any individual is concerned. The freedom of any individual consists in choosing on the basis of established prices what commodities he will produce and sell, and in what quantities, and which ones he will buy and consume. Where goods or services are produced for exchange under rational economic motivation—i.e., for the satisfaction of given wants of the producer—the whole operation is to be understood in terms of the comparative efficiency of different methods of production. An economically rational subject produces one thing and exchanges it for another if and because he gets a greater value or "satisfaction" by so doing. That is, he either gets a greater quantity of the same good, or a more desirable good, than he could secure by using his productive powers directly, in a self-sufficient way, to satisfy his wants. In producing for exchange he is still in effect using his own resources in his own way to satisfy his own wants. In terms of motives, he is behaving on exactly the same principles as a Crusoe, choosing between different modes of using his productive capacity so as to secure the maximum benefits in quantity and kind of results.

Thus what is called market competition is really a purely technological and impersonal category. Viewed in the large it is a method of organizing cooperation in the interest of increasing the effectiveness of activity where both means and ends are given an individual. And in a system of cooperation organized in this way, every individual enjoys complete social freedom; he is free in the sense in which a Crusoe is free (more accurately, in the sense in which a Crusoe would be free if he operated a productive mechanism with the mechanical characteristics of the modern economic order). As stated before, everyone really knows that there is in the buying and selling transactions of ordinary life substantially no psychological competition, and no exercise of persuasive power in the way of "bargaining." He also knows that the prices are fixed by impersonal conditions, which are beyond the control of the other party, as of himself, whether he is buying groceries in a retail store, selling agricultural products to a local trader, or selling his labor to an employer. Yet he commonly alleges the contrary, because he feels unfree. The typical human being, the educated as well as the uneducated, shows an inveterate tendency to assume that because he does not decide the terms of exchange, or influence them by fiat, someone else must be dictating to him arbitrarily. In essence, the attitude represents a survival of the animistic ideas with which primitive man, unable to conceive of objective fact, viewed the world as a whole, inanimate as well as animate nature. The first step in getting men to feel free is to get them to apply the knowledge they already possess, to take a rational or objective attitude, instead of a romantic one, toward the conditions of their lives. Otherwise they not only will be unhappy, but are certain to act in ways which are destructive instead of remedial.

It is true that real economic relations are largely competitive, in the psychological sense, as we have already emphasized. But this has nothing whatever to do with the form of organization. It is true for the same reason that other social relations are competitive, specifically our play, in which we feel especially free. It is because human nature is competitive, and competition seems to be necessary to make any activity interesting. But psychological competition is alien to economic motivation, as already noted, and in the effective market the individual behaves as an economic man. In so far as he does so behave, the market organization both involves perfect liberty and enables each participant to achieve the maximum gain in efficiency which is to be had through mutually free specialization and cooperation. He could improve his position only through one-sided transfers at the expense of others, predation or gift, or through placing his own affairs in the hands of someone more competent than himself to manage them. Incidentally, the free-market economy leaves individuals free to make this arrangement on mutually agreeable terms, and it is a common occurrence. It is to be noted, too, that if any two parties dislike for any reason the "objective" terms fixed by the general give-and-take, they are free to deal on any other terms upon which they may agree—specifically, to set a "fair" price if they think the market price is unjustly high or low. And, further, if any "society" is convinced that the terms of the free market give some individuals too little and others too much, it is free to take from some for the benefit of others, by taxation, or to regulate or suppress any form of trade, without changing the system of organization.

All this, however, as we have already stated, does not mean either that the free-market economy has produced ideal results in reality, or that there is no chance for improvement through social action. On the other side of the case, the side of rational criticism, inquiry would naturally proceed in two stages. First, we should have to investigate the relations between the perfect competition of theory and actual conditions; and, second, we should look into the matter of diagnosis of the evils in terms other than the form of organization. Under the first head, it goes without saying that the actual functioning of the market mechanism is not in strict conformity with the theoretical pattern. This is not even true of physical machines, and far less so of any mechanism of human organization. With reference to the economic organization, it should be evident that individuals have much to gain by breaking the rules, and that the competitive-market ideal will not be realized or approximated without a large amount of intelligent social action through the making and enforcement of appropriate rules or laws. This is the first and main practical problem, whether social policy should in general be directed toward making competition effective or to discarding the system outright and replacing it with one of an entirely different pattern. The second course will naturally be advisable only if another pattern can be found which will be really better, on the whole. (It is a paradoxical but evident truth that for practical purposes a hopeless situation is identical with an ideal one.)

We can only run over in a most cursory manner a few criticisms, of what may be called a mechanical sort, which are brought against the free-market organization and are supposed to justify its rejection. No doubt the two most common allegations treated as conclusive by the romantic critics are, first, that competition is an economic myth of theorists or a fable used to dupe the unwary in the interest of exploiters, that the business economy is and must be dominated by monopoly; and, second, that it is in the nature of such a system to fall into cyclical oscillations, and particularly into periodic depressions so disastrous as to make the system intolerable.

On the first point, monopoly, we can only make a few assertions, without giving the facts or arguments to support them. The amount of monopoly actually present is grossly exaggerated in the popular mind, and the nature and causes of monopoly and its evils grossly misunderstood. A considerable amount of monopoly is not merely unpreventable, and in that sense a part of the cost of freedom and progress, but is functionally necessary. This should be clear from the case of patents on inventions, and similar legal devices, and from the evident fact that monopoly which is not based on deliberate public grant functions in the same way: the hope for a temporary monopoly gain serves as the incentive to experimentation and development. Such gains may be, and in fact are, offset or more than offset by losses incurred in similar activities and must be viewed as the earned reward of taking risks which are inevitable in a progressive society. Moreover, the evils of monopoly are very largely the product of unwise governmental action or are the indirect result of depression conditions. The public, however, seems to think that the remedy for monopoly is more monopoly, deliberately set up in favor of the groups (primarily wage-earners and farmers) which feel themselves victimized by the largely imaginary monopolies of "big business" and "high finance." This assumes that the way to have more, all around, is to produce less.

With respect to the business cycle, it must suffice here to point out two facts. The first is that practically no one makes any gain out of depression; and, in particular, that the owners of business enterprises suffer enormous losses, including wholesale bankruptcy. Consequently, the problem is twofold: the scientific one of discovering the cause and devising appropriate remedies, and the application of the remedies when found—a matter of the political competence of democracy. The second observation, which must also stand as an assertion, is that any "planned" economy which seriously attempted to preserve the fundamental liberties of individuals would embody the same tendencies and encounter the same difficulties. For the roots of cyclical tendencies are to be found in the money-and-credit mechanism; and the socialistic planners do not propose to eliminate purchase and sale in terms of money as the general pattern of economic organization—and certainly could not do so without making the mere administrative task insuperable.

Passing over other more or less appealing lines of argument, the general conclusion must be that the first objective in a social policy aimed at the maximum individual freedom must be to make competition reasonably effective where it is not and in any case to make it as effective as possible in the great bulk of the productive organization. In exceptional cases, where this is not feasible—such as the "natural monopolies" (chiefly public utilities)—the procedure indicated is to substitute public enterprise, governmental ownership and operation. All price control must be pronounced bad, for whatever reason it is employed (though emergencies, especially war, produce conditions under which there seems to be no alternative). The possible alternative to the price economy would be some political system of controlling production and distribution, some form of planned economy, or collectivism, or socialism. But, as we have seen, socialists do not propose to get away from the market organization as the basic pattern of their system. Passing over grave doubts as to whether the two mechanisms, business and policies, could be effectively combined, there is every reason against believing that political machinery would in practice conform any more closely to its theoretical principles, or come nearer to realizing its ideal objective.

Reasoning from known facts and principles indicates that collectivism would aggravate the very evils of the system which is miscalled "capitalism," which it would be particularly intended to cure. And, in addition, a little reflection should make it clear that any government faced with the task of ordering the economic affairs of a modern nation, to say nothing of world relations, would necessarily be a dictatorship, suppressing personal liberty in all fields of social life as well as the distinctively economic. If theoretical arguments on these points left any room for reasonable doubt, the course of events in the European world since the first World War, and specifically the Russian experiment, should be sufficient to remove them.

The issue with respect to the open-market economic order, as already stated, is correct diagnosis, in place of the false one that competition does not work, that it is a "myth" and cannot be realized. The root fallacy is the idea that the complete realization of economic freedom would solve or eliminate the major social problems. It rests on a confusion between freedom and power—or, in a more comprehensive view, on the mistake of taking the individual as given, with respect both to his endowment with economic power and to his wants or dispositions (what he desires to do with power and freedom).

The first step which must be taken as a prerequisite for the intelligent discussion of power in economic relations is to separate analytically economic power in the form in which it appears in the free market from other forms. In an effectively competitive market organization, economic power consists exclusively of the productive capacity which the individual possesses, including personal capacity or labor power and the ownership of external wealth or property. It is a matter of individual sharing in the aggregate social capital—and, of course, of the total amount of that capital, relative to population, accumulated down to any given time. Productive capacity is measured by its economic value, which depends upon the demand of other persons as consumers for the ultimate product. And this demand is made up of two factors, consumers' desires or preferences and their economic capacity, which is their source of purchasing power.

The second step (which might, indeed, have been placed first) is to recognize both that economic power is sadly limited in comparison with human needs (in contrast with the nonsense we hear about poverty in the midst of abundance), and that there is an inherent conflict between freedom and power. For power is indefinitely multiplied by organization; while effective organization reduces individual freedom. Men have to choose as to how far they wish to give up freedom for power in production—or, more accurately, for increased effective freedom as consumers, a higher standard of living, and wider choice in its composition.

Without carrying the analysis further, it should be clear that no intelligent discussion of economic problems, in terms of freedom and power, is possible without a clear understanding of the mechanical and functional relationships in the market economy as a whole, the activities or roles which mutually condition one another and under the given conditions determine all prices and so the terms of association. And a second and equally necessary step must be to know what these given conditions are and to understand the way in which they change in consequence of normal individual behavior under such conditions, before proceeding to consider how they can be changed by planned social action. Any statement made without these preliminary achievements is certain to reflect wish-thinking—either self-interest or romanticism—and if made the basis of action is certain to lead to disastrous results. Without this knowledge and understanding, reformers and agitators are simply "monkeying" with an infinitely intricate and delicate mechanism and the consequences are not in doubt.

The primary "romantic delusion" in the public mind is the belief that a few individuals exercise enormous power and reap vast "unearned" returns through the ownership and management of business enterprise. This notion is closely connected with the ideas about monopoly already considered. To dispel the error, the objective inquirer need only look into the statistics of the distribution of income, and of the mortality (bankruptcy) among business enterprises. He will not be able to find any monopoly gain, or "profit," properly defined. All the evidence, theoretical and factual, indicates that, in the aggregate, business losses at least equal or exceed the gains, allowing for the fair value of services furnished by their owners to production. In a free and progressive economy (with antisocial practices suppressed), it is in the nature of things that some ventures will be conspicuously successful while others will fail. It is also in the nature of things that success and failure will correspond in a general way with social service, reflecting better or worse foresight or competence—but only in a general way—and that the results will be largely affected and distorted by "luck," good or bad.

We cannot go into the conditions, the facts of nature and human nature, which make it necessary for large-scale productive units to exist and to operate under the orders of a centralized directive authority. It is fairly well recognized that both large-scale organization and centralized direction are, in fact, conditions necessary to efficiency in the world as it is. In theory, production might be organized under the form of "democracy," meaning representative government, or a town meeting, or even anarchy. (In theory, an army might also be so organized!) Under the legal order of liberalism, no artificial obstacle has prevented the participants in enterprise from organizing as democratically as they might like. Various types of "economic democracy"—or, more specifically, of producers' cooperation—have been repeatedly tried by their advocates under all sorts of conditions and have usually proved unable to survive. The specific reasons are not far to seek, but are not to be recounted here. In general, the enterprise has taken the form it actually assumes (typically that of the business corporation—which is partially democratic) for the reason that this is the form which has proved least unsatisfactory to the individuals immediately concerned, and to society as a whole. It does involve much concentration of nominal directive or managerial authority, and some really "arbitrary" power. But any candid appraisal must lead to the verdict that the same result is at least as characteristic of any representative institutions which human beings have been able to devise and operate. One need only compare business management with politics, in any unit from the town or city to the nation, to confirm the conclusion that, between the two, market competition is more effective in compelling those who nominally exercise power to act responsibly as the agents of those whose interests they are supposed to serve. Once more, the way to possible improvement in economic organization in its mechanical aspects lies through intelligent action to make competition more effective and not through replacing business with politics, as planners and reformers advocate.

This brings us to the chief valid and serious criticism to be made against the liberal economic order, one which has little to do with the free-market form of organization. The main real problem is economic power, correctly defined, as the ownership of productive capacity. A little reflection on familiar facts will show the fallacy of the idea that even ideal market competition necessarily or naturally implies ideal or good results in the human (social and ethical) sense. The truth is quite obviously to the contrary. Productive capacity, as we have pointed out, is itself a product. The conditions under which, and methods by which, individuals acquire economic power set limits to individual freedom, properly so-called, as an ideal in social relations and organized life; and further limits are set by the way in which they get their wants, also taken as given in the mechanical analysis of the market organization. The conclusion that perfect competition would involve both maximum freedom and maximum efficiency, and ideal "justice" as between given individuals, means only that the fruits of productive activity would be distributed on the basis of the economic power (productive capacity, labor power, and property) possessed at any time by each individual, measured by the economic demand of the other members of the community. This result will not be ethically ideal, or just, in the larger sense of distributive in contrast with commutative justice, unless the distribution of productive capacity itself is ethically ideal. Or the result would be practically ideal if this distribution were really and unalterably given, beyond improvement by social action.

But the first of these assumptions is untenable in terms of accepted modern ideals, and the second is false to the facts. The endowment of any individual with economic power at any time is the product, in part, of his own previous activity. But in larger part, and on the whole, predominantly, it is the product of the previous working of the whole economic institutional system in which the individual has lived. It is therefore predominantly due to factors beyond the individual's control, to the nature and operation of the institutional system itself, which is the primary object matter of social action. The amount of economic capacity in existence in any society at any time and its distribution among individuals depend on a mixture of biological and social inheritance, as well as the previous behavior of the living individuals. No one now thinks either that men are created equal or that endowment with power corresponds with desert or excellence of moral character. In a progressive society the inequitable tendencies of the factors named are further greatly affected by the factor of luck, meaning conditions affecting the consequences of individual action which they could not reasonably be expected to foresee. (Luck is by no means wholly evil, as it is prominent in play and all free activity, and necessary to make activity interesting.) For reasons which cannot be developed here, but which should be fairly obvious, uncertainty and unpredictability play a tremendous and increasing role in individualistic organization, as the scale and intricacy of organization increase, as the interests of men center more in progress or getting ahead, and also as a consequence of a rising scale of living, which takes economic provision further and further away from the more elementary wants, which are fairly stable and predictable.

But the most important fact for the problem of freedom, in its aspect of effective freedom or a just distribution of power, is an inherent tendency of individualistic accumulation to proceed differentially, hence for inequality to increase cumulatively. Those who have more productive capacity at any time are obviously in a better position to save and invest, in themselves (knowledge, training) or in external wealth, and so to accumulate personal or physical capital and to increase their differential advantage over others. The situation suggests the scriptural saying, "To him that hath shall be given." But the importance of this cumulative tendency to increasing inequality is multiplied by the fact that it does not cease to operate at the end of the active life of the individual, but goes on from generation to generation. This is because the family, and not the individual, is from the long-run standpoint the real social unit. For what we call "individualism," "familism" would be a much more descriptive name. In this long view, again, the cumulative tendency is further distorted, and within limits intensified, by the role of uncertainty, the speculative character which economic life inevitably assumes in a society at once free, individualistic, or familistic, and progressive—i.e., where the maintenance and increase of the whole culture inheritance (material and immaterial, resources and wants) are left to the free action of individuals who also enjoy freedom in family life, including the freedom (even the duty) to make provision for their children. It is this situation which gives rise to relatively permanent inequality, the so-called "class structure" of society, and at least a tendency to its accentuation, in the absence of preventive measures.

To change the situation radically would call, as a beginning, for substantial abolition of the family as an institution. The difficulty in the way of such action is not merely that the family as such is considered sacrosanct, or the improbability of finding any workable substitute. It lies even more in the fact that freedom in family life is one of the essential freedoms desired by individuals themselves, and that this freedom, as desired and held sacred, includes the right (and duty) of parents to provide for their children, economically and culturally. Thus there is a profound contradiction between family freedom, or the rights of the individuals of one generation, and the right of the individuals of the succeeding generation to an equal start in life. In other words, there is a contradiction at the heart of the notion of equality or justice between free individuals, in that it involves rights which are inherently incompatible in the world as it is. For the individual is biologically an ephemeral unit; he comes into the world a liability and becomes an individual in the effective sense through sharing, via the family or some equivalent institution, in a culture inheritance (material and immaterial, power, knowledge, and taste) which is the product of social accumulation through the ages.

Moreover, abolition of inheritance through the family of the material or property factor in the culture accumulation—assuming that even that could be accomplished without functionally destroying the family—would be only a relatively short step toward the goal of equal or equitable distribution of opportunity among all individuals at birth. Something can, of course, be done along this line; and a great deal has, in fact, been done by the more advanced societies through drastic taxation of property inheritance, and of large incomes from whatever source derived, and the use of the proceeds to provide nonmaterial culture ("education") to the children of the poor and for the material relief of the indigent. The practical difficulties—political, economic, and social—of greatly extending action in this direction are very great, even if the public understood the problem and attacked it intelligently.

But space does not admit of carrying the investigation further—i.e., beyond the threshold of the problem. We can only hope that enough has been said to indicate the nature of the problem itself. It centers in the combination of the necessity of maintaining and increasing the total cultural inheritance, in which the material and immaterial factors, power and appreciation, are inseparable, with the ideal, also within limits a necessity, of effecting a distribution, as equitable as can be achieved, of this cultural inheritance, in its inseparable factors, among the individuals of each new generation as they come to adult life. Ethical individualism can only be realized or approached under the really unalterable conditions of human life on the earth, by social-political action, directed to making individuals what they "ought" to be, in their equipment with means and in the ends for which they wish to use the means under their control. As a social program, this situation obviously calls for depriving the private family of a very large part of its traditional functions, beginning with the most important of all, education in a very inclusive sense, and especially moral education, and transferring these to "society." This problem is not merely that of transferring the functions of the family to political units or jurisdictions as they now exist, culminating in the sovereign territorial state. In terms of any defensible general ideals, precisely the same problem arises in the relations between states, or between persons across state lines. The ultimate ideal would doubtless envision world humanity as an ideal family, an all-inclusive "brotherhood of man." But beyond the questions as to what that means, and as to the possibilities, it is also clear that no sharp boundary can be drawn around "humanity" itself, either on the side of inclusion or exclusion.

Such changes can only be effected very gradually at best, and only in the light of vastly more knowledge, and through more devotion than anyone now possesses, to say nothing of the great mass of the electorate, by whose action any change must come, if it is to be free action. But the first requirement, not yet achieved or in sight, if freedom is to be increased and life ennobled, is the creation, presumably by general education, of a disposition to attack the problems "rationally," in terms (a) of the facts of the situation and the possibilities of action and (b) reasonable clarity and agreement on the ideals to be achieved. In other words, the first step is to counteract the romanticism in social thinking, indeed the proliferation of varied and mutually antagonistic romanticisms—the cry for action without serious examination of its consequences, which seems to be the humanly natural way of acting, especially in a social crisis.

Notes

1. The writer would have supposed it to be clear without more explicit statement than is given in the text that these paragraphs about the "Four Freedoms" are illustrative and are used for that reason, and in particular that they represent no criticism of this particular specimen of the "manifesto" type of political document. Such writing would never be heard of, unless to be ridiculed, if its use of language did not place popular appeal and emotive power ahead of analytic accuracy. Under less pressure of space limits, this point might have received more development, perhaps with the addition of other illustrations. This note is added in view of a criticism offered by a distinguished political scientist who read the lecture as it was going through the press. The critic construes this section as "a rather unjustifiable attack against President Roosevelt's four freedoms," attributes it to the writer's "tendency to abstraction" and his "unawareness" that similar matter has long been common in bills of rights. All this may be significant as a further illustration of the main theme of this chapter—the way in which language is used, and understood, in political discussion.

7

The Rights of Man and Natural Law

As a student of theoretical economics the writer constantly faces problems of "methodology," of the concepts and presuppositions involved in generalized description and interpretation of social phenomena, where motivation of behavior cannot be ignored. This discipline also stands in a peculiarly close connection with the problems of social action—i.e., of the procedure by which a human group acts as a unit—and the meaning of group objectives. All these are essentially philosophical rather than scientific problems, in the sense of ordinary usage, in which there is a contrast between the two. In this situation it is natural to seek help from specialists in philosophy, a discipline supposedly concerned with these issues, which was age-old when any of the social sciences now recognized began to be cultivated. But the results of this quest are disappointing. The philosophers typically seem ignorant of and indifferent to facts which are essential to any understanding of the problems. What they have to say is so remotely relevant to the issues that it is often fairly to be characterized as empty verbiage or sheer absurdity. The book which gives its title to this article[1] is such an excellent illustration of this situation, such a "good bad example," as to justify reviewing, and quoting, at a length disproportionate to its own, and using it as a basis for an attempt to sketch a serious discussion of the vitally important issues with which it purports to deal.

The author calls his book (in the first sentence) "an essay in political philosophy," and that, rather than a "review," is the intent of this paper. In context it is largely an abridged and in a sense popularized version of

Reprinted with permission from *Ethics* 54 (January 1944): 124–45.

doctrine presented in earlier works, perhaps especially *Freedom in the Modern World* (New York: Scribner's, 1936), with elimination of the more explicit argument for Thomism and Roman Catholic apologetics. It impresses the reviewer as being not too carefully done; the English is much inferior; and, while the translation in this case contains absurd renderings of the French idiom,[2] the French text itself is strangely lacking in the clarity and aesthetic qualities typical of the better literary work in that language. However, the translator's main fault is the usual one of excessive literalness, of crudity rather than of changing the author's meaning. There are two chapters, entitled, respectively, "A Society of Human Persons" (pp. 1–49) and "The Rights of the Person" (pp. 50–114), and a four-page appendix giving the "International Declaration of the Rights of Man" put out by the Institute of International Law at a session at New York in 1929. Each chapter is divided into a number of sections (respectively, 11 and 9), which have titles but no numbers. The author does not follow his subtitles at all closely, and at least three-fourths of the book logically belongs in the first chapter. The early sections of chapter 2 expound the doctrine of natural law, and later ones take up named "rights," concluding with a resume. Only in a general way will this review follow the author's order; our summary and comment will be organized around a few main issues. The main points which call for critical notice are the author's reasoning, his use of history, and his social-ethical position.

1. Logical Method

We may begin *in medias res* with an example of the reasoning, taken from chapter 2, and from a section entitled "Natural Law":

> Since I have not space here to discuss nonsense (you can always find very intelligent philosophers to defend it most brilliantly) I am taking it for granted that you admit that there is a human nature, and that this human nature is the same in all men. [p. 60]

The reviewer would merely change the last part of this sentence so as to make the proposition "human nature is the same in all men" the example of the nonsense which is defended by "philosophers." Critical discussion must begin with the word "nonsense," because of its wide ambiguity and of the need to use it freely in discussing the book itself— the author having set the example. The term does not usually refer to mere collections of words without grammatical sense but rather to statements which convey a meaning which is viewed as "absurd." Here again, however, caution must be exercised. A proposition which in its literal meaning is absurd may still be significant and important. It may even express a meaning more effectively than one which is objectively scientific, and it may at the same time have other important values, such as humor or poetic beauty. M. Maritain's book will hardly suggest these qualities; and it is more pertinent to observe that a statement which is nonsensical, in nearly any meaning of the word, may be intelligently made and published, if the intent of the author is to arouse some emotion or to conduct propaganda to promote some cause or line of action, whether good or bad.

Various minor types of nonsense might be illustrated from the book before us. For example, the statement (p. 11) that "an unjust law is not a law," taken literally is a bald self-contradiction. But if it means that an unjust law is not a just law, it is nonsense in the meaning of verbal truism. What the author presumably does mean is that an unjust law carries no moral obligation to obedience. In this interpretation it begs one of the most important questions at issue. In the Christian tradition, for which our author explicitly speaks, both Plato and Jesus—undoubtedly high authorities—are on record in opposition to the view stated (cf. *Crito*, 50; Matthew 23:2–3; 5:17–18). Again, the book recognizes the distinction between natural law and positive law, and it is a truism that a law in one meaning of the word may not be a law in another meaning. However, the main use of the word "nonsense" in describing this book will be to characterize statements which are so ambiguous that they mean nothing in particular, being true in numerous interpretations and false in quite as many.

The statement "human nature is the same in all men" is, of course, true, to the extent that the word "man" is meaningful as a class name; and, in fact, its members are usually (though by no means always) distinguished without difficulty. In the same sense all living beings, including men, are alike, and all objects. But it is just as true, and as trivial, to say that men are all different—like the members of most important classes. Men (and the members of most other classes) are both alike and different in respects innumerable and impossible to list. A biological species is rarely distinguished from all others by any single differentia, and a biologist of standing is authority for the statement that no valid general distinction can be drawn between life and combustion; and this writer is not in a position to prove him wrong by stating the distinction. One of the most important attributes of man as a species is the extraordinary range of difference between different individuals as to personality and culture. It is these differences which both make men peculiarly interesting and give rise to the major problems of describing men, and also to the practical problems which men themselves face in their effort to live together satisfactorily in the "societies," also of boundless variety, in which they do and must live. The statement that all men are alike is not at all helpful in dealing with any of these problems. Furthermore, the innumerable differences which distinguish any class from others are largely a matter of degree in the possession of traits which in the qualitative sense are common to the classes and with respect to which the members of the same class also differ in degree. Consequently, classification is a matter of quantitative estimation, since measurement is usually impossible, and is a matter of judgment.

Finally, characterization of any biological class must both take account of the whole life-history of a "normal" individual and have special reference to the "normal" adult; and normality cannot be accurately defined. The last point is especially important in connection with the characteristic traits of "man." A careful expositor would hesitate to say without qualification that any particular individual is "the same" at any two moments of his life. And the infallible Roman church has had difficulty in formulating indicia to show at what moment in the biological life of a "human being" he actually becomes (potentially) a "human being." In short, it is about equally true, or illuminating, to say that all men are alike and to say that all are different; and there is a sense in which they have nothing in common. (We cannot take the space and impose upon the reader's patience to comment in detail on the idea that "intelligence," undefined and without recognition of differences in kind or degree, is "the" differentia of man as a species, the unique trait of that "human nature" which is always and everywhere the same.)

Real issues arise when we inquire into the significant differentiae of human beings, those relevant to questions beyond the relatively academic matter of classification. Immediately following the sentence first quoted, our author tells his readers that

> man is a being gifted with intelligence, and who, as such, acts with an understanding of what he is doing, and therefore with the power to determine the ends which he pursues [and] being constituted in a given, determinate fashion, man obviously possesses ends which correspond to his natural constitution, and which are the same for all, as all pianos for instance, . . . have as their end the production of certain attuned sounds. *If they don't produce these sounds they must be tuned, or discarded as worthless.*

[Italics here added by reviewer.] But since man is endowed with intelligence and determines his own ends, it is up to him to put himself in tune with the ends necessarily demanded by his nature. This means that there is, by very virtue of human nature, _an order or a disposition which human reason can discover and according to which the human will must act in order to attune itself to the necessary ends of the human being. The unwritten law, or natural law, is nothing more than that._ [Italics here in original; double emphasis by the reviewer; explanation hardly necessary.]

It should "leap to the eyes" of any reader of a philosophical journal that the argument is a tissue of self-contradiction. The simile of the pianos tells us that the end of all men is to serve as an instrument for a specific use by some purposive subject outside of man himself (under penalty of being "discarded"). Whether true or false, this is the antithesis of determining for himself the ends which he pursues. Further, our author ignores the fundamental facts of the relation between desires and moral ends, as well as differences of opinion about ends. Apart from differences it is probably impossible to think of anyone's having any opinion at all. In one view such differences are the root of all social and moral problems (since conflicts of mere desires cannot be discussed). In another view it is the similarity of men as to ends (desires, needs, or values) which generates conflict, by leading different individuals to seek the same things which they cannot all have; and our author's reasoning also ignores this aspect of social problems.

Also interesting for its reasoning is what the author goes on to say about our knowledge of the natural law. We are told that "the only practical knowledge all men have naturally and infallibly in common is that we must do good and avoid evil." But "this is the preamble and the principle of natural law . . . not the law itself. Natural law is the ensemble of things to do and not to do which follow therefrom in _necessary_ fashion, and _from the simple fact that man is man,_ nothing else being taken into account" (pp. 62–63). Yet "men know it . . . in different degrees, running the risk of error here as well as elsewhere"; "every sort of error and deviation is possible . . ." and our knowledge of natural law is classed with that of arithmetic and astronomy (p. 63). The later discussion of particular rights gives no example of necessary deduction from the simple fact that man is man, but only vague assertions that different rights belong in different degrees to natural law and positive law. In fact, the Encyclopedists are denounced for their rationalistic view of natural law as "no longer an offspring of creative wisdom but a revelation of reason unto itself" and for transforming natural law into "code of absolute and universal justice inscribed in nature and deciphered by reason as an ensemble of geometric theorems or speculative data. . . ." (pp. 80–81). The "logic" by which the validity of positive law and the substance of particular rights are deduced from natural law is that the duty of man to fulfill his destiny implies the right to do so, and to "the things necessary for this purpose" (p. 65).

II. Natural Law in History

A striking feature of our author's technique is his practice of repeatedly laying claim, without argument, to the natural law and human rights and everything good in European civilization or all history as due to and originating in the teaching of the Gospels, or the church, or of "classical" writers which was taken over by the church and somehow reconciled with its theology. As an early example, we read,

> All alike, Catholics and non-Catholics, Christians and non-Christians . . . recognize, each in his own way, the human values of which the Gospel has made us aware, the dignity and rights of the person, the character of moral obligation inherent in authority, the law of brotherly love, and the sanctity of natural law . . . [p. 24]

And again,

> It was first in the religious order, and through the sudden pouring forth of the evangelical message, that this transcendent dignity of the human person was made manifest. [p. 73]

(For other similar expressions see pp. 11, 46, 61, 68, 74, 80 81, etc.) This is historically indefensible; natural law as custom is recognized in all human society, while modern ethical individualism is a product of a recent movement away from the religious view of life; and, as we shall see, the author practically admits the fact (cf. here the statement with respect to the views on slavery of the great thinkers of antiquity and the medieval theologians, p. 105).

In place of direct comment on the historical assertions sprinkled through the book, it seems better to survey the main facts. The expressions "natural law," "natural rights," and "rights of man" are familiar to every student of politics or ethics. Phrases equivalent to the first have been bandied about since the earliest beginnings of the European intellectual tradition among the Greeks. (Outside this tradition the concept seems hardly to be met with.) The appeal to "nature" has always been a slogan, or *Kampfwort*; it has been used to beg the question in favor of any position which a particular writer or school happened to wish to defend or promote—or against any one singled out for condemnation. The "state of nature" has been a symbol either for idyllic social life or for all that is horrible. The political state and positive law have been either primary dictates of the (benevolent) law of nature or man's punishment for sin. The form of the state ordained by nature has been everything from absolutism to pure democracy or antinomian anarchy. All men are "naturally" equal, and free, or naturally unequal, making slavery and social castes and rule by absolute authority a feature of the naturally right social and political order. Natural law has served as a defense for any existing order against any change and as an argument for change in any direction. Prior to the eighteenth century, natural law was chiefly a support for order and authority; since then, "natural rights" have played the opposite role, as the appeal of the individual against government. Finally, the "nature" from which laws or rights are derived has borne every possible relation to "God" or the gods.

While the central idea goes back to the early Greek (pre-Socratic) distinction between what is right by nature and by convention, the first general use of the expression "natural law" *(nomos physikos)* was that of the Stoics. These writers talked in general terms about reasonable ideals of conduct and of social relations on which they thought "reasonable" men would agree. But the Stoics were philosophers and held an essentially quietistic ethical world view. They addressed themselves primarily to philosophers, meaning Stoic philosophers, as their conception of reasonable men. They assumed that such men's interests are centered in the contemplative life, leaving them indifferent to such crass material considerations as practical politics and economics, even to physical pleasure and pain. They were also indifferent to beauty and to "knowledge," other than abstractions evolved out of the inner consciousness. Their ideal, if followed to its logical conclusion (which was sometimes done), means indifference to life and death, or is perhaps equivalent to "Nirvana." The Stoic social ideal is thus anarchy, in the philosophical meaning of the rule of reason, while their "relative" natural law accepted existing institutions. The classical source of the rule-of-reason ideal, for the individual and for society, is Plato. But, in sharp contrast with the Stoic theory of universal human equality and freedom (in an abstract spiritual sense), Plato's ideal society assumed that few men are even potentially philosophers and set up a hierarchical class system, with the philosophers as rulers. Aristotle largely followed Plato, specifically in defending slavery and Greek political hegemony on the ground of natural human inequality.

The teachings of Christianity are especially in point here. The original position was similar in the abstract to Stoicism, but with the inner life of freedom and equality interpreted in emotional or religious, in contrast with intellectual, terms, leading again to a social ideal of anarchy; righteousness, based on love, took the place of wisdom, as the controlling principle or law. But the "historical" Christian position was in practice analogous to Platonism rather than to Stoicism, though it confused love and knowledge. Only a few people are capable of supreme righteous love—or of apprehending the divine reason—and these should be the rulers of society. In fact, the righteous were soon divided into two groups, the religious orders and the church bureaucracy, the latter holding all power, the former theoretically segregated from the sinful world with its power relations and practical problems, for a role of vicarious atonement. This might well have happened under Platonism, if a serious effort had ever been made to bring its doctrine into any practical relation with reality, prior to its absorption in Christianity. The organized church became an authoritarian hierarchy indorsing slavery and a caste system of society, in line with the historical background of Christianity in Old Testament theocracy. But the Old Testament contains little or no trace of natural law; its law is positive and revealed, down to concrete sanitary regulations and military dispositions. Of course, modern research finds the laws given by Yahweh to Moses largely identical with those given by Shamash to Hammurabi centuries before and with those of the Canaanites and Israel's other enemies, who deserved death for their immorality and worship of false gods. The laws are crude, often barbarous, by modern standards (e.g., "Thou shalt not suffer a witch to live," Exod. 22:18). In the New Testament there are a few suggestions of a moral law in the "hearts" of men; Rom. 2:14–15 is an example often cited, and the word "conscience" occurs a few times in a nontheological reference.

Medieval Christian thought vacillated on the question as to how far natural law could be discerned by the reason, or conscience, of "fallen" man, how far he is dependent upon revelation, meaning the Bible. But, in sharp contrast with Judaism, the revealed word had to be "interpreted" by the divinely inspired church and was subject to amendment by law and fiat of the latter as God's spokesman on earth. In any case the law of nature became the law of God, meaning in practice the law, or will, of the church, and this is still the Catholic position (since there is no real limit to matters of "faith and morals"). For the church, the end—beginning, of course, with maintenance of its own authority and prestige—has always justified any means; it was not bound by any law, and resistance or disagreement was blasphemy or heresy and called for suppression by torture or execution. Human reason was out of it, except possibly in some sense for the supreme authorities in the church and as prescribing agreement by others. The writers are not clear how far the church itself follows reason or revelation, or even love. As to the divine source of law, the doctors also disagree as to whether it comes from God's own reason, a reason prior to and above God, or God's arbitrary fiat.

While it would be out of place here to follow the history in detail, it should be noted that in the post-Renascence epoch, particularly in the seventeenth century, the idea of a natural or moral law (now practically separated from theism, as in the case of the Stoics) played an important constructive role in the development of an international law governing the relations between the new sovereign and absolute states. By the next revolutionary period, the eighteenth century—the Age of Reason, or the Enlightenment—the ideal had become thoroughly individualized as well as secularized. The function of natural law was now inverted (as we have seen); it was used to beg the question for what is called either liberalism or bourgeois class morality, according to taste or prejudice. It was now the "nature" of man (whether "created" or not) to be "free and equal," free from the shackles of custom and authority, in his economic, political, and religious and social life, free for the pursuit of happiness—and, it should be added, for actively promoting "progress," material, intellectual, and spiritual.

In its mundane working content, the law of nature has always been primarily commercial, centering in exchange in the market and specifically in contract. Scholars reasonably guess that the first working form, the Roman *ius gentium* (later fused with the Stoic idea of *ius naturale*), actually grew out of a "law merchant" or commercial law independent of governments which was prevalent in the Mediterranean region when the Roman dominion was established. Thus the content has been "natural" in the crude utilitarian sense of a set of rules necessary for orderly economic relations between individuals, or other units, possessing a considerable degree of freedom, and associating on the basis of mutual agreement or consent. In a large historical view, such a pattern of relationships is not "natural" at all, in any meaningful interpretation of the word. Only in a relatively advanced state of civilization—and a civilization of a particular type (historically the type called "commercial")—do people in considerable numbers act or think in such terms. And still more novel and artificial are modern natural rights, extended to include the various "freedoms" and claims of the individual at the hands of government, which are recognized in the legal systems of liberal society, or demanded through legal action.

III. Political Philosophy

An attempt to discuss our author's political philosophy encounters great difficulty in discovering any particular position that he holds to the exclusion of numerous other and conflicting positions. Roughly speaking, there are two ways of using language which has an apparent reference to morals and politics but which ends up by saying nothing or shedding no light on any question which might possibly be at issue. One way is to make statements so abstract that they can be interpreted as taking any side of any question, i.e., statements which amount to saying that their author stands for truth and high ideals and wishes other people to do likewise. This may not unfairly be characterized as the method of "preaching," in contrast both with objective argument and with propaganda, in which the speaker has something to "sell." The other method is to make strong categorical statements on both sides of issues, without recognizing the conflict and the inconsistency. In political discussion this is familiar as the principle of eating one's cake and having it or producing omelets without breaking eggs. The methods overlap; and those who use either may be serious and honest but naive, or they may really be engaging in propaganda, or their naivete may cover any combination of these. Our author's motives are beyond question, but the obvious fact is that he combines platitude with evasion and self-contradiction. And an obvious strain of propaganda also runs through his book, as well as preaching. This he probably would not entirely deny; perhaps there has to be some of both in any writing addressed to a public broader than a small group of specialists and dealing with this type of subject matter rather than with the most objective facts.

The mode of effecting this combination, in the book under review, is to deal only with abstract issues and in highly abstract and ambiguous terms, and to remain blind to the contradictions which are involved in advocating any simple abstract principles of conduct. The subjects dealt with, by sweeping pronouncements, are primarily freedom, law—moral

and positive—authority, and institutions, particularly the political institution of the state, and "the" religious institution of "the church." The
"position" of the author is to come out strongly in favor of all of them,
while avoiding such definition of any as would convey a suggestion of
the essential fact, which is universal conflict of interests and "rational"
ideals and of principles, with all real issues arising out of this conflict.
Thus the essential character of the book is that of a political platform
advocating a moral and social order in which there would be no such
conflicts, or, in other words, a world and a human race utterly different
from those of reality and which, indeed, are hardly in any concrete
meaning philosophically imaginable.[3]

For a serious analysis of the real problems, the essential concepts and
the relations between them might be brought out by a series of questions
putting them in a serial order. Beginning with the ideal of freedom—
with peace and order—the first question would be why there must be
a moral law felt as constraint, hence a restriction of freedom in the most
literal interpretation, and reflecting a cleavage in the will at the core of
"human nature." Next would be the question of why there must be a
positive law to supplement the moral law; and the third, why there must
be authority or authorities. The essential meaning of positive law is a set
of rules "sanctioned" or enforced on the individual by some agent outside himself, some human individual or group or some supposed supernatural power, or the former as an agent of the latter. The distinctive
attribute of such an enforcing agent is authority; but, in addition to enforcing law, authority always has in varying degree the attribute or function of issuing commands, by "fiat," outside the text of any established
and recognized set or code of rules. These are only the most general
analytical questions, leading up to the concrete issues which have to be
decided in social life.

It is not too much to say that all real moral problems, all that are
discussable, arise out of inherent overlapping and conflict among these
different principles. (As already observed, mere interests cannot give rise
to problems, to be settled by discussion, in contrast with force.) Men, as
we know them, inevitably have some freedom (as do all animals, as far
as they are conscious and intelligent). But this is inevitably limited, especially their effective freedom, which requires power, since power is
limited. But (normal) men, as we know them, both crave more freedom
and power than they have and also demand both as a "right," specifically at the expense of other men, as individuals or organized in the

various social groups in which men have to live and want to live. (This demand is probably peculiar to men.) All rights, in the abstract, are rights to freedom and power, for some use; they are conceivable only in relation to other men and as generated by a combination of harmonious and conflicting interests. A "Crusoe," living in isolation, can hardly be thought of as having either rights or obligations or freedom in an ethical meaning, unless these are rooted in a relation to some supernatural being. Finally, all human groups are more or less institutional. Institutions are partly brute historical data, partly defined and enforced by law, including definitions of the rights and duties of agents—of rulers or the group itself or superhuman powers—who enforce law and, within some limits, make law and issue *ad hoc* commands.

The pertinence of these observations here is that the book under review (and the author's other writings, as far as known to the reviewer) contains no recognition of the nature of the social context of harmony and conflict out of which problems arise, or, *ipso facto,* of the nature of the problems themselves, or how they are, or should be, dealt with. To begin with, as would be expected, there is much talk throughout the book about freedom, the dignity of man or of the person, etc. The expression "freedom of expansion and autonomy" recurs with minor verbal variation (pp. 9, 34, 44), and slavery and bondage are condemned (pp. 45, 47, 68, 105). Much of this is quite laudable—from the standpoint of a liberal, i.e., one who accepts freedom as the fundamental social ideal; more accurately, it would be laudable if it could be taken out of its context.

There are three difficulties in the way of taking seriously these noble expressions about freedom and the dignity of man. First, in general, they are platitudinous in the abstract and ambiguous and contradictory in the concrete. The Christian view of freedom was never found inconsistent with slavery until after it was already abolished in any jurisdiction, and, in the writer's opinion, it is not inconsistent. On the other hand, the ideal does not now tell us who ought to have more freedom— practically meaning power—or how the increase is to be arranged. In the second place, the expressions themselves include equal praise of authority and the virtue of obedience. For example: "The common good is the foundation of authority [which] requires that individuals be charged with . . . guidance and that the directions which they determine, the decisions which they make . . . be followed or obeyed by the other members of the community" (pp. 9–10; cf. also pp. 24, cited above, and 56; and elsewhere). It is noteworthy that the authority to be obeyed is explicitly that of individuals, not of law. True, the author goes on, characteristically, to assert that it is aimed at the good of the whole, not the particular good of those who exercise it. Elsewhere (p. 21) we are told that God is its prime source. There is here no more recognition of the need for some mechanism to hold authorities responsible to the governed, in order to prevent abuses, than there is of the inherent moral value of free government, even at some cost in good government. We are not told anything about the relations between authority, positive law, and the state. It is true that in the latter part of the book we find sweeping assertions about the rights of the individual and the state, about universal suffrage and the people's right to choose their political constitution (pp. 85–87).

Reserving these ostensibly more concrete expressions for later comment, we must consider at this point a third difficulty in the way of interpreting the author's position on freedom. At least as important as his insistence upon authority is his reiterated reference to the superiority of the church over the state. His references to "the church," or explicitly to the Catholic church, leave little doubt as to the ultimate locus of authority and shed much light on its character and scope. A section on "Four Characteristics of a Society of Free Men" (pp. 20–22) lists these as "personalist," "communal," "pluralist," and "theist or Christian"; and this is followed by a section entitled "A Vitally Christian Society" (pp. 23–29). In these pages we are told that "the world has done with neutrality," that "states will be obliged to make a choice for or against the Gospel," and that "the Catholic Church insists upon the principle that truth must have precedence over error and that the true religion, when it is known, should be aided in its spiritual mission in preference to religions whose message is more or less faltering and in which error is mingled with truth" (pp. 23, 25–26). Also, the society of free men, as theist or Christian,

> recognizes that in the reality of things, God, principle and end of the human person . . . is . . . the prime source of political society and authority among men; and that the currents . . . sanctioned by it, the feeling of responsibility before God required by it, . . . are the internal energy which civilization needs to achieve its fulfillment [pp. 21–22].[4]

To be sure, we could as usual cite numerous passages which seem to contradict much of the above. The society in question is not theist or Christian, "in the sense that it would require every member of society to believe in God and be a Christian" (p. 21). And one must "distinguish the Apocryphal from the authentic, a clerical or decoratively Christian state from a vitally and truly Christian political society" (p. 23). And earlier (p. 19), in discussing the need for "more limited groups or fellow-ships" within civil society, it is said that "these the person enters of his own free choice . . ." (cf. also p. 22). In the latter part of the book the discussion of rights—particularly the section on "The Rights of the Human Person"—indorses intellectual, moral, and religious freedom as absolute rights of the individual, but explicitly only against the state (pp. 75–77), and even here there is an interesting reservation:

> If this religious path goes so very far afield that it leads to acts repugnant to natural law and the security of the State, the latter has the right to interdict and apply sanctions against these acts. This does not mean that it has authority in the realm of conscience. [p. 82 n.]

The reader is left to draw his own conclusion as to who is to judge when such action is necessary and to determine its character, especially whether it is to be the state or the "higher kingdom" to which such frequent reference is made.

If one carefully balances all the author's confused and conflicting statements about freedom, law, and authority, and about the rights of the individual, of the state, and of the church, it seems fair to conclude that the only social order which meets his specifications is an ecclesiastical authoritarian state. This would not be the theocracy of the Old Testament, in which there was at least a law which no one claimed the right to change or set aside; it would be the Roman Catholic church according to its own claims, substantially realized over much of Europe in the thirteenth century. For the content as of today, particularly the internal government of the church and the "freedom" implied, one who does not have the documents in mind may look up the decrees of the Council of Trent, the Syllabus of Errors of 1864, and the Acts of the Vatican Council of 1870. A careful and repeated reading of the book as a whole suggests nothing so much as the Marxian idea of an educational dictatorship, but with the church in the role of the party. However, the state would not "wither away," giving place to an anarchist utopia, but would be preserved as an administrative organ of the church (as in the ideal of the Middle Ages) in a social order in which authority and obedience would be the moral cornerstone.

This conclusion is in no way modified by the author's repeated condemnation of totalitarianism, with explicit reference to communism and fascism or National Socialism. Of course, he does not recognize and probably does not believe that his own system is totalitarian. Mortal enmity of any group with such aspirations toward other groups differing in ideology or even merely in personnel is to be taken for granted. (But this antagonism may be the means of preserving freedom.) The similarity between the platforms of Roman Catholicism and communism has often been pointed out. But an ecclesiastical authoritarianism is hardly to be preferred to other species of the genus; rather, its very claims to superhuman wisdom and virtue are likely to make it more arbitrary and ruthless than other forms, and this inference could be abundantly documented from the history of western Europe.[5]

The interpretation suggested is more or less confirmed by the social nature and function of religion in general, and in particular by the history of Christianity. The function of religion has been to sanction established morality, law, and authority, not reform, at least in any constructive or progressive sense. Apart from the naive "brotherhood" ideal, embodied in "anarchist" propaganda, in a "social gospel," or in fraternities, some exception would be called for only in the case of theocracies in which the church has become essentially a state, with political and other mundane functions pushing religion into the background. The essence of the original Christian social teaching was literal acceptance of established political forms and obedience to established authority. This is a recurrent note in the New Testament. In the Middle Ages, of course, the church became a theocracy and played the game of political and economic power in the manner to be expected from an organization with absolute authority, direct from God, over this life and the next. Now that historical changes, which both "the church" and the churches set up by the "Reformation" opposed as long and as vigorously as they were able, have established "freedom," in place of obedience to authority, as an unquestioned ideal, spokesmen for religion are quite naturally in favor of that—or at least render lip service to it.[6]

We should observe, again, that the common notion of active freedom is also ambiguous. It confuses freedom in the literal meaning of absence of unnecessary or arbitrary coercion or restraint with possession of power or the necessary means to do what one wants to do. And a thoroughgoing analysis must further consider the possibility that the individual may not want to be free, because "conditioned" to obedience as an ideal. The will to freedom is adequately recognized in the book we are discussing. It also formally recognizes the individual's right to economic means, in a sense far beyond the original Christian ideal of charity and even beyond the traditional defense of property by the

Roman Catholic church. Most of this is in the latter part of the book, in connection with economic rights, and will receive comment later. In chapter 1, we also find a section dealing with "Progress," an ideal inseparable from freedom in liberal thinking. It is notable for expressions which a liberal can commend, if he gives them a liberal interpretation, to which they are more or less susceptible. While there is no specific definition of progress, the political task is summed up as "essentially a task of civilization and culture" (p. 44); and it is even admitted that the political task of meeting the "aspiration of the person . . . towards liberty of expansion and autonomy" is conditioned upon material progress in techniques and organization, and "supposes [presupposes] societies all the more strongly equipped and defended because they seek to be just" (p. 46). A liberal is inclined to ask, first, what else the common task could be and, second, when or where Christianity showed an interest in progress, other than progress backward to the Garden of Eden, with no problems to solve and only one negative duty—to remain ignorant of good and evil—and a life of bliss without effort. Moreover, the study of history raises doubts as to whether any authoritarian organization, or especially one of the ecclesiastical type, ever acts to promote cultural progress except for the benefit of a small elite, or material progress except for similar ends or as a basis of military power to be used for predatory action. Of course, it may be the alternative to chaos and make for cultural progress in the long run.

Finally, our interpretation of the author's position as some type of authoritarianism is confirmed by his repeated derogatory comments on democracy as it is, in the modern world.[7] This is referred to by such designations as

> the old disguised anarchic conception of bourgeois materialism, according to which the entire duty of society consists in seeing that the freedom of each one be respected, thereby enabling the strong freely to oppress the weak. [p. 8]

The antithesis of this description, specifically the last clause, to the entire aim and practice of modern democratic government needs no comment. Again we are told:

> In the bourgeois-individualist type of society there is no common work to do, nor is there any form of communion. Each one asks only that the State protect his individual freedom of profit against the possible encroachments of other men's freedoms. [p. 39]

It is obvious that what is really lacking in democratic society is a common task or form of communion of the type approved by the author, *imposed by authority from above*. It seems that what is objected to is the freedom allowed to the people to find these forms and tasks, or to interpret the common good for themselves—as well as to have ends and enjoyments of their own, under a system of law designed by themselves to protect this freedom, to limit it where clearly necessary, and to facilitate and implement free association.[8]

IV. Natural Law and Natural Rights

We must run very briefly over the early sections of chapter 2 and hasten on to the treatment of more specific rights. The first two sections deal with generalities of the same sort as found in chapter 1, including the discussion of Aristotle's regimes, just cited, and further disparagement of democracy as "the old bourgeois individualism" (p. 55). The citations given early in the review to illustrate the author's logic are taken from the second section, on "Natural Law." In the next section, on "Natural Law and Human Rights," we are told that "the same natural law which lays down our most fundamental duties, and by virtue of which every law is binding, . . . assigns to us our fundamental rights" (p. 66). This is defensible in the abstract, in terms of modern ethical theory, but it is contrary to history (as we have pointed out), and it is not illuminating to quote or paraphrase alternately Thomas Aquinas and Thomas Paine. These sections contain many general assertions about human rights which are highly commendable, or rather commonplace, from the standpoint of liberal social philosophy, as long as they are viewed in the abstract and effectively isolated from the conflicts and problems to which they give rise in the real world. These rights formally recognized include the right to life; to keep one's body whole; to the pursuit of happiness and moral perfection; to intellectual, moral, and religious freedom; to marriage and family life; and to the ownership of material goods. (Interspersed are numerous derogations of democracy, some already cited, and statements in praise of authority and asserting the superiority of the church over the state.)

The section on "The Rights of the Civic Person" (pp. 83–91), in particular, contains (with other matter) a fairly good statement of modern liberal-democratic political principles. Universal suffrage for every adult human person, is "one of those rights which a community of free men can never give up" (p. 85), though it is not explicitly derived from natural law. It implies the right to affiliate with, or to form, political parties, though not in the totalitarian meaning and without the abuses and vices which have caused the degeneration of the European democracies. The qualifications are left at the plane of pious wishing—or to the care of the supratemporal society superior to the state. In the next section, the author refers to the natural right of association, sanctioned by positive law (p. 96; cf. also pp. 19 and 90). Again,

> The right of the people to take unto itself the constitution and the form of government of its choice is the first and most fundamental of political rights . . . subject only to the requirements of justice and natural law. [p. 87]

Other rights of the civic person are

> summed up by the three equalities: political equality . . . equality of all before the law . . . equal admission of all citizens to public employment according to their capacity, and free access of all to the various professions without racial or political discrimination. [p. 88.]

Earlier (pp. 72–73 and note) President Roosevelt's Four Freedoms are approved as yearnings "to be fulfilled by positive law and by an economic and political organization of the civilized world."

> What we know as freedom of speech and expression . . . better designated [as] freedom of investigation and discussion . . . is a fundamental natural right, for man's very nature is to seek the truth. [But] freedom to spread ideas, . . . like freedom of association, is subject to the regulations of positive law. For the political community has the right to resist the propagation of lies or calumnies [and] activities which have as their aim the corruption of morals [or] the destruction of the State and of the foundations of common life. [pp. 89–90]

However, "censorship and police methods are in my opinion the worst way—at least in peacetime—to insure this repression"; among "many better ways," the only one named is the "spontaneous pressure of common conscience and public opinion . . ." (p. 90). In conclusion, we are told that this problem

> can be properly solved only by a recasting of society on an organic or pluralist basis . . . a regime no longer based on the self-propagating power of money . . . but on the human value and aim of work where the class struggle introduced by capitalist economy will have been surmounted along with this economy itself. [p. 90]

This last statement explicitly serves as a transition to the last and longest section, dealing with "The Rights of the Working Person," viewed as the locus of the most urgent problems of the social person in various functional relations. Half the space is again devoted to the same type of moral and political generalities that fill the early part of the book. One of the most remarkable passages in the entire work is the second sentence of the second paragraph of this section:

> The principal phenomenon in this point of view, which emerged in the nineteenth century, is the *consciousness of self (prise de conscience),* achieved by the working person and the working community.

We have previously alluded to this. What is remarkable is, of course, the admission that recognition of those who do the ordinary work of the world as human beings with essentially equal rights "emerged in the nineteenth century" and, by omission of the author's usual contrary claim, the admission that this revolutionary moral advance was not due to the teaching of the Gospels or connected with Christianity. Of course, the doctrine "emerged" somewhat earlier, in the rationalistic age of the Enlightenment; but it became generally recognized in the nineteenth century.

Early in this section, the author warns against two "temptations." The first, "which arises from old Socialist concepts, is that of granting primacy to economic technique, and by the same token of tending to entrust everything to the power of the state." This "leads in the direction of a totalitarianism . . ." and is to be avoided through replacing the idea of planned economy with a new idea of "adjusted economy," and the idea of "collectivization" with that of "associative ownership of the means of production" (pp. 97–98). The second temptation, "which comes from old concepts formerly in favor in certain Christian circles is . . . paternalism" (p. 99). Still another is "corporatism," moving toward state corporatism; but "the notion of 'corporation' or rather of vocational body, as presented by Pope Pius XI," in the encyclical, *Quadragesimo anno,* of 1931, is of course "completely free from these connotations" (p. 100); but no difference is pointed out. The "essential thing" is that reorganization of economy on a structural and cooperative principle must establish itself

> from below upwards according to the principles of personalist democracy, with the suffrage and active personal participation of all the interested parties at the bottom, and as emanating from them and their free unions and associations. [p. 100]

Beyond the advocacy of a radical economic reorganization in accord with vague idealistic principles, admirable enough in the abstract, it seems impossible to make out what the author has in mind. We are told that, "aside from certain areas of altogether general interest, whose transformation into public services is to be expected," the proposal is "an associative system substituting, as far as possible, joint ownership for the wage system, that . . . ought to take the place of the capitalist regime" (p. 98). However, we have previously been told that the rights of labor include "first of all . . . a just wage, for man's work is not a piece of merchandise subject to the mere law of supply and demand; the wage which it yields must enable the worker and his family to have a suffi- ciently human standard of living, in relation to the normal conditions of a given society," whatever that may mean (p. 94). It is hardly needful to point out that these statements are a tissue of contradiction. A wage is the price of a service, regardless of pronouncements by idealists or by the United States Congress in solemn (or cynical) convention; and, if it is not to correspond with the economic value of the service to the pur- chaser and beyond him to the ultimate consumer (the meaning of the law of supply and demand), some other word should be used. Moreover, we are given no light on the question of economic organization, how resources would be allocated, or how even the product of the single enterprise would be shared among the participants, when joint owner- ship has replaced the wage system.

It is probably useless to point out that "supply and demand" is the only possible way of apportioning men and other productive agents to their tasks, between different enterprises or within any enterprise, in such a way as to produce what consumers want or to produce anything effectively. It is the main reliance of totalitarian, as well as free or "capi- talistic," economies. Whether or not consumers have any "rights" (to what they want or in the amount to be had through a sound administra- tion of production), it is now impossible to organize production at all on the basis of any contrary assumption. Moreover, if the productive agents—including all kinds of laborers and of nonhuman instruments, natural and artificial—are not to be attracted into their occupations through the preference of larger to smaller earnings, they must be ap- portioned and organized by the fiat of some authority; and this would simply destroy all freedom of economic choice and substitute dictator- ship, possibly but not probably paternalistic, in a benevolent meaning.

In connection with the rights of labor, we should consider the dis- cussion mentioned earlier of the right to economic means. Apart from a "sufficiently human standard of living," we are told in an early section that *"redistribution"* is a first essential characteristic of the common good (p. 9). A right to the private ownership of "material goods" is said to be rooted in natural law and to be "an extension of the person itself"; but the explicit reason given is its necessity "to make up for the protection nature does not afford it"; further, it "supposes [presupposes] the conditions normally required for human work . . . according to the form of a society and the state of development of its economy" (pp. 71–72 and note). At this point the author refers to a discussion on private property appended to his earlier book, *Freedom in the Modern World*. A careful reading of this appendix, of some twenty pages, will leave any student with an elementary knowledge of economics mystified as to what the author thinks is the meaning of property in organized modern society. In the larger work, as in the one under review, economic rights and ideas are discussed entirely without reference to the most elementary facts of social life or the conditions under which it may be possible for a society to pursue intelligently the objectives of a sufficient production to support its people and maintain a culture, with as much regard as possible for such values as freedom, equality, and justice. Nor is there any more recognition of the fact that property, as things, owes its existence and its perpetuation to saving and investment—or that the same is true in essence of the laborer's capacity to work—than there is of the institutional facts of ownership, which in a free society comes about through production, saving, management, and risk-taking, or through inheritance. (Of course it would be merely immoral to entertain the thought that an excessive birth rate could have something to do with poverty and bondage.)

Finally, a few words should be devoted to the ideal of the "participation of the working personnel in the management of the undertaking," which is emphasized by our author as an essential feature of associative ownership. This is described as *"an association of persons* (management-technicians, workers, investors) entirely different from the associations of capital which the idea of joint ownership might suggest under the present regime" (pp. 98–99). In this connection a few facts may be pointed out. The first is that what are called "associations of capital" *are* associations of persons; hence no other associations could be "entirely different" and perform the same necessary functions. Further, under the mechanism of the competitive market, everyone connected with any enterprise does participate in the management, including especially the consumers of the product, ignored by our author. The mode of participation is impersonal and indirect in various degrees and ways, but it is more effective than direct control has ever been made, for most of the participants in a vast, heterogeneous, and freely changing organization; this is the main reason the "enterprise economy" has developed as it has.

As anyone interested in the facts presumably knows, those who immediately direct operations in any business enterprise are not the owners but the employed agents of nominal owners; but neither managers nor owners nor the enterprise as a whole has any considerable degree of arbitrary power. Actual control is in the hands of those who sell to and buy from the productive unit, primarily the consumers, but also the various employees and the several categories of property owners. It is true that voting power is distributed on the basis of economic capacity, in contrast with the nominally more democratic principle of one person, one vote. The reasons underlying the arrangement lie in the conditions of efficiency on one hand, and debatable ideals of justice on the other, including the merits of private property. They cannot be analyzed in detail here. A critic can only ask for some recognition of facts and confronting of issues, and note that both are conspicuously lacking in the treatment under review. He may point out, as one pertinent fact, that if any group prefers, and can agree upon, any method of more direct control, or any other distribution of control, there is not and never has been anything in the institutions of "capitalist society" to prevent their having what they want, subject to their ability to achieve efficiency, with due consideration of other interests and values. The reason things are as they are lies in human nature and the given conditions of life on the earth.

This does not at all imply either that things as they are, are abstractly ideal or that they "cannot" be changed or improved. It does imply, to some minds at least, that to be improved, the complicated mechanism must be understood and that remedial action must be oriented to facts and to some critical regard for the meaning and relative importance of conflicting ethical principles. Our author seems oblivious to all such considerations, as well as to all the fairly sweeping measures which have been taken in modern liberal society with a view to remedying the evils and realizing the ideals toward which he points in abstract terms. The program has been carried forward as fast as specialists and the public have found it possible to reach agreement on objectives and methods and to act with a reasonable prospect of doing more good than harm.

Our main criticism of the book, to repeat, is that it cites principles that are true but truistical, with the air and implication of enlightenment. Let us repeat also that this practice is not peculiar to our author or his school of thought; it is met with in most political discussion, whether it aims at action or edification. One can always cite a principle—or a proverb or even a legal precedent—to support either side of any question which is seriously at issue. The task of the moral philosopher is not to emphasize ideals—that pertains to the preacher—but to define ideals with a precision not found in common sense or "wisdom" literature. Practical social problems, on the other hand, center in the political order which determines who is to make and interpret the positive law. Here the main question is whether such persons are to be held responsible to a public opinion and will, formulated through free discussion, or simply to themselves. It is a secondary matter whether men in power without this check profess to follow ideals or to be responsible to God. No one wholly repudiates freedom, or law, or authority, or property, or the family, or any right named by our author. But what freedom, authority, and rights actually mean depends very much on whether those talking about them are in power or seeking power. This is true of political parties and leaders in a democracy, as well as of "the Church." The supreme paradox doubtless is that the anarchist ideal—the rule of reason and/or of love—works out in practice to mean authority, backed up by force. But the transition is simple. It is easily assumed that disagreement—with "us" or "me"—rests on some immoral motive, obstinacy, or incompetence, perhaps due to immaturity or defective education.

V. Absolutism and Relativism in Value Theory

We may now turn from the defects of M. Maritain's work to suggest what would be required in a more objective treatment of the central ethical problem. A philosophical discussion of natural or moral law, in the context of modern thought and in a way meaningful to modern minds, must begin by recognizing that it is a "historical category" in the large sense in which the major part of history is anthropology. The philosophical task involves formulating a workable conception of freedom and progress and of the relationship between moral and other value judgments. It is customary to think of these as the "triad"—truth, beauty, and goodness; but some place must be found for the neglected values of play and sport, and perhaps sociability and religion should be recognized as separate types. Play interests and relations have unquestionably played a large role in the genesis in our race of the ideas and sentiments of legality and fairness, and of leadership; and the play spirit, including emulation, is obviously a large factor in aesthetics, morals, and religion, and even in science and philosophy. History and all the main branches of philosophy must cooperate in the task of studying the development of the critical consciousness, in all fields of normative judgment. Further, any intelligent use of the word "nature" must rest on a critical interrelating of nonhuman and human nature, nature and art or artifice, cause-and-effect and purposive action, hence on a tenable conception of man's place in nature. The student must attempt to follow the thread of more and more inadequate knowledge, merging into speculation, back in time to a point where the biological forebears of civilized and reflective mankind were merely a part of nature, and to form some conception of the sequence of change by which "man" has become at once more and more artificial and more creative, in opposition to nature, in his individual and group life.

What such beings as we call men (normal adults) most conspicuously have in common, and in distinction from the other main recognized orders of existence—inert objects, plants, and animals—is the faculty of speech. Growth of this faculty undoubtedly went along with growth in "intelligence" in various meanings, but equally and inseparably with vast changes in emotional traits. The primary use of speech among civilized men today is doubtless the expression and communication of emotion, including playful and esthetic matter, and including also the formulation of unexpressed mental content. The "highest" form of mental activity, and use of speech, is in formulating and expressing reasons for judgments which combine discrimination of the various values, including truth, with the emotional attitude of approval or condemnation. Pure literature (and ornate oral discourse), culminating in poetry, involves this process in a form different from that of science and philosophy and with more emphasis on emotional qualities; but these are also clearly present in connection with intellectual discovery and belief.

These activities are "high" in the sense that they involve a distinction between high and low. What men actually say and think is in all degrees, and, indeed, in innumerable meanings, wise or foolish, beautiful or ugly, good or bad—in content, motive, and result. Moreover, the content is still largely determined by impersonal, non-purposive processes of social life, backed up and modified by coercive force. Speech always means the use of some particular language, which has been created by a particular culture and learned in and through that milieu. The learning and use of language is inseparable from the acquisition of the content, also cultural, whether intellectual and emotional or merely trivial, which speech is used to express to others or to mediate to the individual in his thinking, and from the various ends which expression is used to promote. There is practically no sense in speculating as to what any man would approve or disapprove, in conduct, belief, or taste, apart from the context of some cultural background, some complex of social institutions. Even our beliefs about the most rudimentary "physical" facts are only to a limited degree an exception; and so, at the opposite extreme, are the most "original," romantic, and false ideas of the "crackpot."

The degree to which the attitudes and beliefs of the most independent and critical-minded individual of today are really determined by culture and tradition, "sanctioned" by various "forces," is a fact which one is reluctant to admit and which one comes to realize only through a process of education and self-discipline. At the level of "primitive" society, meaning through most of human history, intellectual and spiritual independence hardly existed. The mores made anything right (and true and beautiful). In the most primitive societies of which we have any knowledge and in any society we should call human, there is plenty of "difference of opinion" and even a kind of discussion, or proto-discussion. But, as far as one can learn from anthropologists, there is in known primitive societies no true critical discussion (or virtually none) involving an appeal from customary and established criteria to such "higher" norms as are represented by the idea of natural or moral law. (Discussion of morality and law undoubtedly emerged long before discussion of scientific or esthetic problems.) In any stable social order all norms generally recognized in practice at any time are necessarily traditional and are called in question exceptionally or not at all. The formulation of ulterior norms, as rational grounds for judging, approving, or condemning established and accepted criteria, goes with a high degree of cultural sophistication. This tendency to criticize what is established is obviously a force making for social instability, and one main function of religion, throughout history, has been that of suppressing or checking it. Criticism undoubtedly "began" in a very limited sector of a society already possessing a relatively high civilization in the sense of concrete achievement—among a few priests or law-speakers, or in some relatively functionless elite or leisure class. It has spread downward with the growth of freedom of discussion, and especially in consequence of democratic government (to be contrasted with the upper-class republics of antiquity), until in our own culture practically everyone freely judges what is in terms of what (he assumes) ought to be.

The general idea expressed by such phrases as "natural law" is that of supposedly rational principles used as norms to criticize law and tradition. (Criticism, of course, includes defense against negative criticism, as well as attack or condemnation.) Natural law is any general unwritten norm or principle which is cited or appealed to on any moral or political issue. In the nature of the case the issue must be one which is not thought to be settled "rightly" by the written law or by custom equivalent to law; hence the issue involves passing judgment on the law, written or customary. However, norms themselves are validated, or become effective, only by acceptance in some community of discourse, or possibly through the use of literal force by an advocate. An individual may, of course, take his stand upon his own opinion "against the world," like Athanasius; but this amounts to assuming he is "God" or stands in some unique relation to ultimate truth; and, again, such a position becomes effective only as it is accepted by others (and/or is backed up by force).

A moral law, in terms of content commanding respect, is clearly a phenomenon of moral progress, on the one hand, and, on the other hand, of the differential nature of progress, the "lag" of generally accepted laws or standards behind more advanced views. To be strictly objective, we should say "cumulative change" instead of "progress"; but, since there is no criterion of validity beyond the "verdict of history," men have to act upon the faith that the trend of change is forward, or upward, toward what is better. The "true" moral law is defined in any society by a "consensus of the competent"; but there is at any moment no objective or absolute test of competence beyond the consensus itself of the competent group and its recognition by wider circles. In this respect the moral law is in exactly the same position, in the abstract, as scientific truth and as judgments of beauty or of any value. All such judgments are forms or species of truth—truth "about" different kinds of subject matter. To the extent that any truth is subject to a supposed objective test, as in natural science, the issue is merely carried back to the validity of the test, which depends on the same social criteria. It is worth noting that the truths of mathematics and formal logic can be tested empirically to any degree of accuracy and universality which is considered worth the trouble; hence, only their "absolute" accuracy and universality is in at all the same position as moral and esthetic truth, i.e., directly dependent (without testing) on a consensus reached through judgment and discussion. The same reasoning applies, of course, to logical demonstration.

We must recognize an ultimate paradox in connection with all judgments. They are meaningless apart from some issue; and, as long as there is an issue, either party can affirm its position as truth only by asserting the incompetence of the opposition—or by backing up its own position with overwhelming force. On the other hand, when an issue is finally settled and no longer in question in any way, the matter of truth or falsity has lost all relevance and all meaning. It may be assumed that reasonable men now admit that force does not really answer questions in terms of truth. But this position, again, rests on the faith that force as expressed in the historical process is ultimately on the side of "real" truth. Through most of human history, truth has been a question of the morality or immorality of belief (or sanity versus insanity) or especially of religious orthodoxy versus heresy; and all these issues have actually been settled by force in the most overt meaning—and this is strikingly true in the history of "Christian" civilization.

It will be evident that "natural law," properly defined, is the opposite of "natural." To the extent that men are aware of it, it is a highly artificial product of social mental life, exceeded in artificiality only by the creative products—or mere aberrations—of individual minds. We may perhaps think of moral progress, in the etymological meaning, as occurring automatically and unconsciously, but such change can hardly be called moral in the higher sense to be distinguished as ethical. A true moral law rests on a recognized conflict between what is and what ought to be, or at least upon some conflict which is not resolved by established customs and norms, and which presents a problem for solution. It reflects a threefold cleavage, in varying degree, within the individual (self-criticism), between different individuals in a culture group (mutual criticism), and within the group as a whole (group self-criticism). A moral law, with any content whatever, about which there is no disagreement or even no serious disagreement is essentially a contradiction; if not self-contradictory in the abstract logical sense, it is at least contrary to all historical reality.

The philosophical problem is one of interpreting moral progress, which, to repeat, involves interrelating this with other aspects of man's spiritual development. The familiar triad may be interpreted to cover the whole field. In all its aspects, progress means advance through effort, in which the activities of individuals and groups can be only partly distinguished, even in abstract analysis. When a society becomes conscious of its problems, these are tremendously complicated by the fact that, within limits, the primary consideration is social order and peace, hence the necessary degree of agreement, with less regard for the abstract merits of the position on which agreement is reached. This makes for conservatism. However, since agreement is the only test of truth, we must assume that the two quests coincide and that deliberate, compromise is only a working approximation to a right answer to an unanswered question. Any forward step must begin with some individual digression, and this leads to real advance only through acceptance on intellectual grounds. Most incipient innovations are certainly wrong and never take root or are rejected by "history."

Progress is thus a matter of the two factors, innovation and critical discussion, leading eventually to a consensus (or to social division, or disintegration, or conquest). The first factor is freedom, under another name. It is an intellectual mystery or surd, yet the most certainly known of all facts, since it is a presupposition of all thinking and cannot be denied without asserting it. (That it is a mystery is itself hardly a mystery, since mind as subject clearly could not well adequately see itself as an object.) Moral freedom is not to be conceived as arbitrary whim, or caprice, or blind chance but as the active endeavor to get right answers to questions; it implies the possibility of error, to which (effortless) mechanical processes are not subject. Innovation and particularly rational freedom are both experimental and narrowly limited in scope. The critical mind itself is, of necessity, formed for the most part by forces antecedent to itself and, at any moment, by its own prior history; it can only in small part be self-created. Complete or absolute freedom operating *de novo* at every instant (as if the actor had no past) is unthinkable. It is equally essential to recognize historical determination and process and the fact that the spiritually developed individual, in a spiritually advanced social milieu, has the capacity to react critically, creatively, upon himself and upon the culture which has largely made him what he is. We must assume that all peoples, or publics, and their individual members, must experience the threefold cleavage of self-criticism, when they reach a certain stage in the historical progress of mental and spiritual development.

If men are to think critically and yet escape moral skepticism and a destructive relativism, they must have faith, on some ground, in the validity of thought and discussion and in the ultimate verdict of history, i.e., in the reality of progress. In the historical past and in our present Western civilization the majority of serious minds have viewed their faith as founded, first, in ultimate real norms which do not change but are merely progressively discovered and, second, in some idea of "God" as the ground of this reality. But there are enough examples to the contrary to prove that neither of these conceptions is necessary. To many competent minds (as to this writer), it is as reasonable to regard values as progressively created, or actualized, in a world in which they have been potential but not actual as it is to conceive of progress as the discovery of an immutable reality. And it seems to such minds more reasonable to view the nature of the cosmic ground of the distinction between the valid and the invalid in all fields, or the nature of the objectivity of this distinction, as an open philosophical problem. It also seems to such minds more reasonable and better to recognize that the validity of all accepted concrete judgments is only more or less provisionally established. This seems to be the only view which is reconcilable with the facts of historical progress, in which new insights have constantly superseded old knowledge or changed it by reinterpretation.

Nothing properly called absolute truth is possible for any principle or proposition, or even the simplest fact. The highest certainty, beyond the direct awareness that thinking is a free activity, is that it takes place in social beings living in a social milieu, i.e., in connection with discussion, and that discussion recognizes problems which are discussable. The precise way in which we conceive or picture ultimate cosmic reality—as far as we picture it at all—is largely a matter of taste and convenience as long as our conceptions make a place for the belief that the effort to solve problems is real and "makes a difference." Experience shows that men confront a real danger of arguing themselves into a world view which denies this essential fact, though ultimate denial would be madness. This fundamental requirement excludes both absolute mechanism and absolute will, and makes absolute values tainted. One may believe in such values only under the explicit condition of admitting that he does not know what they are and that absolute knowledge would be identical with nihilism. The danger here lies in the psychological fact that one who believes in the absolute character of values in the abstract is likely to go on to use that proposition as a premise to establish conclusions which are highly relative.

This reasoning applies still more cogently to the belief in God. Again, a conviction that intelligence and moral will are operative in the cosmos and in human history is admissible and should be useful, provided that God is thought of in such a way as not to negate the essential consideration of human achievement through effort. But this is extraordinarily difficult. God must not be thought of as statically complete or "infinite," in any ordinary meaning. In fact the ideas of omnipotence, omniscience, and infinite goodness are self-contradictory; in the final analysis they negate the ideas of power, knowledge, and goodness. If God, or the ultimate cosmic reality, is to have any of these spiritual attributes—to which "taste" should certainly be added—he must be thought of in essentially human terms of struggle to achieve the several values. It is then necessary to think of cooperation, a working together, between God and men, and this is where the greatest difficulty is encountered.[9] Those who try to make the will of God practically meaningful in moral and social life seem inevitably to fall into the error noted above in connection with absolute values, i.e., they think they know what God wills with respect to controversial issues. The idea or feeling of communication with God (even indirectly through a prophet, or demigod, or inspired organization) seems to have too much attraction for frail human nature, though neither the channels of communication nor the content of the revelation stand up under critical examination. The common result is pride and bigotry, in a sect or people, though usually on matters of form rather than matters of substance.

What has been said should make it clear that the problem for modern thought and life is that of the validity or objectivity of values. The fallacies which men tend to fall into may be approached in two ways. From one point of view the error to be avoided is a false dichotomy between absolutism and relativism, with respect to all values, whereas these terms themselves should be used in a relative and not an absolute sense. From the other point of view it is the treatment of truth, where the error is treatment of scientific and logical truth as absolute and the relegation of moral and aesthetic judgments to the level of relativity. It is better to approach the problem by looking first at the fallacy in the second form. Here the essential fact is that even the truths of science are finally judgments of value. When there is any issue, it is a matter of weighing evidence and the cogency of reasoning; and, when there is no issue, any assertion is nonsensical. Again we confront the paradox of the inherently progressive or "dynamic" nature of intellectual life; truth is the answer to a question; and, when any question is definitively answered, there is no longer any question, and no truth, in any significant meaning of the word. Further, an objective answer to any question, in science as elsewhere, is a social judgment, dependent on verification.[10]

All questions are questions of truth or falsity, whether they relate to matters of "fact" or to "values" in the narrower sense of morals and esthetics. On the other hand, truth itself *(where any question is at issue)* is a value, a matter of what one "ought" to believe, of better and worse reasons for believing; and the obligation to believe what is true because it is true, rather than to believe anything else or for any other reason, is the universal and supreme imperative for the critical consciousness. All discussable questions come down finally to good judgment, including "good" taste and "right" moral discrimination versus "mere" taste or preference. It is true that moral questions involve a further imperative or obligation, that of *acting* in accord with true judgments as to what is good or right, but they are not peculiar in this respect. Esthetic judgments have their creative aspect as well as that of appreciation. And truth about "facts" is also expressed in action, giving rise to the imperatives of economy (versus waste) and of "workmanship," which also involves esthetic norms. None of these distinctions can be sharply drawn. In a special sense the judgment of truth is a moral judgment, since—truth being a social category—the obligation to believe what is true is inseparable from the obligation to "tell" the truth (apart from other grounds for this rule). Yet the different forms of value imperatives also conflict. Literal truth in discourse must very often give place to other values, both esthetic and moral; and, while beauty may be viewed as a kind of truth (or conversely), the two may conflict as well as coincide. There are also conflicts within each category, conspicuously in the case of moral values or duties; but different truths also conflict, in spite of the logician's prejudice to the contrary.

Looking at all value problems, then, from the standpoint of truth, we return to the position stated above: that no such judgment can be "absolutely absolute" or "absolutely relative." Absoluteness or relativity is a matter of degree of certainty, the only test of which is the degree of agreement in a community of discourse, the consensus of the competent (and unbiased). The simpler axioms of mathematics and everyday matters of fact are "relatively absolute," in comparison with disputed rankings of works of art—or any matter which is controversial among competent and serious (honest) students. Of course, what any individual believes to be true is based chiefly on what he believes to be the consensus of the competent, a community to which he does not usually profess to belong for most of the field of knowledge. The only meaning of "absolutely absolute" truth or validity is a judgment on a matter about which there is assumed to be no possible question—a commonplace and a species of nonsense. When anyone makes an assertion as an absolute truth, in the face of disagreement, he merely sets himself up as an absolute authority or as a spokesman for such an authority. The meaning of the position is to forbid discussion by fiat and finally to claim the right to silence opposition by force.

At the other extreme, an "absolutely relative" judgment would not be a judgment at all but would merely describe an individual state of mind. Thus both absolutely absolute and absolutely relative judgments negate discussion and all intellectual life, the first by asserting dogmatically that there is nothing to discuss, the second by limiting discourse to utter banality. In so far as any assertion of the absolute validity of a proposition is meaningful, it is so by raising the issue of the relative competence—or honesty—of those who assert and those who deny it, or of some authority for which they speak. (The authenticity of the spokesman's credentials may also be at issue.)

The meaning of all values is rooted in a process of progressive sociocultural achievement, including resistance to change in wrong directions. A value is something sought rather than finally possessed. This is the meaning of the statement that man is a rationally social being, or "potentially" such. The determination of truth by free discussion is also the meaning of democracy as a social philosophy. Its antithesis is authoritarian society, which is a mixture in varying proportions of traditionalism and arbitrary dictatorship. In another view the issue is between a "liberal" and a "religious" ideal of social life and conception of belief. A dictatorship must be religious in some sense, and a democracy must be rational. However, the ultimate ideal of liberalism or democracy, government by (rational) discussion alone, is antinomian (in the sense of enforced law) and is inherently unattainable. But progress in that direction is the final meaning of social-moral progress. The ideal has the two aspects, free government and a minimum of government by enforced law or by authority, net, maximum freedom for individual disagreement and nonconformity. Where agreement is "necessary," i.e., where other values are more important than freedom (even if lower in ideal rank), it must, of course, be secured by some mechanism of compulsion enforcing the closest achievable approximation to a social will based on a common opinion.

Notes

1. Jacques Maritain, *The Rights of Man and Natural Law,* trans. Doris C. Anson (New York: Charles Scribner's Sons, 1943).

2. E.g., in the second sentence of the book, *dans une guerre* and *dans la paix* are rendered "given a war" and "given a peace"; and on p. 66, *à voir* is translated literally "to see," with nonsensical results.

3. One of M. Maritain's most obvious positions being Roman Catholicism, it is in order to observe that the pronouncements made under "liberal" religious auspices differ chiefly in following more largely the first of our two ways of saying virtually nothing, i.e., advocating high ideals with no concrete and hence controversial implications—though they are also by no means free from advocacy of clearly incompatible things. As an example we may quote the "seven points for peace" of the first American interfaith pronouncement on world order by more than 140 top-ranking Protestant, Catholic, and Jewish leaders: "1. The moral law must govern world order. 2. The rights of the individual must be assured. 3. The rights of oppressed, weak, or colonial peoples must be protected. 4. The rights of minorities must be secured. 5. International institutions to maintain peace with justice must be organized. 6. International economic co-operation must be developed. 7. A just social order within each state must be achieved" (*Pathfinder,* October 18, 1943). At best this could be defended as a beginning toward a breakdown of the problem or listing of its "aspects." We certainly do not wish to be invidious, and the significance of our criticisms is increased by the fact that other schools of thought exemplify the weaknesses pointed out. The religious writers are merely the worst sinners in this respect.

4. There are many other expressions in the same vein: "Above the plane of civil society, the person crosses the threshold of a kingdom which is not of this world . . . a supra-temporal society which is called the Church, and which has to do with the things that are not Caesar's" (p. 19). "Other communities are of a rank superior to the State, as is above all the Church in the mind of Christians . . ." (p. 21). In a later section, among the rights which "belong to natural law in the strictest sense of the word" are included "the rights and liberties of spiritual and religious families" and specifically "the superior right which the Church invokes by reason of her divine foundation" (pp. 82–83); cf. also pp. 75–76, and elsewhere.

5. If the political principles of Catholicism present more of a contrast with fascism than with communism, the similarity in historical policy, in propagating the creeds, and in establishing their political authority by completely ruthless use of force, is striking enough. This again is a natural consequence of the religious basis, and the quasi-religious character of both fascism and communism is a familiar observation.

6. General assertions about religion in this paper relate to recognized religions having a body of belief and practice, and usually an ecclesiastical organization. There is assumed to be a distinction between religion and philosophy or *Weltanschauung,* and space limits exclude discussion of "prophecy."

With respect to freedom, the Christian conception is that this, like truth, is achieved through a voluntary emotional self-surrender to another will, ostensibly the will of God (sometimes apostrophized as truth—cf. Matt. 26:39; John 8:32). But it necessarily meant in practice the will of ecclesiastical authority, where any problem was involved. This, of course, is straight totalitarianism in a theological formulation; but the philosophy of modern political totalitarianism differs from historical Christianity in being activistic, where the original form of the latter was strongly quietistic. The Christian conception of an all-loving and omnipotent divine will and divine love as the fundamental cosmic reality and the supreme and all-inclusive good cannot be logically harmonized with an ethic of action. Effective participation of Christians in economic and political activities merely shows that they do not believe what they profess.

This Christian conception of emotional freedom presents an interesting contrast to the more rigorous quietism of Hindu thought, in which the ideal is self-annihilation of the personal will, without reference to either a cosmic will or a political authority superior to ordinary men in its thinking and interests.

7. The words "liberalism" and "liberal" are not used in this book. But in the parent volume, *Freedom in the Modern World,* we read (p. 63), "Liberalism is not merely false in theory; it is finished in fact, bankrupt by the turn of events."

8. The three political regimes of Aristotle are contrasted in terms of their characteristic values. The democratic regime tends above all to freedom, the monarchical to strength and unity; it is the aristocratic which "tends above all to the differentiation of values and to the production of the noblest and rarest values" (p. 51). It is at once explained that to be faithful to Aristotle's terminology and also to designate properly the author's own "political humanism" or "commonwealth of free men," the democratic regime should be called "republican." No definition is given beyond its characterization as a "mixed" regime and a general statement of the vague and conflicting ideals which it should realize. It is also designated as a "new Democracy" (pp. 54, 86).

9. There is a scriptural reference to God as working—John 5:17—but in its context it has no intelligible meaning; and it is difficult, if not impossible, to give the idea any practically significant meaning. The use of the word "hitherto" in the saying of Jesus cited suggests the position known as "deism." This is an intellectually respectable position and was prominent in the eighteenth century. But the idea that God created the world and man and then turned both loose, the one to follow its natural-scientific laws, the other to struggle along as best he may, amounts for all practical purposes to leaving God out of the picture.

10. We restrict our discussion to discussable questions, such as presuppose an answer that is valid for some group, some community of discourse. We leave aside purely private problems—if there are any such in the strict sense—in which an individual merely has to decide between conflicting purely personal values, no one else being involved. Even the answers to such questions may have a kind of objectivity, but we cannot go into that here.

8

Realism and Relevance in the Theory of Demand

The treatment of demand is the branch of economic theory in which methodological problems are most important and most difficult. This is because it is here that behavior facts are most inseparably bound up with motivation and that objective data call most imperatively for interpretation by subjective facts and meanings.[1] The objective in this paper is largely negative—to criticize certain recent innovations in the treatment of demand which have been generally hailed as representing an advance but which, in the writer's opinion, constitute a movement in a backward direction. The particular reference is to the treatment of demand and utility by J. R. Hicks, pioneered by E. Slutsky, and also followed, and more or less independently worked out, by Henry Schultz and many others.[2] The essential features of the theory are a new psychology of consumption and a distinctive treatment of the demand curve based upon the former. The new interpretation of consumption is more relativistic than the conventional view, specifically that of Marshall, and is adopted for the sake of greater objectivity. It has two aspects. The first is replacement of the conception of "absolute" diminishing incremental utility (of a single good) with a diminishing "coefficient of substitution" of one good for another, assumed to be a purely behavioristic principle, or at least purely relative. The second aspect is a distinctive view of the relation between change in income and change in the psychic state of the subject—his economic well-being. In this second connection the thinkers criticized have not been willing to follow through with a behavioristic complete rejection of subjective magnitudes—or their

Reprinted with permission from the *Journal of Political Economy* 52 (December 1944): 289–318.

reduction to the role of a "force" impelling men to buy and consume and to compare and choose. They still think of the individual as controlling his consumption with a view to securing more rather than less of something called "utility"—a subjective magnitude which is maximized when the consumer's behavior conforms to the economic ideal. They merely insist that this something-maximized need not, and therefore should not, be treated as a quantity in the ordinary "cardinal" meaning, but as only "ordinal"; that is, utilities are subject to ranking but not to real quantification, which is identified with measurement.[3]

In the way of construction we shall attempt to clarify the relationship between the subjective and the objective aspects of the economic values of different consumption goods—more accurately, services— under given conditions correctly defined, and the relation between levels of objective consumption, or real income, and economic well-being. On the basis of this analysis we shall outline a realistic theory of the demand curve. Part 4 of the paper will take up the problem of measurement in connection with economic well-being and motivation; Part 5 will offer a brief re-examination of the problem of consumer's surplus. In the first three parts, it will be assumed that the reader has a general knowledge of recent controversial discussion, and our treatment will be confined to a brief statement of essentials, without elaboration in detail.

I. The Theory of Indifference—Various Methods of Exposition

For a clear, sound, and useful theory of demand, or the demand curve, the first essential is a sharp separation between the comparative economic values of different goods in relation to a given level of "economic well-being" of the individual consumer and a theory of the relation between changes in the level of well-being and changes in consumption. In the absence of any better terminology, we may refer to the first as the "theory of comparative value" (relative in the sense of comparing different goods) and to the second as the "theory of dynamic valuation." It is to be understood that the term "value" is used in the strictly economic sense, without any implication of "objectivity," as in ethics or aesthetics, where valuations may be "right" or "wrong" or be affected with a quality of imperative or "oughtness." As in all economic discussion, we take the consumer's individual evaluations as final. We also exclude the factor of "error" in its more intellectual meanings; we assume that what the consumer wants is what he gets, and describe his behavior under the condition that he "correctly" solves his "economic" problem, actually

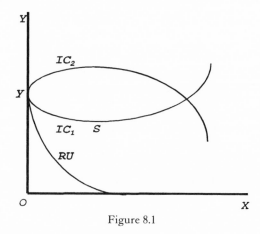

Figure 8.1

maximizing whatever it is that he tries to maximize in the choices which direct his behavior as a consumer.

We first consider different methods of graphing in the simple case of a two-commodity system. In order to make the most useful approximation to the conditions of real life, we assume that an individual A is given a total income (over a short interval of time dt) in the form of a definite amount y, of commodity Y, measured along a vertical axis, and that he is confronted with the opportunity of exchanging successive increments of Y for increments of another commodity, X, measured along a horizontal axis (see Figure 8.1). The conditions are such that A "buys" successive infinitesimal increments of X, seriatim, paying for the first the maximum amount of Y which he is willing to pay, for the second the maximum amount he is willing to pay after having bought the first, and so on. Thus we picture the "generation" of a curve IC_1, the simplest form of indifference curve; for the purpose of distinction we shall call it the "indifference-combinations" curve. The ordinate on this curve at any point on the x-axis measures the amount of Y which A will have left out of his original supply (per unit of time) after carrying the process to any point, while the abscissa of the same point measures the amount of X he will have secured. (The total amount of Y given up is measured downward from y.) Every point on the curve represents a different combination of amounts of X and Y such that to the given subject A (with initial income y) exchange or choice between any two combinations is a matter of indifference. The ratio or price at which the last exchange is made (or the next one will be made) is measured by the slope of the curve at any point—with a negative sign, if, as is usual, we think of the price of X in terms of Y, the price of the good secured in terms of that given up.

If we continue such a curve to the right over a sufficient interval, it will take the general form shown in Figure 8.1. The facts here are not in dispute, especially as far as the descending section of the curve is concerned. The curve will descend over some interval, with a decreasing (negative) slope, to a point at which it becomes horizontal; and then, if the experiment is continued, it will ascend at an increasing (positive) slope. The lowest point S on the curve (the point at which it is horizontal) corresponds to complete satiety with good X; the price of X here is zero, and no further amount of Y will be voluntarily given up for any further amount of X. Under the conditions of a two-commodity system, this point should ordinarily have the same X value, regardless of the subject's initial income, if X and Y are "independent," i.e., noncomplementary but different goods.

Along the ascending leg of the curve the increasing slope shows that it would be necessary to give back to A increasing amounts of Y, previously given up, to "hire" him to consume each successive increment of X. (We assume consumption, compulsory if necessary, ignoring the possibility that later increments of X might be simply ignored or might be disposed of in some other way.) Over the interval between S and y corresponding to the initial supply of Y, the curve will have dual Y values; there will be two equivalent combinations of each quantity of Y with different quantities of X, one corresponding to a deficiency, the other to a superfluity, of X. The ascending part of the curve is unrealistic under ordinary conditions where the subject has freedom of choice; but the hypothetical procedure is useful for depicting the psychology of demand. The curve IC_1 may be extended upward beyond y, giving A more Y than his initial income, to a point at which it would become vertical, indicating that no more of X could be consumed without making him absolutely worse off (or more than would be voluntarily consumed) no matter how much Y were given him at the same time. The facts shown by the indifference curve may also be presented by a curve drawn upward initially and then downward (curve IC_2 in Figure 8.1). This has some advantages, particularly that the amounts of Y given up are indicated in positive instead of negative terms in the significant part. But points on the curves will not then represent "indifference combinations" of X and Y, on the same axes.

Exactly the same facts may again be portrayed by a curve of relative incremental (marginal) utility, as shown in curve RU, which may be called a "curve of indifference-prices" or a "price-indifference curve." On this second curve the vertical axis is a scale of exchange ratios or prices (Y/X or Y per unit of X, at the margin, i.e., dY/dX, in the previous notation); that is, the price at any point is measured by the ordinate instead of by the slope. Hence the ordinate of RU measures the slope of curves IC_1 and IC_2 at any point on X, or it is the "derivative" of either of these except for algebraic sign in case of the former. Curves IC_1 and IC_2 may be viewed as curves of total expenditure drawn under the condition that a consumer buys from a monopolist who exacts the maximum total amount (or maximum price per unit) the buyer is willing to pay for each amount of X. The radical difference between RU, the derivative curve, and a demand curve, showing amounts purchased at given prices with the buyer free to choose the amount he will take at each price, will come into consideration repeatedly as the argument proceeds. Curve RU will intersect the x-axis at the point at which the indifference curve as previously drawn (in either form) becomes horizontal, and beyond that point the indifference-price will become increasingly negative.

The hypothesis of a two-commodity system is, of course, unrealistic and should be used with great caution. Details of the curves would depend on necessarily arbitrary assumptions as to the character of the two goods and the relations between them. To make the discussion more realistic, we should first take the vertical axis as a scale in terms of "money" representing a complex of alternative commodities, at prices which vary together, but inversely with the price of X, so that the money has constant total purchasing power. This change in the facts represented will not change the general form of any of our curves. This is still true if any of the commodities in the complex Y are interrelated among themselves or with X by any degree of complementarity or similarity. And it is immaterial for the general argument just what price changes occur within the alternative complex, among the infinitude of possibilities, to offset the changing price of X and keep the value of money constant. The indifference-combinations-curve method of graphing (for X and money) has a great advantage over the indifference-price method, in that the former shows money income directly on a plane diagram and so makes it possible to represent a whole "system" of curves, corresponding to different levels of income. But its use is limited because it does not correspond with market quotations and everyday ways of thinking, which necessarily run in terms of price and quantity.[4]

II. Consumer's Valuation as a "Dynamic" Problem

We turn to the psychological problem of the interpretive explanation of the curves considered in Part 1 or of the facts which they represent. The curves are taken as portraying objective facts of consumer behavior (though under idealized conditions), with only incidental reference to any subjective state as "indifference." But it is necessary to decide whether they are to be allowed to stand as purely empirical or are to bring the behavior facts into some intelligible relation to facts of subjective experience.[5] The second position is the one to be defended in this paper as a whole. The more philosophical aspect of the argument for considering motives, and not merely the facts of choice, will be developed in Part 4. In the present section we shall merely explore certain psychological relations. Further than this, we need only remark here that such terms as "willingly" and "voluntarily" occur in the earlier exposition and suggest that it would not be easy to eliminate them and make the discussion seem to "talk sense."

The main concrete issue directly raised is whether we should think of the "utility" of a single good—the property which causes it to be consumed and chosen for consumption in preference to other goods—as an independent variable, or as inherently and solely a comparison between the particular good and other goods. In other words, should we view the essence of (final) economic value as purely a comparison or think of relative value as a comparison between the values of different goods? Investigation of the question will take the form of an inquiry into the dynamic problem of the quantitative relation between uncompensated variation in the consumption of individual goods or combinations of goods and variations in desirable experience or state of being in the consumer, i.e., in his "mind." In terms of the established principles used in the analysis of demand, prior to this new controversy, the issue will be found to center in the principle of diminishing utility in connection with an individual good. As pointed out earlier, the Slutsky school deny this principle; they replace it by a combination of two devices, the principle of a decreasing ratio of substitution of one good for another—at a constant level of well-being expressed through "free" choice—and a ranking without "measurement" (or quantification) of states of total well-being, as an individual passes from one indifference level to another.

Our first step will be to inquire into the reality of the principle of diminishing utility for a single good. The investigation may take the form of reflecting upon a series of simple imaginary experiments. To make the analysis accurate and the conditions realistic, in contrast with the vague and misleading assumptions usually met with, we must begin by carefully stating the *ceteris paribus* conditions. We postulate an individual who is consuming a "reasonable" list or budget of commodities, not including the one involved in the experiments, and who continues throughout to consume these in unvarying amount. The first experiment consists in adding to the individual's consumption of these items successive, equal, small (infinitesimal) increments (per unit of time) of the particular commodity or good X, not before consumed, and having him report upon his experience of "satisfaction." These conditions allow full play for all relations of complementarity and similarity ("substitutability") among all the commodities, including the one which is varied in the experiment.

In the interest of precision and clarity, other conditions of the experiment need to be carefully stated and some terms defined. We must sharply separate consumer behavior from all productive activity, and especially from saving and investment, and must be clear about the dimensionality of the magnitudes with which we are dealing. To touch first on the second point, consumption (like production and all "activity") has the dimensionality of a flow or "flux." But the correct physical analogy is not the flow of a material such as water, which exists and can be measured when it is not flowing. Light is perhaps the best physical analogue in this respect. The rate of flow of water is realistically viewed as a composite magnitude—quantity divided by time. With light the relation is the opposite. Only the intensity can be measured directly (though the unit may be defined in terms of other dimensions); quantity is the composite and derivative magnitude, an arithmetical product of intensity *times* time—candle-power-hours. It is a mere concept, essentially fictitious.

The same relation holds for consumption, whether thought of as a subjective or as an objective magnitude. What is consumed is always a *service* (of some agent, human or "physical"). The result, which is the end or purpose and which gives consumption quantitative meaning, may be called want-satisfaction," or simply "satisfaction"; but "subjective service" is a less objectionable designation. Any more concrete definition will commit the economist on psychological or moral issues with which he has nothing to do. It is simply the common quality underlying all direct economic comparisons and choice—"that which" the consumer strives to maximize and does maximize when his behavior is "economic." It must be a homogeneous magnitude if we are to speak of quantitative change; and, since there is no physical attribute which is common to all sources of satisfaction, the end of consumption must be a single variable state or condition of the individual. We assume that what is desired is identical with what is realized and experienced; that is, we abstract from error—connected with the fact that consumption may be treated as a means to welfare as the real end—and from the fact that novelty, surprise, and gratification of curiosity are elements in real enjoyment and in the motivation of choice. This assumption is largely implied by ideal stationary conditions, in which desire and satisfaction, production and consumption are strictly simultaneous. ("Utility" is the attribute of an agent by virtue of which it yields subjective service, and the two terms are not always interchangeable.) Correspondingly, the primary meaning of production is "objective service" or the use of any agent to render subjective service.

The main source of confusion in relation to consumption is the fact that production in this primary meaning is not necessarily equal to consumption over any interval of time. Production may exceed consumption, the difference being (axiomatically) added to "capital"; i.e., it may consist in the production of (additional) capital and not of "satisfaction." And conversely, consumption may exceed production, the difference representing a decrease in capital. (Production of what is consumed includes maintenance of capital.) Since the production of any amount of capital (saving and investment) represents a sacrifice of a given amount of consumption and results in future consumption, it seems natural to think of a quantity of capital as a quantity of consumption stored up in a stock. But this is invalid, for two reasons. The quantity of capital accumulated in any finite interval is not the amount of consumption sacrificed—intensity *times* time—but contains an additional element, a return on investment, continuously compounded at a certain "rate." (This is usually referred to as the rate of interest, but it has no connection with the lending of money—or of anything else—and would have exactly the same meaning in a Crusoe economy as in a pecuniary society.) On the other hand, a quantity of capital does not represent any determinate quantity of future consumption. Until and unless the capital itself is consumed, the total yield grows without limit; and in any case it also is affected by the rate of return or interest. Analysis requires treatment of the production of capital during any interval and its subsequent use to yield consumption-service (or further investment) as distinct acts or processes of production.[6]

Elimination of all investment and disinvestment in effect reduces exchange to the purchase and sale of services, without any transfer of "goods" (all of which are "capital"), and imposes stationary conditions. It also eliminates all lending of money; for, under ideal conditions, such a loan is indistinguishable from a lease for a rental. Similarly excluded are all "contracts" for the purchase and sale of services, involving any commitment for the future. It is most convenient to think of the consumer as not owning any productive capacity, and particularly any money.[7]

Returning to our imaginary experiment, we are to think of our subject as having no alternatives of choice; he is simply given increasing amounts (per time unit) of a particular objective service, which we shall now call os_i. We submit that beyond any possibility of doubt he will report decreasing increments in the intensity of subjective service ss_i from equal increments of os_i (added to his original budget). That is, the variation in his additional satisfaction will show progressive satiation up to a point of complete satiety, and then run into supersatiation with increasing increments of negative satisfaction. It will be represented by a curve of the shape of a round arch or inverted U (preferably measured upward from a false base line). It is to be stressed that the increments of subjective service are not quantified (on "measurement," see below) by comparison with any other kind of satisfaction. Each increment of satisfaction is compared only with the increments of the same kind which precede it in the sequence. The total real income of the subject increases by equal steps, as defined and measured in physical units by an ideal index number, while, in subjective terms, it behaves in the manner described. Thus the curve and its derivative are very different in meaning from IC_2 of Figure 8.1.

The experiment is, next, to be modified in two steps. First, we give the subject increasing amounts, in fixed proportions, of all the items in any fixed budget or list of services. The resulting variation in total satisfaction will certainly take the same form as before. Next we give him "money" in increasing amounts (increasing by equal increments), restricted to the purchase of a given list of items at fixed (absolute) money prices, with freedom to reapportion his expenditure among them at will. The reported result will again be of the same kind—total satisfaction increasing by decreasing steps and then decreasing.

If introspection leaves any room for doubt as to the declining (arithmetic) rate of increase, it is proved by the unquestionable fact that if the money income of an individual increases, under realistic conditions (i.e., if he has freedom of choice), he will not merely buy more of the services previously consumed but, in addition to buying more of these, will spend part of his increased income for services not previously consumed. This is wholly inexplicable and would not happen, except for the fact that the whole list previously consumed is subject to diminishing incremental utility. Mere growth of total income cannot increase the utility of items not previously consumed and cannot increase their relative marginal utility or coefficient of substitution, in comparison with earlier items, unless increased consumption absolutely reduces the marginal utility of the earlier budget items. We cannot realistically interpret the decline in the marginal utility of one good increased in supply relative to others not consumed, hence its decreasing coefficient of substitution for the latter, without taking into account its decreasing absolute marginal utility as its consumption increases, *ceteris paribus*. Further, the negative price elasticity of demand for a good cannot be dissociated from declining positive income elasticity, all prices being constant and with the consumer free to add new items. And decreasing income elasticity can result only from decreasing marginal utility of any whole list of goods or of money to be spent for them at given prices.[8]

The propositions (*a*) that utility and satisfaction are purely relative and (*b*) that the total is merely an ordinal magnitude are impossible even under the assumption that demand curves are to be studied exclusively with reference to a given list of commodities. If absolute marginal utility did not decrease, no determinate apportionment of income would be made. If we think of the consumer's income beginning at zero and gradually increasing, the first increment would be spent on the service yielding the most satisfaction for the initial unit, or one chosen at random. And if increasing consumption of this item carried increasing or constant incremental satisfaction, no other items would ever be added, but all further additions to income would be spent for the same good. (With incremental change constant, adding new items would either involve loss or be a matter of indifference.) It is logically admissible to think that the marginal utility of a particular good may increase with increasing consumption over a narrow initial interval; and this might even be true of total income, under special conditions. But the rational consumer will never stop using freely apportionable income to purchase any quantity of a good within an interval of increasing marginal utility but will proceed at least to the point of maximum utility per unit of expenditure; and (with proportions freely variable) no budget items will be added in the interval of increasing utility of money income. The situation is parallel with that of productive services, where the operations are limited to the range of diminishing physical returns. All facts of complementarity and similarity are essentially the same in the two cases. Subjective service is not physically measurable, but its quantitative variation is factually indubitable; and even if it were possible to explain the facts of demand without it, the procedure would be interesting only as an intellectual "stunt."

We must hasten to take account of a realistic difficulty in reasoning from the addition of new items to a budget, with increasing income in money of constant purchasing power. In this situation an individual will not usually increase his consumption of all previous items but, besides adding new items, will to some extent *replace* commodities previously consumed with new ones, decreasing his purchase of some of the former, or even dropping them altogether. In a familiar illustration, if he has been eating chiefly bread, at a higher income he may not only add some meat but consume less bread. Moreover, he may also replace a lower "grade" of bread with a higher grade. As we classify commodities more "finely," even to correspond with market facts in a high civilization, displacement of items may predominate over increased consumption.

The phenomenon of replacement of "inferior" by "superior" goods or the reverse, as income changes, has received much attention in recent discussion. The correct view is that they are different goods. Even the "same" good bought from a dealer of a different class is really a different thing—certainly, if a different price is paid, whatever the reason. The underlying fact is that any commodity, as named and sold in the market, yields a "bundle" of diverse subjective services, which are to be had only (or more economically) in combination rather than separately. Things regarded as differing only in grade are usually named with reference to some predominant useful quality which they have in common, along with different assortments of other qualities. At the most general level of analysis it should be assumed that each single good (objective service) as purchased yields a single type of satisfaction. This might still be allowed to vary in degree in accord with the price for the ordinary market unit, "quality" differing in that sense. Under this assumption, displacement obviously will not occur in consequence of income change.

III. The Meaning of a Demand Curve

We must now briefly consider the demand curve in terms of its expository meaning rather than its psychological or philosophical interpretation. Here we are concerned with an aspect of the Slutsky view which has little logical connection with the methodological conceptions with which we find it associated. The demand curve in the tradition of modern economic theory shows the functional relation between price and quantity taken (or sold) for a particular good, "all other things being equal." It is always assumed that the buyer confronts a set price at which he is free to purchase as much or as little of the good as he may choose— a fact which differentiates the curve sharply from any of those we have previously considered. Until quite recently, few, if any, writers were at all careful to say what they meant by this *ceteris paribus* condition; and in general it probably did not occur to them that price is ambiguous or that it is not possible for all other things to be equal. The money price and sale of a particular good cannot change while all other variables in an economic system are constant. We have to choose in analysis between holding the prices of all other goods constant and maintaining constant the "real income" of the hypothetical consumer. For, obviously, if the price of a single good, *X,* increases, while the prices of other goods are unchanged (along with the money income of the individual), the "value of money" to the subject will have decreased—in objective and in subjective terms—and vice versa. The strict *ceteris paribus* assumption can be valid only when there is no finite change, i.e., for the partial derivative of a total-consumption function at a single point.

The treatment of the Slutsky school adopts the assumption that the price of X varies under the condition that the prices of all other goods (and the consumer's money income) are constant. Hence, real income must change. Of the two alternatives, this seems to be definitely the wrong choice. It throws together two distinct effects upon consumption, the "price effect" and the "income effect." The treatment then proceeds to separate these by means of an ingenious analysis. The cleverness of it all must be conceded. But it is called for only because of an initial confusion in the statement of the problem, which is wholly unnecessary and should clearly be avoided. The simple and obvious alternative is to draw the demand curve in terms of a change in *relative* prices, i.e., to assume that the value of money is held constant, through compensating changes in the prices of other goods, and not that these other prices are held constant. The "income effect" of Slutsky et al. is merely a particular case or mode of change in the purchasing power of money, or the price level; and it is this problem as a whole that should be isolated and reserved for separate treatment.[9]

As to reality, important price changes generally approximate one or the other of two patterns. Either the price of a particular good changes, relative to the prices of other goods—reflecting some change in tastes or productive conditions—without a significant change in the general price level, or all prices change more or less simultaneously, in consequence of monetary changes. In so far as change is general and uniform, the whole phenomenon is purely arithmetical, particularly since incomes change in the same ratio as the prices of consumption goods. Of course, the two types of change occur together, to some extent; and especially the relative prices of consumption goods and of various indirect goods and productive services (and the present values of contracts and other commitments) are differentially changed over substantial periods by changes which originate in the field of money and ultimately lead chiefly to a movement of the general price level. Boom and depression are incidents of such temporary changes. Real, practical price problems arise only in connection with changes in relative prices, and it is exclusively the connection of general changes with such relative changes that gives the general price level any practical importance. Consequently, the separation of price changes due to monetary causes from those due to other causes is one of the main tasks of price analysis as a whole. An approach to any particular price problem which "jumbles" effects of change in the purchasing power of money (however caused) with effects of change in its relative value for purchasing different things is mere gratuitous confusion. And it is easy to avoid, specifically in the theory of demand. In fact, this confusing procedure is much more complex and difficult than one based on formulating the problem in more realistic terms to begin with, in the manner already indicated. That is, in drawing the demand curve, the utility and the objective purchasing power of money are the factors which should be held constant ("impounded in *ceteris paribus,*" in Marshall's familiar phrase) and not the prices of other consumption goods. This procedure has the further great advantage of eliminating the spurious "Giffen paradox" (see below) and making the theory of consumption logically parallel with the theory of production, which is in accord with the essential facts.[10]

It is a fairly simple matter to explain the general shape—the descending slope—of the demand curve (of an individual for a particular good) in terms of its (independent) diminishing incremental utility in comparison with that of other goods. Quantity purchased decreases as the relative price increases *(ceteris paribus)* because at the higher price the same amount of money buys less of the particular good, while there is a small converse effect on the complex of other goods, which fall in price. Consequently, if the consumer's marginal "dollar" bought equal increments of total satisfaction in terms of all services before the change, it will, after the change, buy less satisfaction if spent for the particular service, os_i, than if spent for competing services; and enough of os_i will be replaced in the individual's budget by other goods to restore the equality. The total expenditure upon os_i may increase, or decrease, or remain constant, according as the elasticity of demand (determined by all the factors which enter into the demand situation) is below, above, or equal to unity.[11]

IV. Satisfaction as a Quantity

We come to the crucial methodological, or philosophical, issue in the interpretation of economic choice, and specifically in the theory of demand. The question raised by the new school of thought has two forms or aspects. The question is whether "total satisfaction" is a cardinal magnitude, a "quantity," or is merely ordinal. This is the variable which the "economic man" strives to maximize in his choices as a consumer with a given income and as a producer with given productive resources, and strives to increase by increasing his income through saving and investment. The question is identical with that as to the reality of the diminishing marginal or incremental utility of a particular good or group of goods, as increasing amounts are consumed by an individual, *ceteris paribus*. The Slutsky analysis of demand, as developed by Hicks and others (after it was suggested by Pareto), sharply separates movement along an indifference curve (with a fixed real income) from movement from a lower to a higher indifference curve with increasing real income. We assume here that the analysis is correctly set up, with the money income of the individual increasing while all prices are constant, and that the indifference curves start from an axis of money.

The "new" analysis admits that the individual moving outward from the origin across his indifference curves is really moving "up hill" along a third perpendicular axis of total satisfaction or well-being, that the indifference curves are projections downward of contour lines on a surface. But it denies the need of assigning any vertical scale of magnitude to change in this direction. It is held that the upward movement can be represented by an index function, all other properties of which are immaterial except that it is increasing. Since that is all we need to know about it, no other information should be used in the analysis.[12] This view eliminates diminishing marginal (incremental) utility of increasing total income, in whatever manner the increase is effected, in terms of actual goods. As we have pointed out, recognition of diminishing utility is another way of saying that we can draw a curve of total satisfaction in a vertical plane through any straight line in the base plane, cutting all the indifference curves, as an x-axis and that it will ascend at a decreasing slope. This decrease in slope is a fact additional to that of ascent and can be present only if a linear scale is assigned to the perpendicular axis.

For convenience we consider movement along the axis of money, observing that the curves are spaced at equal intervals along that axis (but nowhere else) and that money has constant objective purchasing power. For the purpose of the moment, this may be given the simplest meaning—constancy of all prices. For convenience we may take this y-axis or money axis as a new x-axis, and treat the vertical third axis as a y-axis, and ask what variable it may be assumed to measure and what will be its mode of variation. There are obviously four possibilities of interpretation. The first is that the y-axis measures merely quantity of consumption, in units of some ideal index number. The curve would be a straight line diverging from the x-axis itself only because of a different unit than money price for measuring income. Anything that may be happening to the individual internally, in his mind, is ignored if not denied. This would be the rigorously objective or behavioristic view. It is appropriate in statistical economics; but even statistics implicitly assumes comparison and direction of choice by a principle of maximizing something. Second, this view might be modified, or restated without any change in substance, by interpreting the economic tendency or urge (to consume and to proportion expenditures in one way rather than another) in terms of a "force" on the analogy of mechanics, without assuming that any conscious experience or "conation" is involved.

At the opposite extreme (third) is interpretation in terms of the theory of diminishing incremental utility, in more or less the orthodox form. This is the view advocated in this paper. It includes two statements: *(a)* that the subject becomes economically better off, in terms of conscious (or "subconscious") experience, i.e., that he enjoys an increasing "quantity" (meaning intensity) of satisfaction or subjective service; and *(b)* that he can, and will, say that the increasing conscious well-being experienced in passing from a particular indifference curve I_j to the next higher one I_k is less than the increase experienced in passing from the next lower curve I_i to curve I_j. Hence the change in his well-being can be shown by a curve of decreasing upward slope. Fourth, this third position may be modified by dropping the second statement, leaving only the first. This last is the Slutsky position, which is attacked in this paper. It admits and uses comparison between levels of satisfaction but denies or ignores all comparison of differences between different levels—all judgment by the subject as to "how much" better off he becomes through any addition to income. This view is defended by appeal to the principle that entities or fundamental concepts are not to be multiplied unnecessarily—the principle known as "Occam's Razor"; its advocates hold that the statement dropped is superfluous and, if not false, is at least irrelevant. The position has to be judged with reference to the psychological reality of decreasing increments and to its usefulness in interpreting the phenomena scientifically and for practical purposes.

The validity of the decreasing additions to satisfaction or subjective service derived from equal additions to consumption of measurable objective service, regardless of kind, has already been demonstrated in our discussion of hypothetical experiments, and little remains to be said directly on that point. It is obvious to introspection that the successive equal "doses" of the service os_i or of money could be replaced with increasing doses, experimentally so adjusted that the subject would report equal, instead of decreasing, increments of satisfaction intensity. It should go without saying that we assume psychological stability in the subject and the economic or rational character of his thinking and motivation. The increments of satisfaction received from increments of a single good os_i might be experimentally quantified, and in a sense measured, by ascertaining how much of any good, or of the whole collection of goods previously consumed, represented by money, the subject would be willing to give up to secure an additional increment of the particular good at any point in the experimental variation of the latter. This could not be done for money or income as a whole, for total satisfaction can be measured only in units of itself.

There may be no harm in saying that the experiments we have described constitute "measurement," in terms of money, of the added satisfaction derived from successive increments of os_i, provided there is a clear understanding of the conditions and of the meaning of measurement in this connection. The satisfaction derived from os_i, or its "capacity" to yield satisfaction, ordinarily has no clear and direct relation to any physical attribute of the service consumed. Further, as the service enters into a budget, it cannot be said to yield a particular kind of satisfaction or a complex of particular kinds, but simply added total satisfaction. Most physical services actually yield an unanalyzable and varying complex of kinds of satisfaction, involving manifold complementary relations with other goods. We are dealing with a unique universe of subjective comparison. To investigate this new problem, we must consider the relations between objective measurement, subjective experience, and estimation.

The measurement of any physical magnitude (any that is directly perceptible to the senses) is a technical procedure for improving upon the accuracy of a subjective judgment or estimate. The operation does not measure or change in any way the estimate itself as a quantitative experience; and, to whatever degree of refinement measurement is carried, there always remains an element of comparison by subjective estimation. This source of inaccuracy is much reduced, but not eliminated, by the use of the "zero method," whereby the judgment is one of equality rather than of what multiple one magnitude is of another. (The theory of demand and of all forms of indifference curves runs in terms of the zero method; at any chosen position, the subject judges that a small shift in his expenditure makes no difference in his level of satisfaction.)

Physical mechanics is built around the three primary magnitudes of space, mass (or force [see below, pp. 261–63]), and time; and in physics as a whole the units for measuring other magnitudes are viewed as derived from these three elementary "dimensions." (Here we need think only of the classical or Newtonian conceptual system.) Of the three, space is measured in a primary and direct sense, which is not true of the other two or of any other magnitude whatever. It is only space—and, practically speaking, only length, not even area and volume—that we can cut into equal pieces, compare the pieces for equality by superposition, and count their number. The role of estimation in this process is obvious, and the relation between measurement of distance (whether by the crude yardstick method or by one which is in any degree more refined) and its outright estimation need not be discussed. All other magnitudes, including time and mass (or force), are measured indirectly through the measurement of length, by the use of some apparatus based on a theory which brings the magnitude to be measured into correlation with a scale of length. (Usually the correlation is linear—the scale divisions on the instrument are equal—but this is a detail.)

Some aspects of the relation between subjective and objective magnitudes can be brought out by the example of thermometry. Here, again, a length—familiarly, the height of a column of mercury—is assumed to measure temperature as a physical magnitude, defined by dynamic theory, which corresponds *in a general way* with our sensations of warmth and cold. If the correspondence were exact in all cases, we should hardly need thermometers; and if there were no correspondence at all, it is idle to speculate as to what might have been the development of our concept of temperature as a measurable quantity. But the quantitative changes in sensation are none the less real, whether the correspondence with the thermometer follows some nonlinear function (such as the logarithmic relation of the Weber-Fechner law, roughly valid for some magnitudes within some limits) or whether there is no simple functional relation. In the nature of the case there can be no physical measurement of the feeling of temperature (or of the estimate of length); this is a matter of direct experience and of verbal reporting. Yet either judgment—that the temperature as felt shows a linear correspondence with that measured, that they are related by any other function, or that they are not related—proves with equal and complete conclusiveness that temperature as felt is quantitative (in the cardinal sense). The subject "knows" approximately—he can estimate—whether a second change in his feeling is equal to or greater or less than a preceding one, and experimental changes could be adjusted to seem equal; and there would literally be no sense in saying that any such judgment is wrong. We hold it to be self-evident that what has been said of temperature is true of every subjective variable, regardless of its nature or relation to a measurable physical variable as a cause—or in what sense, if at all, we attribute the experience to such a cause. Whenever our minds judge one experience to be greater, more intense, than another, it is always possible to distinguish between (approximately) equal and unequal degrees of change.

An illustration which seems made to order for expository purposes (and has been used) is the grading of examination papers, in any subject from arithmetic to any branch of aesthetics, or grading human performance of any kind. Of course, the effort to grade is an effort to quantify a magnitude which is assumed to be objective in some sense, in contrast with the mere subjective experience or feeling of the grader; estimation of merit must be distinguished from mere liking. But this fact is immaterial for the argument, as long as there is no conceivable possibility of physically measuring the "real" merit of the object or performance, or of describing it in terms of physical qualities. We need not go into the special problem of the objectivity of values as magnitudes or inquire as to how far "real" values enter into economic desire and satisfaction or investigate the relation between the aesthetic merit and the economic (money) value of the same objects. What is essential is only the fact that grading is done, and on a linear numerical scale; this is conclusive for the fact of quantification and removes the main question from the sphere of argument. Manifestly, the activity is one of estimation, not of measurement, in any proper use of the word. The word "measure" ought to be used very cautiously in connection with distinctively human data, i.e., with respect to any but the simplest physical capacities of man, such as speed in running, the lifting of weights, and the like, and the ability to estimate measurable physical quantities. Averaging estimates or guesses is not measuring and should not be so called, though the notion of "reliability" implies objectivity of some kind.

Experiment shows that if the same person holds one hand for a brief interval in very warm water and the other in cold and then places both hands in water at an intermediate temperature, the latter will at the same time feel cold to one hand and warm to the other. But even such a fact has nothing to do with the quantitative character of the feeling of warmth or coldness in either hand or with the validity of its quantitative estimation by the subject. Where measurement is impossible, our confidence in the validity of estimates of magnitude or rank can itself only be estimated. It may well be true that the reliability of ranking is greater than that of estimation of differences in degree, as tested by repetition by the same or a different estimator. The essential fact here is that wherever it is possible to say of three "experienced data" of any kind, A, B, and C, that C is "greater" than B and B is greater than A, it is also possible to compare the differences, i.e., to judge (though perhaps with less accuracy) whether C is greater than B by an amount—a difference—greater or less than that by which B is greater than A. We certainly make such estimates in economic choice.[13]

We turn now to the relation between the first and second of our four possible views of the theory of choice—a purely behavioristic interpretation and one which runs in terms of "force." Early in the history of modern physics objection was raised to use of the concept of force, on the double ground that it is never open to direct observation and that it is not objective but animistic or anthropomorphic. It was (and is) pointed out that we observe or measure only the effects of forces and contended that it would be simpler and more candid to talk only about effects, i.e., equations of motion, in relation to observed and measured antecedents or conditions. The place of motive in economic choice presents a closely parallel problem. In mechanics the issue arises at the very beginning, in the question as to what it is that is measured in the second of the three primary units—grams or pounds. Those who repudiate the notion of force contend that the gram (or pound) is a unit of mass and that the word "force" is simply a shorter designation of the defining relationship, the product of mass by acceleration. The expression $f = ma$ should then be treated as a definition and not as an equality.

This reasoning is plausible, but any effort to follow the procedure advocated runs at once into insuperable difficulty; for, in fact, mass is not measured and not experienced directly, but only as force. In practice, the unit is a unit of weight and is measured with the balance or by elastic deformation (of a steel spring or the like). Theoretically, mass should be measured by comparing the accelerations of two masses when these "interact." But, unfortunately for the theory, interaction itself is never directly observed, or even inferred, without the mediation of some force. It has, of course, long been known that impact is no exception to this statement, that literal impact between rigid solids is both unreal and theoretically impossible, since it would involve infinite acceleration. (In modern theory mass would be infinite at a relative velocity equal to that of light.) The empirical phenomenon of impact involves either elastic or permanent deformation, and neither can be interpretively conceived without using the idea of force as an elementary datum. The palpable fact is that the most elementary mechanical phenomena cannot be thought of in purely empirical terms, in the meaning which our minds seem to crave, namely, *visual* observation. The impossibility of such a "behavioristic" view should be evident to reflection and has been pointed out by theoretical physicists.[14]

It may be admitted that the notion of force "seems" more anthropomorphic and subjective than other qualities of objects which seem to be more directly perceived. When we see or picture in thought an interaction between two bodies, such as the familiar impact of billiard balls, we think we observe (see, literally or in imagination) the change in motion and only infer the operation of force. And the inference seems to involve "reading into" the physical process something from an imagined experience of our own—either tactile pressure or muscular effort. However, reflection makes it a serious question whether we do not observe force at least as truly and "primarily" as we observe anything, specifically, when we see objects. We certainly feel both weight and inertia in our own bodily members and in objects which exert pressure upon us or offer resistance to our efforts to change their state of rest or motion. It is noteworthy that the qualities early distinguished as "primary" are those perceived in this way, in contrast with visual properties as secondary; and it is an accepted doctrine of psychology that the visual recognition of physical objects in their external, three-dimensional reality is learned through the education of the eyes by tactile sensation, pressure, and movement or muscular kinesthesis. In fact, no one has ever proposed a distinction acceptable to critical common sense between what we perceive and what we infer. We think we see objects, but if in thinking we go back of immediate (adult) experience, what we really perceive is light waves or some physicochemical change in eye, or nerve, or brain. The difference between the cognition of force and perception by sight (and perhaps hearing) seems to be that one perceives a force only when it is acting directly on his own body, while vision (and in a sense hearing and smell, but not taste) "report" on objects at a distance. However, we usually do not see anything unless we voluntarily look at it (in contrast with hearing and smell); but we believe things "visibly" exist whether we momentarily see them or not, and the apparent anthropomorphism of force rests on an unwillingness to assume that they similarly exert force.

In human, and specifically in economic, behavior, motive—i.e., desire for things or their services, or for experiences of "satisfaction"—is the analogue of force in mechanics. Objects of choice may be thought of as exerting a "pull" upon the subject and so causing a response in behavior. (Repulsions can always be interpreted in positive terms, and we need not inquire into the ground of the occasional negative quality of the feeling.) But in the field of conduct, the *a fortiori* argument for the reality of the force (motive) is irresistibly conclusive. If interpretive thinking cannot do without the notion of force as a reality in physical nature, it becomes arbitrary in the nth degree to rule motive out of our conception of the conduct of human beings, where everyone is directly aware of it in his own experience and has the most certain knowledge of its reality in others. Our knowledge of what is in other minds is more certain than that which we have of the reality of the physical world, and prior to the latter. All our common-sense knowledge of the world of objects and especially all of our scientific knowledge manifestly depend on valid intercommunication with other minds, since no observation is regarded as valid unless it is or can be confirmed through other observers.

Our thinking about conduct must conform to common-sense introspection and intelligible intercommunication, which always run in terms of "reasons" for action or choice, meaning ends or motives. In the discussion of conduct we cannot separate description from teleological interpretation—the "what" from the "why" in this sense—what is done from what is achieved or expected to be achieved. Motive in relation to conduct—as a form of answer to the question "Why?"—is an intermediate and ambiguous category, much like force in relation to motion. Under critical scrutiny motive tends to "go over" one way or the other, giving place either to a purely empirical (perceptual but not really physical) view of behavior as taking place in accord with scientific laws or to an idealistic, subjectivistic world view. But in the one direction lies naive materialism and in the other "solipsism"—equally impossible positions.[15]

There is a special reason (motive!) against admitting motive into the interpretation of economic choice, in that choices do not seem to correspond accurately with motives. This is true with respect to other persons, and also of one's own choices, viewed with detachment or from a later point in time. This discrepancy is partly a matter of error in choice itself and partly one of error in the assignment of motives, including one's own. Probably everyone makes choices "really knowing" at the time that he will be sorry afterward—or will feel sorry—rightly or wrongly. In physical causality the fact that we know a force only by inference from its effects means that discrepancy between the two is impossible. When any force known to be operating does not fully and accurately account for an observed effect, we confidently impute the difference to some other force, known or unknown. Why we do not spontaneously and finally do the same in the case of human responses raises the ultimate problem of *freedom*. With respect to freedom or will the essential fact is that we "know too much" about human motivation to consider it exhaustively interpretable in terms of antecedent physical conditions as causes. Especially, we know indubitably the complex fact of *error*. We have to assume that the behavior of inert objects is not affected by *effort* or by thinking which is *aimed* at *solving problems* and so is not like human choice, inherently subject to error. This also means that freedom in choice involves more than mere contingency or chance or caprice, and ordinarily more than "arbitrary" thought and action.

The philosophical question of whether the comparison of satisfactions (utilities) should be thought of as a comparison between magnitudes which exist separately and are quantified separately or whether the recognition of utility inherently involves a comparison has a certain parallel in the case of force. We are apparently unable to think of any force as existing and acting entirely apart from some other force, or a "resistance" of some sort (Newton's third law of motion). It is also evident that the idea of economic value, or utility, always arises out of the necessity of choosing between alternative "goods," more or less different in kind. The giving-up of an alternative good is the meaning of cost. The relativity of desires is more intimate than that of forces. But in mechanics forces are dealt with one at a time, and the same is true of desires in economics; any one desire or attraction is a distinct factor and the associated satisfaction an independent variable under any actual conditions of choice. (However, discussion of the psychological effect of variation in the consumption of a single good, under the condition that it is the only one consumed by the individual, in place of reasonable *ceteris paribus* conditions, is one of the "classical errors" from which theory needs to free itself.) Desire for a particular service might, of course, be viewed as a mutual attraction between the human being and the good, as in the case of masses, electric charges, or magnetic poles; but the economist should doubtless follow the common-sense procedure of locating the attraction in the "mind" of the human being. In fact, even physicists speak of the magnet one-sidedly attracting its armature, the earth the apple, etc., where theory makes the attraction mutual.[16]

One or two observations on the use of physical analogy in economic analysis should be added, by way of warning, particularly with reference to the concepts of statics and dynamics and to units and dimensions. We have pointed out that the fundamental economic magnitudes have the nature and dimensionality of flow or flux, not of existent masses. In an economic system the forces and their equilibrium relate to rates of flow, i.e., the distribution of a current among alternative paths, under a (difference of) pressure or potential of some sort. There is no direct analogy with equilibrium between objects stationary in a field of force. The true physical analogy would require an elaborate construction hardly undertaken so far in the literature, to the writer's knowledge. It is not to be undertaken here, but one or two points call for mention.

Of the three elementary dimensions in (Newtonian) mechanics, only time carries over into economics with at all the same meaning.[17] As to space, economists speak of direction and velocity of change; but it seems impossible either to bring these notions into any intelligible relation with the three-dimensional field of Euclidean space or to formulate any usable conception of economic hyper-space. The analogy of mass, in relation to force, presents even greater difficulties; and we probably cannot formulate any usable analogy for physical friction, involving energy loss. The best "model" for an economic system would seem to be one based on the phenomena of electric current, generated by a large

number of interconnected sources and distributing itself through a complex network of circuits. One should, of course, begin with the case
of a single generator feeding a number of circuits, as the analogue for a
Crusoe economy. At the outset the role of inertia would be ignored, as
electromagnetic induction is ignored in Ohm's law stating the relations
for electricity. The relation between potential, resistance, and flow—
maximizing satisfaction under diminishing utility—will be less simple
than Ohm's formula, because electrical resistance is invariant with respect to current; but it is quite manageable mathematically. Another
serious difficulty lies in the fact that in the human case the treatment
of the "source" itself, the human being, as either simple or constant
involves heroic abstraction, even if we could think of our Robinson
Crusoe as using only his own "person" in the satisfaction of his economic
wants, ignoring all other instrumentalities. The difficulty centers in the
concept of capital (the whole complex "source" itself) and its maintenance and/or growth or decline. (Capital theory is the central difficulty
in any attempt at rigorous formulation of economic relationships and
processes.)

Turning from theoretical to practical difficulties, it is actually quite
unrealistic to think of the functional (cause-and-effect) relations between
economic variables as remaining unchanged through a real change in
any independent variable.[18] There is always a significant "lag" in time;
and in the meantime other things will not remain "equal." The demand
curve (our special topic in this paper) affords an excellent illustration,
being undoubtedly the most solidly real of all the functional relations
dealt with in economic theory. The individual curve for a particular
good describes a theoretical position of equilibrium in the relation between price and quantity taken. In reality, any change in the price, unless infinitely gradual, will carry the rate of consumption to a point off
the curve, and it will "tend" to return to the curve at a new point. But
conceptual interpretation of the lag of consumption change behind price
change involves a causal sequence bearing some analogy to the action of
a force against a resistance in which inertia is combined with friction
(opposing the redistribution of a flow among alternate paths). The result
to be expected under stationary conditions would be "damped oscillations," settling down at a new point on the curve. The nature of the
concepts required for interpreting such phenomena calls loudly for investigation, particularly with respect to the possibility of finding any
magnitude which can be assumed to remain constant, on the analogy of
the conservation principles of mechanics (with or without allowance

for energy loss). This line of argument suggests a basis for a pure theory of economic fluctuations. But the realism of such theorizing would be severely limited because the heart of the phenomena in the human case is uncertainty, error, and speculation (with some analogy to mental inertia!) in the thinking by which economic behavior is controlled, and these are not considered to be present in mechanical processes.

For numerous and important reasons, economic theory cannot approach the analytical realism of mechanics—remote from the empirical facts and the conditions of practical problems as are the assumptions of the latter science. Motives are not analogous to forces, i.e., merely concepts for interpreting conduct, which could be left out, to yield an empirical description of the causal sequence in physical or behavioristic terms. As already observed, we "know too much"; we have direct knowledge, not only that motives are present but that they do *not* correspond with hypothetical forces connecting behavior with its antecedent conditions. Their operation disrupts the uniformity of sequence. In the first place, action rarely leads to exactly the intended result, because it is always affected by error, which also is of several kinds. And, beyond this fact, ends are never really given. Actual desires are partly a matter of curiosity—the urge to explore—giving rise to the paradox of expected surprise as an important element in motivation. A different matter is the problem-solving interest, the quest of the "right" answer to some question, which it is a sheer contradiction to treat as an end given in advance. Well-being is largely of this nature, the answer to an unsolved problem, to be sought through "intelligent" experiment.

Finally, the practical significance of economic theory is in the field of social action, not of individual conduct. Particularly in a democratic society the instrumental pattern of means and end hardly fits this problem at all. It would have some application, though even then a very limited one, if we could think of the social problem as that of an absolute dictator, entirely outside of society and viewing his "subjects" merely as passive instruments for his own purposes. (They would have to be "lower" than any real slaves or even beasts of burden.) In free society the primary objective is agreement on terms of association, and the secondary objective is agreement on "right" terms and on the "best" ends and procedures. Actually association itself has only to a limited extent the purpose assumed in economic analysis—cooperation for the achievement of any ends, of individuals or of groups. To a very large extent it is a matter of formulating the rules of a game, in which individuals do indeed pursue ends, but ends symbolic in character, set up to make activity interesting, instrumental to this purpose, and in large part effective because of their conflicting or competitive nature. The intelligence involved in playing games is a very different kind of faculty from either technical-instrumental rationality or the thinking used in apportioning means. Incidentally, the ability to invent games or improve the rules is much less common in the human species than these other capacities—which still do not exhaust the ambiguity of the word "intelligence."

V. Consumer's Surplus

The consumer's surplus idea was doubtless first adumbrated by Dupuit; but the term and the classical treatment come from Marshall and the general observations to be offered here will be oriented primarily to his treatment. It has extremely little practical significance, but a correct exposition is useful in bringing out the relations between the individual demand curve and the indifference curves, with which it is much confused. It may also be useful for the price theory of monopoly, in connection with perfectly classified monopoly price.

Marshall defines the concept as the excess of the price which a person would be willing to pay rather than go without the thing, over that which he actually does pay (*Principles,* 8th ed., p. 124). We shall see that this definition is incorrect as well as loosely stated. The amount by which a person's total expenditure for a good under demand conditions (buying freely at a given price) is less than he would be willing to pay for the same amount rather than do without it altogether does not correspond with the value to him of having the good available at the price rather than unavailable—other conditions being the same[19]—and the latter is the essential idea.

There can be no question of the "theoretical reality" of the concept of consumer's surplus, as defined, and it would need to be considered by a rational individual in the situation used by Marshall as an illustration. That (as will be recalled) is the case of a man choosing between living in a modern city and in a primitive community (central Africa) where the products available are assumed to have the same prices but where the same money income purchases less "value" because some products are not to be had. (To make the comparison valid, we must assume that there are no compensating advantages in other uses of income and that the choice is permanent and the income the same, so as to exclude temporary residence in the primitive community and saving for later expenditure in the higher civilization.) The problem is to find an unambiguous measure or expression for the advantage, in terms of money.

One difficulty in connection with Marshall's theory is that of forming any clear and defensible conception of what is meant by neglecting the change in the marginal utility of money. In the main argument, based on the purchase of tea for domestic consumption, which is introduced "in order to give definiteness to our notions" (*Principles,* pp. 125–27), the object seems to be to set up the assumption that there is no difference between a demand curve for tea (under the conditions of free purchase) and a marginal utility curve or an indifference curve in the price form. This is also clearly implied in the discussion of the diagram in his footnote on page 128. But the whole argument is economically nonsensical; to make the various curves identical or to give meaning to the area under the demand curve, we must practically assume that all the curves are horizontal; and this assumption not only defies the facts but eliminates consumer's surplus altogether.

A second interpretation of the Marshallian assumption is adopted in a brief and ingenious discussion by A. Henderson. It is that "the marginal rate of substitution between X and money is independent of income."[20] This view seems to be neither a reasonable interpretation of Marshall's position nor economically defensible. It would make the demand curve and the indifference curves independent of the individual's income, and, as argued above, this would also make the consumption independent of the price. The most plausible view would again treat the indifference-combinations curves as straight lines, the other curves as horizontal and coincident. (It is geometrically possible to introduce, respectively, curvature and declining slope, as Henderson does.) The assumption that the demand has neither income nor price elasticity is not impossible, as an approximation, for an unimportant commodity over a limited range. That is, within this range, the consumer may buy approximately the amount of X he would consume if it were a free good, while at a lower income or a higher price he will not buy it at all. If the assumption is generalized, it means that the consumer's only response to price or income change will be to add fixed amounts of different goods to his budget or to drop them, as the case may be.

A third possibility is to take Marshall as meaning quite literally what he seems to say, most explicitly in his mathematical note (p. 84n), namely, that "the marginal utility of money to the individual purchaser is the same throughout." That is, money is assumed to have an "absolute" marginal utility in the consumer's equilibrium position from which we start (with or without the opportunity to purchase X freely at a fixed price), and this magnitude is assumed to be invariant with respect to the amount of income spent for X, as the price of X varies from zero to infinity.[21] Whether the change so neglected would really be negligible or not manifestly depends on the importance of X in the consumer's budget. This, in turn, is partly a matter of the total number of commodities consumed, partly one of the intrinsic qualities of X, and partly of its complementarity relations with other goods. Marshall explicitly makes an exception for "commodities some supply of which is necessary for life" (p. 133, n. 1). He apparently fails to recognize that necessity is entirely a matter of degree or that no particular commodity as bought in the market under ordinary conditions is necessary; finally, in assuming that we can know the individual's utility (satisfaction) function for money, he fails to see that income as a whole is in a sense necessary, but not in any definable amount. His suggestion, that we take the necessary supply for granted and estimate the total utility of the excess over this amount, must be applied to money, not to a particular commodity, and must be interpreted to mean an income which would actually yield zero satisfaction.

The problem of consumer's surplus is that of finding a monetary measure or expression for an increment of total satisfaction which accrues to a consumer through having the opportunity to purchase a freely chosen amount of a particular good at a particular price, in comparison with a situation in which the good is not available and all other conditions are the same. In the second situation he will spend the same amount of money on other goods at the same prices (but not necessarily quite the same list of other goods), freely distributing his expenditure among these. The problem lies in the field of value dynamics, surveyed in Section 2 above, not in that of price-quantity relations under given conditions. To begin with, it is impossible literally to measure in money a change in the total utility of an income which itself is expressed in money. The only problem which can be pictured as real is that which is indicated by the third assumption we have been considering. We must measure a change in total satisfaction in units of the absolute satisfaction yielded by an increment of money income under some given conditions, assuming that this magnitude is not changed by the actual change in the use of the increment of income in question. Of course, it would be changed, more or less. If the change is substantial, the result is merely that our measurement still runs in terms of the original value; it will not become relative to the actual new value.

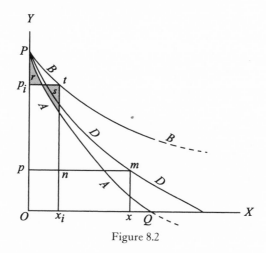

Figure 8.2

To handle this problem analytically, it will be useful to have in mind three curves, as shown in Figure 8.2. Curve A shows the variation in the relative marginal utility of good (service) X, measured by money. It is really an indifference curve, being drawn under the condition that the subject actually purchases each successive small unit of X at the maximum price he is willing to pay, after buying the earlier units seriatim on these terms. Curve B shows the same facts, but with prices averaged out. It is so drawn in relation to A that any three-cornered area, r, is equal to the area, s, for any point, p_i (see shaded areas). That is, the ordinates of B show the highest price at which any quantity of X can be sold to the consumer, if he is free only to take or leave the whole amount. (We do not go into the meaning of curves A or B beyond the point Q, where A intersects the x-axis.) D is a demand curve. We cannot draw this curve from the data of the other two. We know only that it will run between A and B except for the terminal point P on the vertical axis. This means that at any positive (relative) price at which the consumer buys good X at all, he will buy less of it if free to choose the amount than he can be made to buy if he must take all or none at a maximum average price (or the price he will pay for any amount is less than he could be made to pay under the more restricted terms of choice). But the amount he will freely buy is greater than that which would have the same marginal utility in terms of money at his stopping-point if he bought all the earlier units seriatim at the maximum price for each in turn (or bought the whole block at his maximum total or average price). This is because under the demand condition he will have money left after reaching the terminal point of the second condition and will spend some of this for X (if all goods are "simple"). This last fact is a consequence of the existence of diminishing utility and of consumer's surplus.

The consumer's surplus obviously is *not* measured by the three-cornered area bounded by the price axis, the demand curve, and the upper boundary of the expenditure rectangle *Opmx, Ox* being the amount purchased at price p under demand conditions. In fact, *the area under a demand curve has no economic meaning whatever.* Consumer's surplus as a subjective magnitude is the difference between the total satisfaction yielded by the quantity of a particular good freely purchased at any price and that which would be secured by freely spending the *same amount of money* for other goods at (just below) the actual uniform margin. In terms of money it must be the money value of this difference. The second alternative is, of course, identical with spending the same money for good X under indifference conditions (however represented graphically), which by definition makes it a matter of indifference what quantity of X is purchased, including zero amount. The surplus should not be measured by the difference between two different money expenditures for the same quantity of X, since this result differs from the value determined by the other comparison.[22]

To obtain (on this form of diagram) the money measure of the difference—the surplus—we must first locate the point t on curve B, which subtends with the two axes a rectangle of the same area as the expenditure rectangle under the demand curve for the given demand price p. The magnitude sought is, then, the area of the rectangle cut off from this total-expenditure rectangle by the ordinate of this point, i.e., at x_i. It is the area of the rectangle $x_i nmx$. The "indifference expenditure rectangle," $Op_i tx_i$, has, of course, the same area as that under curve A between the price axis and the ordinate at x_i.[23]

Since, as repeatedly emphasized, the curve of marginal utility relative to money, or the indifference curve in any form, cannot be drawn from demand data, all this procedure is purely formal and without practical meaning. Its only use is to clarify certain analytical concepts and to prevent making certain errors. The primary error in Marshall's analysis, and in the textbooks which have commonly followed the same procedure, is that of identifying or confusing the demand curve with the curve of marginal utility in terms of money and of treating the area under the demand curve as the measure of total satisfaction.

A theoretical measure of consumer's surplus could be derived more simply in graphic terms by using a series of indifference-combinations curves for quantities of money and of good X. It must be emphasized that the procedure would still be purely hypothetical since market data do not provide the facts required for drawing indifference curves. These might be had only from actual experimentation with strictly classified monopoly price. But it would also be necessary to establish conditions under which the buyer would not know or suspect the nature of his situation or in which purchasers are, in fact, so numerous that any one is negligible to the seller, while, at the same time, purchase for resale is somehow excluded. Otherwise the situation will be one of bargaining and "bluffing," between a monopoly and a monopsony, and the price will be indeterminate within a range depending on the details of the two curves. However, for the purpose of clarifying analytical procedure (as before) we may impose the arbitrary conditions called for and proceed.

Our figure embodies the same basic diagram and notation employed by Henderson, and before him (in an incomplete form) by Hicks (Figure 8.3). The point M on the vertical axis shows the money income of the individual. The line MP'' is a line of slope p, where p is the price of X. It is tangent to some indifference curve I_2 at P, which point marks the position of equilibrium for the consumer under market-demand conditions, where ON measures the amount of X bought. (For clarity the diagram is drawn off-scale, with vertical distances greatly exaggerated.) Curve I_1 is the indifference-combinations curve of the individual for X and money, corresponding to income M. The vertical distance PR is, indeed, the excess amount of money the individual would pay for ON of X offered as an indivisible block, over the amount FP which he does pay in the free market. But it is not the consumer's surplus. Henderson is correct in saying that "if the individual had spent FR in buying ON of X, he would have been just as well off as if the commodity had not been available, whereas in fact he only had to spend FP on it." But he overlooks the fact that the individual would also have been just as well off at any other point (than R) on indifference curve I_1 (and as well off at any other point than P on I_2). Yet he recognizes that the money measure of the difference in situation represented by the two curves is not the same at any two points on either—unless the curves are arbitrarily drawn in an admittedly indefensible way. The correct comparison with free purchase is clearly the point at which he spends the same amount of money for less X and not where he spends more money for the same amount of X (in both cases paying a higher average price but not the same price in these two cases); for, if X had not been available, he would have spent the same amount on other things.

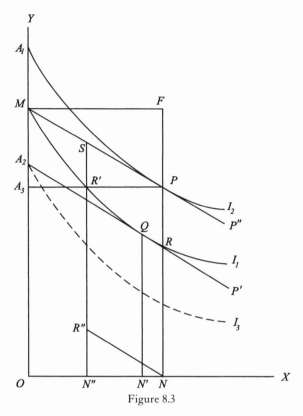

Figure 8.3

To find the money measure of consumer's surplus, defined as we have defined it, we draw the horizontal line PA_3, cutting the indifference curve I_1 at R'. Spending the same amount of money FP under the indifference conditions, the individual would buy A_3R' (or ON'') of X instead of ON; i.e., he would buy $N''N$ less than if he bought under market conditions. The money value of this difference at the given price is $N''R''$ (NR'' being drawn parallel to the original price line), or it is $R''S$. This is less than PR even if the curves are drawn according to Henderson's interpretation of Marshall's assumption, i.e., so as to have the same slope for the same X value, hence a uniform vertical distance between them.

A still more defensible money measure of the difference in satisfaction represented by two indifference-combinations curves is afforded by the notion of a "compensating variation." The term was introduced by Hicks as the best way of looking at consumer's surplus but was mistakenly identified by him with his graphic measure of the surplus, the line segment PR. As Henderson shows, the magnitude has two values, both different from that of the consumer's surplus as defined by Hicks and Henderson and also different from our "correct" definition. The measurement calls for a system of indifference-combinations curves beginning or terminating on the Y-axis or money axis, and it derives its superiority from this feature. (Hicks drew only one of these curves in this way, the one at point M.)

Expressed in words, the compensating variation might, in fact, take any of four different forms. First, we may consider the position of an individual with an income M and without the privilege of buying X freely at a certain market price and may ask either (I-a) what is the maximum amount of income he would be willing to give up in exchange for the privilege, or (I-b) what is the minimum additional income he would accept as an equivalent to getting it? Second, we may consider the position of an individual who has an income M and also has the privilege in question and may ask (II-a) how much additional income he would demand to give it up, or (II-b) how much of his actual income he would be willing to give up as an alternative to parting with the privilege? There are actually but two magnitudes, since I-a and II-b are identical, as are I-b and II-a. Henderson works out, first, I-a (equals MA_2) and then II-a (equals A_1M), which he strangely says is also the Marshallian consumer's surplus. It should be noted that two of the four different magnitudes—i.e., Henderson's second form of the compensating variation (II-a or A_1M) and the Hicks-Henderson consumer's surplus (PR)—will be identical if (and only if) the indifference curves are straight lines identical with the price line or are otherwise so drawn that the vertical distance between them is the same for all values of X. The other two magnitudes will be different from both, as well as between themselves, unless still more implausible conditions are imposed.

The two compensating variations are different because an individual buying X freely at the same price at different income levels will buy different amounts (if it is a "simple" good or one of any probable utility composition). The two values of the compensating variation involve the two intervals between three successive indifference curves. For an individual to be on I_1 with the privilege of buying X freely at price p is equivalent to being on I_2 without the privilege; and being on I_1 without it is equivalent to being on a lower curve I_3 passing through A_2 with the privilege open. But movement from M to A_1 represents a greater monetary difference on the Y-axis than movement from M to A_2, because more X will be bought out of a higher income at the same price, because, in turn, the marginal utility of money is lower compared with that of a given supply of any single good.

The vertical or monetary distance between two indifference curves, or the order of two such distances at other points cannot be inferred from the magnitudes along the axis of money. This is true whether or not a linear scale is assigned to the suppressed third axis (of utility or satisfaction). The indifference curves are projections upon the base plane of contour lines on a surface, defined either by a utility function or by some index function with the properties considered essential. In either case the shape of the curves depends on the character of the good X and its relationships with other goods available for purchase. We can draw curves spaced equally, or in any other way, along the money axis; but their vertical spacing anywhere else obviously depends on their shape. About this we know in general only three facts. They always have a negative slope (within the significant range), they do not intersect (or meet), and they cannot have a uniform slope and vertical spacing for different values of X. This third feature would involve zero income elasticity of demand for X, and this, as we have seen, is conceivable only for a good with a complex utility so arranged that displacement of other goods would exactly offset the diminishing utility of the various component types of satisfaction which it yields.[24]

The utility value of a difference in money income is still another matter. This would be measured along a third axis perpendicular to the plane of a diagram of the type here discussed.

Notes

1. In the pure theory, or ultimate analysis, of economic behavior, production is for consumption and does not involve any motivation other than that which is derived or imputed from the consumer interest. Production and consumption should be defined in such a way as to make this distinction clear. Immediate preferences between productive activities will then be treated as situations in which a certain amount of consumption is simultaneous with production, and the two are inseparable. And saving—net production of capital—will be viewed in the usual (only partly realistic) way as provision for future consumption. The sweeping limitation of such assumptions, in contrast with the inclusive facts of motivation, can be given only incidental notice in this paper.

2. Hicks, *Value and Capital* (Oxford, 1939), chap. 1; Schultz, *The Theory and Measurement of Demand* (Chicago, 1938); see also the contributions of Mosak and Samuelson to *Studies in Mathematical Economics and Econometrics, in*

Memory of Henry Schultz, edited by O. Lange, F. McIntyre, and T. O. Yntema (Chicago, 1942).

3. In the course of this discussion we shall distinguish sharply between quantification and measurement, stressing quantification by estimation without measurement, and will use the terms "quantity" and "ordinal magnitude" to designate the two main concepts which are to be contrasted.

This article will not be encumbered with references to the literature—even that which is known to the writer and which, in view of his mathematical limitations, he feels competent to judge. This applies especially to recent work (including articles by Hicks) based on the assumption of absolute money prices and relative utility, which it is the main purpose of the article to criticize. Earlier references may be found in the books of Schultz and Hicks cited above in n. 2. The aim here is to clarify issues and state a position in non-mathematical and the simplest possible terms. To venture into detailed criticism of the history of doctrine would both extend the paper far beyond allowable compass and make its perusal laborious and confusing. The writer may note, however, that he was first jolted out of complacency and led to rethink the problem by reading a short article by Oscar Lange, "The Determinateness of the Utility Function," *Review of Economic Studies* 1 (1934): 218–25. Also that in the discussion which followed the publication of this article and of articles by Schultz, and Hicks, and Allen in 1934 and 1935, and their independent rediscovery of Slutsky's paper of 1915, Harro Bernardelli stands out as a thinker and particularly one of mathematical competence who has "kept his feet on the ground" and not been swept away by the romantic glamour of revolution and the temptation to indulge in logical ingenuity presented by the "new" form of analysis. Cf. "Notes on the Determinateness of the Utility Function," *Review of Economic Studies* 2 (1934–35): 69–77. It goes without saying that we recognize the high intellectual quality of the work which has gone into the development of the "new approach" and its value in contributing to the clarification of the issues, and also that choice between fundamental assumptions is, to some extent, a matter of taste and may depend on the purpose in view in a particular exposition.

4. We more commonly meet with the indifference-combinations curve for two goods as generated by changes in opposite directions from an intermediate starting point, as roughly suggested in the accompanying figure (Figure 8.4). Only a part of the negatively inclined portion of the curve is usually drawn, the continuous line in the figure. If the curve is projected in realistic form in both directions, it will have the general shape indicated by the dotted portions. Details would largely depend on the goods in question, their absolute and relative importance, relations of complementarity and substitution, etc. Single commodities that are actually "necessary" hardly occur, and this and other special cases need not be considered. In both directions the curve will ordinarily become parallel, first, with the neighboring axis and then with the other axis. This second event might occur before reaching a point of intersection with the other branch, preventing completion of the closed figure shown. In any event

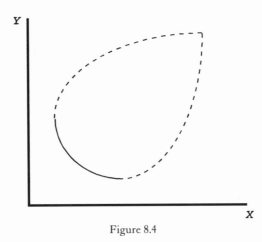

Figure 8.4

the situation represented by the parts of the curve beyond zero marginal utility for either commodity is unrealistic and need not be discussed.

5. The former procedure was followed by Cournot in a pure-theory treatment and is the point of view of statistical investigators of demand.

6. It should go without saying that the "production of capital" means here "net production" or "growth," distinguished from the maintenance of capital already existing, including all replacements, even by a different type of concrete agent (and that "capital" consumption means "net" consumption.) In real life the bulk of investment is "presumptively permanent"; only the yield is expected to be consumed, or not all of that, apart from some emergency—but, of course, there are important exceptions. We cannot go into the special difficulties of investment in human beings or their capacities (and its maintenance) in "free" society, beyond noting that in essential respects these are much like any other capital. This fact and its practical limitation will be evident if one compares conditions in a slave economy with those of free individualism (see also n. 7 below).

7. This assumption again raises the difficulty of the individual's ownership and use of himself as a productive agent. It is really necessary to assume only that all ownership—of things, or capacities, or money—is held constant. Consumption must be separated from such changes, particularly in the holding of money, in order to isolate the special problems connected with that cause. One important desideratum in economic analysis is to bring out explicitly the unrealistic assumptions necessary to generality at every point.

8. There is actually no reasonable ground for doubt that money income of constant objective purchasing-power decreases in marginal utility (and utility per unit) as its amount increases, even if expenditure is not restricted to the purchase of the same goods. This restriction only makes the conclusion more obvious and the decline more rapid than if the individual is free to add new items to his budget. The rate of decline might be reduced by a high degree of complementarity between items previously consumed and new items; but the

general effect of this will be merely a greater variety in consumption at all income levels. It is a judgment of common sense, on a level of self-evidence virtually that of the simpler mathematical axioms that, other things being equal, the addition or subtraction of a dollar per week or month from his income means less to the recipient of a larger income than to one whose income is smaller. Apart from this principle, no one would defend or suggest the justice of progressive income taxation. Equality of sacrifice of "final value" to the subject (however this is interpreted) would then call for absolutely equal taxation, not even equality in the fractional levy, to say nothing of progression. (The statement assumes that consumption is the only significance of income, ignoring such factors as security, prestige, power, justice, etc., which may make equality a consideration for other reasons or on its own account).

As far as the present discussion is concerned, we need not dispute the usual assumption that the desire for income is insatiable, that its marginal utility would never fall to zero or become negative, if it can be used to satisfy additional wants. However, the proposition is doubtful if wants are strictly defined in terms of consumption, excluding social emulation, prestige, and power. And it is surely false if we go on and exclude special costs of change desired purely for the sake of change. However, this factor bulks large in want-satisfaction even at low income levels and introduces an element of unreality into a mechanical or function-and-variable theory of demand.

9. The conception of price changes as relative is, of course, the view which was made classical by the treatment of J. S. Mill and is perhaps the position generally adopted in textbooks—when the authors state their assumptions or make it possible to discern any consistent position.

10. We may digress to point out that the general point of view and habit of mind reflected in the Hicks-Slutsky analysis has wide ramifications in recent literature and has led to utter confusion in the whole body of economic thought. We refer, of course, to the huge corpus of discussion beginning with Keynes's *General Theory* and following the lead of that work. J. R. Hicks's book, *Value and Capital,* is especially interesting as a general treatise which combines the theory of Keynes's treatment of unemployment and money with the Slutsky analysis of demand and theory of utility. It should be kept in mind that there is no logical connection between the confusion of price changes due to monetary causes and those due to other causes with either the use of indifference curves or their distinctive psychological-philosophical interpretation.

This whole episode may be viewed as a reaction against the neglect of monetary changes and their extremely important effects (boom and depression) in the main line of treatises of classical economic theory, including Marshall's. Mill and other classical writers paid some incidental attention to monetary or trade crises but strangely neglected the more important and longer-range repercussions upon production, as well as the converse causal relation between productive maladjustments—especially in the field of investment—and price disorganization. Failure to deal somewhere with these phenomena is doubtless a valid criticism of the classical economic theory as a whole. But it does not follow at all that the omission is to be corrected by jumbling other maladjustments, real and pecuniary, in with the general theory of economic equilibrium. The valid remedy for the defect represents much less of a departure from tradition. It consists simply in adding what has been lacking, i.e., adding a theory of monetary perturbations to the theory of general equilibrium. We need not here enter upon this task, but we may note that, since all the important phenomena could well occur without either commercial banking or any lending of money, the perturbations of the interest rate (or rates) and their causes and effects are a relatively minor topic in the inquiry as a whole.

11. If we consider the whole range of price variation, the elasticity of demand will normally have a high value at the highest price at which consumption begins, and will fall to zero as price declines to some point at which consumption no longer increases appreciably with its further decline. Elasticity must, of course, be measured at a position of equilibrium. It will ordinarily be low if determined in relation to sudden changes; and the fact that these afford practically the only possibility of determining it inductively largely vitiates statistical measurements; for if a change is slow, other things cannot be assumed equal, and we cannot distinguish empirically between a movement along the curve and a movement of the curve as a whole. The elasticity of demand depends on the availability of substitutes; but freedom of substitution is only in part a matter of physical similarity between goods or even between the types of satisfaction which they yield.

It must be emphasized that the demand curve, showing the relation between price and quantity taken, under the condition that the subject is free to buy as much or as little as he pleases of os_i at a uniform price (other things being equal in other respects), is a very different thing from any form of indifference curve. A demand curve cannot be drawn from an indifference curve, nor from a system of indifference curves in the form in which these usually appear. A curve of the Hicks-Slutsky type can be drawn from an indifference map only if objective money or commodity values are given for the curves; a true demand curve could presumably (in theory) be computed from a complete "map" in n dimensions (in algebraic form) and a given income and given pattern of compensating price changes.

12. In the absence of experimental determination of a satisfaction function, we actually work with the supposed essential properties of such functions.

13. The writer knows of only one case of quantitative variation in a physical quality where it is possible to rank but impossible to space the ranks along a linear or numerical scale. This is the case of the hardness of solids as determined exclusively by the scratching test. In this case, and in any case where magnitudes are ranked and only the rank is given, no valid numerical correlation with any other series can be computed. Correlation between ranked series, or of such a series with any measured variable, rests on an arbitrary assumption that all the ranks are equally spaced along a scale.

Estimates of differences are fairly definite only within the range of direct observation. In this fact also there is a difference of degree from the comparison of primary magnitudes.

14. See, e.g., a review article by H. Poincaré, "Les Idées de Hertz sur la mécanique," *Revue générale des sciences pures et appliquées* 8, no. 16 (August 30, 1897): 734–43. Of course, all real, observable, terrestrial, physical phenomena also involve friction and loss of energy. This concept is even more metaphysical than that of force, specifically since it involves the notion of potential energy. The problem of friction and its analogue in economic phenomena will be touched upon later. We need not go into the modern replacement of the force concept by field theory, beyond noting that hyper-space raises equal difficulty for common sense.

15. To the earlier distinction between primary and secondary qualities—the former supposed really to exist in things, the latter only in the mind of the observer—a nineteenth-century school of thought added "tertiary" qualities to take care of values. Apart from the dubious character of the distinctions as drawn, this scheme still fails to take account of another distinction which is even more important for both theoretical and practical thinking. That is the difference between the mere fact of being desired and having "value" in some objective meaning. It is a distinction which everyone constantly makes, and cannot help making, though many will "argue" that value is "really" nothing but desiredness. The truth is rather that all perception or cognition of fact rests on value judgments, in the weighing of evidence not different in kind from those of aesthetics or morals. This "reducing" process may go further; it is also familiar in pseudo-scientific argument that desire itself becomes merely a "tendency to react." Here "tendency" apparently has the meaning of a force, or force component, if it has any meaning at all. In scientific economics, of course, we are concerned only with the quality of desiredness, without regard to any basis it may have in valuation in the higher sense or even to the "satisfaction" which may actually follow upon choice and action.

16. For many problems in price theory, it is convenient and admissible to treat money as an absolute measure of value, hence to view both price and utility changes as entirely relative to money. This assumption gives rise to serious problems in accounting practice. The economist must have in mind, wherever it is relevant, that the value of money does change, in terms both of objective purchasing power and of subjective utility. The ultimate practical concern of the economist (as of all scientists) is with "welfare"; but to deal with this he must first have a sound scientific theory of utility, both in relative and in absolute terms, on the analogy of a force causing and explaining choice but consciously known to the choosing subject. Ultimately, "satisfaction" must be conceived, for the purpose of economic analysis, as only one ingredient or factor in human well-being; others may, in fact, have greater practical importance.

17. Professor Sorokin in his recent work, *Socio-Cultural Causality, Space, Time* (Durham, N.C., 1943), advocates developing a special conception of time for use in social theory.

18. This is a convenient place for the important observation that price theory must explain a change in any dependent variable by a change in a really independent one, i.e., as the effect of some force impinging on the price system from without and to be explained or treated by some other science. No price

change can be validly treated as a cause, except for changes in the situation of some individual or limited sector of the economy, where the price change is due to some cause entirely outside the area considered. Error in this regard is frequently met with, especially in the work of the earlier writers. Much of Ricardo's reasoning is nonsensical on this account. Of course, it is also vital to avoid the blunder of making incompatible assumptions as to the classification and interrelations of dependent and independent variables.

19. For simplicity we assume that all the individual's income is spent for consumption (no saving) and also, of course, that we are comparing an initial with a final state of equilibrium in the individual's use of his income. We need not consider here the highly problematical use of the concept in connection with collections of commodities and/or groups of persons, as in the theory of foreign trade.

20. See "Consumer's Surplus and the Compensating Variation," *Review of Economic Studies* 8 (1940–41): 117–21, esp. 119, n. 1. Professor Lange called my attention to this paper. I have found it helpful, in spite of inability to accept some of the author's conclusions, for reasons which will presently be indicated in part.

21. This assumption seems to be implied by the statement that "in mathematical language the neglected elements would generally belong to the second order of small quantities" (*Principles of Economics,* p. 132, no. 1). Marshall goes on to chide Professor Nicholson for not recognizing "the legitimacy of the familiar scientific method by which they are neglected." In spite of diffidence in challenging Marshall—and Pigou (*Economics of Welfare,* 1st ed., p. 935)— on such a matter, the present writer must suggest that this mathematical argument is invalid. The theory of orders of infinitesimals does not seem to be applicable unless total utility is assumed to be represented by an algebraic expression of a fairly simple type, and this clearly cannot be done. The question of what can be neglected, and in comparison with what, is purely one of fact; and the facts are magnitudes which are a matter of estimation only, and their importance, absolute or relative, varies indefinitely with the particular good in question and depends on many other conditions.

(This matter of what magnitudes are practically negligible is of great importance for other problems in economic theory where unknown functions are involved, notably the conception of perfect competition among producers. It is hard to give much meaning to elaborate curves of total and marginal cost for a firm assumed to be of negligible size, which means that the whole diagram reduces to the area of a point!)

In sec. 4 (pp. 132–33) Marshall discusses as an exception the effect of a rise in the price of *X,* specifically in connection with the "Giffen paradox." Here, as the price of *X* increases, an increased quantity of *X* is purchased—the consumption of bread by very poor families being used as an illustration. As our previous argument has shown, what this case really illustrates is the confusion which results from drawing a demand curve on the assumption that all other prices are constant. What happens in such cases is a consequence of a disastrous fall in the value of money to the buyers affected, though not necessarily connected with a change in its value in the social economy, as measured by any general index number. From the standpoint of the theory of demand, it is the spurious problem of the "income effect."

22. See Hicks, op. cit., pp. 38–40; also Henderson, op. cit., p. 118. It is rather strange that Henderson slips into this error after making the statement in italics on the first page of this article. A minor slip in Henderson's argument is the statement (p. 118) that the consumer's surplus, defined as the difference in two expenditures for the same quantity of X, is "the maximum increase in return which the seller could obtain through negotiating all-or-none bargains with [the] consumer." It is the maximum increase *for the same amount of X*. The maximum without this unjustifiable condition would depend on the cost curve of the seller and on special conditions of bargaining (see discussion of figure 8.3).

23. We might have proceeded by locating hypothetically the one appropriate point on curve A and drawing a horizontal line $p_t t$ of the right length to yield the equivalent equal-expenditure rectangle without drawing the whole curve B. If the marginal utility under indifference conditions is assumed identical with the marginal utility under demand conditions, for the same quantities, curves A, B, and D will all coincide and consumer's surplus will disappear.

Professor Viner has pointed out the fallacy of confusing the demand curve with the equivalent of an indifference-combinations curve (see *Studies in the Theory of International Trade* [New York, 1937], pp. 573–74). In classroom lectures he also presents a graphic measure of consumer's surplus, showing the difference.

24. We should note, finally, that the notion of maximizing consumer's surplus cannot be entertained (as so often assumed) as a description of rational consumer behavior. Any aggregation of distinct consumer's surpluses is without meaning—though conditions might justify or require treating some complex of goods as a unit.

To pursue the analysis further would lead into a discussion of the familiar "antinomies of value" of Wieser et al. The suggestion that total satisfaction be increased by taxing goods of inelastic demand and subsidizing consumption of those of the opposite character would justify the taxation of free goods so as to make the consumer pay for them. It is hard to deny that this might actually increase total conscious satisfaction, but it would hardly increase real well-being to have one's total consumption cut down to famine conditions. In the ordinary course of events, one must agree with the position of Nicholson (see Marshall, *Principles*, p. 127, n. 1), that the consumer is not conscious of receiving the "free satisfaction" described by the theory of consumer's surplus. It is a real antinomy of economic psychology, but an indubitable fact, that our feelings of satisfaction depend more on *changes* in income (or particular prices) than on the absolute level—and surprise, in relation to established expectations, is also vitally important, irrespective of the accustomed standard.

9

The Sickness of Liberal Society

The sickness of modern civilization is a familiar theme and a fact which is obvious and not in dispute. The occurrence of two world wars within less than a generation is proof enough; and quite as sinister is the strong probability that, in the second case at least, international conflict came as the alternative to internal class war, or to chaos, in some of the major countries involved. Antagonism, war, and preparation for war between nations and allied groups can be viewed as the one psychological force capable of overcoming tendencies to conflict between interest groups within nations, groups formed chiefly along economic lines.

Agreement on the fact of social unhealth does not carry far toward common acceptance of a program of action and may, indeed, work in the opposite direction, aggravating the malady. Awareness of social disorder makes imperative a reasonable unity of opinion as to what is the matter and what to do about it, or—in medical terms—on diagnosis and treatment. In the current scene we find the most acute disagreement on these crucial points. There is intense controversy especially between two opposed schools of social-medical thought, as to the very meaning of social health. The one school views our social malady as a too-exclusive reliance upon science, upon knowledge as power, and the accumulation of means for making knowledge effective in terms of "material comfort," to the neglect of the "spiritual" values, intellectual esthetic, and moral. The opposed diagnosis finds a failure to "follow

Reprinted with permission of The University of Chicago Press and HarperCollins Publishers from *Freedom and Reform: Essays in Economics and Social Philosophy* (New York: Harper & Bros., 1947), 370–402, which was an expanded version of the original essay published in *Ethics* 56 (January 1946): 79–95.

through" with the scientific development, especially to apply scientific method to the solution of the social problem, and more specifically the economic organization. The methods of treatment advocated follow obviously from the diagnoses. The first position is typically advocated by our humanists and literary intelligentsia, as well as by the "preachers" in the narrow religious sense, but perhaps derives its most serious support from organized religion. The countermovement is represented by a substantial proportion of contemporary scientists, including the human and social as well as the natural sciences, and philosophers of the "pragmatic" school.

In this essay criticism of these social philosophies will be incidental to a more constructive task. This is the ambitious one of surveying the twofold problem, of indicating the nature of the trouble and the method or methods of treatment most likely to be effective. Our main concern is with the meaning of social health, especially the facts as to what are the ideals or spiritual foundations of modern civilization. These ideals will be referred to as liberalism or individualism. The former term directly suggests the ethical ideal of freedom, and freedom is the fundamental moral value exalted in the modern view of life, individual and social, in thinking and in practice.

Freedom, the Ethical Meaning of Liberalism

The first major difficulty, both for analysis and in the practical application of freedom as the ideal, is, of course, the ambiguity of the concept. The word has been claimed as a designation, and used as a slogan, by the most diverse ethical and social philosophies and programs, ancient and modern; in our day, this applies also to "democracy," its synonym in political discussion. Both the older and the newer antiliberal ideals of social order, the ecclesiastical authoritarianism surviving from the Middle Ages and the contemporary totalitarianisms—communism, fascism, and "naziism"—claim to be or to embody the "real freedom," or democracy, in opposition to liberalism. Further, the new use of the word "liberalism" to refer to supposedly democratic statism—socialism or economic planning—now compels us to restrict the term explicitly to the conception which went by that name in the nineteenth century social-philosophic theory and was the norm of social policy in countries where it was accepted. Our task is to show, in relatively concrete terms, the meaning of freedom, the autonomy of the active personal self, in its relation to the social problem. (A philosophical discussion of freedom would merely lead into endless metaphysical speculation.) The main point for emphasis is that freedom is an ethical principle. Its acceptance does not involve a repudiation of morality or idealism, but rather does involve an inversion of the ethical principle which has ruled in all civilizations prior to liberalism. All these earlier systems of social order have been rooted in tradition and authority, and it is by opposition to these that liberal freedom is to be defined.

The important fact is that liberalism asserts a new ethical ideal, thereby rejecting or modifying ideals which had previously been accepted; this rejection of old ideals has frequently been misinterpreted as an abandonment of all morality and ideals. Our first task is to make clear the content of the liberal ideal. Two points need emphasis at the outset. The first is that freedom is an intrinsic value, as well as instrumental to other goods. It is assumed that greater "well-being" will result if, in general, each person is the final judge of his own and of the means of achieving it. But historical liberalism has probably overemphasized this utilitarian argument. It is also a part of the liberal faith in human nature to believe that normal men prefer freedom to objective well-being, within limits, when the two conflict. Freedom always includes the right to consult others, provided one may choose his own counselors and follow or reject their advice. But the liberal doctrine goes further, holding that men "ought" to prefer freedom; and the institutions and laws of liberal states do not allow anyone to contract away his freedom, to sell himself into servitude for any price, however attractive. Thus freedom is paradoxically limited in the interest of its own preservation. An agreement binding the individual for the future will be invalidated if it is shown that he has entered into it under duress, or deception, or even gross incompetence to manage his own affairs.

The second point is that freedom does not mean unregulated impulse, or "license," but action directed by rational ideals and conforming to rational laws. The ideals and laws are to be discovered in individual and social life and recognized and imposed upon themselves by individuals and groups. Somewhat paradoxically, again, conformity to law is combined with spontaneity in choice. The fundamental notion of obligation is found in problem-solving activity, the raising of questions and quest of the "right" answers. But, at the same time, liberalism exalts a more literal spontaneity, a limitation of the whole "serious" side of life; it has meant an ethical rehabilitation of the play interest, along with a new conception of work. Thus it has brought about an enormous extension of the field of value and of the human interests and activities accepted as ethically worthy. Freedom must mean the freedom to change; hence, a central feature of liberalism is the ideal of progress, viewed as the goal of rationally directed action, in addition to its recognition as an evolutionary and historical fact. Earlier thought, particularly in our own religious-ethical tradition, inclined to view history in terms of degeneration from an original perfect state, recovery of which would be the supreme ideal. Modern ideas place the "golden age" in the future, not in the past, and regard betterment as to be achieved gradually by human action, not through a supernatural cataclysm.

Liberalism conceives of progress in terms of cultural values, intellectual and esthetic as well as moral, all based on material advance. It is a cumulative achievement in the individual life, and in various societies and the world as a whole, through the ages. The maintenance of a civilized standard of living, defined in cultural terms, and its progressive advance or elevation has come to be the serious business of life. This involves the gradual transformation of the world, of society, and of the individual human being, including his appreciations and his creative powers. This is the meaning of "work," defined as purposive activity, in which the real motive is some desired result. But the good life includes play as well as work. In play, also, activity is usually directed toward some end, but the relation is reversed; the end is not "real" but symbolic and instrumental: it is set up for the purpose of making the activity interesting. The value lies as much in the activity of pursuit as in the enjoyment of the result. The work and play interests are actually so mixed on both sides that concrete activities can hardly be classified between the two heads. The ambiguity is particularly evident in the direct pursuit of cultural values, the professional intellectual, and esthetic life. But all work is ideally, and to some extent actually, affected by the play interest.

On its serious side, liberalism might be called "secular rationalism," in contrast with naive theism, ethical and metaphysical idealism, and also with that philosophical rationalism which finds the solution of all problems of life in immutable principles, supposed to be known, or somehow accessible, to all men.

Liberal thinking about conduct tends to proceed in two steps—the critical evaluation of ends and the selection of appropriate means or modes of using means. The main subject of discussion in these pages will be "economic liberalism," or individualism, since it is chiefly in the domain of economic life, the organization of the use of means, that the reaction against liberalism centers and radical reform or revolution is advocated. However, it is to be emphasized that economic liberalism is merely a part, an aspect, of a system of values centering in individual liberty and applicable to all departments of human interest and activity and all social relationships. Economic freedom and other freedoms are inseparable, and authoritarianism must likewise be all-inclusive. The term *"laissez-faire"* actually means simply freedom; and it is for historical and rather accidental reasons that the phrase has come to refer to the economic life, or what is usually thought of under that designation. A thorough examination of the relation between ends and means, or between duty and pleasure, will make it clear that more is finally to be learned about life and morality, even in the economic field, from the study of play and of cultural pursuits than from the direct study of economics as ordinarily conceived and in terms of the assumptions usually made in economic discussion.

Economic Individualism

Discussion of economic problems has been prominent in liberal theory for two main reasons. Achievement of most ends, higher as well as lower, depends on the use of means and is limited by an actual scarcity of means. The world is poor; and so are the wealthiest countries, compared to the resources, material and human, that would be required to give everyone a "decent"—morally and esthetically satisfactory—life or standard of living, to say nothing of what men would like to have. The basic ethical principle, the meaning of freedom and democracy, is the equal right of everyone to the good life, or a fair opportunity to get the means necessary for it. It is wrong for one to have these at the expense of another or by using another as a means. It follows that social betterment requires an increase in total means available—resources or capital—along with an equitable distribution, and also the most effective use of means and improvement in "technology." Liberalism finds hypocrisy as well as falsehood in the older ethical attitude of exalting poverty—which always tended to mean that poverty was an ideal for others, the masses, not for the "elite" who preached the doctrine. The contempt for means and for the common forms of work which persists among the elite today is a survival of the attitude of a slaveholding aristocracy, always supported by religion. (In our own country and within the lifetime of people still living, slavery was defended on scriptural grounds, where it was established; in Europe, official Christianity never condemned it until it was undermined by other forces.) Means are emphasized, then, because progress depends on increase in means and their better distribution.

The second reason for emphasis on means is that according to liberal theory each individual ought to be and in the main can be free to choose his own ends, while access to means is more directly dependent on the social situation. Consequently means present a social problem, a problem for unitary social action, while ends, in the main, do not. These statements are indeed, subject to limitations, which liberal political thought has doubtless tended to underestimate. The subject of qualifications will come up at a later point. Liberal society first came under severe criticism in terms of its own fundamental values, and specifically with respect to the economic organization. Opposition developed, not on grounds of a repudiation of the liberal ideals of freedom and equality (or "just" inequality) and progress, but rather the failure of the liberal order to realize these ideals, in a way reasonably satisfactory to a major section of society, which has felt itself unfree and unjustly treated. (We refer here to the countries which have remained democratic, primarily the English-speaking world; we shall not go into the explicitly anti-liberal, totalitarian social philosophies and movements, now painfully familiar.)

The course of events under liberalism, beginning even in its formative period in the eighteenth and nineteenth centuries, led to increasing discontent and to an attempt to organize the "disadvantaged" classes. Later, other functional interests have been organized. They try to secure economic advantage for themselves, partly through unitary economic action—essentially monopolistic—under existing law, and in part through legal change or government action, by acting as political pressure groups. We must also remember that all through the liberal period there were movements advocating revolution to replace the "capitalist" system with some form of politically organized collectivism. Originally, the collectivist order was to be thoroughly democratic. But after the middle of the nineteenth century, socialism in the "scientific" version, under the lead of Marx and Engels, lost faith in democracy as a method of change. It was felt that the "vested interests" were too strong, and the movement looked to forcible seizure of power by a small "party," claiming to represent an advanced section of the working class; hence the "dictatorship of the proletariat"—meaning a dictatorship of the propagandists. This would theoretically be a transitory measure, to reorganize society and re-educate the people toward the ultimate classless—and hence stateless—society. The ultimate ideal was an anarchist utopia, administered "scientifically," without any exercise of power by men over men. The scientific social order advocated by Professor

Dewey, referred to earlier, is essentially identical except for omission of the transitional dictatorship—without replacing it by anything else; and the professed ideals of the moralistic school, and indeed of utopians or reformers of all ages, are strikingly similar.

The basic ideals of liberalism have been indicated briefly, but in order to deal with contemporary problems, it is necessary also to sketch briefly the main facts and principles involved in the application of liberal ideals to the political and economic order. For the economic system envisaged and partially constructed by liberalism, "free enterprise" is perhaps the most descriptive designation—certainly less misleading than "capitalism." An adequate treatment of this topic would obviously extend first to a treatise on economics and then to a similar treatment of politics and the more basic social sciences, including psychology. We can point out only a few of the main general principles and conclusions; these will be contrasted with popular misconceptions, and attention centered on the merits and defects of the system.

From the standpoint of social and political ethics, free enterprise *in its theoretically ideal form* is an embodiment and application of the fundamental principle of liberalism, i.e., individual liberty, including free association. In economic discussion liberty means the right of the individual to choose his own ends and the means or procedure most effective for realizing them. And association, in economic terms, means cooperation, for the purpose of greater "efficiency," more effective individual action in realizing individual ends—always including community ends freely chosen by all members of any group.

It is easy to show that wherever goods and services are roughly standardized, free cooperation must take the form of regular exchange and will result in the establishment of "markets." The theoretically ideal market is described in terms of "perfect competition." This is a most unfortunate term since psychological competition or emulation is not involved and is in fact inconsistent with economic motives. A free market means simply provision for effective intercommunication, so that every man as buyer or seller (or potentially one or the other) is in a position to offer terms of exchange to every other, and any pair are free to agree on the most favorable terms acceptable to both parties. A free market will establish a price, uniform for all, on every good or service, with the general result that all parties will specialize in production in the manner and degree which secures for each the greatest advantage compatible with the free consent of all. The market rests on the ethical principle of mutuality, with each party respecting the equal freedom and rights of others. The mutual advantage of free exchange is the meaning of the "invisible hand" directing each to serve the interests of others in pursuing his own. It replaces the idea that what one gains the other must lose. Any two parties are always free to exchange on terms other than those fixed by the market, upon which they can agree as better, or preferable for any reason.

Free association also allows for the organization of groups to act as units in production or trade, in the interest of still greater efficiency. These, again, may have any form of internal constitution on which the parties can agree. As things have worked out historically, such groups have been widely set up, chiefly under the "entrepreneurial" form. Either an individual or a more or less numerous body takes the initiative in production—decides all detailed questions, and assumes financial responsibility for the economic result by buying labor and property services at definite prices fixed in the open market. Typical today is a group of comparatively large size, organized in the legal form of a "corporation," with a representative system of control similar to that of political democracy, except for the different basis of voting power. Effective competition between industries will tend to direct production into the lines most in demand by consumers; and competition within any industry tends to compel every productive unit to adopt the most efficient methods—as a condition of remaining solvent and staying in the business. The price of any product will be equal to the money costs of the productive services required to produce it, i.e., to the prices that must be paid for these to meet the competition of producers of other products, fixed by the demand for the latter. Thus the entrepreneur will have neither a profit nor a loss. Product prices will be as low, and prices for productive services as high, as is compatible with freedom of choice of consumers and producers. Any profit will reflect superior achievement by the enterprise-unit receiving it, either in gauging consumers' demand or in technical efficiency, and any loss a similar inferiority. Profit or loss can only occur temporarily; a profit to one unit means a loss by others, and vice versa, and the inferior unit or units must either do better or be eliminated.

This form of organization is widely condemned on various moral and economic grounds. Criticisms usually center in the idea that "profit" is unnecessary and reflects "monopolistic exploitation," of consumers or those who supply productive services (labor and property), or of both groups. Critics ignore the facts about profits that have just been pointed out and are obvious or easily verified. (Theoretical reasons which we cannot go into here lead to the expectation that losses will actually exceed profits, and this conclusion is on the whole confirmed by the best statistical evidence available.) Those who oppose the entrepreneurial or "profit" system have frequently experimented with organization under other forms. These are commonly distinguished as "cooperative," reflecting failure to understand that exchange itself is a method of free cooperation. The results of these experiments have usually been failure (with some exception for the special and limited field of "consumers'" cooperation). The facts are a matter of common knowledge; the reasons are not hard to find and need not be given here.

The Theoretical Merits of Free Enterprise

The brief description just given should suffice to show that the free enterprise system of organization, *in its theoretically ideal form,* combines maximum efficiency with freedom for all. It produces for every individual the largest yield from his "resources" (person and property) that is compatible with the free consent of others. Further, it embodies "justice" between individuals, in the "commutative" sense that what is given up in exchange is equal to what is received; hence the individual's share in the total product is equal to his contribution to it, including personal services and use of property. This is "natural" justice; each receives the consequences of his own conduct. The conclusion is commonly drawn, both by those who condemn the system and those who defend it, that these three features constitute an ethical vindication of it as socially ideal. This conclusion is wholly unjustified, and its rejection in no way discredits the theory itself, as is commonly assumed. Its validity clearly depends upon two sets of facts or conditions and may be destroyed by facts contrary to either set. On the one hand, the system as it actually exists may have "mechanical" imperfections; it may fail to work in accord with the theory. And, on the other hand, the principle of reward on the basis of productive contribution may be rejected on ethical grounds. The facts under the two heads must be briefly summarized.

Two Major Mechanical Weaknesses

The mechanical imperfections of the system as it actually works are only too familiar. Two ways in which reality deviates from the theoretical ideal are especially important. Monopoly, and other tendencies, partly inherent in the "given conditions," physical and human, partly contrived by individuals and groups for their own advantage, make competition more or less imperfect. Popular criticism with respect to monopoly is, indeed, much exaggerated and misconceived. Every monopoly obviously has competition, and the notion that monopoly is always bad may be met by the two reminders: monopoly is often deliberately created by social action, as in the case of patents on inventions; and other monopolies commonly function in the same way, to stimulate and reward useful innovation and compensate for the risk and the losses that they involve. Most monopolies are in fact relatively temporary. Yet monopoly is certainly a real evil in many cases and presents a very difficult problem. No simple legal procedure can preserve freedom and the incentive of profit and at the same time prevent individuals from seeking economic power and organizing for this end or from seeking gain through monopoly and restriction.

Far more important in practice is a second mechanical weakness. This is the familiar tendency for economic activity to expand and contract in more or less regular "cycles" of prosperity and depression, both in particular fields and in society as a whole. Depressions involve widespread suffering and the equal or greater evil of insecurity and fear. The worst feature of the situation, from the political point of view, is the "panic" type of thinking which seems to be natural to human beings in a crisis. The drowning man not merely grasps at straws but is likely to seize hold of one who attempts to rescue him in a way which results in the death of both. It would take us too far afield to show in detail the falsity, or very limited truth, of the two common assumptions that depressions are inherent in the nature of capitalism and that the problem would be avoided under any other system of organization, or at least any which allowed individual freedom of purchase and sale. (Most theories of collectivism, and the practice of both communist and fascist states, do embody these activities as basic to the social-economic structure.) It should, however, be evident that the cycle problem is purely one of scientific knowledge and political competence. It is not one of conflicting interests, since all classes suffer in varying degree from a depression and practically no one is profited.[1]

Ethical Limitations of Individualism

This brings us to consideration of the ethical postulates of economic individualism, specifically the principle of reward according to contribution, or "reaping what one sows." If men's behavior is "economically intelligent," competition will mean sharing in the social dividend in proportion to "productive capacity." We then face the question whether this "commutative justice" is defensible as an ideal of human rights, or how far it is even compatible with social necessity. The ethical limitations of this principle are far more serious than the mechanical imperfections of the market in invalidating an apologetic interpretation of economic theory. The social result of the principle will clearly be any degree of inequality—opulence at one end of the scale and poverty at the other—in accord with inequality in ownership of productive capacity, in its two forms. In an exchange economy, the principle directly implies destitution for any who have nothing to sell in the way of services, of person or property, for which—or for their products—other persons are both willing and able to pay. The principle can be defended only to the extent either that the distribution of productive capacity itself is ideally just or that nothing can be done about it, and both these assumptions are patently contrary to fact.

It is a fallacy, rooted in prejudice and superficiality, but nearly universal in popular and reformist thinking, that economic inequality is, or is mainly, associated with the ownership of "wealth" or property. To begin with, many of the largest incomes are actually derived from personal services: for example, "prominent" lawyers, doctors, and artists, including prize fighters and movie stars. Moreover, the difference is largely unreal, since property and personal earning capacity come into the possession of individuals through practically the same channels—inheritance, effort, and thrift, all largely affected by "luck. " It follows that the familiar sharp distinction between the ethical claims of the two sources of income to their economic earnings is indefensible. All forms of capacity for rendering useful service are largely artificial, but chiefly in the social and historical sense, not that of individual creation. They are components of "civilization," and so, in fact, is appreciative capacity, or economic wants. The whole problem of inequality and injustice is rooted in the two factors of natural endowment and the participation of individuals in a total accumulated social inheritance, and this is mental, or spiritual, or "cultural," as well as "material." And to all these sources of inequality must be added the large factor of accident.

Individualistic Theory versus Facts

What has just been said does not mean that the moral qualities of the individual are economically unimportant. It does not even logically imply that superior inherited capacity ought not to have a superior reward. These propositions set problems that are to be discussed on their merits and in the light of facts and social ideals. But it does follow that the whole social philosophy of individualism is subject to sweeping limitations. Freedom is a sound ethical ideal, but "effective" freedom depends on the possession of power as well as mere absence of interference, at the hands of other individuals or of "society." And it is also relative to tastes or wants. The assumption underlying the individualistic economic ethic is that the individual is either unalterably "given" as he stands, or is morally "self-made" and that in either case he is the real social unit. The element of profound truth in this view is basic to the moral life and to all serious discussion of human and social problems. But it is only part of the truth, and liberal thought, particularly in its formative stage, tended to neglect other factors fully as important. Freedom and power are like the factors in an arithmetical product; the result varies in proportion to each separately and disappears entirely if either factor is zero. Both wants and "capacity" (in both forms) result from a complex mixture of individual effort reflecting moral qualities, with various forces and conditions that are beyond individual control. As is usually the case in human problems, no clear or accurate analysis is possible; "judgment" must be used in comparing and combining factors which seem important but are never measurable.

The limitations of individualism are particularly obvious from the standpoint of economic analysis. The theory of market competition takes individuals as given, with respect to their three economic attributes, i.e., their tastes or wants and their productive capacity, the latter in turn consisting of personal qualities, and external agents and materials owned, and recognized and protected by the existing legal order. In sociological terms it may almost be said that the individual is unreal; any nation or other society which acts as a unit in external or internal policy is a complex of "institutions"—traditions, knowledge or belief, and common-interest groupings—rather than an organization of independent individuals. Our "individualistic" society would be more descriptively called "familistic" and—as it has worked out in the past century—nationalistic and "classistic." The individual is not a datum, and social policy cannot treat him as such.

Again, it is useful to think of social life as a game, and consider its particular features. It is played by groups, or teams—in this case an indefinite number. In fact, inequality and injustice exist far more in the relations between groups than between literal individuals. The family, in some form, is the minimum real unit, and many other communities, up to states and even larger units, are only less important, both as interest groups and in making the individual what he is on entering social life as a functioning unit. The fact that inequality applies "fundamentally" to families and communities, regions and states, rather than to literal individuals is the basis for the rivalry and conflict which result both in international war and in the "class struggle." The tendency to conflict is greatly aggravated by differences in "culture," as well as wealth, and by cultural, group, and national loyalties; such groups always feel an urge to perpetuate themselves and their way of life, and to expand at the expense of others. Secondly, the social game is played for stakes which involve the major values of life. And, finally, it goes on continuously, generation after generation, with "players" constantly dropping out and being replaced. Hence, in addition to the procedure of play itself, the rules must cover the terms of admission of new players. Any new entrant must be trained to play, and dealt a "hand," and must also be given some share in the "chips"—the stakes which the activity must not only distribute but maintain and increase by using it.

In free society the preservation and increase of wealth and culture are largely left to individual, family, and voluntary group initiative. The inevitable result is a tendency toward increasing inequality between self-perpetuating groups of all sorts, as well as (or rather than) between individuals. This is most conspicuous with respect to productive capacity (internal and external) though just as true of all elements of culture. It is a case of "to him that hath shall be given." Any individual or other unit which at any time has more is in a better position to acquire still more. Capacity and taste develop together and inseparably, though wants typically grow more rapidly than the means of satisfying them— human nature being as it is (and probably ought to be). The tendency goes beyond the individual life, through various forms of inheritance, appearing in each new generation as the injustice of an unequal start in life.

Liberal societies have as a matter of course, if gropingly, recognized these problems in practice and have tried to meet them through such measures as progressive income and inheritance taxation. This is designed to reduce inequality, at both ends of the scale. It sets some limit to accumulation, and the proceeds are used to provide a decent minimum for all and especially to provide education and other requirements for the young. The liberal ethic goes beyond law, in many directions. Modern civilization has been as much distinguished from others by humanitarianism and "charity," voluntary and politically organized, as it has by the unprecedented development of science and technology. The attitude toward rights of convicted criminals and toward animals is in point here.

Complexity of the Problem of Free Society

The facts briefly pointed out make the social-ethical problem of liberal society one of tremendous complexity, scope, and difficulty. Liberal society may be defined by the fact of consciously facing its own future as a social problem. It is a human or world problem, not merely a local or national one, and is spiritual as well as economic or "material," even in those aspects which can at all properly be even roughly distinguished as economic. It is rather an accident that the conflicts which threaten peace and order arise in the economic field, even when this is properly defined to cover the use of means for all ends, higher as well as lower, and the distribution of means. A little reflection, along the lines of the foregoing argument, should make it clear that harmony and conflict of interest, giving rise to problems of law-making and enforcement, are characteristic of informal association, play, and cultural activities, as well as of "business" life, and that the problems have essentially the same form in all fields. Without law and obedience to law, and moral ideals and self-restraint going far beyond law, even a casual conversation may degenerate into a quarrel and then a fight. It is increasingly recognized that conflicting economic interest is relatively unimportant as a cause of war. The parties could almost always gain more through peaceful exchange and cooperation, and they really know that this is true. All this is true also of "class struggle," and all clashes of economic interests. Careful calculation shows that even colonial exploitation is not usually profitable economically. In European history religious differences loom large as a cause of war—supplemented by cultural competition and by sheer partisanship. Economic interests, real or supposed, are also involved, but an "economic interpretation" is largely rationalization. In war, as in general, the real motives are unanalyzable and often seem paradoxical and inscrutable and in any case irrational.

The Deeper Meaning of Liberalism

One who approaches the social problem from the economic side, and who at the same time tries to be objective and face obvious facts, must be struck by the limitations of the economic view of conduct. Economic analysis treats production as a "means" to consumption, or at least to some ultimate use of some result. But reflection will show that in "economic" life itself the motives are highly mixed and in large part not distinctively "economic." That is, the "value" to individuals and groups of the goods and services they want and strive to get is not mainly intrinsic; they are symbols of success. Economic activity has at least as much the character of a competitive game or sport as that of providing the means for satisfying substantive wants or needs. This applies both to consumption and to production; people are largely motivated by "keeping up with the Joneses"—and/or getting ahead of them. Economic "success" is largely competitive; and the symbols are in large part culturally determined, and their concrete form more or less a historical accident.

In so far as the ends of action are real, i.e., valued for any intrinsic quality, the content is primarily esthetic, as indicated by the expression "a decent standard of living." But esthetic values also are distinctive of particular cultures and are much affected by the motives of emulation and prestige considerations. Real beauty cannot be separated at all sharply from rarity and costliness, and these clearly reflect the craving for conformity and distinction. But it is "beauty" in a broad interpretation, which makes up the bulk of the cost—beyond purely competitive standards—of a scale of living, even at a "decent minimum" in modern society. Physical comfort, in anything like a literal interpretation, is hardly at issue in civilized life under ordinary conditions. It is a right, both recognized and provided for through charity, public and private, and even for incarcerated criminals. If anyone is physically destitute, it is because of the repugnant social terms on which "relief" is offered. Nothing is more familiar than the voluntary sacrifice of comfort and security for "appearances," or even the mere love of adventure. Esthetic creation, in contrast with the reduplication of existing works, is so much more than a matter of economy in the use of limited means that it seems trivial, absurd, if not repulsive, to think of it from the latter standpoint at all, though it always has this aspect also.

Beyond obvious and fairly narrow limits, it becomes entirely unrealistic to look at the good life in economic terms, or under the form of means and ends, even with the choice of ends not treated as given but also included in the problem; indeed, there are limits to viewing it as a problem in any sense. As an American economist has observed, "an irrational passion for dispassionate rationality" would take all the joy out of life. And it is just as true that an irrational passion for duty can destroy goodness. The castigation and lampooning of Puritanism (or of its caricature) is a familiar theme. That social life is much more than cooperation for increased efficiency has been illustrated by the story of a football club which hired an efficiency expert as a manager; his first innovation was to have all the men play on the same side, it being obviously wasteful to have half of them pushing against the other half. Our ethical thinking runs into similar paradoxes, if pushed too far along any line. J. S. Mill, perhaps the leading representative of liberal social philosophy and ethics as well as economics in the nineteenth century, held that pleasure is the ultimate end but had to admit that, to get maximum pleasure, we must to a large extent forget it and pursue other explicit ends. The observation can be generalized for all ethical theory; all thinking about conduct seems to run into a principle of indirection. Friendliness and generosity toward others lose much of their ethical quality if the motive is merely a sense of duty—and even more obviously if it is personal salvation, in terms of eternal heaven and hell.

To get at the real meaning of liberalism, we need to consider more fully the observation made earlier, that the ideal of freedom involves both a rehabilitation of play and a changed conception of work. Liberal thought recognizes that man is a social being—though in the light of many radical differences between human society and that of nonhuman species, it may be misleading to call him a "social animal." The liberal ideal of society in accord with the principle of freedom is free association. It is useful to distinguish at least four forms or aspects of a good social life. Arranged in a descending order with respect to the degree of reflective seriousness involved, they are work, cultural activity, formal or organized play, and pure or spontaneous, even frivolous, "sociability," typified by casual conversation. The different types overlap and fuse, beyond the possibility of clear distinction, and all have both individual and social aspects. The point here is to emphasize that "the good life" involves all of them inseparably, particularly the last—and that more is to be learned about liberalism by considering the roles of the other three factors than that of work. This last term may be used to include all "economic" activity, everything that is undertaken primarily for the sake of some end felt to be intrinsically or "finally" desirable, or necessary. A vague and largely arbitrary distinction must be made between work in which the value of the end is individual and that in which it is social or involves the "good" of others. The latter seems to be the meaning of ethical value, or "duty," though personal enjoyment or avoidance of pain, beauty, and moral obligation all enter into all four forms of activity, in varying ways and degrees.

The permeation of all conduct by the different factors or aspects may be brought out by noting the paradox in the meaning of play and work, as the main contrast in the rationale of conduct. The difference is largely a matter of the more or less arbitrary attitude of the participant. It depends on whether the end is "real" and the activity instrumental to it, or the reverse is the case. No empirical classification of activity into play and work is possible; it would be hard to find any concrete activity which may not be one or the other, depending on "circumstances." On the one hand, play has its serious purpose; as exercise, it is developmental, and undoubtedly necessary to man for health, physical and mental. But if the player thinks about the activity in terms of its "purpose, it becomes work and not only loses its distinctive value as enjoyment, but may also fail to accomplish the serious purpose. On the other hand, work ideally has the play aspect of being interesting, and doubtless always does have more or less of it, at least if it is above the lowest drudgery. Perhaps the most serious human activity or work is the task of democracy, the discussion of ethical and social problems. But discussion itself is largely mixed with the play interest—and also with esthetic motives. These tend to outweigh the reaching of sound conclusions, and we cannot say that discussion is in general more fruitful in its primary function if attention is seriously fixed upon the serious end, excluding the other interests.

The paradox perhaps comes to a head in the attempt to discuss conduct itself, in the abstract, to give a truthful description of it, hence in the "methodology" of the moral and social disciplines. The urge for scientific objectivity calls for ignoring motives and reducing behavior to purely physical process—the "behavioristic" point of view. But in such a treatment, in a rigorous sense, conduct ceases to be conduct and becomes mechanical reaction—and it is a manifest absurdity to take this view of the discussion itself, which is also a form of conduct. A similar paradox applies to all mutuality in social relations; we cannot verbally define free association, or state the distinction between exchange and "robbery" through either fraud or force. All human relationships involve an unanalyzable mixture of mechanical interaction, free exchange of things or services, and also both giving and taking, by coercion or deception, on both sides. We cannot realistically ignore motives—especially because we are usually more interested in these than in the physical facts—though we can never say at all accurately what the motives are. It is a scientific truism that an individual's motives are known only to himself; they cannot be observed by anyone else. But the facts are often to the contrary; the motives professed, and even actually felt, depend largely upon the norms which are currently "fashionable" in the cultural setup. Men give, even honestly give, moral or sentimental reasons for their acts—affection, patriotism, or religion—when an observer cannot help seeing that the "real" reasons are largely of the opposite sort, and the converse situation is perhaps equally typical. In the Middle Ages thought and expression were dominated by an ascetic-religious ideology; the counsel of perfection was the monastic ideal of poverty, chastity, and obedience. But, as everyone knows, the monks assumed that the world owed them a living, and they expected and normally secured a degree of comfort and security as high as contemporary civilization afforded and far above what was possible for the mass of the population which supported them. Further, the means considered legitimate for securing this support often amounted to pious fraud and violated modern standards of common honesty. In our own day the opposite situation commonly prevails. The modern spirit abhors sentimentality and pretense. This results in the familiar "hard-boiled" pose, where the real motives are often clearly sentimental.

The modern devotion to critical objectivity—as soon as we reflect about that—"brings the eternal note of sadness in." While our better instincts run in the direction of making work into play, our inclination toward "too much thinking" has the opposite effect, converting our play into work. Philosophy as well as science tends to destroy romance and only partly to replace it with another "beauty" of a colder intellectual kind. But all the distinctively human values are romantic; love must proverbially be blind. And beauty also, to a degree; it is hard for the scientific botanist not to lose the beauty of the flower, which, of course, he cannot find with his microscope or by any use of the scientific method, and the argument applies as well to the economic botanist.

The Ethical Significance of Play

We have suggested that for an understanding of the social ethic of liberalism, its general principles and their application to political and economic life, it is highly important to consider carefully the phenomena of play and the cultural pursuits. Both will be discussed without reference to any economic aspect, though this is always present in one form or another and cannot finally be ignored. We have also pointed out that economic life, in the meaning ordinarily understood, really has much of the character of play. It is a mixture of solitaire and competition and also "ritual"; but attention may here be confined to competitive play. The ethics of play or sport is a topic strangely neglected by moral philosophers, even in modern free society, and is virtually ignored in all discussion under religious auspices. (In the Bible one finds no explicit reference to having "fun," or to rivalry or emulation, as a part of the good life.)

The first characteristic of play, as of all social activity, and indeed of that which is called individual or private, is that freedom is conditioned and limited by "law," in several meanings of the word. Even in the most informal sociability, such as casual conversation, not usually thought of as play, there must be a common language and this in itself implies a vast stock of common ideas, meanings, and values, and of accepted formalities. These are necessary to mutual understanding and anticipation by each of the way in which the other will "react." However, this foresight is and must be limited. An element of curiosity and surprise is equally essential to interest in any activity. There is always an element of luck; there are games of pure chance, but a game of pure skill is a self-contradictory idea. The basis of mutual understanding is a common cultural background. This is never perfectly uniform, and cultural as well as individual differences are a source of misunderstanding and strife; the former are the main factors in international relations.

In the pure ideal form of play all the "laws" are taken for granted; the moment they give rise to any problem, the nature of the activity and of the association is fundamentally changed. Law, in the inclusive sense, is the essence of any social group, and the acceptance of the laws is a condition of membership. In free and progressive society, every social problem centers in differences as to what the law either is or ought to be and takes the form of interpreting, enforcing, and eventually changing the constitution and laws. In free association, this is done by "discussion," ideally leading to unanimous agreement. "Government by discussion" is Lord Bryce's well-known definition of democracy. Discussion is an activity not directed to any concrete end but to the solution of the problem, necessarily unknown in advance. A social problem always combines conflict of interest with difference of opinion about what is right. Further, the differences must be associated with a common interest, the interest in perpetuating the group—in play, "the game"—while improving its character. It follows that freedom in social relations has three forms or components. First, every system of law allows some latitude for literal freedom of action by individuals and free groups. Second, social freedom requires equal participation in the activities of law-making—or this is a condition of full membership in a group. Finally, since complete unanimity is not usually to be had, complete freedom implies the right and the power to leave the group, hence to join other groups, and eventually to form groupings at will. In principle, any group is "political" to the extent that its members do not have this third form of freedom. In common usage political groups are defined by territorial sovereignty; leaving one group means physical removal to another and is limited by material cost, by cultural differences, and by the laws governing departure and especially entry into other political units, which practically cover the earth. The first task of law is to define its own scope, i.e., the scope of individual freedom within the law, or tolerance of differences.

In play, not much literal enforcement is possible, without destroying the play spirit. It takes the form of excluding the recalcitrant individual—which is also the ultimate sanction of political law. Breaking the rules, or "cheating," is the primary meaning of crime, and of "sin" as well. But it is human nature to feel a temptation to cheat, in spite of its irrationality (scoring or winning by this means is not really doing so at all). The satisfaction of the individual interest in winning and of the group interest in having a good game are completely interdependent.

All problems of social ethics are like those of play in that they have the two components of obeying the rules and improving the rules, in the interest of a better "game"—or other associative activity. We cannot here develop in detail the extensive parallelism between play and political and economic life. Both present problems of distribution of the "reward" in some relation to capacity, effort, and luck; and the fundamental values to be achieved—morality, intelligence, good taste, and enjoyment—define the philosophical problem. Intelligence is always both a form of capacity to act and a requisite for the use of capacity in other forms—a means and a mode of use of other means and an end. It is a vitally important fact that capacity to play intelligently, from the standpoint of winning, is much more highly and more commonly developed among human beings than is the capacity to improve the rules or invent better games. The difference between sport and action in the larger social arena is partly bridged over when a game is played for "stakes," in contrast with mere points—i.e., for values felt to be substantial as well as symbolic of success.

Perhaps the most important ethical principle of secular liberalism—in contrast with our traditional religious ethic—that is to be learned from the consideration of play has to do with competitive self-assertion. As a matter of course, every party in a game must "play his own hand" to the best of his ability; otherwise, there is no game. The ideals of charity or service simply have no place. Further, rigorous equality in the distribution of the results is self-contradictory (as is the complete elimination of luck, as already pointed out). The ethical ideal is a "fair" and an interesting game. Sportsmanship is a large part of liberal ethics. The conception of fairness calls for a certain minimum of inequality in capacity among the players. This need is often met by classification of players, choice of the game, handicaps, etc. Such devices are obviously needful in connection with the larger social, economic, and political game, and the difficulty of working out and applying them is a major aspect of the whole problem. The moral attitude of liberalism, being defined by the notion of law, is primarily impersonal. It is a matter of respect for the rules and of ideals for their improvement, rather than a feeling toward persons, and the two things are as often conflicting as harmonious. The law is, of course, supposed to express the rights of men, which are in question only where these differ, or seem to differ, from their felt interests. The principle is not "love," which covers a group of special feelings, all restricted in scope, and hardly a matter of duty or obligation. Friendliness and courtesy are, of course, good, and there is always a margin for generosity in interpreting and applying rules in doubtful cases. A game is more or less spoiled if the players are "too much" interested in winning, even in strict accord with the rules.

Cultural Values; Development and Progress

In contrast with casual association and play, the cultural values are the content of liberalism on the "serious" side. The primary values are intellectual and esthetic; morality or "goodness" is chiefly a matter of distribution rather than a distinct value; personal relations, as obligatory, are largely comprehended in good manners or courtesy, which is more an esthetic than a moral category, and in "giving" in special cases of distress. In the liberal view the serious values of life are intellectual and esthetic enjoyment and creativeness. From the standpoint of discussion or of reflective thinking, as we have seen, all values are serious. They are included in "truth," since all questions relate to the truth "about" whatever subject matter is in question. Truth is assumed to be ultimately the same for all, but it is neither necessary nor desirable to have universal agreement. Genuine belief cannot be coerced, and freedom of belief is the ultimate concept in terms of which all freedom is defined. The overt expression of belief can, of course, be controlled through reward and punishment, and even the feeling of believing freely can be established by social conditioning in infancy or by playing upon the emotions. But these procedures are abhorrent to liberal ethics, which calls for a sharp distinction, as a matter of personal integrity, between true intellectual conviction and any so-called belief which is at bottom an emotional loyalty or an esthetic appreciation or which rests on any ground other than the truth. To draw these distinctions clearly is one of the tasks of a liberal education.

The core of liberalism—what most distinguishes it from other views of life—is a manifold revolution in the conception of truth. We need not attempt to answer Pilate's famous question, "What is truth," as we need not give a formal definition of freedom in any metaphysical sense. We assume that there is an intelligible difference between believing on the basis of facts, reasoning, and the critical evaluation of evidence, and "prejudice," or believing by choosing to have faith in some traditional dogma, or myth, or authoritative pronouncement. These usually have no concrete meaning until interpreted with explicit reference to a particular issue, by an authority, itself based on traditional faith or some form of force.

To say the belief is free is to say that truth is inherently "dynamic," subject to change and actually growing and changing. The liberal interest in truth is one of curiosity and quest, not of mystical contemplation or adoration. Truth is the right—or the best—answer to some intelligent question, and when a question is definitively answered it is no longer a question. Hence, any truth that is really "established" is no longer interesting, but a commonplace, even a bore. Truth is the supreme example of the principle that liberal idealism looks at the values of life in terms of pursuit as well as possession; they belong to the activity as much as to the result, to means as well as to ends. Truth is an end when it is unknown or uncertain, and especially if controversial; hence the truth interest is finally a romantic one. Established truth is valued instrumentally, as a means to the acquisition of further truth, or of other values, to be had through thinking and acting. Truth is the solution of a problem, and its pursuit is partly explorative, the goal more or less an unknown. This is clearly the case in mathematics, where we make the nearest approach to "absolute" truth; the answer to a problem is that unknown result which satisfies certain prescribed conditions.

The second feature of the liberal conception of truth is that it is a social category; its only test is unanimous acceptance in some community of discussion. Further, truth as social is ultimately democratic. As in most cases, democracy is indirect, and implies some kind of aristocracy, and some form of leadership. The consensus which defines truth is that of the competent and unbiased, even in factual observation. For most people, and in most of the field of knowledge and opinion, what to believe is necessarily a matter of accepting tradition or selecting the authority to be followed. Thus a truth judgment is moral as well as intellectual. But competence and freedom from bias are to be judged by the whole community of interested persons, and finally by each individual for himself. No sanctity attaches to tradition or to any authority; intellectual leaders secure their position exclusively through appeal to the free judgment of their followers. It follows that telling the truth in social relations is a primary ethical value. However, literal truthfulness in discourse is seriously limited by conflicting goods, and every person is both free and morally obliged to make the best compromise he can between literal veracity and other values. Among the latter, the moral value of courtesy and kindliness is conspicuous, and the conflict is a familiar problem. Fully as important are esthetic values of many kinds. Far more statements are interesting because they are not true, but imaginative and fictional, than are significant because of objective accuracy.

On the vital subject of esthetic value, and its relation to truth and to utility, only a few words are in order here. The concept covers a very wide range of experience, suggested by such words as "amusing," "exciting," "chastening," "cathartic," "edifying," and " thrilling"— "comic" and "tragic," "realistic," "romantic," and "classical." Undoubtedly, beauty is connected with and overlaps both truth and utility, yet some contrast is of the essence of the meaning of the word. The poetic statement that "beauty is truth, truth beauty," etc., is beautiful but not true. And so of beauty and utility—with due respect in this case to Ruskin instead of Keats. Recognition of beauty, natural as well as artistic, its enjoyment and creation, on their own account, as a part of the good life for everybody, is a distinctive feature of liberalism, almost on a par with the free and critical-skeptical pursuit of truth and its appreciation. Other systems of values have used art for didactic purposes and as a part of the "pomp and circumstance" making religious and political authority impressive to the masses. From the liberal point of view, all this represents special privilege and emolument, and prestige, for the elite. (In the Semitic religious tradition, a part of the original Christian inheritance, representative art is explicitly prohibited.)

Liberalism and Religion; Absolutism; Pragmatism

At this point, some negative observations are called for. The social and ethical philosophy of liberalism involves no repudiation of religion, specifically the more basic tenets of Judaism and Christianity, such as the belief in God, moral freedom and responsibility, personal immortality, churches, and even "faith." It does involve a radical re-interpretation of these fundamental doctrines, but it is one which large numbers have been able to accept while retaining allegiance to either of the two great religions of European civilization. The idea of God does not necessarily mean more than some kind of "ground" in the cosmos for the validity of spiritual values. Modern physics recognizes that matter itself is finally metaphysical in nature not physical in the naive meaning. The church is for the liberal a free association of individuals for the pursuit of the religious life, not a supernatural entity with special authority to tell people what to believe or to do, or to dispense "salvation" on arbitrary terms. The belief in immortality will function as extending and enlarging the moral life and providing additional meaning and motivation. Otherwise, it is not practically significant, since the liberal will hold that the problems of the other world can be dealt with only by working as intelligently and conscientiously as possible at those presented by the present life. As to faith, all reasoning finally goes back to premises which cannot be demonstrated, or rationally argued, and usually to following authority with special competence.

Liberalism is also a "faith," a faith in the world and in man. It views the world as an environment in which it is possible progressively to achieve a better life, in terms of the values of truth, beauty, goodness, and enjoyment; and it imputes to men at large the intelligence and the will to work for these values. It is a qualified optimism, in contrast with the doctrines of the vale-of-tears and original sin, which make men helpless, morally and materially, and dependent on miraculous intervention and aid. In practice, the latter doctrines have meant a duty of submission to the authority of some human group claiming to speak for

God, and also claiming the right to enforce, by torture and execution, both belief and conduct. The liberal ethic is democratic; it exalts freedom against obedience and power. Either will be "abused"; but it is held both that the abuse of power generally leads to worse objective evils, and that even doing what is actually good, under authoritative command, is contrary to the ideal of the moral life. Within limits, self-government, by the individual and society, is to be preferred to good government, where a choice must be made. But only within limits; the liberal ideal is always one of balance and compromise, on the basis of "judgment," between conflicting principles and values, as well as interests. The best balance cannot be described in formal rules concrete enough to answer real questions, or not subject to criticism and revision.

In short, as we have stressed, liberalism is a faith in the capacity, and the courage, of man to find and follow truth and right. This implies a faith in the nature of the world as "such that" truth, carried as far as facts and evidence allow, will be finally in harmony with other values, including utility. Truth is to be believed because it is true, and for no other reason, though in particular cases objective accuracy may be subordinate to other considerations, as we have seen. For liberalism, no form of value is "absolute"; but this does not mean that one opinion is as good as another, or that error, moral choice, or good taste are unreal. These things are rather "relatively absolute"; they are valid in the same sense that the objective world is real; i.e., we think in terms of a substance or sub-stratum which may be "eternal and immutable," but its nature is to be progressively discovered, and never fully or finally known. The liberal faith begins with skepticism, and repudiates dogma and wish-thinking on absolutistic grounds or "rationalistic" in the idealistic meaning; but it equally repudiates the reduction of intelligence to will in the rational-utilitarian or "pragmatic" manner. It is assumed that men should know and face the truth, and will wish to, even when it is unpleasant; and also that the world is "such that" truth will be useful, in leading to the enlargement of personality and to cultural progress, and ultimately to "happiness." This does not exclude humor, frivolity, play, and esthetic escape, setting more or less arbitrary bounds to serious thinking and acting. The scientist must both believe that truth will be useful, while pursuing it as truth and not as utility, and at the same time accept it as a moral, and even a religious, value. There can be no science either if scientific workers are dogmatic absolutists or if their motive is utilitarian, not to mention the self-seeking interest of the charlatan.

Freedom of thought implies freedom of action as a corollary as well as freedom of verbal expression, which is obviously necessary to freedom of thought itself. The ultimate contrast is between intellectual freedom and various forms of obscurantism. Freedom of association, or mutuality, in action may be viewed as a form of freedom of expression. If the historical change to liberalism from "religious," i.e., ultimately theistic, idealism, with its logical implication in social practice of ecclesiastical authoritarianism, and a static social order based on caste, constitutes moral degeneracy, the liberal can only say, "Make the most of it." The only "proof" that can be offered for the validity of the liberal position is that we are discussing it, and its acceptance is a presupposition of discussion, since discussion is the essence of the position itself. From this point of view, the core of liberalism is a faith in ultimate potential equality of men as the basis of democracy. There are two possible alternatives. One is a conspiracy to seize power by force. The other is "preaching," which itself is really a form of force and can finally be successful only through "preaching down" or overt repression of other preachers of competing programs or gospels.

The liberal will admit that much is to be said for an aristocratic constitution of society, including slavery, in an idealized form—if it could be assumed that there is any practicable way of having it in an ideal form. This "if" is enough by itself to give away the whole case. An idealized "caste" relation between leaders and followers, in accord with the romantic picture of parents and children in the family, can be defended in terms both of "happiness" and of the possibility of a higher absolute level of cultural achievement. Such a system might endure indefinitely, preserved by conditioning each new generation to accept it, and in obeying to feel free. But there does not seem to be any way for a society once liberalized deliberately to "go back." It would have to give to some particular selected individual or group a perpetual blank check on power; and this is hardly thinkable as a rational performance—apart from actual belief in some special channel of access to a superhuman source of knowledge and taste open only to the ruling caste. If the change comes about, it must apparently be through some self-appointed leader and party seizing power by some combination of force and deception.

The Place of Economic Conflict in the Social Problem

Enough was said earlier of the ultimate unreality of the economic basis of conflict, or the more or less accidental reasons for conflict appearing in this form. All conduct has the economic aspect, as far as purposive action involves the use of scarce means; and all associative life involves power relations. And on the other hand, the ends are never economic, but are a mixture of esthetic and symbolic values. It is a serious question whether, if all economic limitations and conflicts were removed say, by the discovery of some effective magic for producing all material goods and services without effort or the use of scarce means, social antagonism and conflict would be removed, or even reduced, or essentially changed in form. It appears probable that conflict would be more intense, unless other interests and other traits of "human nature" were at the same time miraculously transformed, removing all desire to "get ahead" and all occasion for organized action of any kind.

However, there are obvious reasons why conflict, within and between societies, arises in the economic field. These begin with the two facts, that means are necessary for the good life, and that in any community they are "scarce" in comparison with what is required for a satisfactory standard of living for all. Thus arises the problem of distribution, since men have individual interests (in contrast with bees), and there is no generally accepted or acceptable norm for a "just" distribution, especially because the problem is tied up with family interests and the institution, and with the motivation of production. Finally, a tolerably effective use of means requires organization. And moreover, the progress of civilization and the accumulation of means require organization on a larger and larger scale. It is now on a scale where cooperative relations are largely "impersonal," and the moral forces that operate more or less effectively in the small face-to-face groups (and might operate even in a small democratic group) practically lose all their force. To utilize modern technology, economic organization has in many respects to be worldwide.

When we look at the problem of any society, or of the world, in economic terms, and from the standpoint of the disadvantaged individual and group, the major "real" evils are on one side the esthetic sordidness of life for the poor, and on the other the dreary monotony and lack of effective freedom which affects highly specialized work under the direction of technical and administrative specialists. For completeness, we should add the overwork of those individuals who incur and accept responsibility, and the "boredom" of those who are independent and do not.

For the liberal moral sense, the major evils may be actually worse if they are not felt by those directly affected. A bad condition presents a social problem only if it is socially recognized. The diseases of liberalism may be viewed as results of the general inculcation of ideals of equal rights, combined with failure to impart an understanding of the limits of equality and of the methods and costs of securing that which is possible. This fact raises the difficult moral problem of the role of the "agitator" on the one hand, and the dispenser of philosophic or religious "opiate" on the other. The critical spectator finds discrepancy both ways between discontent actually felt and that which "ought" to prevail. People are satisfied with conditions they ought to rebel against, and dissatisfied with conditions better than they deserve or can reasonably expect—or they are justifiably discontented, but for wrong reasons. According to liberal theory, they ought to be discontented only with what is both bad or unfair, and remediable; it is irrational to object to what cannot be changed. But there is little agreement on these points, or upon rational procedure.

Moralistic and Scientistic Romanticism

Since the essence of liberalism is the reliance on rational agreement or mutual consent for the determination of policy, and since the amount of agreement attainable seems very meager in relation to the needs for action felt in a large-scale, rapidly changing society, it is easy to understand psychologically, though not to approve, the tendency to fly to one or the other of the two positions mentioned early in the essay under the names of moralism and scientism. There is much truth in both these positions; the error is in accepting either as true to the exclusion of the other (and still others), i.e., in the romantic disposition to oversimplify the problem. On the one hand, human nature is undoubtedly "sinful," and, on the other, the mind makes mistakes in the choice of means to achieve given ends. It is easy and attractive to generalize from either fact, and make it explain everything, and particularly attractive to account for the ills of society in terms of either the sins or the errors of other people. And as to the content of sin and error, there is much real virtue and wisdom in respecting tradition and established authority. There is also much truth in the idea that the desire to "get ahead," and especially to get ahead of other people, is the primary sin to be avoided. We can only mention the questions obviously raised—whether the play interest, including the emulative aspect, can be rationally condemned, whether civilization and progress are good, and whether it is possible to have them without the motives which religious idealism views as sinful. These views are as old as history.

The advent of modern science, with the power it has conferred on man to change the world and the conditions of life, has just as naturally produced the opposite romanticism, the "scientistic" oversimplification. It is perhaps true that, especially under the influence of frontier conditions, liberalism had tended to stress activity as such and the cruder levels of achievement, to some neglect of the higher appreciations, the intellectual and esthetic life, and the moral value of fellow-feeling and "aimless" sociability. In any case, the problem of life cannot be reduced to one of means for achieving given ends. And this is particularly true of the social problem. Here, the end is right terms of association, and the essence of it is the definition of the result to be achieved rather than any concrete achievement.

The "sickness of liberal society" is not to be diagnosed either as moral degeneracy or as arrested intellectual development, specifically in the scientific sense. Both moralism and scientism formally accept freedom as an ultimate value; in form, both are anarchistic, though in contrasting senses; but both eventuate in an authoritarian social order. Both theories aim at unity through free agreement, to cure the malady of social discord and strife. But such agreement is not to be reached either through preaching abstract ideals or through adopting the experimental method. The social-ethical problem is an indivisible whole; means and ends must be determined together, and by the same agent—either by society as a whole, implying equal participation in its decision, or by some prescriptive authority. Both the moralists and the "scientificists" really assume that other people "ought" to agree with them and freely accept their leadership in dealing with both ends and means. An anarchistic theory, in any form, is essentially an invitation to all to "leave it to me" (and "my gang"—those who already agree with me) to deal with the problem as a whole. It is, finally, immaterial whether "utopia" is pictured in moral or scientific-administrative terms. The Marxists are merely frank in cutting the knot by proposing a dictatorship—of themselves—for an indefinite period, to work out the solution and "educate" society to accept it.

The alternative to dictatorship is simply democracy in general as we have known it, struggling to solve its problems, along lines already familiar. It means cooperation in thinking and acting to promote progress, moral, intellectual, and esthetic, with material and technical progress as the basis of all, and all under the limitation of gradualism and "seasoned" with humor and play. The combination is the meaning of liberalism.

Notes

1. These mechanical imperfections do not (as the uninformed public tends to assume) invalidate the economic theory which at the most general stage of analysis pictures them absent. Theoretical mechanics similarly has to assume the absence of "friction," and deal with idealized conditions in other respects, which diverge quite as far from literal realism. Analysis must begin with general principles which must be properly qualified in application to practical problems.

10

Virtue and Knowledge: The View
of Professor Polanyi

In his Riddell Memorial Lectures for 1946 at the University of Durham
and in a pamphlet of the same date on academic freedom, Michael
Polanyi, the distinguished physical chemist, now professor of social philosophy at the University of Manchester, presents a novel and interesting
treatment of the ancient problem named in our title.[1] The exposition is
appealing and the substance contains important truth. At the same time,
the argument is, in the reviewer's opinion, seriously fallacious, and the
partial truth in it particularly justifies thorough critical examination.

The same theme, in an abstract view, has been made familiar in
America during the last two generations, in which thinking about
moral and social theory has been dominated by the pragmatism of
Peirce and James and especially, more recently, by that of John Dewey.
This thesis is the identity of problems and methodology in natural
science and in the disciplines concerned with man and society. But between Polanyi and our scientistic-positivist-pragmatist-utilitarian sociologists and political writers there is a contrast more important than the
affinity. Polanyi goes at the identification in the opposite way about,
"from the other end." Instead of hammering at society and its spokesmen because they do not solve all our problems by adopting and applying scientific method, the former chemist tells us that the procedure of
science is that already in use in dealing with social matters. His injunction is, in effect, to go on conscientiously practicing free discussion and
to put faith in it, specifically in two main principles which underlie the
process—fairness and tolerance (Lect., p. 54). We are to trust and be

Reprinted with permission from *Ethics* 59 (July 1949): 271–84.

patient, quit worrying or stirring up trouble, and all will be well; God's in his Heaven, all's right with the world—or will progressively be put right. Science has demonstrated its capacity to solve problems, and we need only understand that those of the social order are of the same kind.[2] Unhappily, both views alike have the strong appeal of the intellectual get-rich-quick scheme, easy solutions for hard problems, and would likely lead to a resort to the sword of political power to cut the knot of a political impasse, which the author thinks he is combating.

I

As to the nature of scientific method, Polanyi's thesis is valid, *up to a point;* and it is of the utmost importance to have it stated, to students of man and society, from a source that speaks with authority. The procedure of natural science is not *merely* observation and inference, looking to prediction and control. Its problems are also value problems; they call for a large amount of creative imagination and contain a large "moral," even quasi-religious, element. Science also requires loyalty to tradition and respect for authority, even submission. Perhaps the author's greatest service to moral science is his emphasis on the "eternally provisional" nature of truth, in the modern world view (Lect., p. 29). He might go further in driving this home, against the idea of eternal and immutable truth, dogma revealed long ago and once for all, to be accepted by a moral choice between virtue and sin. What is now sacred, under the name of truth, is not particular "truths" but the honest pursuit of truth and critical judgment by standards applied in open court before all competent and unbiased judges.

But the effect of the argument is to carry the assimilation of science to morals so far as to obscure the essential problem in the latter field and virtually to deny its existence. The author nowhere faces up to the simple *fact* that the situation in social discussion presents a glaring contrast to the unforced agreement and phenomenal progress of science; and, of course, he throws no light on how or why the situation comes about. There must be underlying differences to account for the contrast; we cannot draw the implied moral that it is all a mistake—or should we say a sin?—that society need only trust, and not press for solutions faster than free discussion spontaneously establishes agreement. That way lies chaos—social, if not individual, madness.

It is true that there is no explicit identification, and differences are conceded; but they are not followed out to their implications. On one

side, observation and experimentation in science are mentioned, but
only to minimize their role. On the other, it is admitted that compulsion
has more place in moral and political decisions than it has in science.
On the first point, we are told at the very outset (Lect., p. 7, first page of
text) that no law of nature can possibly be derived from any mass of data
"by definitive operations." And again, "The part played by new observations and experiment in the progress of discovery in science is usually
over-estimated," and "objective experience cannot compel a decision . . .
between the magical and the naturalistic interpretation of daily life,
or . . . the scientific and the theological interpretation of nature . . . the
decision can be found only by a process of arbitration in which alternative forms of satisfaction will be weighed in the balance" (ibid., p. 14. Is
he a hedonist?). And, near the end of the Lectures (p. 62): "The method
of disbelieving every proposition which cannot be verified by definitely
prescribed operations would destroy all belief in natural science . . . in
fact, belief in truth and the love of truth itself which is the condition of
all free thought." And, perhaps most important of all: "The scientist's
conviction that science *works* is no better . . . than the astrologer's belief
in horoscopes or the fundamentalist's belief in the letter of the Bible. A
belief always works in the eyes of the believer" (p. 47).[3]

What the author says is true, "up to a point," and vitally important.
A belief "works," satisfies, as long as it is held. (Approximately! People
do cling to beliefs, or professions, after they "know" they are false and
no longer carry them into action.) But typically there comes a point!
And our author does not face up to the question as to why world views
change. It would seem to follow that they could not. In fact, it does
not take primitive peoples—or the civilized but "pre-scientific"—long
to be convinced by the various "arguments" of Europeans that the latter's interpretation of nature is "superior" to their own. And the West-
erners themselves are wont to lament the readiness of Orientals, and
even primitives, to leap to the conclusion that the superiority holds
in detail over the whole field of culture and mores. Contemplation of
such facts will surely make it clear that the validity of scientific and of
moral beliefs must be discussed in very—if not quite absolutely—different terms.

It is true, and important, that "there is a residue of personal judgment required in deciding—as the scientist . . . must—what weight to
attach to any particular set of evidence in regard to the truth of any . . .
proposition." But this light is turned into darkness by serious *Uebertrei-
bung* when, from stressing that observation and experiment are not the

whole story in science, the author goes on to argue as if they were nothing and so effects the assimilation of morals and science on which his heart is set. He does, indeed, recognize the question of why scientists agree, the grounds of the "remarkable" consensus that prevails among them (Lect., p. 26). The second lecture, "Authority and Conscience," is on and around this theme, besides adversions in the other two. But the discussion is far from satisfactory. The answer to the question is found in loyalty to a tradition, with a general authority as its guardian, though we are told that the "scientific conscience" is "the ultimate arbiter" (Lect., pp. 41 and 53). The relations are not made clear. We glimpse a struggle between will power, argument, and conscience to pass on intuition (p. 53). The content of the tradition seems to be simply freedom of conscience. And the role of authority is ambiguous. On page 49 it is "inherently restricted to the guardianship of the premises of freedom"; but on pages 35–36 it must also deny freedom to cranks, swindlers, and bunglers (also pp. 58, 65). Sometimes it seems to be just a brute fact that scientists are all loyal to the same tradition; but elsewhere authority plays a large role, through control of publication, of access to laboratories, teaching appointments, etc. (pp. 35, 40, and elsewhere).

As to freedom of conscience itself, the individual has no choice; it is forced upon him. Its "origin" is in his primary education, like learning to talk and acquiring the naturalistic world view (pp. 28, 29, 31). Of course, the opposite compulsion has prevailed over most of the globe and most of its history. We are given glimpses of the change (esp. Lect. 3, Sec. 3, pp. 60 ff.) but are told nothing about its causes or reasons. "Conversion" is mentioned, as a process by which premises are shifted (p. 53), and the effort to convert others is explicitly sanctioned (p. 67); but it is not described or brought into relation with intuition, argument, will power, and conscience. There is no indication that conversion is a social phenomenon or that the author would so designate the replacement of the religious world view by the naturalistic in modern times.

What is said of science applies to all social beliefs and patterns. "The premises [which] will guide conscience . . . in a free society [are to be found] as in the case of the premises of science . . . underlying the art of free discussion, transmitted by a tradition of civic liberties and embodied in the institutions of democracy" (p. 53). "When a child is born to a national community the Social Contract is imposed on it by force. . . . The whole heritage of free institutions will descend upon [him] and confirm [him] in these traditional obligations. They will thus be secured by compulsion, exercised by public opinion either directly or through . . . legislation" (p. 58). It is thus that our community is "pledged to seek the truth" and "must grant freedom to science as one form of truth." And for this reason, "such adherence as it can gain by fair and tolerant discussion is its *rightful* share [my italics]." And, in general, institutional action remains rightful, so long as it is based on democratic decisions swayed by open persuasion (pp. 58–59). Decisions binding on all, by officials elected under open persuasion, are likely to be a far cry from individual freedom, such as prevails in science, notably when they "involve assent to social action." However, *this is the ultimate point to which we can trace the roots of our conviction expressed in affirming any particular scientific proposition as true*" (p. 59; italics in original). It is surely evident that, while the tradition of the free conscience and some of the techniques of discussion (especially some language, rules for conducting assemblies, some of the control of publication, etc.) are common to science and government, the former has *in addition* other essential features, including the "practice of experimental proof" mentioned above.

To see that the two fields differ sharply, we need only compare the last few paragraphs above with the picture that we get at the beginning of Lecture 2. Here "the premises which underlie science fall into two classes"; free discussion is not one of them, and its premises and technique are not mentioned. They are, first, "the general assumptions . . . which constitute the naturalistic . . . outlook" and, second, "the more particular assumptions underlying the process of scientific discovery and its verification." What is there in the social field corresponding to these last? This is the great unanswered—and unasked—question.

The author goes on to describe the role of the authority of the teacher or master over the student or apprentice. But then he turns to emphasize the necessity, for understanding science, of "penetrating" to the reality described by science, whereby "the authority to which the student submits tends to eliminate its own functions by establishing direct contact [with] the reality of nature" (p. 31). As the student approaches maturity his own intuition of reality and his conscience take over responsibility for his beliefs in place of authority. What the author is insisting upon throughout is some sort of balance of the three forces—individual intuition of reality, tradition, and authority. The conception of tradition and authority and their roles is very ambiguous. Within limits, that is inevitable, but it needs to be recognized to be minimized, instead of making now one, now the other (of all three), predominant. Crucial is the fact that the only ground given for believing that science tells us truth about reality is that its "vast growth in the last 300 years proves massively that new aspects of reality are constantly being added to those known before" (Lect., p. 10). This implies that a considerable growth of any sort of tradition proves it to embody contact with some reality or some aspect of reality. We are given no analysis of grounds of belief, particularly of the relation between intellect and emotion, or between either and our eyes and hands! We are repeatedly told that it is a matter of choice between "types of mental satisfaction." The word "conscience" covers all (all that is not covered by "force," tradition, and authority) without discussion of the kind of faculty that conscience is (but it is neither will power nor argument, Lect., p. 53, as already cited).

At one point emotion seems to be rejected as a source of knowledge or assigned a very subordinate place—the statement is equivocal (Lect., p. 54) But what *are* the grounds of disagreement and the valid grounds of agreement? If "scientists" tend to agree, it may be because of the way they are selected, or the term defined—a vicious circle. There is plenty of disagreement about matters within the field of science. And if agreement proves contact with an underlying reality, what does disagreement prove? One phase of divergence of traditions—hence plurality of realities?—that is briefly but interestingly discussed in the relation between the expert and the public (some particular public?). It is, of course, vitally important for the theory of free society. In science it seems that the public is "audience" to the "free controversy" as a public contest (Lect., p. 54); it is to exercise no actual control but, of course, to support the affair. Scientists are selected by co-option. But we have just been reminded (p. 52) that "theories condemned by science, such as . . . astrology and occultism, are . . . upheld by a considerable public." Christian Science and other unorthodox schools of healing challenge, even "contest effectively," the position of science; and "the question remains how . . . rivalries [between rival interpretations of nature] can be competently decided." "The medieval approach . . . aiming at the discovery of a divine purpose in nature has been abandoned" (p. 51). But "the mental desires which science leaves unsatisfied are always prepared to return to the charge" (p. 52). They certainly do so in the mind of the author and in these lectures! Telepathy and extra-sensory perception are referred to as "established" (Lect., pp. 21, 24, 37–38, 55, and elsewhere)—has this tradition really grown, except among a small coterie of "scientists"?—and "certain miracles . . . are affirmed" (p. 52), though witchcraft has been abandoned [has it?], and astrology deprived of all official support." Where, indeed, and how are we to draw the line between knowledge and purely wishful believing (faith!)? The lectures close with the author's statement of his "belief that modern man will eventually *return* to God" (my italics) as the reality underlying his cultural and social purposes. This is a pretty thought and may be fairly harmless; or it may not; *how far* and along *what course* are we to advance backward climbing down our cultural family tree! One vital feature of science is never mentioned: the skeptical attitude necessary to guard against the inveterate romantic tendency to wishful believing, for moral or aesthetic reasons, and to theorizing for its own sake.

In Lecture 1 the author applies his thesis of the identity of various types of guessing right to a diversified and interesting list. Those named here (Lect., p. 20) are discovery in mathematics[4] and natural science, the creation of a work of art, recovery of a lost recollection, solution of riddles, invention of practical devices, recognition of indistinct shapes, diagnosis of an illness, identification of a rare species, "and many other forms seem to conform to the same pattern. Among these I would include the prayerful search for God," illustrated by the long labors of Augustine to achieve faith in Christianity, abruptly ending in his conversion, which is thus identified with scientific research and discovery. Solving moral and social problems is still to be added, to state the author's central thesis, and to these we now turn.

II

Polanyi offers little concrete treatment of the society side of the relation; he writes mostly about science and faith or science and such things as intuition of reality, conscience, freedom, free discussion, tradition, and authority. It seems that no definition of society or of a social problem, or discussion of procedure in this field, is called for beyond what is said about science and elaboration of the assertion of parallelism. (Lecture 3, "Dedication or Servitude," is chiefly a sermon on faith in the reality of ideals, based on this thesis.) Some approach to concreteness may be found in Section 3 of Lecture 2 (pp. 42–48). The author begins by restating his thesis that it "is true also of all complex creative activities . . . carried on beyond the lifetime of individuals" as it is of science, that "it can exist only because its premises can be embodied in a tradition . . . held in common by a community." "We may think for example of the law and of the Protestant Christian religion," and he proceeds to "include such fields as law and religion in [his] further discussion" (p. 42).[5]

The essential thesis of the whole argument is stated just at the end of the preceding section. A "community of consciences jointly rooted in the same ideals recognized by all . . . becomes an embodiment of these ideals *and a living demonstration of their reality*" (p. 42; my italics). Surely, if ideals are "real," it must be in a distinctive sense of the word, or what do we mean by "realizing" our ideals? [6] But the main question is, What is the significance of the boundless differences and antagonisms between innumerable communities with disparate norms, legal, moral, political, religious, and other kinds? And of their changes, appearances and disappearances? And, especially, of the *contrast* between this bewildering diversity and flux, and the situation presented by science? Surely, a new meaning must be given to "reality" if it is to be all things to all men, and change from year to year, or if its main "aspects" are to behave so. And there is the logical difficulty already mentioned: the institutions and practices of democracy have been put forward as the "art" in which the "reality" of free society is embodied. Surely, they are at most a procedure for discovering some reality—if law-making can be thought of as an attempt to do that! Then, if the organization of science is called a "democracy"—which is more apparent, the similarity or the differences, between research and publication, and the making and enforcement of laws mandatory on all by officials chosen by some putative majority, through the procedures of campaigning and voting? How does the state, separated from other states by geographic boundaries, with membership determined by a mixture of residence and inheritance, compare with the community of science, scattered over the world?

Most astonishing, to me at least, is that Polanyi recognizes the plurality of traditions, *and approves:* "[E]ach of us must start his intellectual development by accepting uncritically a large number of traditions of a particular kind"; and this commitment "should make us feel responsible for cultivating to the best of our ability the particular strain of tradition to which we happen to be born" (Lect., p. 69; cf. also p. 57). And we have seen that he approves of a community acting to serve its traditional ideals (p. 65); but decisions to act are never unanimous, and he goes on at once to condemn societies which limit individual freedom. And, while he speaks of a national tradition, the argument must surely be as valid for the church into which one happens to be born—or no church—and so for any belief or practice, including dogmas or loyalties opposed to science. Moreover, in modern civilization, every individual is virtually born into innumerable traditions and communities. If any latitude at all is allowed, he can find a tradition-community within easy reach to justify any belief or practice that he may incline to. Our vaunted individuality is largely a selection and organization—forced, accidental, or chosen—of community memberships. At the end of the *Foundations* pamphlet this theme recurs. It is observed that all contacts with spiritual reality have a measure of coherence and is suggested that any one "may well be merely a national variant of a universal human tradition." Perhaps—doubtless—in some degree; but all the problems arise out of the *differences,* together with reasons, urgent in all degrees, for getting together on a "right" position, or merely for agreeing.

III

For the most part, the pamphlet on the foundations of academic freedom does not bear directly on the titular theme of the Lectures (and of this article)—the methodologies of science and social discussion.[7] The main burden is further "propaganda" for freedom in science (roughly pp. 3–11; it is a central theme of the Lectures also), followed by a "generalization of these considerations to scholarship in general" (pp. 11–18). However, a look at the more concrete and practical essay will illuminate the philosophical problem, especially since intellectual liberty is the cornerstone of free society, inseparable from freedom of action.

Polanyi's discussion of freedom in science is built around the analogy of a number of people attempting to cooperate in solving a jigsaw puzzle. But if this crude analogy is examined, it will bring out the vast difference between scientific and moral problems rather than the limited resemblance. The author concedes "something profoundly different" (p. 8), in that the puzzle is known to have a definite solution, and a new piece either fits into a particular gap or fails to fit in the most obvious fashion, while in science this is not so. But "this is only to be taken as a warning to be careful in using this analogy." We may pass over his discussion as to whether science has "a comprehensive task,"[8] since it is the definiteness of each step that is important, and here the author exaggerates the difference between the puzzle analogy and science. A little modification will clarify the point. Our puzzle may start with a given central section, to be built out in all directions. And it may have indefinitely many pieces, some of which will fit and others not; and more than one may fit at a given point, but only one make it possible to go on later, so that some occasional tearing-up and rebuilding will be necessary.[9] Still, the jigsaw puzzle will grow by accretion, by steps that are not in dispute, and simultaneous, independent contributions can be made. But cultural progress, moral or aesthetic and political, has more the form of qualitative change; it involves change in the norms themselves by which results are judged. Of course, scientific work is not so mechanical as a puzzle-solving analogy suggests, but the difference from moral problems is vast. Another major difference is that scientific problems can wait, where social issues must often be solved in some way, "now," no backtracking possible. Otherwise they may "solve themselves," disastrously, or it may require carefully considered action to keep that from happening. And this irreversibility in time results in the vital, if familiar, difference, the near-exclusion of experiment.[10]

IV

Professor Polanyi's treatment of academic freedom is restricted to opposing interference by "the State," as "an outside authority superseding . . . individual initiatives." Tolerance is, of course, not enough today; governments themselves accept the obligation to subsidize "institutions of higher learning and higher education" (their functional scope is a main issue), and this increases the likelihood of "pressure."[11] Now, to begin with, it seems pointless to discuss the relations between any institution or person and "the State" in a vacuum, without considering where their interests are likely to conflict. A state might, of course, support science simply as a branch of culture or entertainment, as was done for music and drama in some European cities in other days. Perhaps this applies to elementary education, but the reasons here are complex and various. It is more likely, looking at modern history, to want to suppress science, for religious reasons, and the "cultural elite" commonly oppose it as vulgar and materialistic. The main fact, certainly, is that governments support scientific education, and research (two things), from economic and military motives (and health, if that is not included under economic). Anyhow, Professor Polanyi surely does not expect anybody to support an activity without exercising some direction; he (or it) would not if he could, and could not if he wanted to. A decision to support must be selective. Choice of lines for support will be combined, variously and unanalyzably, with choice among persons, on grounds of "confidence," as is true in every delegation of power to an agent or representative, by any principal.[12] Further, the government could not turn funds over to "science" unless scientists were (like itself) organized to act effectively as a unit. But such an organization would probably destroy the freedom of the individual scientist about as effectively as would direct administration by government. And, still further, a unitary organization of all scientists (co-opting its own membership) would have such power in the world of today as virtually to make it the real government—if other vocations would stand for it and if the scientists were disposed and able to compass it.

The serious error in Polanyi's reasoning, at this point, is the assumption that everyone knows just what "science" is, and scholarship—that they have sharp and clearly marked boundaries. But the contrary is the case; and the nearest he comes to facing this difficulty is to devote a page or so (Pamph., pp. 14–16) to the "detail" of "the difference, which at first sight may appear puzzling, between the independent standing claimed here for members of the academic profession and the admittedly subordinate condition [13] of well-trained scientists engaged in . . . surveying and of scholars employed as bibliographers and the like." But "it is . . . easy to dispose of the claim of applied scientists in industry or government offices to academic freedom"; the justification is "the distinction between creative and routine work," illustrated by the jigsaw puzzle! A second assumption is the identity of "academic" and "creative" work. Both the distinction and the identification are evidently fallacious. What a state or political division—specifically, a democratic one—"ought" to encourage or allow an "educational" institution it maintains to publish, where matters in political controversy are concerned, cannot be settled by an easy generalization about truth and its rights. It matters little who may say that the controversy turns on a question of "fact." This is true in all degrees of such questions, most so of the economic. Usually the "facts" are too well known to need "scientific research" or admit of it. On the other hand, perhaps not one issue does not involve questions of value, about which the scientist has no more to say than anyone else. All this applies specifically to the restrictions on margarine; and the protective tariff and price control rest *mainly* on false premises or reasoning. But there is always another side, more or less defensible. Our author's oversimplification may be due to thinking of physical science, where facts *can* be *fairly* well separated from other interests and values; even biology is different, and, in the study of man and society, what is a fact is the chief subject in dispute.[14]

The weakness of the whole argument comes out most clearly in the scanty treatment of the activities directed to "a purpose other than advancement of knowledge" (identified with academic life) which are to be "directed by a central authority." The dichotomy is "illustrated" by the contrast between judicial and "political" appointments (Pamph., pp. 12–13). To support academic scholarship without affecting its independence, the state need only "regard [it] in the same light as it regards an independent administration of justice." Our Mr. Dooley showed more understanding of the facts in remarking that the "suepreem court follows the 'liction returns." The court itself knows better, too, even without such an object lesson as the Roosevelt attempt to "pack" the body. Congress chose to reject the proposal, knowing that "pressure" and human mortality and new appointments would soon bring the court's opinions into line with the policies of the party in power. The dependence of the judiciary on the legislature and/or executive is formally different in England, but not less close.

In the main we find the authorities responsible for "outside purposes" treated as simply "there," as presenting no problem. Of course, Polanyi knows he is speaking figuratively in saying that "the King appoints and pays the judges." And he buries issues in vague language in saying that this does not matter "so long as the King is under the law" (Pamph., p. 13). Just below, he becomes a bit more definite: "In the case of legal appointments the machine is controlled by the principles of justice as laid down by law and interpreted by the legal profession; while in the case of political appointments the King sanctions the popular will as expressed through the established electoral machinery." Now in all discussion of society, the crucial matter is the making of law—or, more accurately, *change* in the law—whether we are describing and explaining, or appraising and advocating or opposing policies. The latter centers in a relation between "reality" as it is and reality as it ought to be— which Polanyi tries to convince us is the same kind of reality, presenting the same problem of investigation. The notion of a kind of reality or objectivity in what ought to be undoubtedly grows out of conflict in what different people *want* reality to be like, the incompatible ways in which they want to change reality as it is, together with the necessity of appealing to something beyond these clashing subjective desires if there is to be any *discussion* looking toward agreement. And the notion of social freedom is a derivative from that of discussion. Discussion is inherently free and is the alternative to unity through giving and obeying commands. We must also keep in mind the relation between law and tradition, which also partly changes and partly is changed, more or less "intelligently"; and law is changed partly to conform to tradition, partly to change the latter.

The root problem is the necessity—if social and hence human life is to exist—of *agreement,* within some limits. The first phase is to agree upon the limits (the sphere of freedom and tolerance versus compulsory conformity), and the second to agree freely, rationally, peacefully, as far as possible, where agreement is necessary, before resorting to arbitrary devices or to force, which are always involved more or less. A central issue is this, of the relation between various professional specialists ("experts") and the general public; in a society that is to be free, the various expert functionaries—including the judges and the legal profession, among others (juries, and/or nonjudicial, nonlegal "political" officials have at least a co-ordinate role in interpreting, and changing, "the principles of justice")—must be "responsible" to the general public, which must itself be a unitary body; it must reach "agreement" in some way. And so must the different branches of "government" if it is to govern.

Polanyi seems oblivious to the essentials of the problem (we assume he is not skillfully evading them). He *assumes* that the legal profession itself acts as a unit; but if it were so organized, surely it would "generously" and for clear and good reasons seek to take over the public and constitutional law functions also, and the executive, and simply be the government, as we said of the organized scientists.[15]

V

In conclusion, we may sum up the reasons for the reluctant judgment that Professor Polanyi does not contribute much to the solution of the terribly important problem which he treats with so much earnestness and intellectual penetration, and withal so sweet-spiritedly. The problem is *free* cooperation, which means *free agreement* (a) on what to do cooperatively and (b) how to organize for making that decision and for conducting the cooperative part of our activities. This social problem arises from the great spiritual revolution of all history. Our culture has taken the fateful step of rejecting the sanctity of tradition and established authority, and it must find norms for judging and changing previously accepted norms. In contrast with the naive faith in "reason" and sympathy of the revolutionary period, we find that the task threatens to overwhelm us. Interests conflict, and free reconciliation calls for value-premises, appealing to men as reasonable beings and so transcending differences of *opinion* about *rights*. (Those who refuse to discuss issues in these terms must be suppressed as criminals; if they are very numerous, free society is impossible.)[16] In short, the philosophical problem (as epistemological) is that of defining the social good, or "justice" in the widest meaning, by describing the social order which embodies the ideal in the highest degree.

Polanyi's solution or program is to proceed in the way in which "science" proceeds. Science has been an undoubted success, and he argues that the nature of all social problems is the same: an explorative investigation of "reality." Our first question, then, is this: Is "justice" a reality, essentially like the everyday world which we observe, utilize, or playfully manipulate—especially in the sense that we get "knowledge" of both in the same way? Surely, to the plain man, they *seem* very different, more contrasting than similar. The conclusions of science are "laws," analytically descriptive statements, superficially unlike moral laws—the "is" *versus* the "ought-to-be," facts about the world "out there" *versus* feelings in "minds." The latter are called "mental facts" and are affected by a kind of "validity," but this is attributed by different people to widely diverse content. As to how we know or learn, Polanyi establishes essential identity by minimizing and then neglecting the observation and manipulation which are the main part of scientific procedure, in favor of "intuitive contact with reality" and elimination of differences by "free discussion." Observation is first an incidental "clue," then ignored.[17]

The direct practical concern is the *organization* of science. For our author the essential thing is its *freedom*. Concretely, this means two things: internally, the individual investigator is free—scientists are not organized under an authority of their own; and they are also free from external control, meaning by the state. Whoever "controls," say a church, is in so far a state, and the whole argument can have only analogical and very limited significance for the organization of the state—"society," in whatever form it *acts* as a unit, on its own members or outside. The idea of the state as free, in the sense of science, is simply the ancient dream of the anarchist. And the contradiction is aggravated because science demands support from society. However, Polanyi has an ostensible way out of the impasse, though it is hardly an improvement. Apparently, he sets up "the legal profession" as another group, on a parity with scientists, to "advance knowledge" in the distinct field of "justice," and he regards all other government functions, the "political," as applying knowledge in accord with "the popular will." The latter he must *assume* to exist as a unit, and to be expressed. Not unreasonably, as there would not be much to disagree about, seriously, once the full meaning of justice was definitively settled.[18] But this is hardly "democracy"; and we still have no indication of how the legal profession is to achieve unanimity; it would surely need a fuhrer or an infallible pope.

Before closing I must say a word about the "theoretical" problem of freedom, perhaps the most crucial point in the argument. At the beginning of the pamphlet (p. 3, first page) freedom is defined (one meaning, beyond mere absence of external constraint) as liberation from personal ends by voluntary submission to impersonal obligations, surrender to moral compulsion. And the third lecture is entitled "Dedication or Servitude." The main question is, To *what* ideal does one surrender or dedicate one's self? And, especially, is it the ideal of impartial pursuit of truth—all valid values—or some concrete belief or end? Here (as observed before) the example of science gets less emphasis than it should. Polanyi himself notes that the surrender theory becomes totalitarian if you regard the state as the supreme guardian of the public good (Pamph., p. 4). But the state is only one possibility; dedication to any absolute is dedication *to* servitude,[19] even if still "liberation from personal ends." The practical consequence appears near the end of the Lectures: "A society refusing to be dedicated to transcendent ideals chooses to be subjected to servitude" (pp. 65–66). Apart from the vital issue as to how a society chooses, or refuses, as a unit, there is here a fatal ambiguity. The totalitarian can take the author at his word and quite cogently turn the argument against freedom of conscience. He can plausibly argue that the freedom of liberal science and culture is a fraud and really means chaos and exploitation; that it is democracy which is not dedicated to anything but leaves all to chance or whim and a selfish scramble of the machine politician and "the rich," who rule by fooling "the mob" through control of the channels of communication. It is also not hard to "prove" that men are freer under despotism than under freedom! And one cannot help noting, in the democracies that remain, a strong tide flowing in the direction indicated, *back* to "freedom" through planning and control by a quasi-sacrosanct "center." There will be some freedom, to vote the right ticket, until a priesthood gets fairly established in power; then "dedication" will be taken care of by conditioning in infancy—plus a residual of liquidation of recalcitrants. All as in the good old days; and all apparently in conformity with Polanyi's system, except that he apparently thinks he can have a plurality of priesthoods, at least for science, law, and religion, dedicated to their respective values, and a public dedicated to accepting the verdict of each in its separate field.

Dedication to ideals a free society certainly must have. But care must be taken that the primary dedication be to freedom itself and competence, on the part of the "public" as a whole. Freedom must be a value on its own account, even when it conflicts with efficiency, in terms of any defined goal, even truth or justice, as eternally provisional. Polanyi's reason for favoring freedom is simply that "freedom is an efficient form of organization," in science at least the only such form; "there is no other efficient way of organizing the team" than "if each is left to follow his own inclinations" (Pamph., p. 5). This is not strictly "true," even when the end is the discovery of scientific truth. And when it is "justice," freedom must be as much end as means. The *right* of every man to be the judge of his own ends and the mode of realizing them is the premise of a really free society. Yet freedom, limited by respect for the equal freedom of others, cannot be absolute. There are grave problems, conflicts of values, including conditions of life prerequisite to the pursuit of all "higher" value, which cannot be covered by any formula.

Notes

1. The present paper is a review article, on these two writings of Professor Michael Polanyi, F.R.S.: *Science, Faith, and Society* (London: Geoffrey Cumberledge, Oxford University Press, 1946); and *The Foundations of Academic Freedom* ("Occasional Pamphlets of the Society for Freedom in Science," no. 6 [Oxford, 1947]). For brevity, the former will be cited as Lect., the latter as Pamph.

2. Our reference to "God" is not dragged in, as will appear later. This article has a task large enough in criticizing Polanyi's position; it could not attempt, in addition, a detailed comparison with Dewey's views. Of course, Dewey's technique would be different—getting "facts" and attempting to arrive at "laws," where Polanyi would think and argue—if the two really mean what they seem to say! Polanyi cannot really think the procedure suggested by his argument is that of science—he did not achieve his standing as a chemist in that way—and the fact sets a difficulty of interpretation. How far Dewey holds the naive positivistic position which his influence has promoted is also a question. Refutation of this is the chief merit of Polanyi's work. For an illustration of positivistic sociology—a good bad example—see *Can Science Save Us?* by George A. Lundberg (New York: Longmans, Green & Co., 1947), reviewed in an article by the present writer in the *Journal of Political Economy,* December, 1947. A brief statement by Dewey is his paper, "Authority and Social Change," in the volume *Authority and the Individual* (Cambridge: Harvard University Press, 1937); a fuller statement in *Liberalism and Social Action* (New York: G. P. Putnam's Sons, 1937). The student will, of course, consult Dewey's *Logic* and voluminous philosophical writings. Dewey and his followers deserve credit at least for "yeoman service" in combating one type of pseudo-explanations, in terms of a theistic or teleological world-view; on this issue Polanyi seems to take both sides.

3. I quote at length, both to put the author's meaning beyond danger of misrepresentation and in the hope that the truth in what he says may register with some of our psychological and sociological worshipers of "science," who make it so much simpler than it is, in its own proper domain. The same thought is repeated many times in the Lectures, with various shades of meaning. On p. 11 it is denied that "our daily experience compels us . . . to accept certain natural laws as true." To believe that "generalizations such as 'all men must die' or 'the sun sheds daylight' . . . follow from experience without any intervention of an intuitive faculty . . . only shows that we incline to regard our own particular convictions as inescapable. For these generalizations are quite commonly denied by primitive peoples," and "they are of normal intelligence . . . [and] not only find their views wholly consistent with everyday experience, but will uphold them firmly" against Europeans.

And on p. 15: "The part of observation is to supply clues for the apprehension of reality; that is the process underlying scientific discovery. The apprehension of reality thus gained forms in its turn a clue to future observations: this is the process underlying verification. In both processes there is involved an intuition of the relation between observation and reality: a faculty which can range . . . from the highest level [of sagacity] present in the inspired guesses of scientific genius, down to a minimum required for ordinary perception. Verification, even though usually more subject to rules than discovery, rests ultimately on mental powers which go beyond the application of any definite rules."

4. It is to be noted that, as we are repeatedly told, the rules of research, like those of other higher arts, cannot usefully be codified but are embodied in practice alone (Lect., p. 19 and elsewhere).

As to mathematics, the reviewer pretends to no special competence but simply presumes to make a comment. The "high priori" character of mathematical reasoning (and logical, if there is a difference) is commonly exaggerated, if it is not an outright fallacy. There are two schools of thought among the "experts" themselves, and "the truth" surely lies with those (I believe the smaller group) who hold that mathematics is a language for describing and reasoning about the world of ordinary reality. Anyhow, it is clear that, up to very high levels of abstraction (if something more is ultimately involved), mathematical propositions can be verified empirically, by counting and measuring, to any degree of accuracy and generality thought worth the expense. (And it would be merely dogmatic, if meaningful at all, to assert their "absolute" validity.) But no such verification is ever possible for any statement about motivated behavior—nearly the whole field of social phenomena.

For an exposition of the "true" view of mathematics, see the essay, "Intelligence and Mathematics," by Harold Chapman Brown, in *Creative Intelligence* (New York: Henry Holt & Co., 1917); also (as I gather from reviews!) *Mathematics for the Million,* by Lancelot Hogben (London and New York, 1937).

5. Two pages later he "illustrates" by "the fields of law, religion, politics,

manners, etc."; but the discussion fits the first statement. The law will be considered later, in relation to more specific statements in the academic freedom pamphlet. The identification of religion with Protestant Christianity is significant (beyond its being his own "tradition"). He makes it the basis for contrasting "two types of authority, one laying down general presuppositions, the other imposing *conclusions*" (p. 43). It is surely fantastic to treat Protestantism as a unit, and the difference between churches is clearly one of degree and of practically all degrees. Further, for the Roman Catholic and larger Protestant bodies, it is less a matter of their claims than of the will (sincerity?) and effective organization to enforce conformity.

The author goes on to refer to two kinds of rules: first, "the vague rules embodied in the art of scientific research," which leave a margin for personal judgment and can be transmitted only by teaching the practice which embodies them; and, second, "strict rules, like those of the multiplication table." But I do not see any significant correspondence with his two types of authority—or see where the two types of rules fit into the system. Surely, a more important distinction would be that between substantive and procedural law and, still more, that between law, as any form of imperative, and scientific law, stating some factual generalization (conditional imperatives are something else, perhaps intermediate, in some sense).

6. On this same page (42, italics in original) we are told that "such processes of creative renewal [law and religion, like science] always imply an appeal from a tradition as it is to a tradition as it *ought to be*." The commonplace question, Is an "ought-to-be" a reality, in at all the same sense as an "is"? is not answered when the author goes on: "That is, to a spiritual reality embodied in tradition and transcending it," with explicit reference to science.

7. Some exception may be made for a brief reference to the law, introduced as a comparison (see below).

8. Scientists do not show much concern about the possibility (hope or danger) of one day finding out all there is to know—or whether the result would be heaven or hell. It is a profoundly important question, but outside the scope of this review!

9. Actually, not much of this happens—i.e., has happened since the "positive" approach replaced dogma and metaphysics in the study of nature. (A step which Polanyi's argument glosses over, or even points to reversing, though this is clearly impossible.) This *was* a change in the norms (referred to in the text below); it was a change in the conception of truth, not a scientific advance but a cultural, moral-religious, revolution. The greatest scientific discoveries mostly leave old knowledge intact as far as it goes, merely showing it to have been incomplete or imprecise, and changing the interpretation.

10. Experimenting with human life is not merely repugnant sentimentally or ethically. An experiment must not itself produce a serious permanent change. The typical outcome of a laboratory experiment on an animal is a "negative result" and a "dead dog." But there are always plenty more dogs, similar

enough to the defunct specimen, and this is not true of human beings, in the qualities on which we crave knowledge. Apart from injury, a "subject" is usually *changed,* preventing repetition of an experiment. And the moral considerations themselves are complex. Human beings would usually have to be coerced or deceived, in contrast with physical objects (and in part with animals, up to the highest). This alone is considered an "injury," and *"wrong,"* and may, besides, influence the results. The "medical experiments" of the Nazis were of negligible scientific import, apart from other unsatisfactory aspects. In a sense, human life is highly experimental; but deliberate and intelligent experimenting is very difficult and dangerous. (To treat social problems as knowledge problems at all, as Polanyi does, is to beg perhaps the most serious philosophic question; about this, "more later"—but not much, in this review.)

11. Now, to begin with, he at once pounces upon a bad example from the United States and, two pages later, he "rubs it in" with an invidious comparison with named European countries. The example is a pamphlet on the dairy industry and the war effort, published by Iowa State College, at Ames, in 1943. Some statements about restrictions on margarine provoked a reaction from the head of a private farm organization. No official action or threat of action was involved, and the leader of the protest was ousted from his job. It is evidently too much to expect a scientist to get the facts and state them as they were, in such a case (if he said anything); anyhow, what the professor says "actually happened quite recently in Iowa" is utterly different from what actually did actually happen. The facts have long been public, but they would not give a European intellectual an occasion to make an example of American barbarism, in promoting "the interests of learning and truth." (For obvious historical reasons, the British elite assume a natural and vested right to treat Americans as rustic relations or backward children spoiled by unearned material success; however, it does not seem to interfere much with pleasant personal relations, or even—despite aggravating circumstances—with political cooperation. The subject has been entertainingly discussed by Dixon Wecter, in an article entitled "Dying in Southern California," in *Pacific Spectator* for December, 1948.) The matter is not so extraneous here as it may seem, since the fundamental issue is the conflict between truth and other interests and values. Viewing the example as purely hypothetical, without reference to authenticity or other unpleasant aspects, it may serve as concrete focus of attention in showing that the argument is irrelevant and untenable.

12. A patient cannot possibly choose his doctor by rational judgment of the latter's competence; he would have to know *more* about medical science *and* the qualifications of all available choices.

13. " . . . of course there is no difference in the personal respect due to the individual."

14. A recent example so brilliantly illustrates confusion of fact and propaganda and I have to quote. In the *Nation* for April 23, Reinhold Niebuhr states it as a fact that the Roosevelt New Deal is simply "the philosophy of

all . . . who wish to bring the power of the state into the service of the people without annulling the cherished liberties of a democratic society." Of course, the "fact" is that the policy makes the state serve *some* of the people by taking things away from others (things rightfully theirs by the rules so far accepted) and either keep them or hand them over to still others. (Though not all the state does or can do, that is the nature of most currently bruited "reforms.") But, though our statement has the proverbial small merit of being "true," to state it baldly is again to beg the question for the other side; for the issue is whether this taking and giving "ought" to be done—or how far, when and how. It is a question of *changing the rules.* One would like to know how Professor Polanyi classifies such activities between the domain of science or scholarship, where freedom must be virtually absolute, and that of applied science, where there is no valid claim to freedom at all. *If he confronted the relevant facts,* he surely could not say that any political rumpus in an American state university, during the generation that I have been watching them, hinged on scientific or scholarly research and publication or that the issue was wholly one-sided.

15. Polanyi seems to share the view, natural to the legal profession itself (cf. G. R. Allen, *Law in the Making*) that if parliament would just stop messing up a job that it lacks the competence to perform (true enough!)—and, besides, it has too much else to do—the lawyers would run the country as it should be done. Such lawyers also fail to consider how they would act as a unit and what would be the freedom and power of the individual. Polanyi ignores the fact that when scientists themselves have to act as a unit they confront the same troubles as other people, the same opposition between a government and a "public," and disagreement within both.

Polanyi seems naive in admitting that his judicial and academic freedom would not work "if the legal profession were profoundly divided into rival schools of thought" or respectable academic opinion sharply divided in assessing the merits of discoveries and the abilities of scholars (Pamph., p. 13). As to what should be done then, he has only the lame suggestion that "the next best thing probably [would be] to please popular opinion or the government in power." He does not recognize that there are sharp divisions, dealt with partly by authority and force, partly by tolerance, itself a mixture of voluntary and compulsory, and possible because unity is not necessary—*as it unfortunately is in the case of a political society.*

16. Prima facie, the main conflicts center in the "economic" life or aspect of conduct. The principle of free mutuality, at first thought to be the solution, turns out to be far from sufficient. The strong (and/or fortunate) have one-sided obligations to the disadvantaged; there are general interests that transcend arrangements between individuals; and—the supreme fact—society is far more than an organization of given individuals, being largely the creator of individuals, as to both capacities and tastes. (Capacities include the artifacts of civilized life.) The economic view is rather superficial; the problem of

conduct is less that of "satisfying wants" than one of making the rules of a game, a game that covers an infinite variety of component games. But it is both—and correspondingly complex and difficult.

17. Reality, in this view, must be "spiritual," and it is explicitly so described, sometimes in the Lectures, throughout the Pamphlet (example: the solution of a jigsaw puzzle).

As noted before, acceptance of Polanyi's identification would still beg one main question—whether doing the right is purely a matter of "knowing" what it is. The Christian tradition has been the opposite, in spite of its infusion of Greek thought. Surely, there is truth on both sides. Polanyi says little about the will, adding to the difficulty of interpretation. His position is some kind of philosophic idealism, but there are several kinds. He seems to view reality as made up of archetypes, known by "intuition," but to regard every fashion in feeling attitude as an "intuitive contact with reality." If not, how do we discriminate? And, if so, all problems are unreal, which is absurd. The root difficulty is that we actually have no easy or certain way to tell the real from various forms of the imaginary or to separate the reality of minds and of thoughts, feelings, etc., "in" minds which do and do not validly refer to some "independent" reality. Yet one may be philistine (or at least pragmatist) enough to hope the day is past when a bright mind can make a reputation as a philosopher by "proving" that the ideal, or imaginary, in some form or aspect, is the really real, more real than the real. Surely, even in philosophy, truth should be a sensible answer to a sensible question. The "physical" world may ultimately be of the nature of mind, but this hypothesis contributes nothing either to the progress of "science" or to the solution of other problems; at most, a dose of idealism may be "useful" in helping some minds to escape the paralyzing clutches of a (self-contradictory) belief in universal rigorous "causation."

18. Polanyi's discussion is not of a sort to tempt one to levity. I may say— and so explain the tardiness of this review—that I first read the material in 1947 and have been struggling off and on ever since to find in it a "position" which would stand clear statement, in the light of "reality" and the author's own various formulations. On p. 46 of the Lectures he explicitly assumes that scientists will be competent and sincere—they "must" be—implying that no more is necessary to merit both freedom and power or to establish agreement as fast as needful. On the next page we read, "We may accord the same competence to legal opinion and to certain bodies of religious opinion, but probably not to astrological or fundamentalist opinion." Will religion, then, make no claim to speak on the meaning of "justice"? And how about the military? "Scholarship" can more or less be fitted in as history, but I doubt if it can actually be written without trespassing on the domains of both morals and science, for social events are much more than "facts" in the natural-science sense. Art is by Polanyi lumped in with all matters involving truth and all forms of better and worse; its creation is thus treated as investigation and portrayal of reality. The relations among the members of this triad call loudly for investigation; the neglect of beauty is a serious fault of our scientific-technical

age—in spite, again, of the Greek strain in our culture—but we certainly do not understress morality; and the worst deficiency in discussion of ethics and social theory is the omission of sportsmanship, perhaps actually the most important and most respected of all our value norms.

19. This is defensible as an ideal, or at least has been officially accepted in Christian Europe down to the age of free science, democracy, and "getting ahead." Modern thought reverses the former relation between freedom and truth. "Ye shall know the truth, and the truth shall make you free" meant "Accept the dogma and be free from your problems" (logical enough); but that, in turn, meant nothing unless it meant acceptance in advance, for all time, of all pronouncements of the authority that interprets the dogma. Today the only legitimate way of getting rid of a problem is to solve it (as far as it can be solved). I should say that I find no disagreement between Polanyi and myself on any concrete issue and no ideological difference, except that I should emphatically point out that modern totalitarian states take the place of the medieval church, their doctrines having the essential features of a religion, a persecuting religion, with a jealous God, like historical Christianity (at least a jealous priesthood, speaking for eternal and immutable truth).

11

Economics and Ethics of the Wage Problem

I

The wage problem, as our society confronts it, must be understood as a feature of the "modern economic order," and of "modern civilization" as a whole. Poverty and insecurity are age-old; they now arise in an economic system in which the bulk of the working population, no longer slaves or serfs, get their livelihood by the sale of personal services in the open market. Moreover, these evils have come to be felt acutely, in a sense not true of earlier types of culture, particularly as imperatively demanding that something be done about them by intelligent, organized action. This awareness and urge to act are not, to be sure, due only to more humane feelings, plus a general "activistic" attitude toward life and a faith in intelligence—novel as these are, in contrast with fatalism, or a faith that evils are somehow unreal or will be made right, somewhere and somehow, without planned human action. An important factor is the "awakening of the masses" and particularly the organization of large wage-earning groups, giving them *power,* economic and political, under a moral and legal order of personal liberty, to insist on their "rights" and to cause much loss to society at large if their demands are not met. To analyze and explain the economic organization is primarily the task of *economics.* This new branch of knowledge labors under a serious psychological handicap in that it requires imaginative separation of different elements in human conduct and social relations, through use of ab-

Reprinted with kind permission of the author's estate from *The Impact of the Union: Eight Economic Theorists Evaluate the Labor Union Movement,* edited by David McCord Wright (New York: Harcourt Brace, 1951), 80–110.

stract concepts. This type of thinking is clearly repugnant to deep "instincts" of most people, while in contrast with physics, for example, its results can be made effective through democratic processes only if generally understood by the electorate. The economic factor must in particular be brought into as clear a relation as possible with two others from which no sharp separation can be made. These are ethics and play. This is by no means all. Economics, ethics, and play are forms of *motivated* behavior (along with many others), and we know that such phenomena distinguish man categorically from inert physical things subject only to the ordinary laws of cause and effect as studied in the various natural sciences. (Intermediate "orders," plant and animal, complicate the problem but must here be simply left out of account.) The fact of motivation, with its accompaniments of striving, success, and failure or *error* in numerous meanings, implies that a strictly "scientific" treatment of human conduct in contrast with mechanical response (in nature or in man) is subject to sweeping limitations. We must further keep in mind that man is a social being, in a sense very different from the colonial insects or the herds of higher animals, where instinct mechanisms control behavior. Men cooperate, in a way inseparable from conflict; and they have social interests, likes and dislikes, which seem to have no ends beyond the "interestingness" of the activities in which they are expressed. Further, men have complex obligatory customs and laws, and last of all moral ideals; they judge acts and attitudes, their own and those of others, with approval and disapproval, implying norms distinct from mere subjective desire.[1]

Economics, distinguished from other human and social "sciences," has for its subject matter that aspect of the phenomena which is referred to by the term "economy" or the verb, "to economize." This latter means the use, or more or less successful effort to use, of *means* to achieve *ends,* and to do it *economically,* or effectively, so as to achieve the maximum desirable result on the whole that is possible with the given means. Economy applies to the activity of any "unit," but in free society primarily to "the" unit, which we speak of as the individual while meaning in general the family. This may be "represented," more or less accurately, by its "head," but the family in some form is the smallest real unit in any society viewed as historically continuing. The state, minor political divisions, and numerous "voluntary" organizations also function in various ways as economic units. We must note at once that people use means not only to achieve final ends, but also in considerable part to increase the stock of means itself, the main fact underlying economic *progress;*

however, the ends are also constantly evolving or changing, spontaneously or more or less subject to complex conscious direction.

Perhaps the first distinction to be stressed is the separation of economic activity from play. In play, the value is in the activity itself, not in
some end to which it is instrumental: or, the instrumental relation is
reversed; the objective in play is not "real," but is set up to make the
activity interesting. Part of the interest centers in *curiosity;* people act
(also are spectators to action, further motivated by a social interest in
entertaining, or receiving approving attention) in order to see what will
come of it, in contrast with realizing a predetermined result. The end,
beyond "scoring," is "to win"; but even this motive operates only during
the game and when achieved (or when the chance is past) ceases to exist.
Play may be solitary as well as social, and either competitive or ritualis-
tic. But what must be said here is that economics deals with activity as
instrumental to ends more substantive and permanent than mere symbols of victory or success. Yet, in everyday reality, both economic activity
and the political action which controls or regulates and supplements it
partake of the nature of play as well as that of achieving desired ends,
"satisfying wants," through consumption.

Economic analysis must *abstract* from other aspects of purposive action, but valid conclusions for policy cannot be drawn in economic terms
alone. Economic analysis not only has no clear boundaries; it must be
built up by successive stages of decreasing abstractness and generality,
proceeding from propositions describing or defining all economic behavior to others that apply in more limited circumstances. Hence, "principles" or "theory" cannot be used to "prescribe," to guide policy, in
contrast with abstractly describing what happens (describing a general
element or aspect of events); account must be taken of many details of
situations that fluctuate from case to case and must be learned from
empirical observation at the scene of action. There is a rough analogy
here with the study of theoretical mechanics, which starts with "frictionless" conditions and other arbitrary standards and proceeds step by
step through the testing laboratory to engineering decisions made on
the ground. In a general way, the economic analogue of friction in mechanics is *error.* Theoretical principles state what people try to do rather
than what they actually do; they describe "perfectly economic" behavior,
while in reality, of course, many forms of error, ignorance, prejudice,
etc., prevent men from achieving the maximum results which might be
had from the resources at their command. And always, maximum effi-

ciency in want-satisfaction is a most incomplete and even distorted conception of "the good life," the general goal of human thinking and striving.

A further essential point by way of definition is that economics does not consider the technical or technological side of efficiency in the use of means. This is left to the various natural (or psychological) sciences and applications of science. Economics deals with the *allocation* of means among alternative ends or modes of use. The whole science is developed out of, or applies, a few simple principles that are "axiomatic" in the sense of being matter of common knowledge and beyond dispute. The main principle is that of the satiability of particular wants, or diminishing utility; this accounts for apportionment in general. Use of means to gratify any single want is carried to the point where the means yield only as much as they would afford in some other use; there further expenditure is divided between the two uses. The general result is that the maximum utilization of means (any one or all) is secured by carrying the various lines of satisfaction to the point where the last final small increment of means (of the total supply) yields an equal "addition to total satisfaction" in all uses. This may be dignified by the name of "the economic principle." Cavils or hairsplitting about the nature of psychological quantities or measurement, and the logical possibility of deducing many of the conclusions from more general and abstract but less realistic assumptions will not be in question here. At a more empirical or physical level a second principle, parallel in form, holds for the use of physical means in achieving any physical end. If any one "factor of production" in a combination is increased, the others being held constant—e.g., if more labor is used with the same land and capital in raising wheat (passing for the moment over serious questions as to the meaning of these magnitudes)—it will be subject to "diminishing returns." And the producer of any good will strive to economize by apportioning his expenditures among the different factors (at given prices) so as to secure equal increments of (physical) product from equal increments of outlay (finally, or "at the margin").

As a device for clarifying these analytical distinctions—especially for separating the economic factor from the play interest, and from ethics and other social interests (subjective wants from more objective values)—it is useful to begin the discussion by considering the economic situation and problems of an isolated individual—the famous and mistakenly abused notion of a "Crusoe economy." We may be somewhat less unrealistic by postulating a society in which each *unit* (individual or "family" of some sort) is economically self-sufficient. There is no exchange or other form of "cooperation"; each unit entirely produces all it consumes or enjoys, using exclusively its own resources, human and external. (The Crusoe device also eliminates all special problems due to the use of money.) After pointing out that the more fundamental economic concepts have the same meaning for a Crusoe, if he seriously strives to practice "economic rationality," that they have for a member of our complex economic order, and also that the social-ethical problem is formally similar in a society regardless of its economic organization, we may consider briefly a social economy organized through the exchange of products alone (no buying and selling of productive services, or intermediate agents) and then turn to an economy of the form we mainly see around us. This of course is characterized precisely by such buying and selling, hence by the presence of the income distribution problem as we know it, with wages, rent, interest, and profit accruing largely to different persons, groups, or classes who thus find their interests conflicting in a special way.

II

A Crusoe (or Swiss Family Robinson) living on an otherwise uninhabited island, or a self-sufficient unit with otherwise "normal" social relations, would carry on production for consumption, economizing means in the satisfaction of wants. It is assumed to have the kinds of means universal in human life: personal capacities (natural and artificial qualities inseparably commingled); external resources (similarly characterized—a point to be stressed); and a "technology," based on a store of explicit or implicit "science." This last is only analytically separable from the personal capacities of human beings as "workers" but often has to be treated as an independent variable. The concepts here involved need to be defined with some care, in view of confusions in everyday use of terms and even in those of economists. In economics, production is a means to consumption as an end. The active human being has to be recognized as both a "productive agent" and a consumer, though no clear separation of these roles is possible. Most, if not all, productive agents require some maintenance and eventual replacement—again a more or less arbitrary distinction. This is as true of the "laborer" as of other agents; those called "natural" and "artificial" differ in degree and in detail, perhaps as much within each "class" as between the two. It is especially hard or unrealistic to distinguish between the maintenance of a laborer and his consumption that is an end, but conceptually the distinction is important (cf. Ricardo and Mill on "productive consumption").

Consumption is subjective enjoyment. What is consumed is the *services* of productive agents. Both enjoyment and service, as magnitudes, are flows, with a time dimension, and are "measured" as intensities (like light or electric current). They cannot be thought of as block-magnitudes or stocks. Consumption of a service may involve in any degree the using up of the agent, from food or fuel at one extreme to "indestructible" things at the other (but with intermediate types as well as degrees). It is services that are directly *valued*. The value of an agent is simply the value of its expected future stream of service, but this is not merely an intensity times a time; the relation involves the *discounting* process, one of the worst sources of confusion in economic theory. (Services may also be valued at a time-point after any interval of flow, the discounting being reversed; house rent paid at the end of the month would be higher than if paid at the beginning, with payment at very short intervals intermediary in cost.) The fact that agents require maintenance (including any replacement) is connected with the fact that "current productive capacity" can be used to increase the stock of agents, instead of satisfying current wants. To be realistic, we assume that our Crusoe (self-sufficient unit) maintains and increases his stock-of-agents, meaning his "capital"—properly including himself and his family as far as they are in fact productive—also, as far as pertinent, his "technology." These relations also imply that all types of productive agents are finally interconvertible, and form a common "fund." (Qualifications necessary for complete empirical accuracy are too complex to take up here.)

Crusoe's choices, as a consumer, and as a producer (1) using given agents to maximize satisfaction and (2) apportioning productive capacity between consumption and capital maintenance or increase, will compel him to reduce both services and goods to a common denominator of "value." The value of a good relative to its service is the *capitalization* of the future service-stream at a rate equal to the rate (the highest rate) at which capital grows in the economy when all its yield (service) and no more is *invested*. The capitalization (discounting) rate reflects the growth rate, which is essentially a technological fact. But investment in technology—and most or all investment contains some of that element—precludes treating this rate as a "given" over any considerable period of time. And, since investment in technology is problem-solving, and advance prediction of the solution of a problem is self-contradictory, it is impossible to assert whether capital accumulation in the aggregate will decrease or increase the rate of yield.[2]

It is clear that Crusoe would need some unit for comparing and computing values, "money" in the sense used above. His comparisons would result in a virtual price system. And he would have to *impute* product among the agents used jointly in producing it, giving rise to "rent" and "wages" as concepts required in accounting and for managerial decisions.[3]

Further, as just suggested, he will be forced to recognize the amount of investment (sacrificed consumption) in his various productive agents, logically including himself and, perhaps separately, his store of scientific knowledge and technical skill. He will have to do this because of the continuous necessity of deciding whether just to maintain his "productive capacity" in each embodiment, or increase or decrease it, as contrasted with enjoying a somewhat smaller or larger current flow of consumption.

Recognition of capital instruments as embodying a certain quantity of investment involves the notion of a *rate* of yield, as distinguished from the rent of the agent itself. (It is perhaps better not to call it "interest" where there is no borrowing and lending, and no money.) Moreover, due to *errors* in decisions, the actual yield of our agent, its rent, will typically turn out somewhat more or less than expected or than what the investment would have yielded in some other use. Hence, rigorous accounting and accurate planning call for recognition of return on investment separate from rents. The difference could be an excess either way, and would constitute a *profit* (always including loss, negative profit), the fourth traditional form of income. It is also a profit when any concrete agent turns out to yield more or less than *that agent* might have produced in another use. This might be called "operating profit," in contrast with "promoter's" or "investment" profit, the form just mentioned. Thus there are really five functionally distinct types of income, if we separate wages and rent, though analytically it would be more accurate to use such a term as "hire" for both. But our point here is simply that, apart from social relations, the elementary concepts would have the same meaning for a Crusoe as for a member of pecuniary society—and would all have to be clearly conceived as a condition of making any practical decision "correctly."

We now briefly note that in a society made up of many self-sufficient units (Robinson Families of any scope) the same problems of economic ethics would arise that we are painfully familiar with. There would in all realism be wealth and poverty, superfluity and distress—in the absence of relief, "charity," voluntary or enforced. Naturally, being realistic, we assume that people would strive to improve their condition through saving and investment in the various forms of capital: ordinary implements and supplies, personal capacities, exploring for natural resources, scientific investigation, and invention. For differences in ability and in "luck" (not objectively distinguishable in the case of decision-making) would at once produce inequality if the system started without inequality. (Economic equality cannot be accurately defined even where an established monetary system affords a suitable unit; it certainly does not mean equality of money income, per individual, or per family.) And, given the least start, inequality naturally tends to increase cumulatively, if people try to get ahead. Those who have more are always in a better position to get still more: "To him that hath shall be given." And this tendency goes on beyond the individual life, generation after generation (more or less counteracted by other tendencies, as tendencies always are). The inheritance of advantage or encumbrance strikes the modern liberal individualist as especially "unjust." We shall return to the question of moral obligation of the strong or fortunate to help the weak or unlucky. Only the facts are to the point here, especially the fact that these obligations are not in principle affected by the complete absence of economic organization of any form on a social scale—no exchange, no one in any sense "working for" anyone else, or being paid by anyone else. We note too that "property" is not peculiar, since any form of power or means can be used to get more of the same form or of other forms.

III

Organized cooperation of the form prevalent today may be thought of as a development in two stages from the society previously considered. The first stage would be an exchange economy in the proper, literal sense. Each family unit would produce a single final commodity, "from start to finish," or render a personal service, and these end-products would be exchanged in markets.[4]

The intermediate stage, the production and exchange of products, need not detain us long. The main facts needing to be brought out are the same negations that were obtained before. The same income forms would be potential, if not explicitly recognized, in the managerial decisions and accounting of the family unit. But there would still be no payment or receipt of wages, rents, interest, or profit, between persons, hence no "real" separation of such incomes. The economic problem of each unit would be somewhat altered. Instead of apportioning its resources among all the products desired for consumption it would try to select that product which would yield the largest return (in money and "psychic" values) and produce and sell this, and would then apportion the proceeds of its sale in buying the chosen variety of goods from others. However, it would not be quite so unmistakable that each unit was simply working for himself or itself, using his own resources to satisfy his own wants (and to maintain or increase capital, or not). We might expect activities reflecting awareness of conflicting interests of producers and consumers of particular products. There might be efforts to negotiate or "bargain" over prices (presupposing not-quite-perfect markets), to exert "pressure," or to "monopolize"—unless we explicitly frame our assumptions to exclude such antics. Assuming ordinary conditions, there would as before be rich and poor, for the same reasons, and there would be the same "tendency" for inequality to increase (by differential growth, not actual depression of those low in the scale—ignoring the possibility of going into debt). And the same questions would be raised about the ethical obligation (and/or social necessity) of succor of the disadvantaged by (or at the cost of) those better off, through voluntary individual action or through social organization, using more or less compulsion.

IV

Our modern economic order is not, typically and properly, an "exchange" economy. Specialization has been extended beyond the level at which the social unit produces and sells a product. People typically get their living by selling *productive capacity* to a *productive unit* or *enterprise* which carries on production and sells the product (or products—in reality often partial products). With the money received from some productive service or services the individual (social unit) buys his assortment of products for consumption, from whatever producers he finds to offer what he most wants on the best terms. Besides these typical individuals there are, of course, some—in part the same persons—who perform the new function of conducting enterprises, i.e., acting as *entre-*

preneurs. Today, they are characteristically organized in groups as "corporations," meaning roughly the holders of voting common stock. The entrepreneur function is twofold: (1) to take the initiative in production by hiring resources and committing them to a particular product and mode of production; and (2) to take the "risk" or chance of being able to sell the product for enough to cover costs, including the market value of whatever services of person or property the owners furnish to the business (in addition to abstract "deciding"—but this is another separation that can only in part be carried through).

Under this organization, the four or five forms of income are to a large extent (far from completely) separated, going into the pockets of different persons performing the different functions: wage earners, lessors of various kinds of property, lenders of liquid capital, and entrepreneurs of the operating or the investing species. The income of the latter functionaries, called "profit," is in any one case as likely to be negative as positive, depending on his foresight and luck. The expectation or hope of a positive excess of receipts for products over outlays for productive services is the *incentive* to take the "risk" of loss, but it is misleading to call profit, when it occurs, the "reward" of risk-taking. We should not use this term for gambling gains, though business risk-taking has affinities with gambling which are in point here. Analytically, it is desirable to restrict entrepreneurial "risk" to that which cannot be insured against or eliminated by grouping cases; it is commonly thought better to call it by the different term "uncertainty."

It is the entrepreneur who immediately pays the other three forms of income which to him are the costs of production. (Virtually always he himself receives some revenue from both labor and property; the latter may, in this case, be called either rent or interest.) To bring out the nature of the profit system (better called profit and loss system) and the relation between entrepreneur and wage-worker (and, presently, the receiver of rent or interest), it will be useful to proceed, as usual, by considering a hypothetical simple case. To get rid of the common confusion of profit with ownership income, we begin with a case where no property is involved. Let us think of a number of persons who wish to "cooperate" in such an activity as farming a piece of land, where the land itself is a "free good," and other agents, tools, etc., are also free or negligible in cost. They must somehow agree on numerous technical details of the operation, their roles, etc., and on the division of the product. They could, of course, argue out or "negotiate" these matters as they go along, or negotiate contracts ahead of time. But they might also agree that one of the men is to take charge and the others simply to follow his instructions. Even then the division of the product might be made in any manner by agreement. As things typically work out in human affairs, the most effective and satisfactory arrangement is that some person or limited group "hires" the others to work under his (or their) direction, assigns to each a specified amount of the product income created, and himself takes "what is left," if anything, or takes the loss if there is a deficit. The fixed share of product is the meaning of wages, the "residual" share is that of "profit," and the directive function, coupled with responsibility for the result to the other parties, is "entrepreneurship." It is assumed that the laborers will work for the would-be entrepreneur who offers the best terms, and that he is "responsible." The qualification implies that the entrepreneur must have some resources as a surety for performing according to agreement. This does not necessarily mean that he must own property (other than personal capacity or labor-power), but property is the usual form of security. Insofar as the wage-workers are not actually made secure, they share in the entrepreneur function, regardless of how far they know what they are doing. It is because human beings do not completely "know what they are doing"— particularly the consequences very far ahead—that life presents problems; and one result is that the entrepreneurial function in economics exists and comes to be in all degrees specialized in a limited number of individuals.

The principles involved are not changed if some of the "cooperators" furnish property services instead of personal ones to the enterprise—or furnish both types of "productive capacity." The entrepreneur himself, as so designated, inevitably furnishes at least a small amount of both types, even though he may be actually bankrupt and his services really of no value or of negative value. In current business life, the relationships are further obscured and complicated, without affecting the basic principles, by two or three facts. One is the explicit *delegation* of the managerial function to an agent, paid a salary. The real, ultimate entrepreneurship cannot be delegated. In these cases the actual entrepreneur function is that of appointing the agent, fixing his powers and duties and his remuneration, and assuming responsibility for the results of his acts (or, as just noted, the function may be foisted off on unsuspecting laborers and property owners who take the risk of loss without intending to do so and who also make the responsible decisions in committing their resources to the use and the control in question). The appointment of agents obscures the relation between the entrepreneurial and "labor" functions. The hired and salaried manager is a "laborer," whatever the level at which he formally makes decisions.

A second source of confusion is in the entrepreneur–property owner relation. It is common practice for an enterprise to secure property services by borrowing "money," liquid capital, and constructing whatever equipment it wishes, instead of leasing equipment from owners. These latter might construct it *ad hoc* and lease it, as individuals and families produce and hire out capital in the form of more or less specialized labor power. As we have already intimated, there are two forms or levels of the entrepreneurial function: (1) "commitment" of productive capacity to a particular form; (2) direction of the use of equipment in a particular way. The role of the "capitalist" in relation to that of the property owner is not simple. It is not unusual for one person, or a group (partnership, company, corporation), to "own" property which is "mortgaged" to any part of its full value. Who, then, is the "real owner"? Only a complex legal analysis can give the answer, and it might require a trial before a court to decide various issues.

Further complications arise when the entrepreneur is an organized group, a company, or a corporation. In the first place, a group of substantial size inevitably acts through agents, who may or may not be "members," and the principal-agent relation never makes a clear division of power and responsibility. Moreover, the modern corporation may issue a bewildering variety of "securities" and may make contracts and incur debts on all sort of terms, involving a sharing of both assets and control, as well as earnings. With respect to a typical large corporation, it is often hard to say where "membership" ends and outside contractual relations and claims begin. Much actual power to control the operations and to appropriate the income may reside in a labor organization, i.e., in its officials, who may in any degree really "represent" the actual employees.

It is a common misconception that property employs labor; the entrepreneur is the employer (in the mediative sense, representing the ultimate consumer) of both property (or "capital") and labor. He "owns" the enterprise; but it may have no net worth. Property and labor work together, operatively, nominally for him, really more for the consumer who not only gets the product but exercises the final control; and finally, each works for himself. As everyone knows, business enterprises, so often condemned as exploiters of consumers and laborers, incur losses as well as make gains. It is indeed a question whether on the whole and on the average, or as a class, they secure any income at all. Whether losses are greater or less than gains cannot be certainly determined from statistical evidence. Inference from the gambling motive (where people regularly buy "tickets" at far above known actuarial value), and from such other empirical evidence as there is, suggests that over-all net gains cannot be substantial and may well be negative. Even including monopoly revenue, more or less distinguishable from "legitimate" profit, no statistical study is accurate enough to find any "profit" share in the national income. Entrepreneurs in the same and in different industries compete in one set of markets for the purchase of productive services and in another set for the sale of products. Effective competition "tends" to raise the former set of prices (entrepreneurs' costs) and to lower consumer goods prices. It seems that the "spirit of enterprise," akin to the spirit of gambling but including both emulation and the creative urge, has been strong enough to bring costs up and prices down at least to equality, on the average. Of course, either gains or losses may be large in individual ventures, though over time these tend rather rapidly toward "mediocrity," the ordinary return on investment, which contains no "pure" profit, and to fluctuate between gain and loss. Since entrepreneurs usually have other sources of income than "pure profit," there is no paradox in this share being zero or negative.

Theoretical analysis must start from the conception of a "perfectly competitive" economy organized through a system of theoretically ideal markets. Here all profit (and loss, negative profit) is excluded. Such ideal or "frictionless" conditions would make all costs equal to selling prices, the whole value-product being distributed among those who supply the various productive services. The prerequisite is errorless foresight of future conditions in all business decisions. Omniscient direction becomes identical with automatic adjustment to conditions. If a particular entrepreneur had perfect foresight, he would clearly never incur a loss; and if his competitors had it, he could never make a gain. This condition is a necessary hypothesis, though absurd if taken as realistic. Since productive commitments must precede consumption changes by an indeterminate and various but usually long interval, "responsible" decisions are required, subject to a wide range of error in numerous factors. In a society of self-sufficient individuals or families each would make these for himself and take the consequences. Tremendous gains in efficiency are to be had through specialization and cooperation, and there are other reasons for organized action. Concentration on particular products gives place to concentration on particular operations, dozens or even thousands of which may contribute to a completed product. Things have

worked out most to the satisfaction of all parties concerned when implemented through individual initiative under control of exchange in
the market at prices fixed by "demand and supply." Organization of a
large labor force and distribution of product through explicit negotiation or quasi-political process on the pattern of representative government, called "producers' cooperation," is often advocated on ethical
grounds but in practice has never succeeded so as to reach any considerable development.

In any free-market economy, insofar as "competitive" conditions
prevail, each participant unit is in effect like a Crusoe, working for himself, using his own resources to satisfy his own wants. Production for
exchange is indirect production of the product received; it is intelligently
done only because it is more efficient than direct or self-sufficient production, yielding to both parties a larger or a better product from the
same resources. The effect of organization through free exchange is
merely to increase efficiency, and it does this to the maximum extent
consistent with the human limitations of the parties and the amount of
freedom they have. ("Of course" freedom in association means freedom
on both sides, not freedom of one to coerce or defraud another.) The
theoretically ideal free market organization enables everyone to use
whatever resources (personal or external) he has in the way which yields
the maximum value (given the known techniques) to the most willing
and able consumer, and hence to their owner, and it gives the owner
this yield as compensation.

With the world as it is, and men as they are, infinitely varying in
knowledge, wisdom, and managerial capacity, a gain in efficiency comparable to that due to specialization in occupations is to be had through
specialization of management, particularly with modern technology calling for production in large, integrated organizations, in contrast with individual or "family" units. Under these conditions, analysis requires a
"proximate ideal": that of "effective competition" between entrepreneurs
(in the markets for products and for productive services) under the condition that the entrepreneurs and others have such ordinary human
qualities as they do have, not omniscience. But it is assumed that there
are numerous competitors, on both sides, with offers ranging widely (no
collusion). In this situation, the same conclusion as above would hold.
Each works for himself at maximum effectiveness, except that in consequence of uncertainty and error, some enterprises will make a gain
and others incur a loss. Which predominates will depend on the "eager-
ness" of the entrepreneurs; if optimism predominates, they will on the

whole incur losses—and this latter statement seems to accord with the facts, specifically in the United States.

This is the *meaning* of a *free* economy. No one has any arbitrary power over another, since every buyer and seller has a choice of equally good opportunities. And, by the same argument, every member is made secure—secure of being able to sell, at their full value, whatever productive services he is in a position to render. Or he can use his productive capacity himself to gratify his own wants directly. He can also pledge future income to realize present goods, either by borrowing or outright sale of productive capacity—to the extent that the legal system of society actually allows. In fact, this opportunity is normally available to property owners, but to a more limited extent to those who only possess productive capacity in the form of their own personal abilities. In the freest economy, needless to say, anyone's ability to consume depends either on his having productive capacity for direct use or sale to others (or for sale of its product), or on a one-sided transfer. Those who cannot produce can consume only at the expense of someone who can and does produce (except for eating up capital); this is axiomatic, regardless of the system of organization or absence of organization. The main ethical problem centers in the "right" to consume on the part of those who for some reason do not produce—or to consume beyond what they produce, as measured by free choice of other consumers.

V

Finally, we may offer a brief critique and a few observations on policy. The most important general observations which the economic theorist has to offer bearing on social policy are the truisms that "business is business," and that "charity is charity." The two truisms involve different conceptions of "justice," or "rights." (And "law is law" and involves still other norms of justice and right.) But such truisms are repugnant to large numbers of people and are accordingly repudiated. The cry for "Justice, not charity!" may be valid or nonsensical, depending on the definition of justice. In general, the definition of justice is what men dispute and fight about; not many demand more than they have a "right" to—i.e., think they have.

There is a kind of "natural justice" in the principle of the exchange (open or competitive market) economy, i.e., that each shall consume what he produces, i.e., adds, to total social production, as production is organized. (The family is the unit, and voluntary charity or help is always allowed.) This norm would apply "ruthlessly" to an isolated individual (Crusoe) and must axiomatically apply to any community considered as a unit (allowing for some consumption of capital for a time, at the expense of the future). On the other hand, rigorous application of this norm to individuals in a society would be not only immoral but impossible and absurd; it is meaningless, or grotesque, or hideous in relation to babies, for example.

The next proposition is akin to the first and, like it, self-evident. Any unsatisfactory condition in an economic society may be due either to the fact that the "competitive system" does not work effectively in accord with the theory as stated, or to the antithetical fact that it does. Low wages, for example, or wages "too" low. The worker in question may be getting less than his "productive contribution," or may be unemployed because of imperfections in the organization machinery (or interferences with its working); or he may be getting all he is worth (to any ultimate consumer), but this may be inadequate for "decent" support, or less than a socially tolerable minimum, apart from humanitarian considerations. For the baby, and many others, it is zero, and for others it is or "ought" to be zero or small, while their consumption ought nonetheless to be high according to the standards of need and of justice which prevail in our society. However, we cannot say that anyone "ought" to have more than his own contribution without saying that somebody else has an *obligation* to *sacrifice* consumption of some part of his productive contribution, to make up the difference. The main problem is to locate, appraise, and apportion this obligation, determined in relation to needs and possibilities, and to find a way to effect the redistribution without such cost or loss of productiveness (destruction of incentive) as would nullify the gain.

Perhaps the first task of economics teaching is to counteract the tendency of the general public to say that "competition does not work" or has ceased to work, or is a myth, because many people do not get the incomes they "need" or are thought to need. Competition merely tends to give everyone his productive contribution, which is limited by his resources; and these latter bear little or no relation to his needs or those of his dependents. There are, indeed, serious "mechanical" weaknesses in the organization. Competition is "imperfect," for many reasons (not only monopoly of various kinds and related conditions). Much technical monopoly is accidental, or inevitable, or even functional (cf. patents and copyrights; most monopolies are similar in stimulating innovation and are also limited and temporary). The importance of this evil is vastly exaggerated in popular thinking. Moreover, labor unions and farmers, supported by public opinion and often by the law, are now the monopolies that do the most damage. Another and most important phenomenon is the "business cycle" of boom (partly pseudoprosperity) and depression (real), with unemployment, loss, and suffering by all classes, not merely wage-workers. In the first place, much if not most of the real imperfection of the market organization is due to ignorance and prejudice on the part of the individuals acting in every functional role— as consumers, workers, owners, and entrepreneurs in every branch of production, including trade. And much more is due to stupid governmental action and other well-intended interference. Unquestionably, selfishness, greed, and power-lust play a large role. They always will, particularly in any large organization. And the individual wage earner is at a disadvantage here since he is not often in a position to get away with much. But he is not the only victim, and it is far from easy to gauge these things, to separate and define legitimate rights or remediable evils, before discussing remedies. It is especially hard to identify evils remediable democratically by law and administration based on general free approval. The government is the largest organization of all, and "politics" is certainly not less liable to error, and prejudice, and skulduggery of every kind, than is "business." It is discouraging to see how much that is really wrong is due to ill-advised governmental action—action largely demanded by public opinion or at least by the majority; some of it is, of course, "put over" politically by selfish—or indeed by honest and well-meaning—"special interests." The fallacies of "protectionism" in foreign trade and "inflationism" internally are grievances of the economists as old as the science of economics itself, and little if any price-fixing is ever defensible; at the moment, the rent freeze on residential housing is doubtless both the most stupid and the most popular example.

The more serious problems of the free economy lie in the very meaning of economic freedom; but these can be dealt with here only by summary and rather haphazard mention. In fact, while they can be discussed endlessly, what can be said with confidence and in general terms can be put in relatively few words. The essential fact is that, fundamentally, society is not made up of individuals, but rather of institutional groups, beginning with the family as the minimum real unit: that is, considering society as an ongoing complex and looking either backward in history or forward in policy. Again, the heart of the matter, the veritable foundation of society, is the rights of babies—and the locus of the corresponding obligations to give them their rights. Here, obviously, the "individuals" directly in question can have no obligations themselves, and "freedom" for them has no meaning. Otherwise stated, the problem centers in the relations of right and duty between the family and, in the first instance, "the state." But the state—a free state—has nothing to give anyone except what it takes from someone else (if not from himself!)—and only part of that, since the transfer itself necessarily involves costs. The state, in free or individualistic society, serves as a sort of legalized Robin Hood, an intermediary for enforcing the "right" of the weak or unfortunate to be supported at a "decent" level at the cost of the stronger or luckier.

Now it is indisputable (as we have noted before) that within some bounds this right and the corresponding obligations exist. They are not merely dictated by humane sentiments; their acceptance—up to a point—is an absolute requisite to the existence of any society whatever, both sentimentally and practically. What point? is the first question. And the question impinges on every individual as either more or less "weak or unfortunate" or "strong or lucky" as the case may be. We cannot measure either of these variables—cannot even (as already noted) define economic inequality at all sharply. Obviously "individuals" cannot be allowed to be the judges of their own rights and the obligations of others to them or to their children and other dependents. And there is no impartial judge, and little hope of approach to agreement. Further, it is necessary, in the world as it is, to distinguish between inability and unwillingness on the part of those living below approved standards to provide for themselves and their own, and necessary to apply different treatment; and here there is an almost complete absence of objective norms. Yet the incompetent (morally blameless), and the unwilling too, have children, whom society must (both ethically and in self-defense) safeguard and provide for. Reasonable freedom to reproduce is perhaps the most sacred freedom and right, and it carries the heaviest responsibility.

The notion of freedom is meaningful only in relation to "given" individuals, given as to their ends and means, their tastes and their wants, their capacities internal and external. But in fact individuals are not "given." Both the wants and the capacities with which they enter responsible adult life are determined principally by the institutional complex which is society on the basis of innate physical, mental, and moral qualities and what must be classed as "accident." It should be stressed, because it is so generally ignored, that this cultural determination is just as important in connection with wants or tastes as in connection with "means," and that it is true and important in practically the same sense for the internal qualities that make a human being economically productive (his labor power) as for his endowment with external "property." The moral contrast between property rights and "human" rights will not stand examination.

The first requisite for intelligent discussion of wage policy—action to raise wages where they ought to be raised, or to supplement them by relief where they are inadequate—is a genuine interest on the part of the public in intelligent discussion itself, and in truth and understanding, in contrast with action by snap judgment, aimed at symptoms of maladies. Problems must be approached without prejudice in judging facts and the consequences of acts, as well as with high moral ideals. Science must be separated from wishful thinking, and cooperation for mutual advantage through business separated from charity, either voluntary or politically enforced. This has little appeal to the romantic-sentimental nature of man; but it will only confuse council and do more harm than good to define "wages" as what anyone thinks he or someone else ought to have, regardless of the person's contribution to production. And what one ought to have cannot be asserted without considering who is to contribute to his income, fixed by the value of his service to some willing buyer.

Short of slavery, neither the government nor coercive organizations of workers can force anybody to employ labor on any terms; they can only prohibit employment on specified terms. The result ordinarily to be expected from any coercive action to raise wages will be unemployment, i.e., no wage at all, or else the displacement of some workers into a still lower-paid occupation. There is no sense in minimum-wage laws apart from provision for supplying the prescribed income in some other way, and this would make any prohibitive measure superfluous. And the only discoverable reason for existence of large national unions is to coerce the public, rather than the employers. According to the first principles of economics, employers as a group, in an entrepreneurial economy, have nothing to give or to be taken away. Some make gains, which are offset by losses on the part of others. Forcible expropriation of profits where and when positive profits arise must reduce the general inducement to risk resources in employing labor at all. It is simply impossible for all labor to benefit significantly at the expense of all employers. But the public statements of top labor leaders and other advocates of wage legislation express indifference as to where a demanded wage increase is to come from, whether from others better off than the beneficiaries or worse off. The "just" objective, of course, defined in terms of relative capacity in comparison with need, is to assist those badly off at the cost of others enough better off to justify the violation of freedom, as well as all the political and social costs and losses. It will be self-defeating to take away gains where there are gains and not reimburse for losses, destroying the incentive to strive to be better off. Men will not carry on business on terms of "heads you win, tails I lose." That policy must soon lead to a general stoppage or to dictation of all economic life by some authority, with loss of personal freedom and political responsibility.

It is impossible to say, even in theory, who will finally pay any particular wage increase forced from an operating firm. The first impact will be on the proprietors, but they may or may not have anything to lose; and anyhow, it may be passed on to creditors, consumers, or salaried employees, depending on circumstances that will hardly be ascertainable even by careful investigation of the particular case. The firm will in general employ fewer workers and turn out less product. We know that any increased consumption for some must come either from increased production, or from the consumption of others, or from saving. Workers might save a little out of an increase, and there are conditions in which higher wages may stimulate greater productivity, but both cases are unusual. The main effect of an enforced wage payment, beyond the competitive rate (the value of the service to the final consumer), will be to reduce the incentive to entrepreneurs and property owners, actual or potential, to save and to make investments and expand production. If people whose incomes are "inadequate" are to get more, apart from voluntary charity, the means should be secured by taxation levied in a morally and prudentially defensible way and amount, so as not to have too much negative effect on production. Wage earners are by no means the only persons receiving inadequate incomes; they are not as a class identical with propertyless persons, and many of them receive incomes which make them fit subjects for levies to support others. Whether persons owning a little wealth but not enough to support them at a tolerable level should be forced to consume all of this before receiving any aid at the cost of others is one of the difficult questions of social policy.

In any attempt at redistribution of income, many considerations have to be taken into account. Presumably the question of "desert" should be given some weight, on the side both of the provider and the receiver of aid. But this is a factor where even a crude working definition is hard enough, and anything like measurement is hardly possible at all. In what are commonly thought of as economic terms, the first main consideration rendering an income a proper subject of taxation is its size, relative to the socially recognized claims against it. The latter include the number of persons it must support, their health and various special needs, the extremely difficult matter of separating real net income from expenditure properly required by one's business or profession, and the like. Society sometimes requires its functionaries to keep up appearances, to maintain the dignity of a calling, by living even more expensively than they themselves prefer. A second consideration is the security of the income, its steadiness in time and its prospective permanence. The major fallacy in popular thinking is the notion that size and security of income correspond simply to property versus personal services as the source. (This is apart from confusing property owning with entrepreneurship, which affords the most precarious and doubtful income of all.) There is probably a considerable correlation; but it is certainly not enough to justify treating "owning versus earning" (property rights versus human rights) as a principle in the determination of policy. These matters must be decided by discussion on their merits and in accord with facts, in specific cases, by collaboration of specialists in ethics with students of taxation who are up against the detailed facts and practical difficulties. General analysis tells us chiefly that most concrete measures of reform are crude substitutes for taxation and subsidy, and are hard to defend either in ethical terms or in terms of their economic or social-political effects—if their actual effects are brought out into the open.

Before and above all, the problem of social justice must *not* be discussed, as it so commonly is, on the assumption that a given social dividend is to be divided up among the individuals of a given population. The dividend is a current product, with the possibility of drawing a little upon the future by consuming capital—surely to be treated as a recourse of near desperation. But it is only too easy to sacrifice the future to the present by measures which undermine the incentive to activities contributing to growth. An intelligent social policy must strike some balance with respect to action that redistributes income more equitably, but at the cost of reducing the total below what it would otherwise be. And, on the other side, the sharers are not at all "given," either in numbers or in any of their important and relevant characteristics. A drastic redistribution, conforming to some abstract ideal of justice, may both decrease the amount to be distributed and increase the number of claimants; and the moral effects of "indiscriminate charity" constitute another problem about which little is known except that pauperization and disintegration of personality often result. Our moral sentiments seem to be as much out of accord with the possibilities of the world in which our lot is cast as they are in conflict with the basic natural propensities that make up immediate self-interest. He that would love his fellow man, and express his love in a way that will do more good than harm, must indeed learn to be (in scriptural language) as wise as a serpent and harmless as a dove. Freedom, justice, order, efficiency, and progress are value imperatives all essential within wide limits, but there is conflict among them—conflict practically between each one and all the rest; more of one can be had only by giving up more or less of the others. And there is no formula to tell the policy maker where or how to strike the best attainable balance.

The conclusion, which it is not pleasant to reach, but which must be drawn, is that the most needed lesson for public opinion at this historical juncture is not to expect too much. We must "live in the world" as it is until (and if) we can change it. Neither accepting it nor changing it is easy, and, if our powers are limited, attempting much or rapid change is certain to be to make things worse instead of improving them. The forces of nature show no detectable preference for the human virtues of gentleness or justice, or for any "good intentions"; and the basic drives of human nature are those required for survival in a world of the kind this one is. Freedom of the individual in particular is a historically anomalous product of conditions peculiar to the Western world in the past few centuries. It seems to be natural to human beings to turn to a "savior" when they are in trouble of any kind. As a great Founding Father of the American Republic well said, "Eternal vigilance is the price of liberty"; but he should have said "intelligent" vigilance. If we care for freedom, we must respect it, and not hasten to pass laws and set up authorities for enforcing them unless there is very sound reason to expect the result to be an improvement over that "natural liberty" which is anything but natural in view of history as a whole.

This means that laws must be chiefly in the negative form, like the Decalogue, made up of thou-shalt-not's, but summed up in the proposition that none shall infringe the liberty of others; that is, relations shall be by mutual assent. Intelligent, positive policy has as its first requisite a clear understanding of how the free economy works, and of whether the evils we see are due to freedom, or to its absence, or—which is largely the case—to some unalterable condition of life. With respect to wages, the only proper meaning of the term is the price the most willing and able buyer will pay for the most valuable product the individual is able and willing to turn out (or contribute toward); and this is the wage which "tends" to be established in the free market. In no wise does it imply ethically ideal results; for, in the demand for labor, "able" counts as much as willing and might does not make right. Ability and even will (tastes and interests), is in large part the creation of brute facts and forces along with ethical factors. Society is not made up of given individuals; as we have seen, both productive capacity and wants are socially created at least as much as they reflect activities of the individual for which credit or blame can be imputed; and "luck" is perhaps the largest factor of all. Social policy must aim first at giving the worker his wage, in the proper meaning. Beyond that, interference must be directed to supplementing the wage where needful and feasible. But, more especially, social policy must strive to enable the individual to earn as much as he is potentially able to earn through property and personal services, and to achieve security, through reducing the vicissitudes of economic life and through an honest application of the insurance principle.

Finally, social action must not simply be sweepingly identified with state action, as there is such a tendency to do. That can easily lead to submergence of all freedom in a totalitarian regime and to the destruction of civilization, if not of humanity, in international strife. There is no formula, no easy or satisfactory answer to the problem of the distribution of responsibility between the individual, the family, the local community, the nation-state; and the world order, which is slow in coming, must imperatively be somehow built up. And there are innumerable other important groupings, political or nonpolitical in various ways and degrees. There are grave dangers in the tendency of reform to transfer functions from individual, family, and voluntary associations to the state. The family is particularly threatened, and the problems of rich and poor nations, of inequality and alleged exploitation between regions and peoples, are coming to be as serious as the same differences and conflicts within a particular state. Nations no more than individuals can live to themselves alone, in the world of modern technology and humanitarian feeling.

Any serious effort to discuss the social problem, of which the wage problem is merely an inseparable aspect, and to consider all the factors which patently have to be considered and give them their due weight must tend to emphasize caution and conservatism. The time has passed when the world needed simply to be aroused to action, on the assumption that what to do was no serious problem, evils being due to people not doing what they knew it was good to do. There is of course plenty of "sin" in the world, and "vested interests" resist change; but it is not to be assumed that "reformers" are either more disinterested or wise than opponents of particular measures, and it is an infinitely harder problem to change things for the better than to preserve law and order in roughly their wonted course. The modern social order is an infinitely complicated and sensitive mechanism, and there is vastly more chance of injuring than of improving it by tampering with it at random, or without the clearest understanding of what one is doing, however well-meant the action may be. At this time, ill-considered measures of interference are a greater danger than indifference to evils. One of the first conclusions from any candid investigation of our problems, from the standpoint of inadequate wages as from any other standpoint, must be the inevitability of gradualness, or of disaster as its alternative.

Notes

1. Men also, of course, pass *aesthetic* judgments, distinct from individual liking, not liking, disliking. In this sketch we can only note that in economics the distinction is ignored; matters of taste are treated as matters of desire merely.

2. Eliminating invention and exploration, and all discovery of techniques or resources, accumulation would presumably be subject to "diminishing returns" to the extent that there would be particular forms of capital not subject to equally free increase through investment. But it is wholly unrealistic to postulate any particular (final, historical) equilibrium rate of return, particularly the zero rate.

3. Use of different terms for the yield of human and nonhuman agents is a source of confusion, though sometimes useful. Analytically, it would be better to imagine our Crusoe as a slaveholder, doing no work himself and regarding his labor force as capital goods merely, yielding a rent (or, alternatively, interest on his investment—see text). But this would seem more "unrealistic"; in our age it is hard to picture human beings treated simply as inert instruments by "owners."

4. More realistically, they would be bought and sold against "money" of some form. In this sketch, we must assume that money is "neutral," thus separating it from the disturbances that arise from its use: specifically, from its changes in "value," and speculation on its future value—the primary cause of

"business cycles" with all their attendant evils. We also "assume" a perfect market, with a definite uniform price of every product to all buyers and sellers, and, for simplicity, exclude middlemen and all speculation.

The idea of a two-stage development has some historical reality, in that a "handicraft economy" intervened between the medieval system of relatively self-sufficient manors and the modern age. But the idea is to be taken as an analytical device. It is nearer the truth in general, to say that individualism developed through disintegration of a social matrix of custom and authority, not the progressive organization ("contract theory") of previously discrete persons.

12

The Role of Principles in Economics and Politics

The more-than-generous words of introduction by the chairman may suggest or illustrate the underlying theme of my remarks to follow — the conflict of values. Needless to say, the value qualities of an introduction lie in the fields of morals and esthetics. No one would think of applying the category of truth. And as to utility, the "function" of an introduction seems to be, by a little amiable and gracefully stated prevarication, to add to the embarrassment of the speaker—if he has enough modesty or candor in self-appraisal to be subject to embarrassment. I say this, not to return unkindness for kindness, but for the serious purpose stated of illustrating what I believe to be a profoundly important principle in connection with principles; and I wish I had more time than I shall be able to take to consider in particular the conflict between truth and other values, specifically in a liberal ethic and culture.

Let me add that I am modest and candid enough to be "plenty" embarrassed already. It is not only my inadequacy to the occasion and dislike of disappointing an audience such as this. The occasion comes to me at a time when members of our profession cease, by the usual official standards, to be useful and are pensioned off—decently and quietly laid on the shelf. And, standing at this vantage point and surveying the history of our society, of West European civilization, and of the world, during the generation and more in which I, with colleagues in economics and other branches of what is called social science, have been diligently "improving" that society and the world, I find little cause for

Reprinted with permission from the *American Economic Review* 41 (March 1951): 1–29. Presidential address delivered at the Sixty-third Annual Meeting of the American Economic Association, Chicago, December 25, 1950.

jubilation or enhancement of self-esteem. And if I turn to view the standing of my profession in the world, or that of my special branch of it, dealing with principles or "theory" in the profession as a whole, I get no more comfort from what I see. So, I have proposed for the address which custom demands on this occasion, a bit of general stock-taking. Such an endeavor is itself reasonably in accord with custom, if somewhat strange for a "learned society," and I hope it is a custom not dishonored in the observance. Custom also allows the speaker, perhaps especially one of the age of this incumbent, to take a somewhat personal or reminiscent tone, and to verge toward the character of a sermon rather than that of science or scholarship.

My embarrassment, not only at standing before this audience, but in all teaching and writing about economic principles, is not new, as its source is not. I have been increasingly moved to wonder whether my job is a job or a racket, whether economists, and particularly economic theorists, may not be in the position that Cicero, citing Cato, ascribed to the augurs of Rome—that they should cover their faces or burst into laughter when they met on the street. Thus, for reasons which I hope to develop, briefly, my interest has of late tended to shift from the problems of economic theory, or what seem to be its proper concerns, to the question of why people so generally, and the learned elite in particular, as they express themselves in various ways, choose nonsense instead of sense and shake the dust from their feet at us. And also, why the theorist is so commonly "in the dog-house" among economists, as classified by academic faculty lists and books and articles in learned journals carrying the word "economic" in their titles.

And I also note that the period of my career as an economist has been marked by a series of "movements"—I will not say fads—in economic writing and teaching, consisting largely of attacks on traditional views of the nature and function of economics, in which the term "orthodoxy" commonly appears as a "cuss-word," an epithet of reproach. The critics, aggressors, have more or less explicitly advocated the abolition of an economics of economic principles and its replacement by almost anything or everything else, other principles if they can be found—psychological, historical, statistical, political, or ethical—or no principles at all but factual description of some sector of social human phenomena called "economic" for reasons not clear to me. I cannot comment in detail on these fashions in thinking. The latest "new economics," and in my opinion rather the worst for fallacious doctrine and pernicious consequences, is that launched by the late John Maynard

(Lord) Keynes, who for a decade succeeded in carrying economic thinking well back to the dark age, but of late this wave of the future has happily been passing.

This same period of history has also seen a growing disregard for free economic institutions in public policy—increasing resort to legislative and bureaucratic interference and control, the growth of pressure groups employing both political and "direct" action to get what they want, and with all this the debasement of the state itself, completely in much of the European world, from free forms to ruthless despotism. It is surely legitimate to ask whether there is some connection between the movement of economic thinking and that of political change.

Now all thinking involves "principles" in some sense, at least the formation of concepts and fitting of concrete data to concepts through propositions. Surveying the quality of economic thinking in matters of policy which seemingly tends to win out, one faces the unpleasant question whether, if people will not think more or less correctly, it is good for them to think at all. Perhaps it might be better to go back to the good old days when men believed and did what they were told by hoary tradition and constituted authority. For so the great mass always lived, prior to the advent of our historically unique West European civilization a couple of centuries ago. Perhaps the "principle" of authoritarian dictatorship is right after all—or inevitable, which for practical purposes comes to the same thing—as large groups even in this country insist and preach. And I do not mean only the Communist Party and its sympathizers; there are others, far more numerous, who are among its most vociferous opponents. For one totalitarian party will naturally hate another with different leaders and slogans far worse than they will hate those who stand for freedom.

My doubts and discouragement—for there is no reason to avoid such words, since I propose here to place truth ahead of other values—are not new. It has long been my habit to mention to classes the sinister import of such intellectual phenomena as protectionism in foreign economic policy; and the perpetual popular demand for making capital cheap by manufacturing money; and for creating a demand for labor by enforcing all sorts of inefficiency, waste, and even destruction. The free-traders, as has been said, win the debates, but the protectionists win the elections; and it makes little difference in our policy which party wins, the avowed protectionists or the professed free-traders. Inflation is of course to be brought on as a more pleasant alternative to taxation, and then suppressed by law and police action. Try to get people to see that if the value of money has been depreciated by, say, forty-five per cent, any price, charge, or tax that has not risen in money terms by over eighty per cent has actually been reduced. If the rulers of democracy, the demos, will not heed simple arithmetic, what is the use in talking and writing about problems which really are problems?—not to mention developing higher mathematical formulas in which the "given" magnitudes must be largely guessed at. Why engage in public discussion at all, unless one is content with what seems to be our role to serve as an antidote to the poison being disseminated by other social scientists, even economists? Is it not insulting one's own intelligence?

The serious fact is that the bulk of the really important things that economics has to teach are things that people would see for themselves if they were willing to see. And it is hard to believe in the utility of trying to teach what men refuse to learn or even seriously listen to. What point is there in propagating sound economic principles if the electorate is set to have the country run on the principle that the objective in trade is to get rid of as much as possible and get as little as possible in return?, if they will not see that imports are either paid for by exports, as a method of producing the imported goods more efficiently, or else are received for nothing?, or if they hold that economy consists in having as many workers as possible assigned to a given task instead of the fewest who are able to perform it? Of late, I have a new and depressing example of popular economic thinking in the policy of arbitrary price-fixing. Can there be any use in explaining, if it is needful to explain, that fixing a price below the free-market level will create a shortage and one above it a surplus? But the public oh's and ah's and yips and yaps at the shortage of residential housing and surpluses of eggs and potatoes as if these things presented problems—any more than getting one's footgear soiled by deliberately walking in the mud. And let me observe that rent-freezing for example, occurs not at all merely because tenants have more votes than landlords. It reflects a state of mind, a mode of reasoning, even more discouraging than blindness through self-interest-like protectionism among our Middle Western farmers.

One must grant that some critics of rationalistic economics seem to have something in their contention that theories based on the assumption that men are reasoning beings run contrary to facts. But, from the standpoint of policy, the question is, will they be more reasonable in more sweeping political action, considering that it is absurd governmental policies which lead to the criticism in the first place? However, one notes that protectionism and "featherbedding" of organized workers, and even monetary inflation are not (not often) carried to the logical point at which all exchange and specialization through exchange would stop, or all accumulated resources be eaten up. Explanation of policy might conceivably get farther if we did take a more psychological tack and instead of reasoning logically, ask why men believe and practice nonsense but in general act so much less irrationally than they argue— and what follows from that. Presumably our lucubrations must have *some* relation to the public interest if we are to expect public support; but why they pay us for it anyway is one of the deep economic mysteries, one might say another striking example of popular economic irrationality. However, any politician can always find an "economist" to endorse any position or policy he sees fit to advocate, and perhaps this is the proper function of our "science" in a democracy.

Let me say here that I feel like apologizing for the negativistic and even complaining tone of my remarks so far—for there is no transgression more unforgivable than refusing to be "optimistic," and "constructive." But I started out by mentioning the conflict of values and especially that between truth and other values, and have said that on this occasion I propose to give a considerable preference to truth over other standards. It is an advantage of getting old, which I believe even Cicero overlooked in his great apology for age. A certain independence goes with getting to a point where one will hardly be hunting a job or running for office or (probably) even courting the ladies. One may then indulge in the luxury of a moderate amount of candor, even of calling a spade a spade. And unpleasant truth—and truth is likely to be unpleasant, or we should not place so much stress on optimism—may be useful, up to a point. I would not carry it too far, but occasionally, and in homeopathic doses, as it were. I am reminded of a deep philosophical observation made by a high politico in a speech some years ago, here in Chicago I believe, as reported by T. V. Smith: "The time has come to take the bull by the tail and look the situation square in the face." It has occurred to me that one of the interesting "facts of life" is that the expression itself refers to things so ugly or unpleasant that they are to be kept out of sight or explicit mention. If time allowed, I should like to follow this out with some "research" into the reasons why our professional stock in trade is referred to as "the dismal science." At any rate, I do wish to stress the importance of negative conclusions, particularly in relation to action, the advisability of *not* doing things that will make matters worse, and the fact that principles of economics do have in a high degree this unromantic sort of value. And perhaps this applies to knowledge in general. A humorist once popular in this country stated my favorite "principle" in education: "It ain't ignorance that does the most damage, it's knowin' so derned much that ain't so."

I also spoke earlier of philosophizing, or preaching, in contrast with more objective discourse. A sermon should have a text; and I have found a suitable one in the gospel according to "Saint" the Marquis de Talleyrand-Périgord: The only good principle is to have no principles (Le seule bon principe est de n'en avoir aucun). Talleyrand, to be sure, is not regularly listed among the evangelists. But he was in fact a bishop in the Church, and another churchman, of the civilized eighteenth-century French pattern, the abbot Galiani, had earlier stated the same creed. And anyhow, the saying suits my purpose as a text. It is, no doubt, usually enjoyed and dismissed as a witty cynicism; but I propose to treat it quite seriously, as a starting-point. Not literally, I admit. It is an epigram; and an epigram has been defined as a half-truth so stated as to be especially annoying to those who believe in the other half. I wish to stress both halves, the value of principles as well as their limitations. Accordingly, I must re-word the text into one of rather the opposite literal import. The right principle is to respect all the principles, take them fully into account, and then use *good judgment* as to how far to follow one or another in the case in hand. All principles are false, because all are true—in a sense and to a degree; hence, none is true in a sense and to a degree which would deny to others a similarly qualified truth. There is always a principle, plausible and even sound within limits, to justify any possible course of action and, of course, the opposite one. The truly right course is a matter of the best compromise, or the best or "least-worst" combination of good and evil. As in cookery, and in economic theory, it calls for enough and not too much, far enough and not too far, in any direction. Moreover, the ingredients of policy are always imponderable; hence there can be no principle, no formula, for the best compromise. That laws must be stated in sentences partly accounts for the familiar "principle," "The law is an ass." And if people don't have good judgment, or won't use it, it is "just too bad," for themselves and for others over whom they have power.

After so much by way of "preliminary," I am at last ready for some consideration of economic principles. These have, or surely ought to have, two kinds of significance: in explaining what does happen and in providing guidance for bringing about what is thought desirable or what "ought" to happen. In the first role they assimilate to principles of science; in the second, they raise questions of political principle, since action must be primarily political, and both economic and political principles are inseparable from ethics. Political principles are of course affected by the same ambiguity; they both explain and direct, and this is also true in a sense of the ethical. The problem is complicated by the tangled relation between the two concerns, explanation and critical evaluation; for these also are inseparable, yet are finally contradictory. A complete explanation shows why an event is inevitable, given the antecedent circumstances; hence it excludes purposive control. Here I propose, after a brief reminder of what the main economic principles are and what they mean, to consider them in the light of three questions: their value or usefulness, their limitations, and the possible alternatives—all with respect to explanation and guidance of action. I need hardly say that all these topics raise the deepest philosophical issues, and that only a few general and superficial observations, selected rather arbitrarily or at haphazard, are possible here. But let me note at once that Talleyrand was referring to moral principles in connection with political action, and it is with respect to these in particular that I wish to sound an emphatic warning. The most pernicious and abominable principle of all, though it has been stated and preached by the highest authorities, ecclesiastical and lay (from Athanasius to Kant), is the principle of acting on moral principles—"Do right though the world perish." That is—as will be found to be true of moral principles generally—it is false and pernicious if it is taken to mean anything in particular, anything beyond the best compromise, the best combination of good and bad, and in both means and ends, where the problem has the means-end form.

Economic principles are simply the more general implications of the single principle of freedom, individual and social, i.e., free association, in a certain sphere of activity. The sphere is that of economizing, i.e., conduct in which quantitative means are used to achieve quantitative ends, or rather provisional ends, goods and services quantitatively comparable as means to a general end, also quantifiable. But economics deals only with the apportionment of means among the provisional ends or the proportioning of these, leaving to engineering and kindred studies the all-or-none choices among technical processes. The general end has no good and accepted name; it may be called economic well-being if it is recognized that both terms require definition. It is simply the common denominator necessarily implied in comparisons between uses of means. Acceptance of the principle of freedom makes it superfluous to define the end, and the less that is specified about it the better. The provisionally final ends, as noted, are the *impersonal* goods and services desired and sought, produced and consumed, at any time and place. However, we must not fail to include *additional* means or resources, produced with some fraction of those in existence at a given time; maintenance of these, including all replacements, is of course part of the production of the flow of consumable things.

The free association in question is *exchange*, in *markets*, an instrumentality necessary to specialized production, and distribution of the joint result. The meaning of economics in the traditional or orthodox sense is the analysis of this system of cooperation in the production and distribution of impersonal goods. "Competition" has no necessary or proper place in the organization and its use to describe the free choice by each of his cooperators is a linguistic accident calamitous for understanding. All "personal" association, by contrast, involves power, and personal values are not subject to exchange. The form of purchase and sale of friendliness or enmity is viewed as immoral, though there is much pretense both ways—as in most human relations. Exchange or its terms may be much influenced by personal considerations (really mixed with giving), and we actually in large measure exchange dinner-parties, various presents, etc., as well as disfavors. (*One* reason why a science of human behavior, in the literal sense, is impossible is that, in contrast with physical objects, our behavior is so saturated with varied make-believe and deception, not clearly separable from the "realities.") A special and very important form of exchange occurs when one person places his economic capacity under the direction of another, on terms fixed by agreement—the principle of "entrepreneurship." Such direction is a distinctive service in that it cannot be measured until after the arrangement is liquidated, hence cannot be treated as a means-of-production or "capitalized" as can be done with other services, including the personal type, as far as contracts can be enforced.

The "perfect" market (mis-called perfectly competitive) is unreal but conceptually necessary. It is the embodiment of complete freedom. There are no power relations, since everyone has a choice among a number of equally good alternatives. The freedom in question centers in the right of each to be the judge of his own values and of the use of his own means to achieve them. There is no implication of selfishness or any other judgment of the moral quality or artistic taste reflected in any want or act. We usually speak of "individual" freedom, but it applies to any group acting as a unit. The family, "represented" by its "head," is the usual minimum unit, and there are other units in unlimited number and variety. Wants and resources are treated simply as "given" attributes of any individual or other unit; "technology" must either be included among resources or added as a third given—the latter the more useful procedure. On the average, an economic subject's own person, with all its capacities, is the chief means under his control and is in the majority of cases nearly his only resource. Differences between personal capacities and external "property" are the creation of the legal system, and would be absent under a slave economy. The virtual outlawing of enforceable contracts for personal services creates a serious disadvantage for one whose resources are in the personal form, for he cannot freely "realize" future value by sale or pledge and is consequently dependent on a continuous market as well as continuity in the capacity itself. But the benefits of freedom are presumably thought greater than the evil.

The principle of freedom is apparently accepted in modern civilization—consequently called "liberal"—on three or four grounds, which overlap somewhat. First, and most commonly cited, it is instrumental to the realization of other ends accepted as rightful. Modern thought locates value in the individual rather than making him an instrument to the purposes of the state or its ruler. And it is assumed that the normal adult person is ordinarily a better judge of his own interests, values, or well-being than any agent of society (bureaucrat) given authority over him is likely to be. Second, freedom itself is a thing men want, and have a right to, even possibly at the cost of a formally better management of one's affairs by an overlord of any kind; the normal person prefers within wide limits to "make his own mistakes." Third, it is a "value," a thing the individual ought to want, even ought to have if he may not choose it, a part of the modern ideal of the dignity of the person. Thus the laws of liberal states do not allow men to sell themselves (or their children) into "involuntary servitude," even if they so choose, though everyone is free from day to day to place himself or his property under the direction of another, on terms satisfactory to both parties. This is the entrepreneurial relation, which is in a real sense the central feature of the modern free economy. Finally, there is a fourth, "pragmatic" reason, for extending the scope of freedom; policing is costly to the public authority, and coercion itself needs to be economized.

From the standpoint of explaining actual behavior, one can only "submit" that people want to economize and that their efforts to make

resources go further are more or less successful; also that correct apportionment of resources among uses is a way of economizing, as are specialization through exchange of products and the organization of effort
under specialized direction. A large sector of individual and social behavior is then more or less fully "explained" by these principles. How
far they go, and what other principles or unsystematic occurrences may
have to be considered, I obviously cannot take up in detail here.

Certainly economic principles are subject to sweeping limitations as
to their explanatory value. They tell us nothing about concrete economic
facts, *what* wants people have, *what* goods are produced and exchanged,
what resources and techniques are employed, *what* distribution takes
place. The justification of treating these data in a purely abstract way is
the significance of theory for policy, and I shall come back to that. Further, it is easy for a critic to "riddle" the principle of abstract rationality.
No one thinks, I hope, that consumers consciously strive to maximize
satisfaction, well-being, or whatever it be, by acting in relation to a
known function connecting the state in question with measurable quantities of things available at given prices. Effort to get the maximum return in money for productive services seems more realistic, but the view
that production is purely in order to have consumption, unaffected by
interests of its own, is clearly indefensible. Yet comparisons between uses
of means are made and apportionments effected; and the logical principles inherent in these acts are useful for interpretation even if they do
not accurately picture the conscious motives. It suffices that men largely
behave "as if" they were trying to conform to the principles. These have
great value in the prediction of effects of changes, effects both on and
through price movements, changes that happen or are contrived. And
the alternative, which is statistics on a behavioristic basis, is subject to
much the same limitations, rooted in the vagueness and instability of
motives. Certainly the main effort in statistical economics, the prediction
of changes in business conditions, has not produced results justifying
much elation.

More detailed consideration would carry us into the question of the
possibilities and limitations of a natural or positive science of human
conduct. Many limitations are plain to see, and they are related to the
essential fact, which is that such a science is not what we need; indeed
the idea is an absurdity. For if even two people predict one another's
behavior and act on their predictions, both predictions will be falsified,
and the activities of both parties misdirected. From the standpoint of
explanation alone, motives correspond to forces in mechanics. These too

are unobserved, metaphysical; we read them into the phenomena or interpretation, because our minds work that way. Forces, however are known and measured only by their effects, hence always correspond exactly with the latter. But we have other information about human motives, and "know" indisputably that they do not correspond closely with results, that the connection is affected in all degrees by *error* of numerous kinds. Particularly, where motivation takes the form of using means to achieve ends, either may be more or less "wrong," and the two errors are only vaguely separable. In this field, knowledge is so vague and evidence so conflicting that no one can tell with any accuracy at all, even afterwards, to what degree any action is really economic. Still further, we know that the goods and services produced, traded, and consumed do not correspond to final or real wants. These are largely not individual, as the theory requires, but inhere in social relations, such as "keeping up with the Joneses," and "getting ahead of the Joneses"; or they are symbolic, even deliberately "set up," as in play, to make action interesting and yield the feeling of success or victory—thus reversing the means-end relation assumed in economics. Or the motive is no particular result but mere gratification of curiosity as to what the result will be. And all these symbolic relations are extremely unstable and change unpredictably.

Since a fetish of "scientific method" in the study of society is one of the two most pernicious forms of romantic folly that are current among the educated, this theme ought to be developed at a length which is impossible here. (The other "folly," which will receive more attention presently as my main theme, is the idea that devotion to moral principles offers the solution of social problems.) "Science," in the meaning of the natural sciences, can of course do something toward both explaining and directing social events; and nothing is further from my purpose here than any belittling of the importance of ethics. What I insist upon is an understanding of the meaning and limitations of simple or stable principles in both areas. In the naive form in which both doctrines, scientism and moralism, are usually preached, both are antithetical to the principle or ideal of freedom; they imply, and if taken seriously would lead to, absolute authoritarianism. The notion that evils are due to sin works out, as European history makes clear, in having the right people (as shown by their being in power) enforce their orthodoxy on all by burning or otherwise liquidating the heretics, schismatics, and infidels, as occasion demands, though mainly by effective indoctrination and conditioning for submissiveness before the age of responsibility. The principle has merely been taken over by the Marxists from historical ecclesiastical Christianity, with unimportant changes in moral or political content, though with sweeping but practically irrelevant change in the professed underlying metaphysic. As to a "science" of human conduct, I have mentioned some difficulties, notably that one of the most distinctive traits of man is make-believe, hypocrisy, concealment, dissimulation, deception. He is the clothes-wearing animal, but the false exterior he gives to his body is nothing to that put on by his mind. My evangelist, Talleyrand, also remarked that speech is the medium by which men disguise their thoughts. The "real wants" or wishes, referred to before, run largely in pairs of opposites; besides conformity and distinction we find familiarity and novelty or fixity and change, adventure and security, and so on. Mostly they have no specific content, and anything that happens or is done will fit one or the other of some pair. Such principles cannot explain any concrete occurrence, the obvious weakness of the "instincts" that were the groundwork of a "psychology" very popular some years ago.

Another obstreperous feature of human phenomena is that men have "attitudes" toward law as such, both descriptive and imperative law, and both positive and negative attitudes. If there is a law, either a uniformity or a command, and someone finds it and publishes it, one of the first results is a general impulse to violate it. Man is a "contrary critter"—in contrast with the conformism of physical nature. And on the other hand, men love to make laws for their own sake, to conform for a while, until tired of it, then break them and make new ones. Much of the apparent uniformity of behavior is such ritual. And there may be substantive reasons for non-conformity, or for temporary conformity that ultimately causes disruption of the pattern. A familiar example is boom and depression in various prices and in general prices—the purchasing power of money. An accepted prediction of change will cause the change predicted, for a time, then an inevitable reversal. It is true that many generalizations can be made about men and about all known societies. Professor Murdock has listed some dozens of them. But they are of a general, abstract type. All men have a language—but what language? and what will they say in it or with it? And so with numerous institutions. Every society has a technology which "works" up to a point, keeps people alive; but in spite of the conformity of the physical world to uniform natural laws, the fact tells us virtually nothing significant as to what to expect in the way of concrete "economic" behavior, corresponding to the prediction of planetary orbits, eclipses, etc., or the outcome of physical operations. (But if a physical operation is experimental, problem-solving prediction of the result or the course of the operation itself is a self-contradiction.) All peoples and most individuals have some religion. But the careful student, Professor Lowie, finds it impossible to give a general definition of the word, and the dictionary definitions, vague as they are, do not cover actual usage. The simple fact is that we commonly recognize and describe human behavior forms as expressions of some feeling, intent, belief, not as bare acts. And our terms often contain an inseparable value judgment as well; there is no specific intent, not to mention a specific act, of murder or theft.

All this about the abstract and interpretive character of economic theory or principles has little to do with their significance. That is because their main value is connected with policy determination, under the fundamental ethical principle of freedom. Assuming that men have a right to want and strive to get whatever they do want, and to have the tastes and "higher" values they do have, as long as their conduct does not infringe the equal rights of others, the business of the economics of principles, of utility, productivity, and price, is to explain that, and how, the organization through buying-and-selling enables everyone to do whatever he tries to do (whether rational or not, as judged by anyone else) many times more effectively than would be possible if each used his own means in a self-sufficient economic life. Everyone is free, as a Crusoe is free, and also enjoys the nearly boundless gain in the effectiveness of action possible through organization. In fact, the individual's range of choice is extended in a new dimension beyond that of Crusoe; he can produce anything he pleases, or make any specific contribution to production, and independently consume anything or any combination produced by anyone anywhere in the economy. No other possible method of organization will afford this twofold freedom. And anyone is also free to stay out of the system and live his own self-sufficient life, as far as he cares to stand the loss in efficiency—which usually in fact would rapidly become too great to be borne. And all are free to give and receive goods or counsel, and to cooperate on any terms other than those set by the market which they, the parties concerned, may agree in preferring on moral grounds or for any reason. Distribution, what the individual (family unit) gets out of it all, is also in principle the same as with a Crusoe; it is what he produces. That is, what he—the productive "capacity" he furnishes—adds to total output, which is the only meaning the product of a unit can have when production is a joint activity.

In fact, the "imputation" process under market-competition is valid in the sense in which any single causes produce an effect where causes act jointly, as they always do. It is the *difference* caused by the single contribution, as isolated by the mathematical operation of partial differentiation. (Consumption is usually treated, not very accurately, as unorganized.)

Stating all this at length makes me feel that I ought to apologize to you, and to myself; for it is really at the level of truism and triviality. Of course there are "assumptions": that free association implies mutual advantage and that freely chosen advantage to individuals is "good," in contrast with obedience or ascetic self-denial or self-torture (as men professed to believe even in Europe only a few centuries ago). It is assumed that in general normal adults are rational enough to be trusted to manage their own affairs, and decent enough to allow others to do the same; but this means only in comparison with the dictates of some human authority, political or ecclesiastical, chosen in whatever way, who might be in a position to order them around. The ethic of liberal civilization holds (I repeat) both that men want to be free and have a right to be, and they ought to be free, even if they themselves feel that their affairs might possibly be technically better managed for them as slaves by some possible master. Of course even these assumptions in an extreme version are made only for the purposes of theory; everyone admits that in practice governments have to set some limits to individual freedom and freedom of association, and to perform many functions on behalf of the community as a whole. If only economics could really teach people the simple and obvious fact, which most of them already know but refuse to accept, that anyone producing for exchange is producing for himself, as much as a Crusoe, but merely a thousand times more effectively because he does it indirectly by producing for the needs of others. If this were realized, it would surely put an end to all the insane or diabolical revolutionary propaganda and most of the stupid criticisms of the "capitalist system" that menace our free institutions. Why it is necessary to teach this, and accordingly so hard, if not useless to try, is the major real social problem. I can give it little consideration here. But I must note an apparent "innate disposition" in men to think that somebody is getting the better of them, that they are working for somebody else, even where it is, if possible, more absurd than the idea of the wage-worker that he is working to make profits for some greedy capitalist. Doesn't the student regularly talk about working for his professor, and even the patient aver that he is coerced by his doctor, whom he hires and fires and even defies, at will—except for the natural consequences? The much-abused "profit-system" is of course merely a pattern of cooperation, on the terms most satisfactory to the parties concerned, or the only terms they can agree upon. "Property" has intrinsically nothing to do with it; it may be and is the same where only labor services are involved at all.

I wish I had time to follow up in particular the relation between doctor and patient. The similarities and differences as compared with, say, the relationships of an industrial corporation should be interesting, even instructive. Two or three obvious facts which need emphasis must be barely mentioned. The doctor in whose hands one places oneself as a "case" will inevitably have much power, variously and precariously limited by moral, legal, and other restrictions and compulsions. The only real freedom the patient can have is the right and opportunity to choose and change at will his doctor. And the significance of this is limited, since in the nature of things the patient cannot act very intelligently in the matter. He would himself have to possess the specialized knowledge of the medical profession, and much more, in order to appraise it in others. But the case of individual patient and individual doctor (or other professional counselor) is simple in comparison with the problem presented by the vast and highly organized productive units required for the exploitation of modern technology. Here centralized direction is imperative anyway, apart from specialized competence in the directive function. Hence the final word of the candid economist to the public must be—don't expect too much, in the way of freedom, *or* justice, along with the immeasurable increase in technical efficiency that results from these two facts of modern civilization, special competence, and centralized direction. In particular, don't expect too much of "the state"; be very critical in appraising the prospects for good and for harm to result before calling on "Leviathan" and giving him power. In the scope of this address, this, the most vital conclusion, must be stated rather than argued; but it remains true that the chief reliance of the "employee" must be freedom of choice among employers, unsatisfactory though it is, as in the case of the patient and the doctors.

Given the principle of freedom, as active freedom of association, the notion of scientific control of society is a palpable contradiction. (It applies in varying degree in the treatment of defectives, young children, and criminals.) For a *dictator,* the problem would be *formally* parallel to that of scientific technology; but even in that case, the content of control would be utterly different. For, unless he could completely drug or hypnotize and so eliminate the minds and wills of his subject-slaves, the autocrat-proprietor of a society would have to rule *through* those minds and wills. Hence the operation would employ such techniques as persuasion or coercion, suggestion, cajolery, flattery, and, above all, deception—which is at the heart of what is called "force" in human relations—and also, inevitably, some real discussion. But these things have no meaning for the relations between purposive human beings and the inert objects of nature where scientific technique is literally applicable. (The higher animals, notably in domestication, present an intermediate situation which must here be ignored.) In a democracy, the notion of control is not merely unethical, it is excluded, *ipso facto.* The self-contradiction of a number of persons mutually predicting one another's behavior and acting on their predictions has already been pointed out, and that of mutual control is even more obviously absurd. The problem of democracy is to establish a *consensus,* by genuine discussion, with intellectual appeal to super-individual norms. Mere expression of individual desires is not discussion and can only exacerbate conflict of interests and intensify the problem, not tend toward solution in all-around agreement. Objective norms belong to a third level of reality, distinct from and above individual desire or end-and-means, as the category of the instrumental is different from and "above" mechanical sequence or cause-and-effect. And judgments about norms and ideals are affected by a different category of *error,* though the facts that norms are objects of desire and that means-and-end parallels cause-and-effect make clear analysis impossible.

Genuine "free" discussion is a difficult thing to deal with conceptually, and more difficult to realize in practice. The problem presents two aspects: first, agreement on the range in which agreement itself is considered necessary, as marked off from individual freedom and diversity, and second, the specific content of uniformity in its sector. On any considerable scale, discussion itself must be organized; and this organization presents practically the same problems as the matter to be dealt with, specifically the limitation of freedom by rules and authority in order to secure the greatest possible freedom and the performance of function.

The supreme and inestimable merit of the exchange mechanism is that it enables a vast number of people to cooperate in the use of means to achieve ends as far as their interests are mutual, without arguing or in any way agreeing about either the ends or the methods of achieving them. It is the "obvious and simple system of natural liberty." The principle of freedom, where it is applicable, takes other values out of the field of social action. In contrast, agreement on terms of cooperation through discussion is *hard* and always threatens to become impossible, even to degenerate into a fight, not merely the failure of cooperation and loss of its advantages. The only agreement called for in market relations is acceptance of the one essentially negative ethical principle, that the units are not to prey upon one another through coercion or fraud.

This picture of the open-market, free-enterprise organization must sound very one-sided, and it *is* one-sided. Presumably, no competent mind has ever believed in it exclusively. If there have been real anarchists, they were not economists. And the society pictured by the pure, idealized theory of the market economy is, or would be, one held together by the single moral principle just stated. This is entirely proper as a postulate for theoretical analysis at a certain stage of abstraction. But the idea that freedom, or any single principle, contains the solution, or the best solution, of social problems, is of course unrealistic, and is directly contrary to the thesis of this paper, as stated at the outset. Exaggeration of the significance of freedom, or over-emphasis, to the neglect of other principles, was the great error of the liberal age, and is partly responsible for the reaction we now witness, which threatens extinction of freedom and of all defensible values. It should go without saying that freedom alone would not produce an approximation to the conditions required for a market itself, the freest possible market. And modern economists have not thought otherwise. The accusation that Adam Smith, for example, believed in a universal harmony of interests among men, is merely one discouraging example of what passes widely in learned circles for history and discussion. At a minimum, rules must be made and enforced by some agency representing the whole market collectively; and the policing must be paid for on a principle other than direct individual payment for service received. And at most, as I have emphasized, the market deals only in impersonal values. To realize its ideal character, the system would have to be operated through vending machines, avoiding personal contact between the parties to exchange. At this point, I turn to more detailed, though brief and inadequate, notice of the limitations of freedom, from the standpoint of policy, or of freedom as a policy. This will be followed by an even briefer glance at the alternatives and the final practical problem, making up the classical three parts of the argument.

There is a paradox about the general problem of economic organization. One can state a case which sounds much like an "air-tight" justification of market freedom or *laissez-faire*. But if it is easy to "riddle" the notion of means-end rationality as an explanatory principle, this is still more true of the apologetic for reliance on the free market as an ideal social policy. We also encounter a logical paradox in the concept of freedom. On one hand, it is not discussable, being the presupposition of discussion, and freedom in conduct is inseparable from that in communication. Yet we are brought up short by a glance at our own history. For it is only in the small island of our own modern (post-Enlightenment), West European culture that the axiom is accepted; in history as a whole, including rather especially European history in the preceding epochs, political or economic liberty, and even more, religious-moral-intellectual freedom, was emphatically rejected on principle, if it was ever contemplated as a possibility. The aristocratic, slave-holding town-republics of ancient times hardly call for mention as exceptions. Though we can learn from their experience and discussion because some problems of democracy arise within any ruling class (unless it is an established hierarchy headed by an absolute authority like Hitler, the Pope, or Stalin, with effective provision for the succession). The rise of the strange phenomenon of modern liberalism is undoubtedly to be explained in part as a reaction against the peculiar dogmatism, intolerance, and obscurantism of medieval "Christian" Europe. But much of the former spirit is with us yet; and the superposition of an ethic of extreme freedom and individual rights on an extreme authoritarianism of obedience and duties based on status is surely a chief source of the moral-intellectual confusion of our age, of which we hear so much (and so much nonsense). And a kind of pendular principle in history no doubt helps to account for the new turnabout which has carried so much of the world back to despotism.

My own view of the social-economic policy is not greatly concerned with the notion of treating the individual satisfaction-function as a welfare-function and proceeding to the notion of a social maximum in terms of some relation between individual maxima. It is too clearly indefensible to treat "happiness" or the "good life" for the individual as a definable end to be achieved by a definite technique; and even more indefensible to view the objective of social-economic policy in terms of the amount and distribution of measurable impersonal goods and services. Wealth and poverty are terribly important things, but that view of their significance seems to me an absurd over-simplification. Freedom itself, as a value *per se,* is far more important. In "economic" life, in the ordinary empirical reference, the motivation of competitive sport plays a role at least as great as the endeavor to secure gratifications me-

chanically dependent on quantitative consumption. Some business efficiency expert is said to have advised reforming football by having all the
men play on the same side, instead of half pushing against the other
half. The real problem centers, of course, in the fact that activity has
both characters; it is a game, but one in which the most vital substantive
goods, comfort and life itself, are stakes, inseparably combined with victory and defeat and their bauble-symbols. The social problem is to make
the best possible rules for this complex and paradoxical game, which
everyone is compelled to play. And it must go on almost without inter-
ruption, and it is impossible to play a game and discuss the rules at the
same time. The intellectual problem involved in rule-making is different in kind from that of play itself, and neither—it is important to
notice—has much relation to scientific technology, or means-end rationality; nor to our traditional religious-ethical principle of charity. For
when charity comes into a game, the game goes out; though in relation
to the other aspect of the process, the production and distribution of
goods considered intrinsically useful, it does have a part to play. I may
suggest that the ethic really believed in and reasonably practiced by the
modern man centers in sportsmanship, and the related principle of
workmanship.

Even with much and costly social action, there can be no very close
approximation to the theoretical perfect market, particularly in one important area, the labor market. This fact does not at all justify most of
the action being taken in that field, by unions or by government; in
general, the argument against price control and other interference is
made stronger, not weaker, by the "imperfect competition" which is
used as a defense for it. And the action we see is designed to make the
market still more imperfect, and to benefit a select stratum already comparatively well off, at the expense of their weaker brethren. The effects
cannot be traced and measured in detail, but it is a safe "principle" that
in a power contest the weakest get the worst of it. The chief "mechanical" defects in the market system arise less out of "frictions" than out of
speculative situations. When in order to act rationally each must first
know or guess at what everyone else will do, the result is complicated
cyclical tendencies; in particular, speculation in the future value of
money gives rise to "the business cycle," sometimes an actual social disaster. Monopoly is another evil, though the public misconceives its nature and grossly exaggerates the extent and power of business monopolies. A majority of producers and dealers have some short-run monopoly
position; but in general, monopoly is temporary and functional, on the

same principle as patent-rights. Protective duties foster monopoly; but where monopoly really bites is in the legal brigandage of organized wage-earners and farmers. The business interest itself is far more dangerous to free society through political action as a pressure group; but it stands no chance in competition with voting masses "agitated" and organized for power and plunder—all the worse for their self-righteous motivation. Obviously, anything like nation-wide collective bargaining and striking is coercion of the country, not of any opposed economic interest; and as noted, the heaviest cost falls on other "workers," especially those still weaker. (Perhaps I should use a more polite word; but I said I would exploit the privilege of age to put truth ahead of manners; and what does anyone, including the "honest brigand" want but his "rights," to be judge of his own case and have coercive power to enforce his own verdict?)

Far more important than all the mechanical imperfections of "market competition" (the real ones, not created by stupid or unwise public action) are limitations of the principle of economic freedom inherent in unalterable conditions of life and associative action. Our economic ills are not due to the failure of competition; on the contrary, the result of perfect functioning of the system would be socially quite intolerable. The free market, with reasonable help from state authority, can make tolerable provision for the economic cooperation of individuals and other "units," as far as it is "cooperation," as far as their interests are mutual. By the same argument it *cannot* solve any other problems, and there are many other and grave problems that insistently call for solution. So in other fields: free association will solve the problems "up to a point," but not completely or by itself. Social problems are not only hard but finally insoluble. Yet many of them will inevitably get some kind of "treatment"; it is a question of better or worse, or of making things better, more or less, or making them worse than before, even to downright disaster. As I remember hearing "Tommy" Adams say in a classroom, we must not call any problems insoluble which must be solved in some way and for which some solutions are better, or worse, than others.

The most serious limitations of the free-market economy, and major problems set by it, arise from the fact that it takes the "units," individuals, families, etc., as "given," which is entirely unrealistic. In the economic aspect specifically, it "assumes" given "wants, resources, and technique," in possession of each and all. The market is an agency of cooperation between such given units; it is no agency for improving tastes (wants) or manner, or especially for conferring productive capacity to meet wants or needs; it will not redistribute capacity and hence product to accord better than the realities do with any norm of ideal justice. Business relations clearly do work to dissolve clannishness and dogmatic allegiances, and to promote tolerance, and a degree of generosity. But in the distribution of economic resources atomistic motivation tends powerfully toward cumulatively increasing inequality. For all productive capacity—whether owned "property" or personal qualities—is essentially "capital," a joint creation of pre-existing capacity (or the result of "accident"). And those who already have more capacity are always in a better position to acquire still more, with the same effort and sacrifice. This applies about as much to personal capacity as to property, though the latter is a more convenient way of passing on "unearned" advantage to heirs or successors. It is a gross injustice—by one of several conflicting norms of justice generally accepted in liberal society. But it is also the main reliance for the motivation of accumulation in all forms, hence of progress, all forms of which are directly or indirectly dependent on means and their economical use. And the tendency goes on beyond the individual life, from generation to generation, through the family and transmission of advantages. It is modified but hardly mitigated, and certainly not simplified, by the large element of "luck" in human affairs. Any serious effort to interfere with the process would weaken the family in other connections, and if it were replaced by some other primary group, the anti-equalitarian tendency would still be as strong.

No doubt we all agree that extremes of wealth and poverty are unjust, especially when they do not correspond with personal effort or sacrifice—and are bad in other ways. The question is, what can we do about it? Can the rules of the economic game be so changed that the winnings, symbolic and real (and the former are not much inferior in importance) will accord better with some accepted or defensible criterion of justice? And can it be done without wrecking the game itself, as a game, and as a producer of the fruits on which we all live? The intricate conflict of values here cannot be spelled out in detail—freedom with order, efficiency and progress, interesting activity, but especially freedom *versus* justice. The ancient provision against misery was to stress as sacred the obligations of family and neighborhood, and "charity," alms-giving, by those having an excess over "needs." But in the main, men were told and conditioned to believe that somehow everything is really for the best, and the evils of life have to be borne—patience and fortitude. Alms-giving tended to mean supporting the clergy and endowing religious foundations, while an uncertain fraction went to relieve poverty (real or feigned), and that did an uncertain amount of good—certainly made little impression on poverty as a whole. Modern society has largely shifted the load of relief from the family and local group, which can no longer so well bear it, or be made to, and centralized it more and more on the national government through progressive income and inheritance taxation. A vast improvement has come about, chiefly through assuring to poor children support and some equipment for earning a livelihood, with family limitation offsetting improved sanitation and medical care. This of course does not meet either ideal requirements or the popular demand—perhaps even social necessity, considering, again, the children, now future citizen-voters as well as producers of more children, and soldiers. But specialists seem to agree that taxation, for peace uses, can be pushed further very gradually at best, if the practical limit has not already been approached, at least for a government that is not to employ powers incompatible with basic freedoms. So what? I have no answer to that one, especially for the crucial matter of how far society can allow free production of children and agree to support them "decently" and of necessity their parents along with them. But the classes that produce babies can outvote those that prefer "substance and culture" to large families, particularly if the latter are soft-hearted and encourage them to demand "justice." Moreover, the prolific can muster the larger armies, and perhaps the tougher too, where the distinction conforms to national areas; and it is here the conflict between freedom and equalitarian justice now is the great world menace.

With no pretense that my message is a cheering one, I can only, in the interest of what seems to me plain truth, go on to emphasize the difficulties of our problems and the danger of action that will make things worse instead of better. As is now evident, the "liberal" nineteenth century, following the rationalistic eighteenth, was wrong in its view that mere individual liberty, religious-intellectual, political, and economic, would yield well-being and happiness. It did indeed accomplish wonders, supplemented by the kind of state action accepted by its original advocates. And people seem much more actively dissatisfied than before. J. S. Mill's *Principles of Political Economy* and Marx-Engels's *Communist Manifesto* appeared almost simultaneously in the middle of the "wonderful century," wonderful especially for the common man. But Mill was very critical of the institution of property; and the *Mani-*

festo called on the workers of the world to unite for the violent over-throw of all pre-existing social order, because "you have nothing to lose but your chains." Madness, criminal madness, of course; but how many of the bright and educated have fallen for and preached it, in democratic countries where the masses are well off beyond historical comparison! And it has become the accepted political creed in the largest nations of the Old World who now threaten us so dangerously with "liberation" in accord with its tenets. Is it human nature to be more dissatisfied the better off one is? I shall not venture an answer to that one, either.

All I can do is to indicate the nature of the problem of free society, as I see it, point out some false leads and some things that "have to be," "or else." I do not predict; it may be a case like Uncle Remus's rabbit that was "bleeged to climb a tree," to get away from a dog. *If* free society is to exist, the electorate must be informed, and must have and use economic and political intelligence, and of course possess the moral quali-ties actually needful. On the intelligence factor I cannot take time to say more. I hope I have said enough to show that the problem is not of the kind so successfully attacked by natural science and technology in the interest of control by man over the natural environment. It must be "social" intelligence, of the general sort exemplified in the discussion by a group of the problem of improving a game—but with complications due to the vast scale of national and world society and the complex of conflicting interests and ideals involved. For help as to intelligence, we now instinctively turn to institutional education. This can certainly im-part information, up to varying individual limits, and schools have also been successful enough in increasing knowledge—some say too suc-cessful!—and the somewhat opposed functions of transmission and re-vision might perhaps be better coordinated. But does education make people intelligent? As to certain "intellectual skills" no doubt it does, again up to varying limits. But as to good sense, the "gumption" re-quired to select and reject between sound measures and crude economic nostrums such as I mentioned at the outset, the arbitrary interference with freedom of trade, fixing prices by fiat, and preaching revolution, the evidence is not encouraging. The "smart" and the educated seem to fall for these as readily as the man-in-the-street. Indeed it often appears that the result of costly training is to make people more ingenious in thinking up and defending indefensible theories. The crackpots of all kinds and degrees are not recruited from the dumbbell or ignoramus classes. Even outside the "moral sciences," it is not these who spend their lives squaring the circle and inventing perpetual-motion machines.

What schools can do on the side of moral qualities is another question. But first let me say here what I have long believed, that the crucial problem in our whole intellectual-spiritual life, our culture, is the relations between the great values, perhaps especially truth and goodness or knowledge and virtue. I have time only for these and to note the relative neglect of the third member of the trio, beauty and taste—taste that is good or bad in contrast with "mere" taste—and the even more neglected role of play or fun, entirely left out of the good life in our Hebrew-Puritan tradition. You will recall that Socrates-Plato thought that virtue is knowledge (meaning reasoned knowledge, like mathematics, not science) in opposition to the Christian (Pauline) view that we know the good but choose the evil. (But Aristotle at least partly disagreed with Plato, and a famous saying of Ovid sides with Paul.) My point is that I see the main task of education in our age as training to separate believing and believing-in from liking for other reasons—at the crudest level, to distinguish sound from sense and, in general, truth from esthetic or moral or any "romantic" attraction. In any case indoctrination is a vicious trap, and a liberal must wish it were impossible. The first test of a free society is that it teach its youth to question and criticize and form opinions only by weighing evidence—and to admit ignorance where there is no evidence—instead of implanting eternal and immutable truth with abject submission to the inevitable authoritative interpreter, by some prescriptive right. And on the other side, it is an equally pernicious idea that by education a society can lift itself by its bootstraps. Who is to educate the educators? Only some absolute authority, manifestly. And control of education is the first aim of the totalitarian. His ideal is a priesthood as the custodians of Truth, "conditioning" each generation in helpless infancy to unquestioning belief and to go through life like little children.

One of the hardest lessons which in my opinion our democracy has to learn is to make necessary reservations about much of our ethical tradition propagated under religious or church auspices. It should be superfluous to point out that this is an inheritance from an age when virtue in the common man was thought by everyone to consist precisely in the acceptance and submission I just spoke of—conformity to a sacred law and obedience to consecrated authority, Holy Mother Church and Holy Father King. What our Sunday-school moral adages mean is simply the command to be good children and mind Momma and Poppa. They sound well, and their sentiment has a place; but if we ask what they mean, from the standpoint of democratic citizenship, they are simply irrelevant. When they were proclaimed, the idea that the ordinary man (not to mention the woman) should make and unmake the laws and literally hire and fire the rulers, would have provoked only loathing and terror, if it had been dreamed of as a possibility. Even the "Golden Rule," to treat others as you would be treated, is also an epigram. First, it should of course be as the other himself would be treated, or as "you" would be in his place, and with him in yours. But for the slave master, what the slave would want would be to change places: "Let me be master and you be slave"—which would be no improvement in the system. But such is the romantic view of God: one who puts down the mighty from their seats and exalts the lowly, who fills the poor with good things, but the rich he sends empty away. Well, turn about may be fair play, but again we get no light on how to improve the social order. Taking slavery or any institutional framework as given, humane behavior is laudable. And that is exactly what our religious ethic did, and does: it takes the established order of things as given, in fact as divinely ordained: "Let every soul be subject unto the higher power. For there is no power but of God: the powers that be are ordained of God" (Romans, 13:1). And of course this explicitly included subservience of wives to their husbands. The only exception recorded is the right of the propagandist of the "true faith" to preach, in defiance of the authorities (Acts 5:29).

Again, as always (in accord with my theme), there is another side. Liberalism can be equally naive and as given to empty words. No adult in his right mind ever believed that men are born free and equal—except for that complete and in that sense equal helplessness, for which freedom is without meaning. The socialists and communists have called religion the opiate of the masses, and in a broad historical sense that is correct. But two other truths have not been so clear to either side in the controversy. First; some pacifier, reconciler or escape was necessary in a society that accepted the "static" philosophy of life that actually was accepted everywhere prior to the awakening" in Western Europe in the seventeenth and eighteenth centuries. Then were born the ideas of freedom and of progress in and through knowledge and intelligent action under free cooperative association. For man is a romantic animal; and until a people is prepared to make changes by intelligent agreement, supernatural sanctions are required to make them accept what is established and not criticize or try to change it. The second fact is that—disregarding the question of how much intellectual maturity West European peoples had attained by the age of the Enlightenment—

it is certain on general grounds that the basic framework of social order must always be accepted custom interpreted and applied by agents having a large amount of power. The possible amount and speed of free and intelligent social change will always be quite narrowly limited. This is particularly true if intelligent change is taken to mean change in the direction of the ideals of justice and freedom, justice implying some kind of fundamental equality—and other values generally accepted in our modern liberal world view. As I would like to show at greater length than is possible here, no close approach to realization of those ideals is within the realm of possibility. Consequently, men will always require, as a condition for maintaining any high civilization at all, some "opiate," or some effective agent to prevent their demanding their rights. The only alternative to belief in supernatural sanctions of an existing system quite far from just is that intelligence shall be fully aware of its own narrow limitations and be supplemented by a high order of tolerance and self-sacrifice, the patient acceptance of the best all-round choice among evils. Especially, as the world is built, the chances of loss are overwhelmingly greater than the chances of gain in any effort to escape the ills we have by flying to others that we know not of. Since order is the absolute requisite of civilized life, we must stick to the order that is, until there is a reasonable agreement on changes that will be on balance beneficial.

The balance will always be hard to strike and entirely a matter of judgment, not of formula, a balance between principles that conflict, while each claims to be absolute. The danger now, in the world and in the West, is that freedom will be thrown away for a promise or hope of justice but with an actual result of neither justice nor freedom, and very likely the suicide of civilization in war without rules. The world could be heading toward a new age of essentially religious wars, ideological wars. Historically this would be nothing new, except for its scale and for the destructiveness of modern military technology. Otherwise, Europe is reverting to form. For as I have said, Communism, in its social program or pretensions, is largely a revival of historical-ecclesiastical Christianity, with the church more effectively merged in one all-powerful state. From the downfall of the Roman imperium to the age of liberalism, Europe lived under one or more dogmatic, intolerant persecuting, and violently proselyting religions—claiming possession of the formula for salvation, they could not be or do otherwise—and much of the time in a state of war between two or more such religions. In Christianity, surely, we find the supreme "irony of history": that an original teaching centered ethically in humility, meekness, self-denial, and self-sacrifice became organized into corporations whose dignitaries have hardly been matched for arrogant grasping, using, and flaunting of power and wealth and for insistence on prerogative to the borderline of worship. One turns to Dostoievsky's famous speech of the Grand Inquisitor for an adequate portrayal of this situation and its sinister indications of the nature of human nature.

The plea of Communism, like that of Christianity, is justice, under absolute authority ignoring freedom. (The former does extol progress, and progress through science, both of which Christianity despised; by the same argument, Communism is overtly less devoted to law and tradition, more openly claims the right to ignore or break the law.) For Liberalism, the primary value is freedom, self-limited by laws made by the community, ideally by general assent, in practice by representatives elected by a voting majority—one of its dangers. The laws of a liberal state will also be general, non-specific, but in a sense quite different from the Golden Rule or Law of Universal Love. The familiar figure is rules of the road, in contrast with instructions where and when and to how to travel, whether arbitrary or conformable to a traditional practice. But such freedom must be sweepingly limited by measures not only of a "police" character in a broad sense, but also designed to equip the individual and family for social life by implanting wants and tastes in general conformity with the culture, and endowing with a minimum of productive capacity (or ultimately with final goods) without which freedom is a form empty of content. To take these units as "given" is flagrantly contrary to essential facts of life, and means ignoring the major social problem. It is along this line that eighteenth- and nineteenth-century liberalism went to an extreme that has provoked a reaction which threatens to engulf all freedom, and justice too, in the modern conception of it, if not to destroy civilization. Liberal states have been engaged, however, through their short life, in correcting this imbalance between freedom and justice; and more intelligence, better judgment is our need, rather than any radical departure in method.

The prime requisite is simply critical intelligence. And it may well appear as if the race at large hates this type of effort, naturally, instinctively. Anyhow, we have been conditioned in the opposite direction virtually throughout history, with the first breaking away from the ideals of conformity and submission to sacred law and authority during the past few centuries. The real heart of modern liberalism is a radical change: a virtual inversion in the conception of truth and believing, a transfer from a moral-religious to an intellectual-moral basis. What the world really needs to learn from science, for handling social problems, is not its techniques but its moral code. In the religious age, truth was absolute and belief a matter of right and wrong, hence naturally to be controlled by reward and punishment. For liberalism, truth is always provisional, and rests on the "best" evidence—incidentally, not logical demonstration, but that is a long story. Right belief was a virtue, finally the condition of eternal salvation. The principle was stated, particularly with reference to our own religious tradition, by Lord Bacon: "The more absurd and incredible any divine mystery is, the greater honor we do to God in believing it" (and in similar terms by Tertullian, around A.D. 200). Liberal moral values fit the same description as the liberal conception of truth; not virtue versus vice, but the best possible at any time and place. This means that the object of devotion and pursuit is not ends but ideals, progressively redefined as they are progressively realized, and always with the mode and spirit of pursuit and definition—freedom, but under critical direction, not caprice—as the most essential value.

A further consequence is that liberalism is fact-facing above all. It does not pretend that existing economic conditions are just, but recognizes that justice can be approached but never attained, and freedom likewise, and any other social ideal in its ideal form. It just is not that kind of world. It is childish if not hypocritical to preach that all discord is harmony not understood, that "in erring reason's spite, One truth is clear, whatever is, is right," or accordingly, that omnipotent goodness and omniscience rule the world. As T. H. Huxley said, the ways of the cosmos are not our ways. Rather it is man's work to remake the world, as far and as fast as he can, according to his sentiments and ideals about which the Cosmos gives no evidence of the least concern—and to be careful not to defeat the whole project by trying to go too far or too fast with it. Also, to enjoy what goodness and beauty we can find, without letting these appreciations confuse and corrupt our judgments of truth. Any of my students or former students in the audience will please forgive me for repeating here a statement I often quote from Clarence Darrow, characterizing divine justice. Said he, "God made one man a genius and the other a fool—which always seemed to me a raw thing for God to do—to the genius." Of course, it is a raw thing for both of them; but the world *is* like that, and we must take it or leave it. Nor is much freedom possible, either, in any social order, and notably in the large-scale organizations, efficient and yet constantly changing, that are required to exploit modern technology. You're in the army now, even in peacetime, especially in the mass-production industries. You can only be reasonably free to elect some other work, in view of the "net advantages." As to justice, other things are distributed even less in accord with merit than wealth and income, and we can do little against the monstrous vicissitudes and caprices of the natural world. To secure any form of social justice, we should have to begin with a much more equitable distribution of parents and more remote ancestors, and manifold other circumstances that largely determine the character of one's life long before birth. And even when one reaches the fullest responsibility, it is possible to have but a fraction of the knowledge necessary for really intelligent action. As to "happiness," it is easy to agree with Darrow, and Meredith, and many more, that the idiot or, as Whitman put it, the animals, have the best of it. But *that* happiness, at least, is not what makes human life worthwhile.

We must, as I have suggested, be good sports, enjoy the game whether we win or lose, not cheat even to win, and not even be too sore when the opponent wins by a little cheating. And we must try, all along, gradually to improve the rules, as well as to obey and help enforce them. The main injunctions that can be given are negative, especially not to go too fast, not to oversimplify, not to grasp at easy solutions for hard problems. I think the greatest danger is that suggested by my text—a "moralistic" approach, attributing social evil to sin, with the implication of cure by liquidating somebody, or at least firing some scapegoat, and seeking a savior. People are not bad, in the main, but they are ignorant and do not understand. They have not been taught to approach problems in terms of knowing and understanding, but to obey some ancient rule, as interpreted by those in power, or follow some new prophet. Democracy calls for leadership, but that does not mean finding the right man or party and giving him or them irresponsible power. We surely know what a dictator will do, once in power; he will, indeed, use "science" to make everyone be good and do right.

I have used up my time without saying much about the alternatives to the free economy; but that would be an endless task, and also one for a corps of experts. Let me repeat that how people expect to cure the social ills by a radical shift from business to democratic politics is a question for which I see no answer except in terms of the psychology of romantic prejudice and screwy thinking. Most of the evils inherent in

the market organization plainly inhere still more in political campaigning, legislative debates, and administration, perhaps even judicial trials.
Especially the tendency to centralization and concentration of power—
which can only go so far until voting and political discussion will be
empty forms if the boss allows them to go on at all. Yet freedom is not
enough; it was carried too far, and more and more political action is
called for, though it is dangerous; if only it can be in the main right
action, or not too far wrong! Democratic action is *hard*. It means government by discussion, and the organization of discussion itself, as I said
before, involves the main problems. Not much intercommunication is
even theoretically possible. As the world is built, the cards are heavily
stacked in favor of centralization. Even in one direction, communication
is bad enough; among economists, for instance, the typical reply to a
criticism is, "but I didn't say that." I myself have been made a bad example for views I supposed I was arguing against all through the years.
As to intercommunication—even with two persons there is an insoluble
problem of dividing the time for both between speaking and listening;
and it is said to give rise sometimes to friction, even causing dissolution
of the holy marriage bond. With larger numbers, the limitation increases rapidly, in I know not what form of compound progression. One
person can, indeed, be heard by a considerable number and, with mechanical aids now available, by "the world," as well as reached by
print—if so disposed. But, though no prophet, I will predict that no
invention will ever enable one to listen or attend to more than one other
at a time, or to "send" and "receive" communications at the same time.

   To conclude: Time was, no doubt, when society needed to be awak-
ened to the possibility of remedying evils, and stirred to action, mostly
negative action, establishing freedom, but some positive action too. Now,
we have found not only that mere individual freedom is not enough, but
that its excess can have disastrous consequences. And a reaction has set
in, so that people have too much faith in positive action, of the nature of
passing laws and employing policemen, and the opposite warning is
needed. At least so I hold; perhaps it is a prejudice—how can one
tell?—I mistrust reformers. When a man or group asks for power to do
good, my impulse is to say, "Oh, yeah, who ever wanted power for any
other reason? And what have they done when they got it?" So I instinctively want to cancel the last three words, leaving simply "I want
power"; that is easy to believe. And a further confession: I am reluctant
to believe in doing good with power anyhow. With William James, I

incline to the side of "the slow and silent forces," slow as in all conscience they are—and though time is fleeting.

There is much more that should be said, but certainly not on this occasion. When I started this I knew, from experience, that I'd never finish it. Life seems to consist of "unfinished business." And, having already imposed on you too long, without waiting for the peremptory order that is given to naughty corporations, I simply cease and desist.

13

Science, Society, and the Modes of Law

To speak on so general a subject, one must put away modesty and not ask whether he has anything to say that is at once significantly true and new enough to his hearers to be interesting.[1] Even more after Dean Harris's very appropriate words, I feel badly cast for my role on this occasion. Doubting whether I have ever done anything properly called either "science" or "research," I am hardly the one to "whoop it up" for scientific research as the method for dealing with social problems. And I could wail at the impossibility of the task of giving any view of those problems in the scope of a lecture. Far too much must be said if one is to say anything not too misleading or open to misinterpretation. About man, individual and social, practically anything one could say would be more or less true and relevant; hence opposite statements would be more or less equally so—which calls for endless explaining. Moreover, there is a serious divergence between what is true and relevant and what is interesting or even acceptable. There are proprieties, a form of law, as well as truth, which forbid boring people or rubbing prejudices the wrong way—prejudice commonly meaning others' beliefs with which one disagrees.

Sticking to safe generalities, one fact about man is that he is a romantic and opinionated animal rather than inclined to truth-seeking or fact-facing. A rational being—indeed! he says so himself, as a compliment, hardly meant as truth. People will have answers, even to questions that make no sense; and they will "do something"—will "monkey" where they do not understand. They demand absolutes, and there is

Reprinted with permission of The University of Chicago Press from *The State of the Social Sciences,* edited by Leonard D. White (Chicago: University of Chicago Press, 1956), 9–28.

none—truth no exception. If we all started telling the truth, the whole truth, and nothing but the truth, the world would be a shambles before sundown the first day. And in morals, "Do right though the world perish" is the most monstrous of absurdities. Typical of man is one extreme or the other—to be marvelously intelligent or amazingly stupid—and well satisfied with himself in either role, and similarly with heroism and meanness. The great psychologist, P. T. Barnum, made fame and fortune on the maxim that the public loves to be swindled. I know of no "research" on the interesting question of how far that is true of all success; but we may note that Voltaire said his clearest idea of infinity came from observing the credulity and gullibility of the human race.

Whatever truth, or entertainment, such reflections may hold, you are warned not to expect too much from this lecture. It will consist of jottings, not very defensibly selected or put in order, and ending only by command of the clock, that despotic ruler of civilized life. Nor will it be very constructive; unhappily, clearing away rubbish must often precede building. Myself when young did have ambition to contribute to the growth of social science. At the end, I am more interested in having less nonsense posing as knowledge; that is, of course I am in favor of nonsense, good nonsense, and in its place, as well as poetry, romantic fiction, compliments, and jokes—modes of expression with values other than objective accuracy. The great task of education in our field is, in my view, to get people to make those distinctions—just what romantic and impatient man is loath to do. A once-popular humorist said, "It's not ignorance does the most damage; it's knowin' so derned much that ain't so." That is quite literally true in economics, I am sure—the field in which my professional life has mostly been spent.

Even in relation to the natural environment, where some realism means life or death, men constantly look for miracles and tilt at windmills. In that field a few have very recently turned to an interest in truth; and so we have natural science, tolerated because it produces marvels— it has been defined as magic which works—and others use its results without understanding them or caring to understand. If driving a car required knowledge of thermodynamics, cars would not be causing the traffic problems of today. Respecting democratic society, however, knowledge must be possessed by the masses if it is to be useful. And the other side of the contrast is as important; it is a romantic delusion that application of "scientific method" to its problems could produce similar marvels of prediction and control. That prejudice I particularly have to antagonize. To begin with, it is infinitely harder in social problems to free our terms from ambiguity, and few care to try. So we must stumble on, using language which, as the philosopher Paulhan remarked, was made by ignorant barbarians. And to another Frenchman, Talleyrand, speech seemed to have been given to men to disguise their thoughts.

What I shall attempt in this hour is to point out some features of free society and its problems which seem to me to need more attention than they get—problems that often have no solution but yet must and will be solved, for better or worse. Since the essence of society is order, legal and moral, the argument will center on law, its meanings and roles, and their changes through past time. To be stressed is the unique problem of free society—to combine freedom with order. It is soluble only through some compromise. Order, or law, is, of course, universal in nature—until man appears, with his mysterious freedom, the capacity to break law, and turn the very laws of nature to his own purposes. Finally, I shall come to the even more remarkable capacity of making law—of a different kind. As devotees of freedom, we must accept the fact that order is a necessity, freedom a comparative luxury. And as regards the legal order, it is unanimity that is imperative; if free agreement is not reached, it must be imposed, or chaos will ensue. A free society must agree on the maximum of freedom to be had with the needful minimum of order. Democracy could be defined as the socialization of the problem of law, and it is only democracy which confronts social problems, properly speaking. They must be solved by free agreement of the citizens in balancing among degrees and kinds of orderliness and in balancing stable legal order itself against more literally free association. Human nature being as it is, freedom and order reciprocally limit each other, although there is no effective freedom without order. Order is also a condition of security; the degree of freedom for each individual implies a corresponding insecurity for all others. This is the crucial conflict of values, among others which cannot be ignored. Compromise is inevitable; complete freedom would be chaos, and the limit of order would be the condition of ice. But, in fact, a perfect crystal is impossible, and perfection is a romantic illusion where values are involved; at higher levels, as in works of art, formal imperfections contribute to the value.

The long history of science itself, with what it replaced, reveals the nature of man as a romantic and superstitious animal. As all students know, the attitude toward nature, primitively and through the ages, was "animistic." Events were explained by "spirits" in things—by acts of will—and prediction and control were sought, and supposedly achieved, by performing rites and the arts of magic. Myth and ritual took the place held in our thinking by both science and history. Of course, these went with the practice of the techniques, more or less effective, by which people really lived; and, strangely, they were not allowed to interfere—too much or too often—with really effective action. But the latter procedures were routine, a matter of course (like the language spoken, which will come up later); it was myth and dramatization which were the active concerns. Nor has this attitude been outgrown, but only in part overgrown, in our day. Man is a religious animal; he now typically thinks, as the savage did not, that the religion into which he has happened to be born is "true" and all others "false." And these, be it noted, are the "beliefs" men will fight about. Montaigne observed that men assert most confidently where they have the least grounds, in fact, especially where they have none, but believe arbitrarily "by faith." Bacon neatly stated the principle: "The more absurd and incredible any divine mystery is, the greater honor we do to God in believing it."

A little attention to the history of words could be illuminating here. Most, if not all, the terms we use with an impersonally objective meaning had only the opposite import before modern times; and they still have it, with their new meaning—one source of the ambiguity we must contend with. "Truth" meant "fidelity" or "loyalty," and "false" the opposite. How can we think straight, using the same word for a true statement and a true friend, not to mention a true religion or philosophy? Our word "why" is an old ablative of the relative pronoun, meaning "by whom" or "for what"; and we use "reason" for both cause and motive, as well as a valid ground for a belief or act. Even in mechanics, the simplest and most empirically objective of sciences—the model for those who spell "science" with capitals—European man believed for two thousand years in the metaphysical physics of Aristotle, contrary to all experience. The impact theory of Descartes on the eve of the revolution was not much better, and the revolutionary Galileo was a thorough scholastic until over forty, well past the age at which most physicists make their great contributions. Strangely, it was the disclosure by the telescope of the satellites of Jupiter which overthrew medievalism in the learned public mind a lifetime after Copernicus. Everyone should know the kind of arguments used against Galileo's discovery. The head professor of philosophy in the University of Padua disposed of it thusly: There are seven openings in the human head—two eyes, two ears, two nostrils, and a mouth; these correspond with the seven planets; therefore, the number cannot be more or less. Moreover, your Medicean Stars (as Galileo called them) are invisible to the naked eye; therefore, they do not influence human affairs and so are useless; therefore, they do not exist. And it was a lucky coincidence of circumstances that Galileo was only forced to recant and put under house arrest, not burned alive as Giordano Bruno had been a few years before, for talking a little sense, by our standards.

What happens to impress me most is the history of medicine, and one might start with the words "medicine man." What people have done to themselves and others to cure disease is a tale of horror which seems even worse than war and almost as bad as religious persecution (incidentally, a near-monopoly of Christianity, distinguished as it is in history for authoritarian dogmatism and intolerance). A doctor and student of medical history was asked at what date doctors may have begun to cure more people than they killed; he replied that it might take another generation or so. Not to go into revolting details, one may think of bleeding people for practically any symptoms, which was general practice until recently in Western civilization. And nostrums and quackery are still about us, despite hesitant efforts at legal control. Still, as I have noted, we have had the recent growth of an objective attitude toward physical reality, even including the human body as physical and organic. On the side of mind and social relations, where morals and politics are involved, the rampant theorizing and disputing over the rudiments testify that the objective or critical attitude continues subordinate to other motives. In our field, interest centers largely in the discovery of effective techniques of propaganda—for each to use on all the rest, one must infer, since the results are published.

Rather the worst, to my mind—still harping on human romanticism as requiring a skeptical attitude—is that, having at very long last recognized that inert natural objects are *not* like men, beings of mind and will, moved by exhortation, persuasion, and deception, many of the best heads draw the strange conclusion that men are *like* inert objects, mechanisms responding to situations strictly in terms of cause and effect. A social scientist of distinction in his field once said to me in a matter-of-fact tone, "You know, I *think* there is no such thing as *thinking*." And much that is currently published in psychology and sociology advocates or rests upon the absurdity of behaviorism. One may ask: Is it for that that society selects the brightest *minds* and spends hard-earned money of taxpayers, or public trust funds, to give them an expensive education! Perhaps we should drop modern education and go back to ancestral lore, nursery jingles, proverbs, and the sort of reasoning used against Galileo—and under threat of hell-fire renounce progress for the beaten paths as the sum of human wisdom. If, that is, we cannot leave one absurd extreme without going whole hog for the opposite one, as bad or worse. But if men must be strictly scientific, in the sense of the natural sciences, these people are right; the way is to deny or ignore the most patent, relevant, and vital facts. After all, the myth and magic, divinations and incantations of savages were fairly harmless, while the opposite is true of natural science, if misapplied. That can easily destroy civilization, or the race itself, if men do not reach a working agreement on problems of the laws of values, which have to be treated in quite different terms. Up to a point, on both sides; for, of course, there is a place for science in the study of man, and, as I have no time to argue here, science itself is not empirical or its laws rigorous in the naive sense that positivists, pragmatists, and scientificists assume. Its problems are finally value problems also.

It is true that we all confront, in a sense, the same practical tasks, prediction and control. But as should be self-evident, self-prediction and self-control, individual or especially collective, are categorically different matters from the relations of purposive man to inert objects. Man looks at nature from the outside, the standpoint from which alone scientific prediction is possible. He looks at himself and his society from the inside, which makes nonsense of the simple instrumental approach. I have little faith in *a priori* truth, or any absolutes, notably generalizations about impossibility. But I think I know that no one will ever learn to lift himself by his own bootstraps; nor, more pertinent to the social situation, will two persons be able to lift each other at the same time. Similarly, a scientist cannot by scientific method predict his own behavior in investigation. To do so, he would have to know the answers in advance, and then the questions would not be questions, or the problems problems. Further, prediction of the behavior of predicting runs into the familiar logical impasse of the infinite regress. And socially, if even two people predict each other's behavior and redirect their own accordingly, both will be falsified, or at least one must be. To the claim that social changes are scientifically predictable by a member of the society, a fair answer is the challenge to predict the stock market and make a fortune enough times to show that it was not by chance. And it is a logical impossibility, not merely the matter of accurate observation and measurement. Nor does probability theory help much; on that it should suffice to observe that one cannot get insurance on a contingency where there is a substantial moral hazard, which practically means where any human choice is involved. (As will be noted later, there are economic laws of the market which are valid and useful for prediction and control.)

Modern physics has proved what anyone should have seen—that the notion of absolute causality was a logical-metaphysical prejudice all along. If it were true, we could never know it. Physical causality is now conceived statistically, recognizing the fact of contingency in the world. In biology, of course, the case is more extreme. To talk sense in that realm, we must use teleological terms like function, a will or urge to life, competition, and adaptation; and in the higher species we must recognize hesitation, effort, and error, which distinguish them from mechanisms. Human conduct manifests still higher categories of activity, in sharper contrast with passive process—explicit desires, critical evaluation, will, and choice. Man not only errs but "sins," and shows bad taste; he is the pretender, trickster, hypocrite, and liar of the known world, and equally unique for cruelty and obscenity. Absurdly, we call people brutal or beastly for deeds and traits foreign to animal nature. In short, man is subject to laws of a *pre*scriptive kind, contrasting sharply with the *des*criptive laws which he figuratively says "govern" natural phenomena and by which he partly understands and predicts and uses natural events. These other laws he makes, in part, as well as breaks— no one can say how far or how they are made, or found or, indeed, how laws are broken. At least they are chosen by decision, an activity of mind—in part by each person for himself, in part collectively, by groups, in emotional and intellectual intercommunication in cultural life, which changes and is changed through historical time.

Thus what man, the romantic, wants from social science he certainly will not get, not in a society with any freedom whatever. Prediction and control cannot be mutual; but what each naturally wants is to predict and control the rest, and wants social science to tell him how. For instrumental intelligence—and intelligence is basically instrumental—it is a real dilemma. To act intelligently in relations with others, each needs *first* to know how the others *will* act. Social life is possible for intelligent beings because of three facts. The first is law, a legal-moral-customary order sharply restricting the range of conduct to be expected; the second is collusion or preconcerting of activities involving mutuality. In free society "the law" is ideally a generalized form of preconcerting; but, of course, much of it, of which language is the type, "just grows" without raising any questions. Third, men as more truly rational, do not expect or want to live so very intelligently, in the instrumental sense; our days would be dull indeed without a large element of uncertainty and surprise. About collusion, either agreement *ad hoc* or on enduring rules, scientific method has virtually nothing to say, beyond information on what is possible; it cannot tell what should be done, as desired or as a matter of duty. If companions get separated in a crowd, neither can find the other by scientific prediction; they must agree in advance on a course of action.

A note: One-sided control—the only correct use of the word—has a place in a democracy. It applies in the relations between adults and children, and between the agents of society and criminals or defectives—cases involving individuals who are not responsible members of the community. The fields of medicine and education present special cases of power relations, needing extended consideration impossible here. Control is also meaningful for a dictator, up to a point in contrast with the citizen of a free society. But the fact of his subjects having minds—opinion, feeling, and will—would still set the dictator's methods off sharply from those used to control inert objects. Even our relations with the higher animals are in part persuasive, even mutual, not purely mechanistic.

The great source of difficulty in interpreting man and society is that scientific laws apply but are limited by the prescriptive kind, with several subspecies, to which man is also subject. Science itself as a human and social activity works under at least two kinds of law that fall in the normative class. First are the laws of clear and valid thinking, of logic and criticism; about these I cannot say more in this lecture, or of aesthetic norms which are also operative. More to be emphasized is the scientist's subjection to moral laws. He must be honest, have intellectual integrity, be "devoted" to truth. Science has a high and austere code, bordering on the religious. Verification presupposes valid intercommunication, in which the moral factor bulks as large as the intellectual (and the aesthetic is never absent).

More or less apart from the main dichotomy, a third general type of law calls for notice—the historical. Accepted historical laws are few; but such law undoubtedly pervades both the phenomena of nature and those of man. In the natural domain, sciences like cosmology and geology find order in the temporal sequence of events—largely exemplifying the great law of the degradation of energy—and they yield some literal prediction, of the future, by projection or extrapolation. The ordinary laboratory sciences, of course, predict only hypothetically—"If *A*, then *B*," or they go on to measure covariation. It is chiefly such laws that are directly useful to man; the process of discovery shows how to interfere in their working by acts that man "can" do, and so to "control" a course of events. For conduct, these become hypothetical imperatives: "If you want result *B,* you must perform act *A.*" Such laws are not wholly wanting in society; if an enactment is to be obeyed, it must carry some penalty for infraction, and the most conspicuous case is the laws of the market or of "demand and supply." But the whole matter of the instrumental view of rule-making by groups needs special consideration impossible here. Historical laws are closely dependent on the generalizing sort, but I must pass over that, too, and over the reasons why the historical laws of nature are of little use. In biology we have evolution, a historical law which does not enable prediction, still less control, though the opposite is true of the underlying general laws of heredity, adaptation, and survival. In fact, the use of strictly historical law is solely to tell us what will happen "regardless," what we cannot do; hence the given conditions of action. But the first would be true of physical laws if they held rigorously for man himself. Absolute laws of matter would be purely historical, and no one would know them; ideas of knowing and using would be nonexistent in a universe of process, devoid of meaning as well as of rights or values.

In considering history and its laws, we must remember that history also has *its* history; like science, it developed along with mind and culture. We contrast "scientific" history with the romantic, animistic, supernaturalistic myths of the ages down to yesterday, for critically authentic history is also a recent innovation. (A note: Here and at other points, some exception should be made for the Greeks; but all their advances and more were lost in the succeeding Dark Age—Gibbon's "triumph of barbarism and religion.") As to method, we learn history largely by prediction; but for the past, this is valid, since we *are* on the outside of the people and events we study. The absence of intercommunication limits the data (and, of course, there is no possibility of control), but predictions backward are not affected by people being told what they are going to do. That limitation of social science is commonly an intention of the predictor—to exhort or warn or deceive—making prediction a technique of control. History is of the essence in the study of society. All direct knowledge, by observation or report, is, of course, of the past; the future is only inferred, and the present is a mere imaginary line between the two. Further, while everything has a history and is the product of history, this is true in a quite special sense of man and human society. The late Ortega y Gasset said (paraphrasing Dilthey) that "man has no nature, what he has is . . . history." But it has been a history of seeking a nature, of progressively creating humanity, in and with cultures. Finally, the task of our society is historical—to direct intelligently the future course of history.

An honest view of that problem must face up to how little anyone knows about history, especially its causality or laws, or about how to learn from it or apply it. We recall Hegel's sad witticism that we learn from history that men do not learn from history. Here, again, a major obstacle is the romantic character of human interest. Apart from still being, in varying degree, makers or purveyors of myth—for reasons good or bad—historians naturally write mostly about what they and their readers are most interested in. That is, the deeds of the great, glorious victories, and tragic defeats in war or political struggle. Man, we must note, is a social animal, but in contrast with other social species he is also antisocial, a lawbreaker and gangster; as spectator or participant, he likes a good fight, and a good war may redeem a bad cause. Further, it is about the spectacular that records are most available. These features of history are unfortunate for the student of social process in quest of historical law. We are more concerned with the commonplaces of past situations, activities of which the contemporaries were unaware or only passively aware. It is things like language that, because they are hardly affected by purposive action, yield the most definite laws, either scientific or historical. What students of society need from history is a descriptive portrayal of human development in the large: how beings we could call human emerged out of some animal species and gradually became civilized; and civilization's fitful advance until it produced societies more or less intelligently committed to ideals of truth, freedom, and progress.

What to my mind is most important in the long sweep of change is the recurring emergence of novelty, with the new generally not replacing the old but superimposed upon it, giving rise to ever-increasing complexity. Most notably, man requires a pluralistic interpretation, as a being full of contradiction and paradox. He is a physical mechanism and an organism, subject to the laws of both these kinds, and somehow joined to them is a mental or spiritual nature with unique attributes and subject to different laws. Not much will ever be known about human beginnings, the transition from the merely animal to the human. And we must look back beyond man, at least to the appearance of consciousness and the mental faculties we find in some degree in the higher animals. Consciousness can never be "explained" in terms either of physical process or of biological utility. There is no reason of either sort why men should not live and behave exactly as we do, as unconscious mechanisms—which the behaviorist pretends to "think" we are. Consciousness is "epiphenomenal"; we only know it is there, and seems to be active, notably in the scientificist's act of denying it. Another revolutionary change was the shift from a biological to a cultural basis of continuity and development. The inheritance of behavior patterns, like other traits, and including social behavior, as "instincts," through the gene mechanism, somehow gave place in large part to transmission through imitation of the mature by the young. This process, culture or custom, could have been at first as mechanical and unconscious as the older method, a matter of psychological conditioning. If so, it presently turned into the activity of learning, joined by teaching. The new system could be biologically useful, in enabling transmission of learned behavior, thus affording more flexibility and rapid adaptation than the accidents of favorable gene mutation.

The advent of culture gives rise to historical laws in the broad human meaning—descriptive laws of culture change—without voluntary action, as in the case of language, mentioned before. Acquisition of speech was the great advance, providing a tool of thought—fantasy and emotion as well as reasoning—and the main vehicle of cultural continuity and change, of which it is now the most prominent example. Language illustrates culture's virtual independence of physical and biological conditions or laws. The people who carry a culture pattern play much the role of the soil which supports many forms of plant life indifferently. Purely historical laws of culture change are hard to isolate and do not yet amount to a great deal, outside of linguistics. But they show up with a vengeance, negatively, in limiting our ability to make changes. Language itself goes its own way; our society is helpless even to get absurd anachronisms out of English spelling—not to speak of establishing a common medium of communication between peoples, so much needed in science and scholarship and for world organization. In other fields we have in varying degrees more freedom in lawmaking. But I shall come to that after touching on another revolutionary emergence.

At some time, far back in prehistory, developing *Homo* became aware of the customary law to which he had previously conformed automatically. When he realized that he was bound by laws, being human, he resented it, found it interfered with various private urges, and began his unique career as a lawbreaker; he became antisocial as well as social. When custom ceases to be mere historical process and becomes compulsory, as mores, we cross the great divide into the new age of prescriptive law, as morality. (I can only mention the development of felt desires opposed to customary requirements, and other prescriptive laws, notably of logic and of taste.) In a familiar way of putting the change, man "fell" from innocence into sin. I will not raise the great question of life, whether it was really a fall or a rise, and will be reversed in heaven. As I picture the primitive attitude, it would have been a blend of feeling the law—moral law—as in itself compulsory, like, say, wearing clothes, with viewing it as a command to be obeyed, subject to infliction of penalties. In accord with their animistic world view, primitive men thought of law as command by supernatural powers which (or who?) would punish not only the individual culprit but also the society which tolerated him in its midst—at least without retributive treatment and rites of reconciliation and purification.

Such feelings and fears, however, were not enough to prevent lawbreaking. And since man had become social, of biological necessity, and since a society must have laws in order to exist, laws which are consciously obeyed if they do not function automatically, evolution, so to speak, "had to" produce means for enforcing the most necessary rules. Thus arose religion and politics, the beginnings of church and state; and the relations between the two, especially their conflicts, with men's love and hatred for both, have been the red thread running through history ever since. The institutions have been supported by aspects of men's highly ambiguous attitudes—they love order as such as well as hate it, and, in particular, resent lawbreaking by other people, though this may also be admired. If men had in fact been rational, if they had had "common gumption," they would have seen that laws are necessary; hence those that exist must be obeyed until others, supposedly better, are proposed and accepted. But that is not "human nature." One thinks of Marx, the arch-romantic, who denounced religion as the opium of the people—descriptively enough, but without asking how its necessary function would be performed without it—for men cannot be ruled or kept in order by force alone. With the rise of agencies for enforcement, jural law is differentiated from that which is moral only; but that difference is one of social mechanics rather than of categories. Liberals, too, have been romantic in imagining an impossible amount of freedom to change the laws; men can never be "liberated" from custom or convention, for law must be predominantly a matter of habit, use, and wont. And it must also be in considerable part formally enforced.

We may now take a backward glance at some features of the transition which seem to be somewhat neglected. The development of mind tends to be considered too much in terms of intelligence, itself treated as a

biological function; and with the biologizing of man goes the mechaniz-
ing of biology. Changes in the life of feeling need more emphasis.
Nearly a century ago, Darwin made a good beginning of studying emotion in animals, but it seems to have been little followed up. Man is
strikingly unique as the animal that laughs and weeps. More remark-
ably, people will pay others to make them laugh, and pay even more to
be made to cry, if done in some proper way. Emotional changes, some
of which had a physiological and even an anatomical basis, underlie our
moral and aesthetic values, as well as individual desires and aversions.
Somewhere and somehow occurred a remarkable inversion of the instrumental relation between "mind" and body. There must have been a
time, an epoch, when the brain and nervous system were, in fact, instrumental to the life of the organism and the species. In civilized man this
is reversed; the mind thinks of the body as a means to its own life of
"experience." Indeed, it often seems ashamed of having a body at all;
this is called the coffin of the spirit and is "mortified" for the latter's
well-being, or "salvation." The mental life is less a matter of reasoning
than of feelings, wishes, and value judgments, which provide the ends
of reasoning, such as it is. Hume's dictum that the intellect is the slave
of the passions is, in general, true, though I have reservations when he
adds that it has no right to any other role. That also I must pass over,
and, of course, I cannot go into the confused, romantic, and paradoxical
character of human passions. I would stress that neither our desires nor
our higher values, which, largely opposed as they are, together define
what we mean by the "useful," show any consistent relation to biological
advantage of the individual or the species. They seem about as often to
be antibiological. Man is the animal who "works," virtually meaning
that he has an aversion to useful activity as such; and it is most true of
civilized man. He is the slave-maker, and then the builder of machines
to replace the slaves—after civilization has made him softhearted. I
puzzle especially over many of our higher values, as I would guess that
on the whole idealists do more harm than the criminals. The soft heart
proverbially needs the hard head; but this has little romantic or sentimental appeal.

I must hurry on to say a little about the most important topic, the
last and rather the greatest revolution in the modes of law—the coming
of democracy. That was just beginning to be talked about when Hume
wrote, a short two centuries ago, though a major turning point in its
direction had occurred a century before, in the victory of Parliament
over Stuart absolutism. Hume disliked democracy and did not live to

see it; he died a few days after another high point, the adoption of our Declaration of Independence, in a war which was a prelude to the French Revolution. A still earlier turning point was the Protestant Revolt. This destroyed the unitary ecclesiastical absolutism of western Europe, but it did not destroy either authoritarianism or its supernatural foundation; both were transferred to nation-states, under autocrats ruling by the grace of God. Nor did the Age of Reason, with its political revolutions, introduce democracy, which came gradually in the nineteenth and twentieth centuries. Our own Founding Fathers feared it—the famous Declaration was written by and for slaveowners. Just so, none of the protagonists in the terrible "religious" wars following the "Reformation" wanted even toleration, not to mention the general liberation which finally resulted. History, like nature, moves in mysterious ways its wonders to perform. None of the thirteen states adopting our Constitution in 1787 had universal *male* suffrage; and no one then thought of free secular, non-dogmatic education, even for literacy, as a requirement for citizenship in a free state, or as a human right.

It is hard to realize the historical suddenness and vast sweep of the change, in a few generations, from the medieval system—the most extreme totalitarianism known, at least in the Western world before Hitler and Stalin—to our libertarian and equalitarian democracy of today. The accepted human values were largely inverted—an *Umwertung aller Werte,* in the Nietzschean phrase. Culturally and spiritually, the basic fact was the freeing of the mind from dogma for the progressive pursuit of truth and well-being, material and ideal. Everyone should know Professor Bury's two books—at least the earlier chapters—*History of Freedom of Thought* and *The Idea of Progress.* I mention them, as I cannot go into detail. The two great drives back of the whole movement (not the immediate motivation of the heretical religious revolts) were the development of science and the economic interest in trade and production, both of which seem to be naturally individualistic. Modern science is unique in looking toward applications—as preached by Bacon and inaugurated as a movement by his younger contemporary, Galileo. The role of the "Renaissance," reviving classical pagan learning, was important but is, I think, commonly exaggerated.

For our purpose here, the central fact is the revolution in the conception of law. From its historical beginnings through the ages, the law had been sacred, hence in theory eternal and immutable—and so was, of necessity, the authority for its interpretation and enforcement, that is, the uneasy partnership of autocratic church and autocratic state, both divinely ordained and sanctioned. (Note previous reference to reservations for Greece and Rome.) The essence of democracy is the freedom of the people to change the laws at will, by equal participation, and to have them enforced by agents held responsible in the same way. In norms of conduct, a new age began when men first thought that their laws could be wrong, contrary to a "higher" law. For this we unfortunately still use the words "moral" and "ethical," giving them, as usual, a radically new additional meaning. The coming of freedom to change, of course, ended the sanctity of law. The idea of improvement had been impossible before, since the laws, jural or moral in the original sense, contained the whole meaning of right and wrong. Verbally, the right means the regular. At this point, man took or underwent his second great "fall," in the sense of the first; as he had then fallen from the innocence of insouciance into responsibility for obeying laws, he now took on the far more onerous responsibility for determining the content of the law itself.

There was, indeed, a transitional stage when "positive" law was distinguished in theory from "natural law," opening the way to some change in the former—but never very much, and only by the sacred authority. I can only mention the curious history of the ambiguous concept of "nature"—standing for fact versus norm, or used in contrast with the supernatural or the artificial. In culture, it is hard to separate the natural and the artificial, and only in that sense does natural law or natural right have meaning. Life has its scientific laws, as part of nature; but conformity with any sort of standards is unnatural, against nature. Men have the rights recognized in the legal and moral order in which they live. My right to life means only that no one has a right to kill me, unless he has that right—mayhap the duty. I feel some impatience with the solemn cant that passes for inspired wisdom on the most vital questions. The notion of men being born free or equal is one example, and another is that loving people tells how they ought to be treated, which is commonly not as they wish to be. And what "you" would like, with no conditions stated, would as typically lead to misguidance. The phrase "natural-law" is current today—used to cloak dogmatic pronouncements on what ought to be law or ought to be done. If free society endures, this will be outgrown, as legal thinking is struggling free from the conception of law as a command. When people "command themselves," individually or collectively, a different word is called for.

Advisedly I say "individually or collectively." It is essential to free society that, even when law is made by free agreement as far as possible, its scope still be minimized, leaving each person to "command himself." Limits to freedom must be set only by general agreement—not the fiat of whoever can contrive to carry an election—to meet the need for common restraints or for group action to realize group values. But there's the rub! With the progress of liberal civilization, individuals pursuing their wants and needs or ideals run more and more into conflict; and more and more do human needs become social, requiring a consensus in action. Basic like-mindedness is requisite for discussion itself—the method of democracy, and Lord Bryce's familiar definition. Conflict is not only, or even mainly, because of "sin." The minimum requirements for harmony expand, making agreement hard, and threatening resort to force. Agreement must come in part through compulsory legal action, while the basic consensus is the task of education. Hence above all, the schools must be kept free and not allowed to be used for indoctrinating the young with dogma.

The broad crucial task of free society is to reach agreement by discussion on the kind of civilization it is to create for the future; hence it must agree on the meaning of progress. The living adult generation legislate for their children, and also beyond them for the unborn. For that task, attitudes toward persons are not in point; even for infants already born, freedom has no meaning, and equality means all equal to zero, or to digits in a census of units biologically defined. Discussion of legal change must run in terms of general values or ideals. The politics of democracy cannot be a contest between individuals or interest groups in getting what they want at the cost of others. Right must be defined in relation to obligations as well as to possibilities. One of our worst verbal confusions is using the same term, "value," for both subjective desires and ideals which, in seeking agreement, must be recognized as objectively valid, hence as "cognitive." Social problems arise out of conflicts at either of the two levels; but they can be discussed only as differences in critical-intellectual judgment of norms. Mere assertion of opposed claims cannot tend toward agreement, but must intensify conflict.

In a realistic view, the problem of legislation is hardly one of means to ends, or of efficiency—and not at all in the sense of scientific technology. A useful analogy is the making of rules in games or sports. The individual interest will be in winning, but the general interest is the ideal of a good game. I once heard of a business efficiency expert who suggested for the improvement of football first to put all the men on the same side. Sportsmanship, incidentally, looms very large in the ethic of free society and has been very important in the history of democracy; but little is said about it in either connection, by moral philosophers and preachers or by historians.

Society in its rule-making must of course give a high place to efficiency, which also is largely ignored in idealistic and religious ethics. I digress to say explicitly that in referring to anachronisms in religious teachings on morals I do not condemn religion. People should of course have any religion they choose, provided they allow others that right, do not indulge in "offensive" practices, and keep it out of politics; this last was, of course, the clear intention of Jesus and the Apostles. But I would make one remark on the obvious: Surely all who have bowels of feeling share Henry Wallace's view that babies everywhere should have their bottle of milk at feeding time. And that may well be a condition of peace in the world. It will not come about if the number of babies exceeds the number of bottles of milk per feeding period; and the contribution of church ethics to that situation is more babies and fewer bottles of milk.

Efficiency as a social problem is the province of economics. The history of the free-enterprise economy has shown its capacity to promote efficiency, up to any reasonable expectations, but there are other values to be considered. The system is widely criticized, damned as "capitalism" by agitators for radical change. Undoubtedly there are evils, some more or less remediable by intelligent political action. A primary criticism relates to unjust distribution. There are many formulas for justice in that sense; they conflict among themselves, and no one could ever be fully realized or pushed very far without unduly neglecting others. And compulsory redistribution infringes on freedom; but conflicting definitions of that are also in dispute. The citizen must learn critically to compare and balance among possible alternatives, first knowing what these are. The economic order is also condemned for the aesthetic and cultural values it fosters. It is blamed for a civilization denounced as ugly, crass, or trivial, as well as for enslaving the working masses, not giving them real freedom or the good life.

I only mention these things, without passing judgment, at the end of an overlong discourse, in order to suggest the kind of problems we face, in one important area, in trying to realize the revolutionary ideal of a society combining freedom with order. The problem involves "laws" of all the values of the familiar triad—Truth, Beauty, and the Good—in their broadest meaning, everything that enters into a high civilization and the good life for man. We tend to include it all in a vague concept of social justice—again a complex new meaning for an old term. Its historical meaning, as the word shows, was accord with law, which was assumed to be known. That made good conduct a matter of will, of conformity and obedience, to law, established authority, and "conscience." In consequence of our second "fall," however, the issues in conduct are as much intellectual and aesthetic as moral. No longer is good will the whole story; rather, the view of modern man is expressed in the proverb, "The road to hell is paved with good intentions."

As a final word, I stress again two main difficulties or dangers. The first is in the survival of traditions which do not fit the facts and problems of our free society. Traditions, even freed from sanctity as they must be, are still hard and slow to change. Intelligent action demands, first of all, that men accept that method, eschew wishful thinking, face the problems, and try to understand them. Our older maxims of sentimental, personal-relations morality were formulated in and for a society with "static" ideals. Whatever their adequacy in the original setting, they have little to say about the main problems of a society dedicated to progress in truth, freedom, and well-being. The second menace I have dwelt on at still greater length. It is "scientificism," another fatal oversimplification—the insistence on attacking problems of social change entirely by methods adapted to the understanding and use of the natural environment. They are irrelevant to the more crucial problem of democratic society, which is agreement on cultural norms. These must supply—not goals, for goals are always provisional, to be redefined as they are progressively realized—but must point the *direction* of change, that we may have progress and not stagnation or retrogression.

Notes

1. The writer would not have these paragraphs go into print without some words of disclaimer and admonition. They were prepared as a "speech," which implies other limitations as well as that of length. The paper does not purport to give a balanced discussion of any of the subjects touched upon. This applies in particular to the main theme, a critique of the use of scientific method in the study of society, which is a frankly one-sided treatment. It places the emphasis where I think it is needed—on the "limitations" of scientific prediction and control in this field of action. This in no way implies that there is no place for systematic inquiry into social phenomena, with such classification and quantification as can be validly carried out. That brings up the whole subject of methodology, which would call for a long treatise. It would have to begin with the

wide differences in the meaning of "fact" and of "observation" in the main divisions of knowledge—especially the meaningful and communicable, and of intelligibility to a more or less general public in contrast with a small elite. (The latter, in the limit, may become hard to distinguish from a cult.) As briefly indicated in the paper, the reference to economics and its laws is particularly inadequate. In that field regular quantitative comparisons and the working of markets do result in at least some approximation to that "measurement" without which "knowledge is meager and unsatisfactory"—though the magnitudes cannot be used intelligently without an understanding of the way in which units are established and the conditions which enter into them. A large and important area of fact and of law which could not even be mentioned is the plurality of cultures and related political units, culminating in the notion of international law.

14

Philosophy and Social Institutions in the West

I

Discussion of this topic is best approached in historical terms.[1] The variety of philosophic views held in either the East or the West makes it hard to speak of "the" philosophy of either region; the regions themselves have vague bounds as well as internal differences, and there have been important historical changes in both. But these have been vastly more "fundamental" in the West than in the historical East, before Westernization set in. The general history of culture in Europe—and particularly Western Europe (and its "colonies"), the region actually to be considered—has been distinguished by a fairly sharp periodization, recognized in the textbooks and treatises. Ignoring less important "breaks," account must be taken at least of classical antiquity (taken as a beginning), the Middle Ages, a period of monarchical States which has no familiar name better than mercantilist, and, finally, the age or period of Liberalism. They were separated by fairly short and distinct intervals of revolutionary change—the "decline and fall" of the classical civilization, the Renascence, and the Enlightenment, or Age of Reason. Each of the four epochs was marked by fairly characteristic institutions and world view, more or less definitely expressed in its philosophy.

My main concern will be the fourth epoch, as what I mean by "the West," and with the ideas and ethos embodied in liberal institutions, rather than explicit statements of philosophers. I shall pay little attention

Reprinted with permission of The University of Hawaii Press from *Philosophy and Culture: East and West,* edited by Charles A. Moore (Honolulu: University of Hawaii Press, 1962), 549–68.

to classical antiquity, as its great advances in civilization were lost in the succeeding Dark Ages of extreme primitivism. And I shall argue that the resurgence of civilized life following the Middle Ages was less a literal "renascence," a rebirth, than a new birth, a development along different lines. Of course, there were significant survivals, and more important revivals; but I think they served more as a stimulus than as a model for imitation. So I shall use the term "renascence" chiefly in the chronological sense. I hold that—at least apart from the field of fine arts, which I do not discuss—importations from the East and creative innovation in the West itself were together more important for the major changes and the sweep of history than was the rediscovery of classical culture. The importations, about which more will be said presently, are a reminder that account should be taken of the Near or "Middle" East, from which the post-classical West took its dominant religion, out of which its philosophy slowly differentiated. And, incidentally, the more important revivals finally accepted in the field of ideas were largely transmitted to the West by Muslims and Jews.

History merges into evolution; and in that connection some further observations are in order, partly to indicate a personal position, which is bound to color more or less the whole presentation. There is much truth, along with literary exaggeration, in the statement of Ortega y Gasset (he was paraphrasing William Dilthey) that "man has no nature, what he has is history." Philosophy must surely deal with "man," the human mentality, and should have cognitive truth and relevance to general human problems, intellectual and practical. It is not merely a form of entertainment or one of the fine arts. Looking at man as the resultant of age-long development, his nature clearly consists of "layers," which have been added more or less successively, one at a time, yielding, as it were, a stratified deposit. He is a physico-chemical body, a living organism, an animal—he is biologically the "highest" species, so far, in an ascending series. On all this, a uniquely human mental nature has been superposed by later evolution. One thing that strikes me as decisive about Eastern and Western thought (modern Western) is that the latter takes account of the fact that man is basically an animal, while the former fails to do so, or does it in a radically different way—in the idea of *saṁsāra*. However, this difference in particular is one of Western history rather than of geography: Plato believed in the transmigration of souls, and the doctrine seems to have been prevalent earlier in Greece.

It surely follows that the concept of reality, particularly as regards man, must be *pluralistic,* associated with conceptions of "emergent" evolution. The essence of the emergent view is that "stages" of evolution introduced categorical novelties, somehow (usually) superposed upon what existed previously (rather than a replacement) but not to be accounted for in terms of the same concepts. A brief sketch may ignore the earlier breaks, even the appearance of organic life; but it must note the supreme discontinuity, the emergence of consciousness. This clearly cannot be explained in "physical" terms, nor in those of the main accepted theory of organic evolution—the chance occurrence of "mutations" and natural selection of those highly exceptional ones which happen to be favorable for the survival and increase of a species. Thus new strains arose, sometimes becoming distinct varieties, and occasionally new species. In the human species, when it was established, this had not occurred. There is much prejudice to the contrary, but truth-seeking students are dropping the conception of races of man, since no one can list them, or name any one that will be generally accepted as valid. The next emergent to be stressed is "culture" (in the anthropological meaning). Somehow, animal instincts were attenuated into vague "drives" and were replaced as to concrete content by "social inheritance," through imitation of their elders by the young of each new generation. This substantially achieved the advantages of "inheritance of acquired characters"; and these are so great, in flexibility and speed of adaptation, that biological evolution apparently ceased, many thousands of years ago—or may since have been more or less retrograde.

It is "culture" that primarily distinguishes man from other animals, particularly as associated with the acquisition of language, for there lie the differences most significant for the project of synthesizing or reconciling, or understanding, the divergent philosophies. In contrast with biological convergence, resulting in a practically uniform human species, culture has shown the opposite tendency, to wide divergence, which is illustrated by the multiplication of languages over the earth. Another vital fact about culture and the attending mentality is that its change and differentiation—again illustrated by language—cannot in the main be explained in terms of biological usefulness for survival and increase. Human behavior comes to be motivated, taking the form of conduct, which commonly involves use of means to achieve ends. The mental attitude and activity of "reason," by which men adapt acts to ends, itself shows a limited tendency to universality. But more important for understanding human nature are the emotions, which provide the ends. These diverge widely and obstinately, particularly as they come to be less and less directly or visibly connected with the biological "ends." First, with advancing civilization, thinking tends to become less instrumental, in any realistic sense; more "playful" seems to be the best description. But, in addition, when men do think instrumentally, they rather typically use their minds to circumvent Nature, and also society and its laws, on which they are utterly dependent, for in them man lives and moves and has his being. Instrumentally, civilized man has largely inverted the natural and undoubtedly the original relation between his body and his mind. In place of the mind's serving the body, functionally, biologically, he treats the body and its life as a means to some preferred kind of mental experience.

All this cannot in general be termed "bad," as it involves the whole higher purposive life of man—good or bad according to the case and the standards of judgment—which exhibits the most important culture divergence. Greater uniformity of basic standards has now come to be imperative for world civilization or humanity; and that is, I suppose, what is practically meant by the project of "synthesizing" Eastern and Western philosophy. ("Reconciling" would seem to be a better term for it.) Certainly, culture differentiation, in relation to world-wide mobility and communication, with conflicting loyalties, has created "awful" problems, and so has the remarkable diversity among individuals in desires and ideals that has appeared in the "free" society of the modern West— no longer held in unison as formerly, though on a small scale, by the more disciplinary institutions of preceding epochs. (But it went far enough in Greece to cause decline, after a short century or so of brilliance achieved under comparative freedom—a fact that is ominously suggestive, in the light of kindred symptoms that the liberal epoch may be taking a similar course.)

Treatment of the body as the slave of the mind has often gone on to the repudiation of the body as far as possible—the notion of a "war" between the flesh and the spirit. This has had profound consequences, social as well as intellectual; it has been used to justify slavery, or an equivalent class or caste order, in which the "good life," that of the philosopher or priest, is essentially parasitic on the mass of society. Here one should go back of philosophy to religion and consider the relations between the two. What can be said is somewhat speculative, but it seems clear that religion is historically primary and philosophy differentiated out of it—much more fully in the West, until the separation is in practice essentially complete under liberalism—another major contrast with the East. (In medieval Islam, philosophy grew out of medicine.) In the first epoch of Western thought, the Greeks made progress in this separation, but it was lost in the Dark Ages, as philosophy disappeared in dogmatic theology, to reappear gradually as we approach modern times. Primitive religion was typically magic, and "crudely" utilitarian in conception and intention. (This is still seen in the West, in numerous superstitions—for an unbeliever including prayer, for any tangible result.) Religion is directly relevant for our "historical approach," because the West considered is Western Europe, which at the close of the classical epoch became a theocracy. Conditions were different in the Eastern part of the Mediterranean region, where the "Roman" Empire survived into the Renascence centuries, and under Islam, as this power took over there (and in much of what had been the Western Empire) and finally extinguished Byzantium (except for Russia). As far as I know, the nations of the (far) East have never been under ecclesiastical rule, and hence could not undergo a revolution against it; and the fact of such a reaction in the West goes far to account for its difference from the East, after it occurred.

As has been suggested, I find the best way to characterize (recent) Western thought and institutions is to contrast them with conditions in the Middle Ages, and to do that by summarily sketching the course of change through the transitional interval. I contend that "medievalism" was, in essentials, more "Eastern" than the culture of the East itself. In particular and first of all, it was more "religious" in several respects. In both, thought was "mystical," but in the West theistic-supernaturalistic, whereas the East was intuitional, in a sense that seems to me much like early Christian gnosticism. Both systems (groups of systems) centered around the objective of "salvation," to be achieved through "believing" the "truth," and so being made "free" (for Christendom, see John 8:32). Salvation was "from" the world of everyday experience, which was viewed in complete pessimistic terms, but "for" another life very differently conceived in East and West, as was the belief or knowledge instrumental to it. In the West, "faith" was equally independent of evidence, but had to be supported and supplemented by revelation, from an anthropomorphic Deity called Creator or Father of everything. The West had "Heaven" and "Hell" in place of reincarnation in a higher or lower order of life, or eventual "release," hard to distinguish from oblivion. It seems fair to describe the Eastern view as unworldly, in contrast with the Western as otherworldly. Any delineation pretending to accuracy would have to consider innumerable subdivisions of doctrine, and make subtle distinctions in the meanings of terms; and it should also go into the relations between scholastic theory and everyday practice—and between the lives of different orders of society.

Monasticism played a greater role in the life of "Christian" Europe, though the general pattern was imported from the East, and was given a more extreme interpretation in Eastern than in Western Christendom. Its devotees are necessarily parasitic, but the Roman Catholic version produced a dualistic ethic by which the masses could be saved in a life beyond by one of vicarious atonement in this world. In both regions, devotion to a religious ethic of renunciation allowed the utmost luxury of living on the part of potentates. The Roman Church invented the doctrine of Purgatory, with intercession by the living for the souls that had passed on; the agency of the Church was needful and its service in procuring forgiveness of sin came to be sold as "indulgences." This grew into the scandal that helped to precipitate the "Reformation." I have not run across any of this in accounts of Eastern thought, which was, in general individualistic and internalistic, while the Western (pre-liberal) system centered on a corporate body, "the Church," as the authoritative dispenser of salvation and custodian of all significant knowledge. Both powers, or missions, were held to have been conferred by a divine commission, with the revelation of truth. Another item, familiar in the West but seemingly not found in the East, is belief in miracles, in the past and as current events—another ground for the characterization of the West as differing from the East in being similar in principle but "more so."

The concrete transformation that occurred in the West, by which its modern culture is to be described, amounted to an inversion of fundamental values—an *Umwertung aller Werte,* to use a Nietzschean expression. Conformity and obedience in an essentially "static" spiritual and social order—the latter naturally one of more or less rigorous hereditary classes or castes—was replaced by another pair of intimately connected ideals, freedom and progress, i.e., freedom for progress and progress through freedom. Freedom is inherently individualistic, while social as well as individual progress was to result from individual freedom. India, if not China, had a more rigid class structure, but inheritance of status in Europe was similar in principle. The level of culture, for the masses, was in both regions about as low as possible, but the East had a far more cultivated aristocracy. The extreme character of the culture revolution in the West is no doubt partly explained as a "pendular" reaction; it was, of course, influenced by the surviving tradition of classical greatness, and more by increasing contact with the Byzantine and

Islamic East, where much of the ancient culture had survived and received some further development.

As already indicated, the transformation, which I shall call the "Liberal Revolution," occurred in two fairly distinguishable stages. In the first, at the time of the Renascence, two major changes came about. The first was the secularization of political power—though the Roman Church had been as much a political as a religious body. Further, it was a partial secularization, but turned out to be crucial. The second event was a first step toward progress and freedom of thought, represented by the new scientific movement. Both need discussion at a length impossible in this paper. The fundamental achievement of the revolution as a whole was "Freedom of the Mind" (Professor Bury's phrase) from tradition and authority; but it came gradually and fitfully and in relation to several movements. The secularization, such as it was, came rather earlier than the liberation, as the culmination of a long struggle between political and ecclesiastical authorities (in Italy, Ghibellines versus Guelphs). Concentration of feudal power in the hands of territorial princes gave rise to "States" in something like the modern meaning, and these succeeded in securing dominion over "the Church," or whatever churches survived the awful turmoil of the Wars of Religion following the so-called "Reformation"—the revolt of what came to be known as Protestantism. It is a puzzling fact that generally in history (prior to liberalism) the authority on which order was based has typically been exercised by an uneasy partnership of these two forms, contending about as much as they have cooperated, often in open war; and this is strikingly true of European and West-European history, since the "conversion" to "Christianity" marking the close of the classical era. This point has been stressed by J. N. Figgis; Gibbon called the conversion "the triumph of barbarism and religion," and Fr. Cumont has argued that classical polytheism had already disintegrated under the spread of the "mystery cults," of which Christian "churchianity" was essentially one.

The victory of the States was about as definitive in countries that remained Catholic as in those that became Protestant: his Catholic majesty the King of Spain also kept a firm hand on his clergy. But, for other reasons, the sequel was very different in Britain and on most of the Continent. The secularization was limited in that everywhere the new States were absolute monarchies under dynasties ruling by divine right *(Dei gratia),* and they had no intention of being less autocratic than the prelates of the Church had been—and were much less "enlightened" than these were before the Protestant Revolt brought on the

Counter-Reformation (Council of Trent), which took them back to medievalism. The partial secularization was important because the military competition in which the States found themselves forced them to tolerate and even quietly encourage both science and trade (science as the basis of a rational and progressive technology), as sources of new wealth, the sinews of war. Historically, too, the political authorities have tended to be less dogmatic in opposing change than the ecclesiastics, more disposed to consider ways and means to their ends—which centered in power, as in the case of the Church. In any case, in Britain after the Civil Wars (which were largely wars of religion) the course of history was set toward democracy, while, on the Continent, the settlement in the treaties of Westphalia (coincident with the execution of the Lord's anointed, Charles I) fastened on the peoples the twofold "sovereignty" of the State over the individual and of the prince in the State. Britain became the main home of the liberal movement. After the definitive triumph of Parliament over Stuart absolutism in Britain, there is not much for us to notice here, in politics; through most of the eighteenth century, Europe was preoccupied with dynastic and colonial wars. Toward the end of the century began the second stage of the "revolution." Trade and science progressed, chiefly in Britain, where they had much more freedom, and the two undoubtedly furnished the main dynamic of progress toward liberalism. There, too, the literal "renascence" was much less distinct from the Enlightenment, the enthusiasm for ancient learning and art less prominent in comparison with scientific and political interests.

The second great event of the Renascence period, and doubtless the definitive one in destroying and replacing the medieval system, was centered in science. In Britain in particular (Gilbert and Bacon) this was from the first bound up with applications, in sharp distinction from science in antiquity. But the first great specific step toward progress through the liberation of the mind was the Copernican Revolution in astronomy. Its importance lies not, as commonly pictured, in the new picture of the solar system, but in the fact that it forced recognition of radically *new* knowledge, and so finally destroyed the belief in eternal and immutable truth, particularly as given once for all by revelation. (Copernicus had forerunners in antiquity, whom he recognized, and other in centuries then recent, which had been voices crying in the wilderness of a dogmatic-ritualistic religious culture.) As put forward by Copernicus, timidly and in a "half-baked" form, the new view might not have taken hold; that result may well be attributed to Galileo and his telescope, which revealed visual proof to anyone who would look that neither the Bible nor Aristotle could always be believed.

Incidentally, it is a puzzling fact that religions have had to teach weird mythologies, purporting to explain the origin of things and the whole past, taking the place now filled by science and history. But that raises the large question of what religion is "for" anyway, its "function," or "why" otherwise intelligent people strenuously hold one doctrine to be true and others false. But men's reasons for believing, or asserting, are not a cheering inquiry, and are too complex to go into here. I merely note that critical reflection is a late product of advancing civilization— when it occurs at all—and that human and social problems arise in large part because man is naturally more romantic than rational, and at least as much anti-social as social. (Hobbes is more right than Aristotle.) He is the lawbreaker of the known world, and the "liar," and shows strong anti-social traits even in the small-scale tribal society that is his natural milieu—and far more in the large and heterogeneous agglomeration of a modern nation—or the world, which increasingly has to become an orderly society, if civilization or the race is to survive. Man was evolved in, by, and for an environment very different from that which modern civilization has quite suddenly produced; to live in the latter he needs to learn many new things and new ways and acquire new attitudes.

It is significant that man first adopted the rational attitude toward Nature, and fields of natural phenomena about which he does not propose to do anything in the way of control, of changing the "natural" course of events. Astronomy is the type; and Vesalius's empirical treatment of anatomy, which is also practically unamenable to change, appeared in the same year, 1543. Also, about the same time came notable advances in mathematics, another subject matter of the same character. That reminds us that underlying the new intellectual advance were many technological innovations, and many of the most important were imported from the East. The lens itself is said to have been long known in China, and it was the telescope and microscope that most directly forced the revolution in knowledge. Probably most important of all, in the long run, was the "Arabian" arithmetic and algebra; the former intellectual achievement was brought from India and introduced into Europe at the beginning of the thirteenth century (two decades before the birth of Thomas Aquinas, who gave its definitive form to "medieval" thought). In Europe it was put to practical use; without it, neither modern science nor modern business would be possible. Yet it made headway slowly; it was just coming into use in Britain three centuries later, when the "voyagers" were discovering "the world," previously unknown in Europe and its existence denied. Next in rank would be paper and printing (they should be associated), already known and used in China for many centuries; and there were gunpowder and the magnetic compass, and still other achievements.

The great original innovation of the West was the twofold tie-up of science with technology, and in science that of empiricism with measurement and mathematical analysis. Here the work of Copernicus had to be substantiated by Galileo and completed by Newton; and Francis Bacon must also be named—he was preaching progress through the mastery of Nature by science at roughly the same time that Galileo announced his discovery of the "Medicean Stars" (satellites of Jupiter) and the sunspots. It may have been the Reformation in Britain that saved him, and Newton also, from the fate of Giordano Bruno just a few years before—or at least that of Galileo, who was forced to recant, and spent his later years in house arrest under clerical surveillance. But none of these men looked toward democracy, or general freedom of the mind, or challenged the supreme place of religion in society. Newton spent his later years working out fantastic interpretations of the Book of Revelation; and Bacon wrote the famous pronouncement that "the more absurd and incredible any divine mystery is, the greater honor we do to God in believing it." That seems to be the essence of religion, in the tradition of Christendom; it is the duty of unquestioning belief, regardless of facts and logic, without asking why one should believe one doctrine rather than another. It is no wonder that the inquiring and critical attitude made headway slowly, even in the knowledge of Nature—or that the "war" started over again in 1859, when Darwin and Wallace promulgated the theory of biological evolution (where skirmishing still goes on)—or, especially, that a critically objective approach to social problems is still struggling to be born.

Nor is there anything surprising in the tooth-and-nail resistance to such progress put up by the custodians of "sacred" and (therefore) eternal and immutable truth. (Sacred truth cannot change unless God changes his mind, which seems to be a contradiction in terms.) In particular, believers in salvation by belief in a prescribed creed and performance of prescribed ritual will persecute, torture, and kill recalcitrant "heretics" if they have the power; any other course is a confession either of insincerity or of impotence. This practically applies to any belief in absolute right or truth; yet the "intellectuals" of the Western world still commonly repudiate the relativity of knowledge, which is simply one of the obvious facts of life. This idea that there is such truth need not be harmful, if not associated with belief that somebody knows what it is; but it seems to be virtually inevitable psychologically that those who believe in it go on to assert that they have it, or know who has. Then, in case of disagreement, it is surrender or fight, or the defeated party surrenders after a fight, if still alive. That obviously cannot be the meaning of freedom in society; final truth must be something to be pursued rather than possessed. This has come to be recognized in science, but it percolates slowly into men's minds with respect to truth about man, history, morals, or politics, where its own "truth" is much more obvious and important.

The more conspicuous changes came about in the second stage of the revolution, at the time of the Enlightenment. Most conspicuous of all were the democratization of the absolutist governments and radical economic changes resulting in part from what is referred to as the Industrial Revolution, centered in Britain in the late eighteenth century. Another movement which is not much talked about but which I think contributed much to making that country the home of liberalism was the vogue of sports, before and after the seventeenth-century Restoration of the Stuart Dynasty. "Sportsmanship" seems to me actually and necessarily a fundamental moral ideal for a free and progressive society, and it is categorically alien to the main previous moral tradition, particularly as taught under Jewish-Christian religious auspices. Empirically viewed, the grand result for the nineteenth century was a dualistic social order of political democracy and the system of free markets and private enterprise as a largely independent "economic order" in that sector of men's active life. Both were manifestations of the general ideal of individualism (so-called), and there was a close connection between the two in the historical events of the period. These included commercial and colonial wars, particularly between Britain and France. The victory of the former, statistically a much smaller and weaker nation, was largely that of free enterprise over political bureaucracy; and it was the resources created by the new industries and commerce which made possible the defeat of Napoleon. Of course, many factors complicated the situation.

Outstanding in the political history of the period were the American and French revolutions. Of these, the former was surely the more important in the historical long run and along with and in the light of other American happenings was probably decisive for the future of liberalism. The war was won with the aid of the French monarchy, but its result was a republic which grew rapidly in power and prestige, and was progressively liberalized. The suffrage was extended—finally made universal for normal adults—slavery was abolished, and free education introduced, now everywhere acknowledged as indispensable to free government. Another major American contribution was formally complete religious freedom, through separation of Church and State, which has been laggardly followed elsewhere, or hardly at all. A free society must be a secular order, since civilized men will not freely agree on supernatural dogmas. The problem is agreement where it is important, at least where it is necessary.

II

With freedom of thought and expression goes freedom in conduct, virtually as a corollary. The libertarian world view is this-worldly, centering largely in the effective use of means by individuals to achieve freely chosen ends, and so achieve a better life. Its moral essence is the right of each to be the final judge of his own ends, meaning both personal desires and ideal values, in a spirit of fair play; there is no implication of "self-interest" in a bad sense. In fact, the contrary is implied in the faith in progress through freedom. It means voluntary association, on terms fixed by agreement or assent of the parties. Each must, of course, respect the equal freedom of others; it cannot mean the right of one person to infringe on the freedom of any other. That restriction has always been taken for granted, to be enforced by compulsion where conscience and intelligence do not suffice. The "basic" freedom is that of discussion, in which ideally all meet as equals. Next most important is voluntary cooperation for the more effective use of means, which implies the organization of activity through free enterprise, already mentioned; but any plurality of people are free to arrange for any terms on which they may agree.

The whole change in the social ethos may be summed up as the replacement of the maxim "be good" by that of "be intelligent," taken primarily in the broad instrumental meaning of acting—choosing among the alternatives open—as individuals and groups in such a way as to achieve the best results, selected by critical evaluation. In more comprehensive terms, the maxim is, Be good intelligently. In the intellectual life, it calls for believing only on the basis of a critical appraisal of evidence. In so far as medievalism had a place for intelligence, it meant "rationalism," something very different from instrumental rationality. It purported to mean knowing by "intuition," plus a little deductive inference; the beliefs stressed actually arose in the creative imagination, were supported by wishful thinking, and became embedded in a tradition finally sanctified and enforced by the most cruel penalties that could be devised. Allegedly rational knowledge had to be supplemented by revelation, and both were declared and interpreted by the divinely commissioned Church, whose major premise in action was maintenance and extension of its own power. In morals and politics, "reason" meant "natural law." Whether this or "divine law" has a close parallel in Eastern thought, I do not know. The injunction to follow Nature permeates the thought of China, and could, I should say, be interpreted into the Indian systems by an appropriate definition of the concept of "Nature." (In the West it is vague enough to be used in a formula for promoting nearly any doctrine.) It is doubtless "natural" for any society to have *some* law; but as to the relevant question of *what* law, the only one to be called natural is that which actually exists at a time and place—or perhaps a *jus gentium,* to be found in a number of systems somehow coming into contact. "Natural" is also used to distinguish between the fiat of a legislator and either customary law as a "growth" or the laws some writer thinks "necessary" for any social order to exist. In their enthusiasm for freedom from tradition and authority, the Enlightenment thinkers went to absurd extremes, to virtual anarchism, dominated as they were by an utterly "romantic" conception of the innate rationality and goodness of men. The result was a reaction, beginning at once, early in the nineteenth century; and it has been growing ever since, shifting the mainly negative view of the role of law and government over to more and more positive action. (More will presently be said about that.)

As to problems, medieval and Enlightenment theory alike had no room for any, in the strict sense, either individual or social, but the views rested on opposite grounds. The former envisaged a "static" moral and legal order; and, if laws are immutable, men will naturally know what is right, learning that as they learn their language. They would not, indeed, *do* right, because of original sin, and so needed rigorous control by authority—and to question its identity or jurisdiction was the worst of crimes. Also, the "given" laws, or the divine source of law and authority, provided the technique for enforcement as well as the norms to be sanctioned. Thus, only moral choices between good and bad were open to anyone, and the world "problem" refers to questions to be dealt with intellectually. Enlightenment inversion of the notion of original sin also endowed the individual in a different way with all necessary knowledge, and also with good will, logically leaving neither a role for authority nor problems for anyone to solve. The position logically implied the anarchist ideal. This, I understand, was the position of Confucius; but I am acutely aware of ignorance of the theory and practice of law in the East—and that is where I think one finds the "true inwardness" of a social order.

Any serious inquiry into the philosophy of the West, from the Greeks to the present, would have to give extended consideration to the theory of knowledge, particularly from the standpoint of intelligent social action. Knowledge should be brought into relation with error and sin (intellectual with moral judgments) and with choice, or "the will"; and these should be considered in relation to aesthetic taste, the third member of the familiar value-triad. Aesthetic criticism is chiefly a creation of the modern West. Beauty is interesting in ways variously connected with social life, but has relatively minor practical importance for problems of community action. Disagreements in this field rarely give rise to serious conflicts. Beauty has not been considered an absolute, as have truth and right, nor in particular as divinely ordained and sanctioned—and the matter of taste hardly enters into the conception of the Deity, whose perfection in knowledge and goodness is so much stressed. The popular view is that of *de gustibus non disputandum,* which has only limited validity in that field, and has some, if less, in the other two. Investigation of values and value theory might well start from the question how far intelligent people ought to agree in their valuations of the several species. It would soon appear that the distinction between facts and values also has limited validity—in both directions: values are facts, in a sense, and any serious question about facts is a question of values— of "evaluating" evidence. The important distinctions are those between different species of value. Again, for special reasons, but very different ones, disagreements in the field of "science" as knowledge of Nature also only exceptionally present serious social problems, in comparison with factual disagreements about man and society, which much more intricately involve value judgments, though all matters of truth are value problems.

What remains for this paper to undertake is a survey of nineteenth-century revisions of the institutions and the underlying and supporting philosophy that came out of the Enlightenment—changes forced by historical events. The theory of liberal society is "individualism," which is generally used as a close synonym for liberalism; and that is proper enough, logically and etymologically, since freedom pertains primarily to an individual mind and will. In fact, the "Anglo-Saxon" tradition in particular has carried repudiation of any "social-mind" concept to an indefensible extreme, for the reality of group will, choice, and action is inherently a part of the notion of a free society. Rousseau is famous for stressing this point, though he failed to work it out and apply it intelligibly to a workable social order. The theory of a society based on mutual agreement (misleadingly called "contract" by Sir H. S. Maine) between individuals began almost at once to break down in Britain, in a way that it seems would have been foreseen, and a reaction set in which has been extending itself ever since. It stands in manifest, not to say absurd, contradiction with unalterable facts of human life. The breakdown began at the most obvious point, in the relations between adults, or adult "society," and young children, where the theory itself is, to repeat the word, simply absurd. And this is more or less the case with some helpless men, and many wretched women; the scandal of women's work in mines, added to that of children in the textile mills, started official reaction with the first British factory-acts. Since that time, the movement has continued and expanded, through more and more political "interference" in the working of the "economic order." That has been the main current of such change as can at all be attributed to deliberate action promoted and directed by thinking on a national scale and with respect to internal policy. Action touching international relations must be ignored here, in spite of its current magnitude and the repercussions on internal policy of war and preparedness for war.

A major result of the liberal revolution, establishing the freedom of culture in its various aspects and of economic life and political democracy, is a revolution in the nature of thinking about social change. Very recently and suddenly, in historical terms, societies have begun to think, with general participation, about their own nature and problems, and consciously to direct action to deal with the latter. Prior to the advent of the idea of progress, such serious thinking about society as was done at all was done by a few individuals, and was chiefly apologetic for the established order of things; it involved little historical explanation, and that of a very naive kind. Anything like modern objective and interpretive history, or especially is a very recent development. The idea of progress stimulated both study of the past in a new way and effort to look to the future with a view to prediction, adaptation, and control. Democratization of government expanded all this to the social scale and made it "responsible." Popular sovereignty virtually created the right to change the laws in any fundamental way, inhering in "the people," practically without limit. The revolution itself, particularly in the second stage, which wrought the major changes, must be attributed in part to thinking and discussion of a sort, along with impersonal culture-historical forces. Even for the Renascence change, one can find, or make, a theory with some validity, rooted in intelligible motives; and, at the Enlightenment stage, "individualism" has quite a simple theory. The difficulty is that in many respects it is out of accord with basic and unalterable facts of life.

The fundamental discrepancy, already suggested, is that individual liberty takes as "given," as making up society, individuals with their actual interests—desires and ideals, and their actual capacities for acting, including internal abilities and "property." The social theory, in short, is mutuality or reciprocity between given individuals. This is largely false to facts and impossible, on two obvious grounds. First, responsible individuals as they are, capable of active participation in social life, are not given; both their wants and their capacities are in concrete content products of the working of social processes. Second, an implication of the same fact, freedom has no meaning for infants, unformed and unendowed, or for other dependents, who make up half, more or less, of the population of a continuing society. Human beings are *not* born either equal or free—unless equal to zero; they have potentialities, which are highly unequal, but have "natural" rights only in the sense that any society does and must grant and secure to its members *some* rights, if it is to continue to exist as a society. (My right to life means only that no one has a right to kill me, unless he has that right!) The real question is, *what* rights, in detail, and how are they to be implemented? One general right required in order to be human is some degree and kind of freedom, together with some opportunity for action; and this must include some control of means, without which freedom is empty—and also some endowment with civilized tastes, implanted through culture contacts and education. Again the question is, *what* freedom, and what power? Both must exceed strict necessity, biological or social, if the future adult is to have a responsible part in the life of a free society, and a reasonable share in the benefits of advancing culture. In a democracy, with "government by discussion" (Lord Bryce's definition), fundamental equality is implied.

Neither freedom nor equality, nor even an effective right to life, comes to people by natural process. They are not found in animal societies, and only to a minimal degree in most human communities known to history. The common situation has been slavery or closely equivalent hereditary status. The American Declaration of Independence, famous for the principles cited, emanated from slaveowners and was issued on behalf of a nation which maintained slavery for nearly a century afterward. This exemplifies the glaring inconsistencies that characterize the political thinking and practice of Western liberalism, making it hard to find any fairly definite and effective working philosophy. Its first pretension is to exclude inheritance of status in favor of equal opportunity for everyone born to find his own position in society. This presupposes an equal start in life, and no detailed analysis is needed to show that both are impossible. But no democracy tries very hard to live up to its professions. The necessity of compromises between ideal freedom-and-equality and other values or needs is aggravated in practice because the revolutionary struggles against tyranny made freedom a "word to conjure with." Its resulting potency for propaganda use has led to other goods and rights being fallaciously defined into the term—especially the right to possess and control economic means, which should be judged on its own merits as a different dimension of the field of voluntary action. In consequence, the meaning of the words "liberal" and "liberalism" has been inverted; they have largely had their original reference to liberty replaced by its opposite, State paternalism. The fallacy is evident: the correct *definition* of freedom is negative—no interference by others with anyone's doing what he wants to do and can do, or could do in the absence of "coercion," which is the term needing definition. "Positive freedom" implies *power*. But the definition does not mean that freedom will give people happiness or well-being, or the rights they "ought" to have and that a society ought to grant or secure. A Crusoe is entirely free, but is not therefore to be judged better off than he might be in a social order subjecting him to many restraints and obligations.

Ranking ahead of freedom and the means to make it effective is *order:* some form of "law" is essential for a human society to exist— though it may reject freedom by establishing a despotism. The latter has in fact been presented as the best possibility in post-medieval Western thought (by Thomas Hobbes, in mid-seventeenth-century Britain). The self-interest of a dictator would make it expedient for him to supply some other values. Every person would inevitably have some freedom, and some control over means—even a slave. A third requisite is some degree of *efficiency,* hence, a workable economic organization. A fourth is personal *security,* which is implied by order; but order and security come into conflict with freedom, and freedom's relation to efficiency is ambiguous—though freedom is empty without these complements. Fifth, as has been stressed, freedom is tied up with *progress.* The sixth essential is *justice,* a human craving that must be met in some form and degree if a society is to persist—especially a free society, which radically changes its nature, from a basis in hereditary status to chosen relations between individuals. In practice, those of economics set the most serious problems, more so than that of dealing with crime. Finally, for intelligent management of its affairs, a free society must consider "culture," in the meaning of a "high" civilization, with progress, aesthetic and "spiritual," and science for the sake of understanding as well as for use as a means.

Manifestly, the problems of a free society, now confronted in the West, can be met only through compromise, not merely between conflicting individual interests but between many "valid values," most of which must imperatively be recognized and implemented, up to some point. A society can be free only in so far as its members can freely agree on courses of action, or on some procedure for indirectly reaching agreement, beyond that produced by subconscious historical forces and "free" discussion. But, the problems and human nature being what they are, ideal discussion presents difficulties; and, worse, thinking has been *ad hoc,* opportunistic, a patchwork of expedients, largely misdirected. People "naturally" tend to deal with symptoms, evading serious diagnosis and a long-run view of consequences. Human nature, as it has evolved through the ages under utterly different conditions, is averse to the effort to solve problems through intellectual cooperation. The recognized need for agreement prompts trying to get others to agree with "me"—hence persuasion, sales talk, rather than real discussion. It tends to run into moralizing, blaming somebody, then into a quarrel and appeal to overt force. Modern liberalism makes the first serious attempt in history to base social order on free choice rather than tradition, and to minimize compulsion—especially in large units. The West (and the world) still fails to realize the difficulties raised by the commitment to freedom and related values.

The method of action, to repeat, is discussion; it is inherently "free and equal," the type for intelligent association. But discussion, regardless of the subject matter, confronts severe limitations, even with "the best will in the world." First of all, it depends on *inter*-communication; but, while one person can (more or less effectively) communicate "to" a large number (with modern aids to any number who will pay attention), one can attend to only one other at a time, and no invention will change that fact. In consequence, discussion must be organized; but that presupposes both law—"rules of order"—and an authority with power to enforce the rules. Moreover, the knowledge, or the possibility of knowing, necessary for intelligent action, is very inadequate.

For group action, the members must *agree* on several items: first, on the ends to be sought, the social ideal envisaged for the future. (This means a *direction* of progress, not a "goal"; there is no "perfection" in human affairs.) Another requisite is agreement on what can and cannot be done. This depends on knowing historical laws of cultural change; but it is hard to know the facts of past history, and far harder to learn from them to distinguish what is inevitable and must be taken as given from what can be changed, still not mentioning the main use, to predict the future. A third necessity is knowledge predicting the consequences of any action considered, the difference it will or would make, in contrast with inaction. This is clearly relative to the "natural" course of future history, which hardly has definite meaning for human beings and especially for large political units. Only a very few "antinomian" anarchists contemplate absence of all politico-legal action by "States," and their picture of social life envisages quite primitive conditions. (When a theoretical anarchist gets a chance at power, he usually strives to become a dictator; Marxism is another example, and its prototype, the historical Western Church, is essentially another.) However, common sense is not wholly in the dark about the effects of such laws as a democracy "can" enact and administer—it has surely been more right than wrong on the whole—and systematic fact-finding and analysis can add to such knowledge. The problem raised is that of the validity of "social science"; this, unfortunately but perhaps inevitably, is split up into several competing disciplines, vaguely defined and at best overlapping in context. Most directly relevant would be criminology and economics, with the other in an auxiliary though necessary role, while as to relevance all are auxiliary to jurisprudence, including "politics," as the master social science. (The possibility of a general science of "man," biological and psychological, or of society—sociology—is a problem too vast to be considered here.)

Criminology is less able than economics to predict the consequences of legislation in their respective fields. As to method, the latter is really two sciences, one abstract-deductive, based on axioms, the other empirical. Both yield solid and useful knowledge, though far less accurate and reliable than the physical sciences. The greater predictability of the results of political-economic action over criminal law is connected with a

different technique of enforcement. A government in power can forcibly deprive individuals of property or income and use the proceeds to
subsidize, or to conduct by its own officials, any activity that it judges
needful and not performed (or not in the best way) by the market machinery. The distinction from punishment is not sharp, and may be
"psychological." Pecuniary fines are used as a penalty for law-breaking,
and the victims, even of a mild prison sentence, have sometimes described the sacrifice as the price paid for an indulgence, and averred that
this was worth the cost.

The hardest knowledge-problem is the one first mentioned, agreement on ends—what institutional change is desirable, considering the
cost. Intelligent social action must not only adjudicate conflicts between
its living members, but must look to the distant future, to the living
children, and beyond, to the well-being of the unborn and the level of
civilization. The problem is "progress," and in particular moral progress, or progressive morality. This is so different from "morals," as a
relation between "given" right and wrong, that a different name is imperative. "Ethics" might serve for this distinction. "Morals," in use as a
close synonym, would be kept for its etymological meaning, conformity
with the *mores,* or customary law, viewed as not subject to change.
Ethics will then cover all the values entering into a "higher" civilization, standing for the best dynamic balance where these clash among
themselves.

The most serious ethical problem actually calling for action is that
of economic or "distributive" justice. It is the most controversial aspect
of the relation between democratic politics and the economic order of
markets and free enterprise—though it cannot be sharply separated
from other aspects of this general problem. As already noted, freedom
involves a radical redefinition of the concept of justice. In pre-liberal
society, its final meaning was conformity to law, jural or moral, taken as
given. (This meaning is embodied in the word, as *jus* means "law.")
Liberalism poses the vastly harder problem of justice "of" the law itself,
implying higher standards—not absolute, but subject to constant revision. Like other rights and duties, economic justice is no longer a matter
of inherited status, but of relations between free individuals, all, in
theory, equal before the law. As we have seen, such equality is impossible, notably as between adults and children. Inherited inequality is
clearly unjust, by individualistic standards, but it can at best be minimized, not abolished. The family and social milieu into which anyone
is born must largely affect the way of life open to him. And, in fact,

democracies do not try as they might to reduce the injustice or provide "deserved" inequality or equality of opportunity.

The main thing to be said, at the end of a long paper, about distributive justice is that the problem is typical in having no possible "solution," other than the "best" compromise among conflicting ideal principles. The first of these is the norm of "productive contribution"—each participant in a social economy to receive what his activity adds to the total output. This result the enterprise economy will achieve, in so far as it works in accord with the theory of "perfect competition." This norm, that each shall receive the consequence of his acts, has moral-ethical validity: "What a man soweth that shall he also reap." Moreover, only limited divergence from it is possible, since only what is produced can be distributed and consumed. The market machinery actually works far from perfectly, and the first set of social problems arises in that connection. But far more serious are the ethical limitations of individualism as such—most obviously as regards the rights of unproductive dependents. A difficulty is presented by "property," especially inherited wealth. Too much has been made of this. There are other ways of accumulating productive capacity, and of passing it on to heirs, and, besides, there is no clear difference in principle between inheriting property and family advantages or contacts—or even genetic traits. The general problem roots in use of power in any form to acquire more power. Thus arise a tendency to cumulative growth of inequality ("To him that hath shall be given") and the unequal start in life that is the outstanding individual injustice. Much has been done to mitigate the evils—most notably through free education of the young, at the cost of the parents judged most able to meet it, and through inheritance taxation. Such action involves applying norms other than the productive contribution of individuals. The most obvious principles are "need," in relation to ability to meet others' needs, and "equality," at least reducing the extreme inequality that "naturally" results under free competition—much distorted as this is by various "machinations," power-seeking, monopoly, and "luck," or things beyond individual control. All three principles have to be taken into account, thus limiting any one; and there is no formula except good judgment for the best balance, or for the best way to achieve it.

To conclude, I add some notes on the alternative to free association, particularly in markets—which is "politics." Government is the agency by which a democracy acts as a unit and takes responsibility for its destiny. The "first commandment" for intelligent action is, "Compare the

alternatives," beginning with understanding what they are. Much unnecessary evil comes from the disinclination of people to do that, particularly in this case. They commonly prefer subjective snap-judgments,
rooted in self-interest, or some "romantic" prejudice—rather typically
blaming uncritically the economic system and looking naively to "the
government" to correct any alleged wrong. Objective comparison would
show that the two organizations are much alike in basic respects—politics is much more irrationally motivated by competitive persuasion—
while in others one or the other can do things or yield advantages the
other cannot. Human nature being at all as it is, a primary objective
must be to minimize the scope of necessary agreement. That obviously
means two things: first, dismissing uniform belief about supernatural
reality, and all compulsory dealings with supernatural powers; and, second, in matters economic, maximum reliance on the free market, except
where political methods will *clearly* yield better results. The market
order has the supreme merit of freedom. It provides for voluntary cooperation of individuals in using what means they have to achieve their
freely chosen ends, without agreeing on ends or methods, and with
"boundless" increase in effectiveness. In a competitive market, no party
has arbitrary power over another, since each may choose between equally
good opportunities by dealing with the "other" who offers any better
terms. Accordingly, it is a first task of society—not an easy one—to
enforce by law and government a close approximation to effective competition. An exchange *is* an exchange, and is advantageous to both parties if they are competent to manage their own affairs. Only this system
can provide freedom of choice to both producers and consumers. For
reasons already suggested, by itself it falls far short of meeting even
social necessities, still more of ideal justice; but further development
would call for a treatise on elementary economics, which cannot be
thought of here.

On the other hand, the most democratic government cannot afford
comparable freedom. At the utmost, some majority dictates to minorities, and in political reality to express and enforce a majority opinion is
often impossible. For freedom, there must be a presumption of voluntary association—in particular, the free market. However, many necessary things can be done only by society as a unit, and others political
action can do better. One necessity is suppression of organization for
power in contrast with efficiency. Beyond what has been said, further
elaboration is impossible. The only general prescription is intelligent
comparison of agencies on particular issues and adoption of the best

method in each case. More of such effort would do good, especially in stopping much palpably stupid action.

Two important generalizations are very inadequately understood by the public. The first is that a free society under modern conditions is largely a tissue of *agency* relations. In particular, the personnel of government are the agents of the public in all matters delegated to them, and the "management" of business enterprises are the agents at once of the consumers and the final producers, those who supply the labor and property services employed in the operations. The problem is to find the best method of choosing agents and holding them responsible to their principals. In both business and politics, the method is competition; the difference lies between centralized decisions under rules hard to change and decentralization with flexibility. In both fields, the agency structure is required for effective management of the large and complex units needed to apply modern technology or to deal with its problems. But the agency relation prevails widely, is nearly universal, in consequence of the specialization of knowledge required for its growth. An illustration, where no organization in the usual meaning is present, is the relation between a patient and his doctor. The latter is the agent, but, while the relation persists, he has *power* over his principal—in this case, power of life and death—and every agent has more or less discretionary power. The only freedom possible to the patient is that of choosing his doctor, and changing doctors at will; but—the second generalization— this choice cannot be made very intelligently. The patient would have to know extant medical science—annulling most of his need for the service—and also know both the technical and the moral qualifications of the available candidates.

All these conditions apply to the employer-employee situation, and that of the consumer to the enterprise, and also, though not in quite the same sense, to the citizen and his representatives in the government. Everywhere, the freedom possible to the common man is that of selecting an agent who will be his "boss" to a greater or less extent, over a longer or shorter period. Competition governs the selection, even in the case of the doctor, and fixes the delegated powers and the payment to be made. What needs to be understood is the severe restriction this ubiquitous agency-relation places on rational freedom in general—for similar considerations apply to the basic freedom, that of knowledge or belief. Most of what anyone knows, or thinks, if not an accident of tradition, is taken from some chosen authority. Thus, most serious questions place the free man in the paradoxical position of having to judge between others he recognizes as more competent on the issue than he is. But this limitation is the condition of having the residual freedom that is possible, with the vast progress in most fields of endeavor that has been seen to follow its establishment.

Notes

1. It is suggested that Part 1 of this paper (the first half) be regarded as "background" and only Part 2 as matter for discussion.

15

Laissez-Faire: Pro and Con

My title might have been "Laissez-Faire in Some Recent Discussion—Political but Especially Literary-Academic," as will soon appear.[1] My interest in economics, as I need hardly say here, has been that of a teacher, especially of its general principles. What should be taught in schools, and how? And, especially, What is the role of general principles, and what are their limitations? I cannot say much about principles themselves but must stress that the most important are things everyone knows, that are self-evident. However, that does not make it easy to teach things—for reasons that would need long discussion. I have repeatedly said that the way to sounder economic thought and action calls less for "research" or discovery than for more common sense instead of nonsense. My reflections on education recall James H. Robinson's remark in a lecture on the subject that "reflections" is an ambiguous term—and I mean here partly aspersions. One of my favorite quotations is Josh Billings' saying that "it's not ignorance that does most damage, but knowin' so derned much that ain't so," that is, prejudice.

Laissez-faire of course simply means freedom, in the particular case of economic policy: freedom of economic conduct from dictation by government. Our society professes freedom as its basic ideal, yet *laissez-faire* has of late become almost a dirty word, and the situation needs investigating. Of course governmental action, if effective, limits freedom, and few of us are anarchists. It should not be necessary to argue either for or against *laissez-faire* in principle; the issue lies in the amount

Reprinted with permission from the *Journal of Political Economy* 75 (December 1967): 782–95.

of freedom, or of control, and the kinds, which depend on circumstances.

Political control versus *laissez-faire*—letting events take their natural course—is for analysis the first question on policy, but it is realistic
only as raised by the need to decide concrete issues of action. My interest
is in economics as a science, but as one useful for guiding conduct; and
the action in question is social, which means political. I must stress that
the science itself deals with individual conduct, but in society and as
preliminary to that of politics. I speak of "conduct," not "behavior," to
stress that it is purposive and in the distinctive sense of direction toward
an end to be achieved by efficient use of means. But it is an *intended* end,
and of course should be "good"; but a science *describes,* leaving judgment
of ends to the disciplines dealing with values, chiefly ethics and aesthetics. Economic science is *instrumental;* the ends are taken as "given"—
and so are the means, to the acting subject, when he makes any choice.
Being "scarce," they must be economized, selecting ends in their order
of importance and using the best available technology. That, too, is
treated by other disciplines: engineering, and others.

Economics is descriptive in a sense; but ends are not known, either
to the chooser or to others, by sense-observation; so it is not "empirical"
in the meaning of sciences of nature. And the same is partly true of the
means, as far as they are personal capacities. Economic knowledge
comes partly by inference from observed behavior but chiefly through
mental intercommunication, and so is very imperfect. Knowledge of
nature also depends on intercommunication, for verification by comparing reports of different observers in that field is essential; that subject,
however, belongs to philosophy, the theory of knowledge. Still less does
vision or touch tell whether ends are good, especially because men have
other purposes than the economic, which is maximum satisfaction of
wants through efficient use of available means, internal and external: for
example, play and aesthetic enjoyment. And we note that if wants are
bad, efficiency is harmful—a vital consideration for freedom and policy.

Again "reflecting" on education—meaning schooling—during a
lifetime of working at the trade and considering its results, one thing
has disturbed me more and more. Schools can teach information and
many skills, but they do not seem to be successful in developing good
judgment. They can even teach *logic,* but I like Charles Kettering's definition of that as an organized way of going wrong with confidence—
and especially, he should have added, of misleading others. Men's errors
mostly lie in their premises, not in bad logic; one can prove nearly any-

thing from plausible premises merely by treating half-truths as the truth, and that is commonly done in political discussion, as I shall show. Students seem to acquire skill in forming and promoting such arguments (the familiar figure is throwing out the baby with the bath water). The main vice is absolutism: holding that a statement must be either true or false and that, if false, the antithesis must be true. A case often brought to mind is Marxism, with its false premise of two social classes at war, and the inevitable victory of the "proletariat." This is misnamed as a materialistic interpretation of history and the result as "communism" and "people's democracy"; both are mere embezzlement of language. The Russian system is anti-democratic, negates freedom, and is farther from communism than that of the United States, falsely contrasted as capitalism. It is capitalistic, but so is Russia and any economy using human artifacts. In control are not capitalists but entrepreneurs and, finally, consumers. Marxist economics is a tissue of absurdity, but, sad to say, much nonsense has also been published by advocates of *laissez-faire,* as I shall go on to show.

Laissez-faire, that is, economic freedom, if taken in anything like an absolute sense, means anarchism and is indefensible; yet significantly, bright and idealistic people have advocated it, even under that name. That its opposite, dictatorship, is odious should not need arguing in a society claiming to be conceived in liberty. (And dedicated to equality, according to Jefferson and Lincoln; more must be said about that.) But both extremes are in fact impossible, and it is absurd to argue for either *laissez-faire* or "planning" against the other as a general principle. On the one hand, man is a social animal—willy-nilly—and social life sets many limits to freedom. On the other, even Stalin's Russian dictatorship allowed much freedom, especially economic, to the common man. The organization was based on markets and prices, like our own; the consumer got a money income and chose among purchases at set prices; the worker could choose among occupations at set wages and on other fixed terms, and some property ownership and accumulation at interest, and some bequests were allowed. But it was far from a free system in our meaning of the word.

The issue between *laissez-faire* and government control could not arise outside of an economic and a political order related in a way that makes sense under modern conditions. (It could arise, in theory, for the rulers, under an unfree government; but we need consider only free enterprise and a democratic state, which presuppose cultural freedom also.) All these concepts are of recent historical birth. In the sweep of human history we find little personal freedom until the past few centuries, and no democracy in the meaning fitting a modern nation-state. A sketch of the history, to show how it all came about, might begin with the Middle Ages, in western Europe, with attention centered first on England, or Great Britain.[2] Medieval society was essentially primitive, tradition-bound, under laws held divinely ordained and hence immutable, since God does not change his mind. The masses were subject to a feudal nobility, and the legal order was topped by a church that claimed divine authority to loose and unloose on earth and in Heaven; but it pretended not to make laws, only to apply laws divinely given. It dispensed forgiveness of sin, and salvation from eternal fire, after burning alive on earth as punishment for disobedience in belief or conduct. Any claim to freedom was heresy.

In the modernizing movement, two rough stages may be distinguished. By the Renascence period, feudal power was concentrated into monarchies, with sovereigns claiming to rule by divine right. Conflict with the church was inevitable and arose as the monarchs began to enact some laws by decree. At this period, modern science was born, beginning with the new astronomy of Copernicus and Galileo, followed by Newton. Despite the church, it spread to other fields—medicine and mechanics—and became the basis of modern technology. The Crusades had led to a rediscovery of ancient learning and to growth of commerce. The monarchies had to encourage these individualistic activities because they needed the new wealth they yielded, as "sinews of war." The clash produced the Protestant Revolt, and Wars of Religion—the real start toward freedom, though the monarchs did not mean to be more liberal than the church or its popes had been.

The crucial social change of the period was a partial secularization of politics—especially the desanctification of law—allowing it to be changed. Full freedom to legislate, crucial for a free society, came later, with democracy, at a second stage, which transferred sovereignty to the people. This stage reached a climax in the late-eighteenth-century Enlightenment, marked by the American and French Revolutions. The growing power of wealth had forced the sovereigns to incorporate "commoners" into their councils, along with the nobility and clergy, forming parliaments, notably in Britain. There the Reformation took a special course, and the revolutions of the seventeenth century, with the victory of Parliament over Stuart absolutism, was a step toward liberalism. Abolition of monopolies based on royal grant and replacement of feudal dues by national taxation, controlled by Parliament, were important. And there was some movement toward religious toleration, freeing the mind for thought and expression, which is basic for all other freedoms. French "excesses" caused some reaction of feeling in Britain; the new American republic fell short of full democracy with equal manhood suffrage, and the country had still to get rid of slavery. In France and on the Continent, the revolution was followed by the Napoleonic despotism, the Council of Vienna, and a generation of repression. But in the West, formal political equality made progress during the nineteenth century and was completed with woman suffrage after World War I (except for Switzerland).

The whole movement from, say, the twelfth century to the early twentieth constitutes, I contend, the greatest cultural revolution known to history. It is comparable to the "fall" of classical civilization with commission to the mystery religions, ending in establishment of medieval "Christianity." It effected a "transvaluation of all values," replacing the general ideal of conformity and obedience with that of freedom and progress—freedom for progress and progress through freedom.[3] The phrase implies the dynamic of intelligent action, *not* "inevitable" historical progress—apart from Herbert Spencer's later naive interpretation of "evolution," which was brilliantly opposed by T. H. Huxley, the great popularizer of Darwinism.[4]

In this paper I cannot discuss progress in history, which would call for an impossible digression on historical causality and social ethics. At the moment, I merely note that the intelligent action called for is both individual and collective, and that the *laissez-faire* principle assumed individual intelligence at an impossible level, and if taken rigorously would restrict social action to the policing of freedom. This was and is commonly taken to mean "individual" freedom, an absurdity which will presently be spelled out.

The phrase *laissez-faire* is of course French; it arose in the eighteenth century, before the revolution, in connection with foreign trade, which the king wished to control in the supposed national interest. At this time, the new "science" called "political economy" was growing up, chiefly in Britain. It was effectively founded by Adam Smith, with his book *The Wealth of Nations*, published in 1776 (nearly coinciding with the American Declaration of Independence, the great manifesto for political liberty, as Smith's book was for economic). The expression was not used by Smith or his early followers, but their writings were essentially propaganda for the doctrine in domestic economic relations as well as foreign.[5] As to foreign trade, all "good" economists since Smith have favored free trade, that is, *laissez-faire,* against "protectionism." But the public and its chosen political spokesmen have not—and do not. And this illustrates one main thesis of this paper, that people very often rank prejudice as truth over unquestioned fact and the simplest logic. Of course, taxing imports reduces exports, unless these are given away; and the effect is simply to curtail specialization where it is of the greatest advantage, between distant regions with different resources and skills. The French writer Bastiat neatly disposed of the economic issue in his mock petition of the lamp makers for prohibition of windows because their business was crippled by competition of the cheap foreign light from the sun. (There may be political or cultural reasons for regulation, exactly as with domestic trade.) Protectionists, indeed, are not absolutists—but why not? If the principle is sound at all, all trade should be stopped, making everyone economically self-sufficient. Exchange of product *A* for *B* is a method of producing *B,* and managers have the same incentive as in any other case to choose the more efficient process. Similar reasoning condemns most price fixing; our farm program obviously creates surpluses, or forces arbitrary restriction of production, and soon becomes a handout to landlords, not farmers. Nor can wages be raised above the free-market level without causing unemployment, lowering other wages—hurting the weakest; it requires support by relief and retards economic growth. Strangely, again, wage demands are limited—but then men's practices are commonly less stupid than their arguments—a point for educators.

Smith does immediately follow his "obvious and simple system" statement with three general qualifications (loc. cit.), three and only three tasks for the sovereign. They are *(a)* defense against foreign powers, *(b)* establishment of an exact system of justice to prevent members from oppressing others, and *(c)* maintenance of certain public works and institutions. Defense is, of course, a euphemism, and justice must be defined. Smith's long discussion of public works contains important points, particularly on education, where he stood for a bare minimum of local public action. That cannot be taken up here. Nor is it possible to follow the official extension of the *laissez-faire* policy to the extreme advocated by Smith and his successors. In foreign relations, this was completed after the repeal of the corn laws in 1846. Meanwhile it had been carried to extremes domestically, and intolerable conditions provoked a reaction toward government control that has been growing ever since. It began with "factory-acts" to protect children and helpless women, where its application was never defensible.

Apart from advocating *laissez-faire,* the writings of the early economists contain much irrelevance and even nonsense: for instance, Smith's statement that monopoly price is "the highest which can be got . . . squeezed out of buyers," which Ricardo repeats and at once adds two more "howlers" of his own. Use value was rejected as the cause of exchange value by ignoring that men buy water and diamonds by increments and not all-or-none. It took the best minds a century to discover that wants are progressively satiable—and many writers still see only relative weakening, which is plainly "absolute" for any one good— other things being equal. And the diminishing utility of money income is still questioned, in defiance of common sense.

In eighteenth-century Britain there was some excuse for preaching *laissez-faire* and—one might urge—leaving necessary qualifications to be worked out in the light of later developments. This is not the case today, but such preaching has currently been revived at the literary and academic level. In these circles the limitations now call for emphasis, while for "the public" it is still urgent to stress economic freedom and especially to oppose the vast amount of stupid governmental action— notably forcing higher wages, directly or by encouraging monopolistic labor unions (while opposing business monopolies, which do much less harm and are often unreal or inevitable, or in fact beneficial). In the "literary" field, the special reference is to two books, which were the chief impetus to the writing of the present paper. Some notice of these will be a good introduction to the main problem, especially the limitations of *laissez-faire* theory and policy. The first of the two books, by date, is F. A. von Hayek's *Constitution of Liberty;* the second, Henry Hazlitt's *Foundations of Morality.* The latter is more "extremist," but I have reviewed it at length (1966), and I shall here give more attention to Hayek's argument—without pretending to "review" the book. Both books state strong and, in principle, largely sound debating arguments for freedom.

First, a note on Hazlitt's position, the more extreme. Both stress the necessity of a framework of law for the free economy. (Hazlitt says "good" law and a "high" standard of morals, p. 307.) Both are weak— Hazlitt more so—on the content of needed law, and say nothing or little about social procedure for getting proper laws. Hazlitt excludes legislation, leaving changes to spontaneous historical growth (p. 64), and Hayek tends to the same conclusion (see especially p. 198), but is not consistent. On content, Hazlitt quotes Hayek (p. 67) for limiting state coercion to enforcement of "known" law. Hayek equally stresses *generality* and says that laws should be known in the sense that decisions are predictable, the judge having no choice in making them (p. 153). One may ask why any case would ever be brought to trial! Hazlitt says that society is "nothing but . . . combination for cooperative effort" (pp. 35, 309), which is the "essence of morality" (p. 359). He illustrates by a card game (pp. 307 ff.), where the end of the players is victory, hence opposed; no production of a useful result is in question, and would destroy the spirit of play. On the economic order, he says, "The system of capitalism, of the market economy, is a system of freedom, of justice, of productivity . . . infinitely superior to its coercive alternatives" (p. 324). The absurd assumption that men left free will do nothing but, or nothing opposed to, economic cooperation through exchange in markets will excuse omitting further discussion of this book. The importance of the half-truth in both men's arguments will be stressed later.

Turning to Hayek's book, it merits credit as an imposing work of historical scholarship,[6] which this writer lacks the learning to criticize in detail. Over four hundred large and packed pages are followed by 110 of notes in small print, and an index of names listing over eight hundred authors quoted, some twenty times or more. (A pretentiously elaborate subject index is disappointing in use.) However, my first criticism has to do with history. The treatment of the beginning of personal freedom is in a chapter (chap. 11) entitled "The Origins of the Rule of Law," and for the author this concept virtually defines liberty. The first sentence defensibly locates the beginning in seventeenth-century England (p. 162), focusing on the struggle for judicial independence— from the crown!—(p. 171), with incidental notice of Parliament and legislation. "In the dispute about authority to legislate, in which contending parties (not named) reproached each other for acting arbitrarily, i.e., not in accordance with recognized general laws (assumed to exist), individual freedom was *inadvertently* advanced" (p. 163, italics added). Since freedom is to mean the rule of law, not of men (p. 166 on Aristotle versus Hobbes), it means freedom from government, in contrast with free government. It is defined as "the opposite of coercion" (p. 133), surely meaning absence of the latter. Like justice these are relations between persons (p. 99), and coercion "occurs when one man's actions are made to serve another man's will, not for his own but for the other's purposes" (p. 133). (Can no one be coerced for his own good?) The Middle Ages are mildly extolled for "more liberty than is now commonly believed" (p. 160—retracted as to personal liberty in the next sentence). It was of course the power of *the crown* to legislate that was threatened by the opposition to absolute monarchy, until *Parliament* established legislative supremacy in the Civil War and the revolution of 1688. Supremacy over the executive followed naturally and *for democracy* over the judiciary also.

Hayek does not mention the crucial events that led to or constituted the Liberal Revolution, establishing free society, that is, democracy in the broad meaning, especially a political order minimizing compulsory law as well as exercise of arbitrary power, and restricting the latter to acts by lawful agents of society, approved or accepted by public opinion. Surely the crux of political democracy was and is vesting of sovereign power in "the people," to be exercised through enforcing and making laws by representatives; these are chosen freely—as freely as possible— by majority vote (sometimes plurality) where public opinion (or will) is seriously divided. It is "rule of law" indeed, but where direct force of public attitudes does not suffice, by men authorized to interpret and enforce existing formal law *and moral tradition,* making legislation necessary. The law-makers are chosen through free discussion and voting, and so held "responsible to public opinion," in the only possible way. The true maxim was well stated in William Penn's "Frame of Government" for Pennsylvania: "A government is free to the people under it (whatever be the frame) where the laws rule *and the people are a party* to the laws."[7]

The reason why Hayek in his pretentiously detailed history does not mention such crucial matters as church power, the "Reformation," and religious tolerance leading to the primary freedom, that of the mind for thought and expression—and especially the growth of representative government—is clear to any attentive reader. He is scornful of politically organized freedom. His book is organized around the thesis that there have been and are "two different traditions in the theory of liberty: one empirical and unsystematic, the other speculative and rationalistic—the first based on traditions and institutions which had spontaneously grown up and were imperfectly understood, the second aiming at the construction of an utopia, which has often been tried but never successfully" (p. 54). This is a calumny on democracy, and most of the famous utopias were based frankly on autocracy—a few on the naive (anarchistic) assumption that men would spontaneously agree on all political and social issues. Hayek's own main general pronouncements are anarchistic in the proper meaning—that is, excluding "rulers" and ostensibly "limiting" legislation (p. 205) but logically excluding it.

One should, however, compare his treatment of democracy (especially chap. 7 on majority rule); this makes many concessions to the merits but is mainly a "tirade" on the fallibility of majorities and their lack of moral right to make political decisions. "We have no ground for crediting [them] with the super-individual wisdom which . . . the products of spontaneous growth may possess." Both "may" of course be wise or unwise. "That whatever government does should be agreed to by the majority does not [make it] morally entitled to do what it likes; and for those who use 'liberty' in the sense of political liberty . . . the ideal can say nothing about what the aim . . . ought to be" (p. 104). This logically excludes even the aim of preserving liberty and implies that the government should do nothing unless, as already stated, to enforce laws perfectly and universally known (which would hardly need enforcement). "There can clearly be no moral justification for any majority granting its members privileges by laying down rules which discriminate in their favor" (p. 107). Perhaps this has happened in some degree; voters follow their interests "too much," rather than objective judgments of abstract right; but they would need super-human judgment never to do so, and a law which has any effect "discriminates," benefitting some and injuring others. However, it is hard to be consistently absurd, and as suggested before, Hayek in some chapters opens the door to much that humane liberals, common-sense "pragmatists" and even popular clamor would have government do. (See especially chap. 15, "Economic Policy and the Rule of Law," and chap. 19, "Social Security.")

A matter on which our author is notably absurd is his treatment of equality (chiefly in chap. 3, "Common Sense of Progress," chap. 6, "Equality, Value, and Merit," and chap. 20, "Taxation and Redistribution"). His position is clear from two statements: "Equality of the general rules of law and conduct is the only equality which we can secure without destroying liberty" (p. 85). Objection to the use of coercion, to bring about a more even or a more just distribution does not mean that one does not regard these as desirable, but "the desirability of a particular object is not sufficient justification for the use of coercion" (p. 87). The error is in the extremism, absolutism—as with most impossible generalizations that literate and earnest people state for propaganda ends. To begin with, even equality before the law is impossible, and so is any close approach to it where people are very unequal economically. Then, the very concept of economic equality is absurd in many respects; it has not been seriously advocated; and this cannot be done intelligently. Equalizing money income among "individuals" (if that can be imagined) would not make them equal economically and would mean gross inequality among families. (Only about half the population of the United States receives incomes, and those of quite wealthy persons or families may be zero or negative for any year or other interval.)

The supreme absurdity in Hayek's book is reached in his discussion of opportunity and particularly equality of opportunity (especially pp. 90 ff.). True, it was absurd of Commons and Dewey to spread an ideology that identified freedom with power (if they did); but it is also absurd for Hayek to ignore the close connection between the two. Freedom, correctly conceived, *implies* opportunity, unobstructed opportunity, to use power, which must be possessed, to give content to freedom, or make it effective. It is a common fallacy to demand power under the name of freedom, and usage boldly needs the expression "effective freedom" to take account of power and of knowledge and other dimensions in the scope of voluntary action.[8] The social problem of freedom centers in power and its use in relations among persons and between them and society or its agents. The definition of freedom formally as the opposite (or absence?) of coercion, including fraud (p. 149), does not mention persuasion—a highly important form of power over others that is very unequal and is recognized in law as "duress." Nor does Hayek recognize that unequal power over things confers power over persons, or that the main general problem of freedom is unequal power, practically covering significant human inequality; nor, again, that freedom and power pertain to *free* beings, that mechanisms neither coerce nor are coerced. Determinists confuse the ability to choose with ability to do or get what one chooses. Hayek accuses others of inconsistency in using the concept of influence to prove that the will is not free. It does limit freedom, as he recognizes (pp. 74, 76), but denies the reality of a self and apparently of "will" (p. 439, n. 7). But he readmits them under the name of personality; his argument against denying causality has never been in dispute, but causality does not negate all freedom. Absolute freedom or unfreedom is inconceivable. Appeal to facts and logic need not be coercive—though any form of influence may be used for the user's ends, good or bad, or those of the subject, or for other good or bad ends.[9]

Hayek's treatment of inequality is also a flagrant example of false generalizing. Again, no one—"in his right mind"—denies that great inequality is inevitable, in many forms, or that many of its implications are good. He defends property inheritance—also never denied within limits. But it is mere dogma to assert that "bequest of a fortune is so-cially by far the cheapest" of ways in which parents may give their children special advantages (p. 9). As if all the other ways were not already used along with it. Obviously, in exchange and other formally free relations, great inequality of power which is the only issue, whatever the form—gives the stronger party some control over the weaker and may mean his helplessness. But for Hayek, even that does not prove coercion. He does not note that inequality tends to grow, especially economic; for one who at a moment possesses more wealth is in a better position to acquire still more. And free inheritance continues the tendency over generations. The facts have forced preventive or offsetting social action on a vast scale. The tendency is *not* disproved, as has sometimes been alleged, by the modern rough statistical constancy of the ratios between larger and smaller incomes. If all have grown at about the same rate, the differences grow at that rate, and it is differences not ratios that are felt, since they determine what the richer families can do and the poorer cannot.[10]

Monopoly power, we read (p. 137) is not coercive unless it means strict control over a necessity of life, and then only if it is used to compel or prevent some particular act. The treatment violates even Hayek's indorsement of state power to enforce known and general laws. For anti-monopoly is deeply imbedded in modern law, jural and moral; the issue lies only in methods of dealing with it. The condemnation is often ignorant, or stupid, or prejudiced, greatly exaggerating both the amount and the evil; much monopoly is inevitable, and much is good. This fact should be noted as a ground for less action and more discriminating treatment.[11]

The *laissez-faire* postulate is correct for economic analysis, but its purpose and the conditions assumed should be made clear. In "methodology" there is an analogy between price-theory economics and the analytical mechanics of Galileo and Newton. (Relativity and quantum theory raise new issues.) The great difference is that motives—the analogue of forces—cannot be measured, or their laws approximately verified by experiment. (But forces in physics are not observed; they are "metaphysical," and their laws are empirically as unrealistic as the utility principle.)[12]

It is rather in another context, dealing with equality and inequality, that Hayek reaches the peak of fallacy. Only a few points can be sketchily noted here. His main treatment is found in two chapters: chap-

ter 6, "Equality, Value and Merit," and chapter 20, "Taxation and Redistribution." In the former, we read that "equality of general rules of
law is the only equality . . . we can secure without destroying liberty"
(p. 85), a typical absolutizing of a half truth. Of course social action does
reduce freedom, but only killing people can destroy it. The variety of
human nature is used to argue against equality (pp. 86–87) interpreted
as "strictly egalitarian demands," a meaningless expression, as already
noted. "A more even or just distribution" is admitted to be desirable, but
desirability "is not sufficient justification for the use of coercion" (p. 87).
In particular, acceptance of the family as an institution is made to defend all inequalities in education that result from allowing parents absolute authority (pp. 89–90), regardless of means or inclinations. The
opposed conception is said to be that the government should assure to
all an equal start and the same prospects, instead of providing the same
circumstances for all and allowing all to try (p. 92, somewhat rear-
ranged); any objection to inequality is said to countenance envy, "cam-
ouflaged as social justice." In some cases, to be sure, there is the cred-
itable motive of making differences in reward correspond to moral
merit, but this is an indefensible contention (p. 93), of course, if taken in
an absolute sense; but it is equally indefensible that a society can completely ignore merit. However, as noted before, Hayek's chapter 19, "Social Security," also contains statements interpretable as largely opening
the gates to much action contrary to his general principles. Notably, on
pages 300–301, he expressly takes for granted "public relief which provides a uniform minimum for all instances of proved need" obviating
all "want of food or shelter"—proved by a means test (p. 303). Objection
to this is "wholly irrational." Elsewhere, as at the beginning of the chapter, relief is restricted to "circumstances beyond [the person's] control,"
allowing for insurance, for which there is "perhaps" a case for compulsion (p. 298). But insurance is a "misnomer" unless each pays for what
he gets, that is, according to the "risk." My dictionaries indicate no such
restriction on the word, but it is impossible under private enterprise—
which "insures" that those who need insurance most cannot get it
(surely a convincing case for public action).

   Chapter 20 is an essentially silly "tirade" against progressive taxation, or any use of taxation to "redistribute" incomes, considering all
taxes (p. 397); but nothing is said about the definition of income (except
for the absurd statement that a majority of people consider it as "the
only legitimate and socially desirable form of reward" [p. 318]). The

contention is for proportionality, that is, taxes to take an equal fraction of all incomes. This, we read, is the form of equality on which all tax-payers are likely to agree (pp. 314, 315). But they never have; and a near approach to the policy is impossible to absurdity. The particular taxes directly levied on income have sometimes been proportional to account-ancy income after "exemptions," which are not mentioned here. "Agree-ment" means anything from complete ignorance to "volunteering" (very rare for donating to government), or abstaining from insurrection. It does not imply closely following rules professedly, formally, or passively accepted. It is usually wise not to ask what people really agree on— even two parties in conversation—or disagree on, when disputing. The argument that equal sacrifice is more reasonable than equal rates of taxation is met by a sophistical rejection of utility analysis in general, especially the diminishing utility of income. Denying the possibility of comparing utilities between persons is indeed something of a fad among theorists who stress "Occam's razor" and logically reject all motives, or treat them as forces known as a measurable physical response. That clearly eliminates the idea of economizing itself. Of course (as noted before) utilities (and other motives) cannot be measured; no one thinks they are measured by prices. But the notion that a given increment of monetary income is no more important to a poor man than to a rich one is simply absurd; it is for the proverbial birds. Hayek also holds it to be an illusion that progression shifts the burden "substantially" (!) from those with low incomes to the more wealthy (p. 311). This is defensible for the very highest bracket in the bulk of actual income-tax payers, but Hayek goes on with the dogma that the policy makes "the masses" ac-cept a much heavier burden than they otherwise would, and says that "its only major result has been severe limitation of the incomes that could be earned [*sic; obtained?*] by the most successful and thereby grati-fication of the envy of the less well off" (p. 311). It seems that all human sense of right and wrong—the latter more real—is also "illusion." Hayek expressly repudiates "social justice," (in the book, see the index, and elsewhere, noted above). For him, justice is still defined, once and for all, by laws, and those are produced by spontaneous historical growth, not "made" by either men or God.

I have tried to show that, on the contrary, the concept of free society held in the modern West is rooted in the right of the people to change the laws. It is primarily on that right that there is agreement; for free-dom or peace, they must somehow agree on changes to be made. That is where the problems lie, and they are hard. This view arose with the transfer of sovereignty to them from divine-right monarchs who at the Renaissance had seized supreme power from the church. This, as noted above, had claimed at once unlimited right to make law and that it only administered law which was divine and immutable. Hayek makes much the latter claim for "the state," without the divinity, but allowing change by spontaneous "drift," in the manner of language. No ground for state power is given, and about its nature we are told only that when on exception it must act positively, this should be done "democratically" by agreement of the majority. And we find bare mention of a "hierarchy of government" (p. 212) permeated by a relation between principal and agent. In its one rightful coercive role—enforcing known and general laws—it means judges, with nothing said about their selection or tenure, which of course fixes their real responsibility. We learn only what ought to be—according to Professor Hayek's ideals and wishful thinking.

I must bring this paper to an end without, as I should like, going on somewhat more constructively. It must be understood that I have no wish to "pick on" Professor Hayek or Mr. Hazlitt, or to deal harshly with the founding fathers of economics. Of course I have selected statements which illustrate my main point, stated at the outset. It is that the main fault in economic opinions and public action is too much "nonsense"; and hence the main and easy road toward more truth is common sense, and silence or inaction where no positive doctrine or course can be shown to be "better." The problem is not *laissez-faire* versus political planning and control in general, but comparison of the result of market freedom with that of possible action by democratic procedure on specific problems. The citizen must understand the general principles of the two systems but *not* draw practical conclusions from an abstract analysis of either. The basic principles are facts about human nature; and the major difficulty is that this is a tissue of paradox. Most generalizations about it are true—more or less—and also false, since conflicting statements are similarly true.

Men are and ought to be free; but even that statement should not be made as "the" truth. Exchange is free by definition, but unlimited market freedom would have "intolerable" consequence, as is shown both by general reasoning and by historical experience. Ideal enterprise and democracy both imply cooperation, but with human nature and conditions as they are, not at all necessarily fair cooperation or to the general advantage, individual or social. The major fact omitted in individualistic analysis is simply "competition." Rivalry has no place in the general theory of economics, but is in fact a major motive in both fields because it is a major fact in human nature. Man is a contentious being, antisocial as well as social. When people are most free, they *play,* usually in a contest of some kind, in which the individual end is victory, not the production of a useful result. Here, what one gains, the other must lose—the opposite of intelligent exchange, though commonly asserted of market relations (as by many great writers in the past). But rivalry is much more prominent as a motive in democratic politics than in economic activity. Even judicial process so much exalted by Hayek in particular, is in reality largely a contest between advocates more interested in winning the case than in legal or moral justice, let alone social well-being. Men are most disposed to cooperate in organizations for more effective competition—most of all, sad to say, in *war*—where they are most social-minded. The most one can say for freedom is that there is a presumption in its favor unless there is sufficient ground for believe that coercive action will yield a better result in a particular situation. But the antisocial side of human nature must be taken into account in any serious and intelligent discussion of economic policy.

Notes

1. This paper has been somewhat revised from a draft prepared as a talk to a student-faculty seminar at the University of Chicago; it was also presented on two other university campuses.

2. Ancient Athens gave us the word "democracy" but not with a meaning similar to ours. It was a tiny city state with a social order based on slavery and subjection of women. It was not governed by chosen representatives, and the moral code permitted infanticide and other practices now abhorrent. And its independence was short-lived.

3. I go back to the twelfth century because there was something of a "break" in the thirteenth, a partial "renaissance" connected with the translation of Aristotle's main works into Latin and his replacement of Platonism in the official philosophy of the church (led by Thomas Aquinas). But the peak of church power also came in this century, followed by "schism" of the papacy, the great councils, and so on.

4. In Thomas Huxley's Romanes lecture of 1894 on "Evolution and Ethics"; it was published with the addition of more pages of Prolegomena and footnotes in his *Essays,* vol. 9.

5. The history of the phrase in English has been written, especially by D. H. MacGregor (*Economic Thought and Policy,* 1949, chap. 3); it is supplemented by Edward R. Kittrell in an article in the *Journal of the History of Ideas* (1966).

Smith and the others did not argue for freedom in terms of economic principles—maximum want-satisfaction, and so on. That was to begin a century or so later. Smith, after criticizing other systems, essentially treated as self-evident "the obvious and simple system of natural liberty" (*The Wealth of Nations,* Modern Library edition, p. 651). As to the end, he was ambiguous. On page 352, he said, "The great object of the political economy of every country is to increase [its] wealth and power." But on page 625, "Consumption is the sole end and purpose of all production"; and on page 397 we find there are "two distinct objects: first to provide a plentiful revenue or subsistence for the people, or more properly to enable them to provide [this] for themselves; and second, to supply the state or commonwealth with a revenue sufficient for the public services."

6. Hayek, on close reading, disappoints as a treatment of freedom. This reader finds no serious effort even to state clearly the practical problems of personal freedom or free society. The book "straddles" on the philosophical problem of freedom versus universal causality (pp. 72, 73). "Of course" human acts are caused, "largely," but as certainly, not completely. How far does not matter, since animal behavior is based on release of potential energy, in which there is almost no quantitative relation between cause and effect; "trigger action" may multiply an effect indefinitely. Furthermore, it seems rather pointless to discuss personal freedom apart from control of means of acting, and opportunity to act, and an interest in acting, as is done here. More serious—man is a social being, and freedom in society rests on agreement on forms and terms of association, that is, free agreement on the laws, or "government by discussion." This concept is not mentioned, as far as one notices. (The word "agree" does occur [pp. 314, 315] but is not on solving a problem.) The book, apart from historical content (which this writer lacks learning to criticize in detail), is propaganda for "government by law" but against law "making"—law is to be left, or "almost," to spontaneous change in tradition (like language; which is barely mentioned [pp. 24, 57, 59, 434 n.] but not developed or the analogy pressed). Of course, a large and basic element in law—its premises, the mores—does have that character and so is beyond the reach of social action (except by vague reflex influence of "jural" law).

In a recent lecture at the University of Chicago—repeated from a tape recording—Hayek attacked the idea of social economic justice. He held that we are committed to the enterprise organization and must take what it brings, working without political interference. The substance of this is absurd, but it is right to reject the ideal of social justice. It is hopelessly undefinable, meaningless; and there is some prospect of agreement on concrete *in*justices and on procedures to lessen them.

7. The statement is posted in Independence Hall in Philadelphia and is found in any fair collection of documents of American history. Here copied from *The People Shall Judge,* prepared by the faculty of the College of the University of Chicago (1949).

8. A quotation from R. B. Perry (p. 424, n. 23) does state that one's effective liberty is proportional to his power. The concepts cannot be measured, and

other variables must also be recognized. Hayek dismisses the idea with an irrelevant and silly wisecrack.

9. If rigorous causality prevailed, human beings could not possibly know it, since that would require absolutely accurate measurement of cause and effect; and we do know the contrary, by direct experience. Were there no error, there could be no knowledge. Physics now builds on chance in nature, and freedom adds "action," a creative element. Surely paradox cannot surpass men using free choice to deny that it exists—in effect to say that they are not saying anything.

10. These remarks bring to mind the familiar saying of Lord Acton: "Power tends to corrupt, and absolute power corrupts absolutely." Hayek often quotes Acton but, significantly, not this passage. More strangely, he omits one strongly supporting his position on inequality. Speaking of the French Revolution, Acton wrote, "The finest opportunity ever given to the world was thrown away because the passion for equality made vain the hope of freedom" (*History of Freedom,* p. 57.) One does not know how seriously to take the French Revolution slogan, "Liberty, Fraternity, Equality." None of the three can be measured or be absolute or be advocated as complete; but still they are important ideals, for the opposites are certainly bad and have prevailed far enough to force much preventive or offsetting social action. (Life's evils are generally more objective than its goods; the Commandments mostly read "thou shalt not.")

In general, Hayek follows the "individualism" of most price theory, implying absolute power of parents over children. He does grudgingly admit that freedom cannot apply to infants and irresponsible persons, but explicitly passes over the problems involved (p. 77). Clearly the family is the more real unit.

11. The early economists also wrote nonsense about monopoly—including J. S. Mill (*Principles of Political Economy,* 1923, p. 449). They condemned it, assuming a basis in governmental grant, which called for no positive action; public ownership is not mentioned. Smith said that monopoly price is always the highest obtainable, which Ricardo repeated, adding two more absurdities in the next sentence (Sraffa, *Works and Correspondence of Ricardo,* 1951, p. 294). Smith and Mill (Ricardo?) made statements showing that inwardly they "knew better," though they thought that protective duties create monopoly (which they do facilitate). They wrote about monopoly as if they did not know the meaning of the word, which had been used in English for some two centuries. (And Mill wrote nonsense about "scarcity value" [pp. 478, 479], as if there were any other kind.)

12. Further inquiry along this line would try to explain why modern minds accept the "unreality" in physics—as far as, at long last, they have come to do so—but so often reject economic analysis, to hold that its laws can be overruled by political action, and to advocate such action. Of course economists in describing economic conduct do not say that men always act on economic principles. But the law of falling bodies describes "free" fall, which does not occur; and bodies are made to rise—by applying the same law, much as in

manipulating human behavior by coercion or deception. (It still largely exemplifies instrumental rationality, in view of the alternatives, as the acting subject thinks them to be.)

It should be noted that human beings do not naturally recognize objective cause and effect; their inclination was a product of the "liberal revolution" and has spread slowly and incompletely; bright minds still invent perpetual motion devices. Acceptance is opposed by language, which must use words that got their primary meaning from the primitive animistic or anthropomorphic world view and are now ambiguous. A descriptive cause is called a "reason"; "fact" means "deed"; and words for "why" commonly mean for what purpose, as English "why" once did. But in human conduct the relation between positive causality and free choice is subtle and much confused—witness Hayek's treatment.

References

Dalberg-Acton, J. E. E. (Lord Acton). *The History of Freedom and Other Essays.* London: Macmillan & Co., 1922.

Hayek, F. A. von. *The Constitution of Liberty.* Chicago: Univ. of Chicago Press, 1960.

Hazlitt, Henry. *The Foundations of Morality.* Princeton, N. J.: D. Van Nostrand Co., 1963.

Kittrell, Edward R. "Laissez-faire in English Classical Economics," *Journal of the History of Ideas* (October–December, 1966): pp. 610–20.

Knight, Frank H. "Abstract Economics as Absolute Ethics," *Ethics* 76 (April 1966): 163–77.

MacGregor, D. H. *Economic Thought and Policy.* New York: Oxford Univ. Press, 1949.

Mill, John Stuart. *Principles of Political Economy.* Ed. by W. J. Ashley. London: Longman's Green & Co., 1923.

Smith, Adam. *The Wealth of Nations.* New York: Modern Library, 1937.

Sraffa, Piero, ed. *The Works and Correspondence of David Ricardo.* Vol. I. *On the Principles of Political Economy and Taxation.* Cambridge: Cambridge Univ. Press, 1951.

University of Chicago. *The People Shall Judge.* Chicago: Univ. of Chicago Press, 1949.

Index